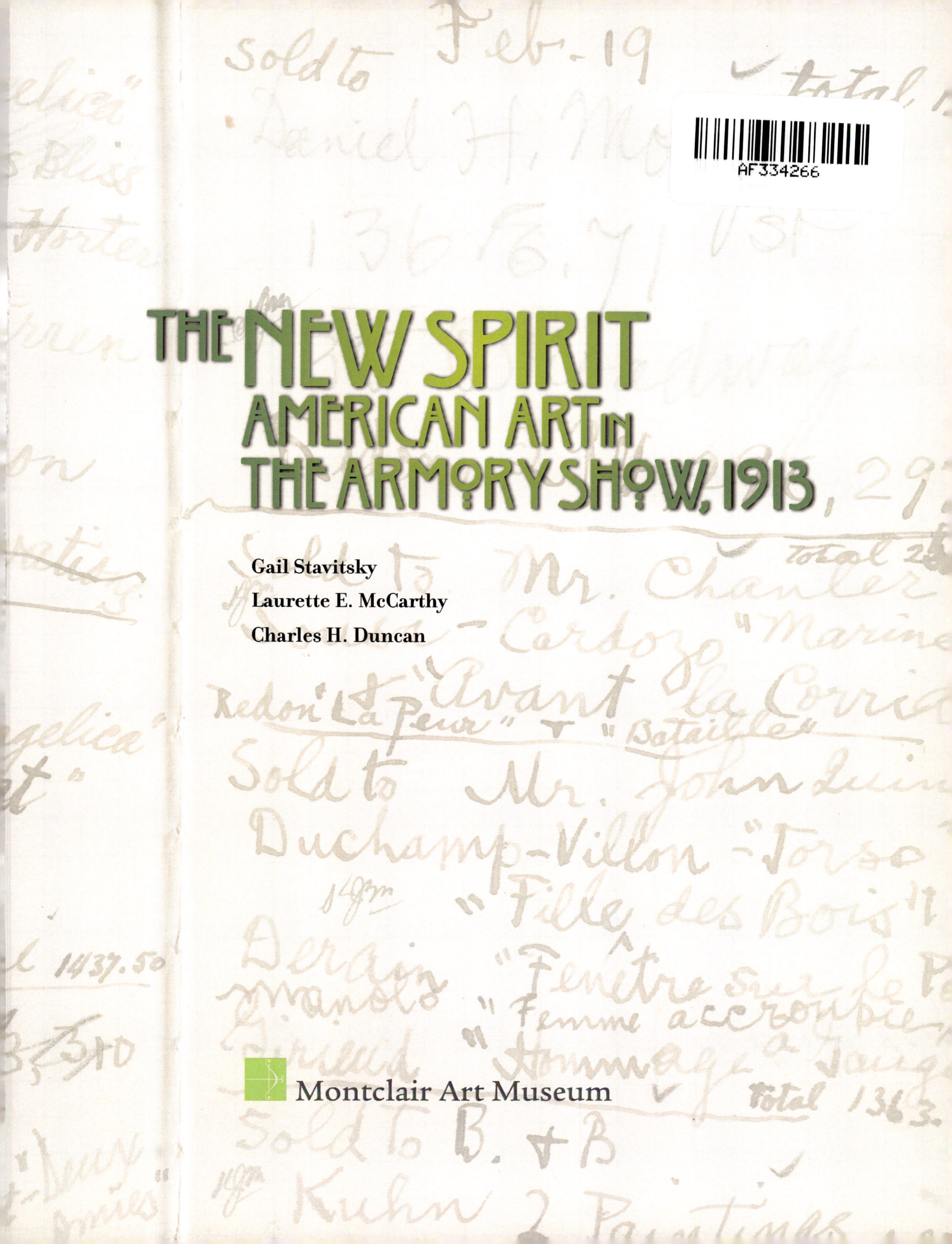

THE NEW SPIRIT
AMERICAN ART in THE ARMORY SHOW, 1913

Gail Stavitsky

Laurette E. McCarthy

Charles H. Duncan

Montclair Art Museum

The New Spirit: American Art in the Armory Show, 1913
By Gail Stavitsky and Laurette E. McCarthy
With an essay by Charles H. Duncan
Montclair Art Museum February 17–June 16, 2013

ISBN 978-0-9883113-0-5
Library of Congress Control Number: 2012951030
© Montclair Art Museum
3 South Mountain Avenue
Montclair, NJ 07042-1747
(973) 746-5555
www.montclairartmuseum.org

Distributed by: The Pennsylvania State University Press
Design: Rich Sheinaus/Gotham Design
Printer: BookMobile

The New Spirit: American Art in the Armory Show, 1913 is organized by the Montclair Art Museum.

The New Spirit: American Art in the Armory Show, 1913 is made possible with generous support from J.P.Morgan.

J.P.Morgan

This exhibition is supported in part by an award from the National Endowment for the Arts. Additional support is provided by Exhibition Angels: The Vance Wall Foundation, The Susan V. Bershad Charitable Fund, Tracy Higgins and James Leitner, Jacqueline and Herb Klein, Toni LeQuire-Schott and Newton B. Schott, Jr., Adrian Shelby and Edward Bindel, Margo and Frank Walter, and the Judith Targan Endowment Fund for Museum Publications.

All Museum programs are made possible, in part, by the New Jersey State Council on the Arts/Department of State, a Partner Agency of the National Endowment for the Arts, and by funds from the National Endowment for the Arts, the Vance Wall Foundation, the Geraldine R. Dodge Foundation, and Museum Members.

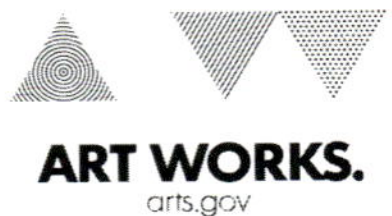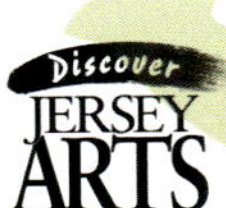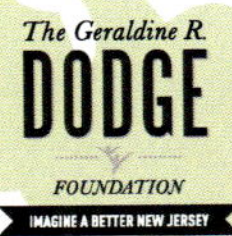

Photo credits
Except where otherwise noted, all photographs were provided by their owners. © 2012 Estate of John Marin/Artists Rights Society (ARS), New York: Cat. 24, fig. 9. © 2012 Delaware Art Museum/Artists Rights Society (ARS), New York: Cat. 33–35. © 2012 Succession H. Matisse / Artists Rights Society (ARS), New York: Cat. 40. © 2012 Albright-Knox Art Gallery. Image courtesy of the G. Robert Strauss, Jr. Memorial Library, Gallery Archives, Albright-Knox Art Gallery, Buffalo, New York: fig. 12. © The Metropolitan Museum of Art. Image source: Art Resource, NY: Cat. 2, 6, 17. © The Museum of Modern Art/Licensed by SCALA / Art Resource, NY: Cat. 39, 41. © Virginia Museum of Fine Arts, Photo: Travis Fullerton: Cat. 4. Photography by Sheldan C. Collins: Cat. 30, 32.

Back cover credits
John Sloan's admission ticket to the Armory Show, John Sloan Manuscript Collection, Delaware Art Museum: Cat. 43; Invitation to the Beefsteak dinner, John Sloan Manuscript Collection, Delaware Art Museum: Cat. 44; Backing board with Armory Show label for Robert Henri's Drawing (*Where We Dined in the Latin Quarter, Paris, in 1896*), 1904, Delaware Art Museum: Cat. 45; Assorted Armory Show postcards: see pp. 155-157.

Front cover credits
"Information" Button from Armory Show Material, The Museum of Modern Art Archives, New York: Cat. 41; Armory Show Poster, 1913, Elmer McRae Papers, Collection Archive, Hirshhorn Museum and Sculpture Garden, Smithsonian Institution, Gift of the Joseph H. Hirshhorn Foundation, 1966: Cat. 42; *International Exhibition of Modern Art*, Association of American Painters and Sculptors, New York, Exhibition Catalog, 1913, Walt Kuhn Family Papers, and Armory Show Records, Archives of American Art, Smithsonian Institution: Cat. 57; *International Exhibition of Modern Art* Button, 1913, Walt Kuhn Family Papers and Armory Show Records, Archives of American Art, Smithsonian Institution: Cat. 65.

TABLE OF CONTENTS

DIRECTOR'S FOREWORD

"American art will never be the same again." (*The Evening Post,* February 17, 1913, 9)

THE INTERNATIONAL EXHIBITION OF MODERN ART has been traditionally regarded as one of the most important moments in the history of American art. Originating in Manhattan before traveling to Chicago and Boston, the show was organized by some of the region's most prominent and active visual artists. In its four-week premier at the 69th Regiment Armory, the exhibition introduced close to 100,000 visitors to current European modern art on a large scale, with over 1200 works representing over 300 artists. Its impact was immediate and, like an earthquake, produced shockwaves that radiated outward and caused a massive shift in the landscape. Until now, public attention has focused almost exclusively on the now-famous European participants in the Armory Show, and American art, which made up two-thirds of the exhibition, has been relatively overlooked. This exhibition attempts to focus for the first time on the significant role of American artists in the planning, implementation, and critical reception of the Armory Show, and proposes to alter opinion on the important impact of their efforts.

We are indebted to independent scholar Laurette E. McCarthy, who approached MAM's Chief Curator Gail Stavitsky about the pending centennial of the Armory Show, after their successful collaboration on the exhibition *Cézanne and American Modernism*, for which Stavitsky served as lead curator. Specializing in American modernism, McCarthy is the foremost authority on American artist and critic Walter Pach; her book, *Walter Pach (1883-1958): The Armory Show and the Untold Story of Modern Art in America*, was published by The Pennsylvania State University Press in 2011. Since 1993 she has been conducting research on the Armory Show and has become one of the leading experts on the topic. Thanks are also due to the Archives of American Art's Mary Savig, Liza Kirwin, Charles Duncan, and Susan Cary for their generosity in arranging for the loans of unique archival materials documenting the Armory Show, featured in our Shelby Gallery. All have been terrific partners in this singular undertaking.

It takes a tremendous commitment of financial support to realize the scholarship and planning required for an ambitious project such as this. We salute J.P. Morgan for making this show possible. This exhibition has also received important support from the National Endowment for the Arts. In addition, we deeply appreciate the vision of all those individuals who have so generously supported this exhibition and publication: The Vance Wall Foundation, The Susan V. Bershad Charitable Fund, Tracy Higgins and James Leitner, Jacqueline and Herb Klein, Toni LeQuire-Schott and Newton B. Schott, Jr., Adrian Shelby and Edward Bindel, Margo and Frank Walter, and the Judith Targan Endowment Fund for Museum Publications.

Projects like this exhibition and catalogue provide all of us on the staff of the Museum with an opportunity to work together in our various professional capacities to bring a complex creative idea to fruition— the exciting sum of many parts. We are fortunate and grateful for all of our staff—educators, registrars, preparators, fundraisers, marketers, guards, and facilities crew—who are passionate about their role in the production. Among them, Gail Stavitsky has skillfully led the curatorial team at MAM since 1994, and continues to inspire us with her scholarship and insight.

As the Montclair Art Museum prepares for its own centennial celebration in 2014, this unique exhibition allows us the opportunity to imagine our founders and community in 1913, constructing an art museum, dreaming of their future, and beginning to feel the impact of those shockwaves emanating westward from Manhattan!

—Lora S. Urbanelli

CURATORS' ACKNOWLEDGMENTS

MANY INDIVIDUALS PLAYED CRITICAL ROLES in the realization of this exhibition. Museum Director Lora Urbanelli has been an important and steadfast advocate since its inception several years ago. Special thanks are extended to our colleagues at the Archives of American Art—Liza Kirwin, Interim Director, Susan Cary, Registrar, Mary Savig, Archives Specialist, and Charles H. Duncan, Collections Specialist—for our unique collaboration with regard to the display of archival objects in Shelby Gallery and Mr. Duncan's catalogue essay.

Francis M. Naumann, independent scholar and director of Francis M. Naumann Fine Art, was especially helpful in many ways, sharing his knowledge, expertise, and recent discoveries of archival materials in the Pach papers that he donated to the Archives of American Art. Our colleagues at the New-York Historical Society, Marilyn Kushner and Kimberly Orcutt, were very generous in making available primary and secondary source materials that they have been accumulating in preparation for their centennial exhibition opening in October 2013, *The Armory Show at 100*. We are particularly grateful to Eleanor Goodman and Brian Beer of the Pennsylvania State University Press for their enthusiastic support in distributing this catalogue. In addition, we truly appreciate Amy Sgarro's thoughtful, thorough editing of the manuscript and Rich Sheinaus's beautiful design of the catalogue.

We are grateful to the staff of the Montclair Art Museum, whose invaluable assistance ensured the successful realization of *The New Spirit: American Art in the Armory Show, 1913*. The complicated logistics of loans for this exhibition were overseen by MAM's Registrar, Renee Powley. Curatorial Assistant Kimberly Fisher ably coordinated all aspects of this project. Arthur Harder, Preparator/Exhibits Designer, was responsible for the superb exhibition design, assisted by Peter Brauch. Esther Harper, MAM's former Deputy Director for Development, and Michelle Shea, Manager of Institutional Giving, took the lead with the fundraising efforts, assisted by John Fox. Our thanks are also extended to Michael Gillespie, Director of Marketing and Communications, assisted by Catherine Mastrangelo, Media Coordinator. We would also like to thank interns Alycia D. Piazza and Nicole DeAugustine for the extensive research that they conducted.

The following colleagues at museums, libraries, archives, galleries, and elsewhere provided generous and critical assistance: Katherine D. Alcauskas, Julie Aronson, Rich Aste, Arlene Balkansky, Claudia Beckwith, Avis Berman, Christine A. Berry, Lisa Blanchard, Josephine Bloodgood, Marisa Bourgoin, Charles Brock, Kathleen Burnside, John Cauman, Heather Campbell Coyle, Shannon Connelly, Sarah Cash, Martha Clawson, Mimi Cohen, Janis Conner, Mac Cosgrove-Davies, Karen Convertino, Michael F. Dressler, Michelle Elligott, Stacey Epstein, Roberta Favis, Betsy Fahlman, Julia Feldman, Elisa Flynn, Emily Foss, Eliza Frecon, Paul Gallagher, Cindy Gresser, Jennifer Gross, Barbara Haskell, Rachel Talent Ivers, Pamela Ivinski, Barry King, Melinda Knapp, Nancy Kuhl, Susan Larkin, Louise Lippincott, Alycia Longwell, Lisa MacDougall, Dana Martin, Nancy Mowll Mathews, Diane Matyas, Virginia Mecklenburg, Richard Miller, Patrick Murphy, Sasha Nicholas, Maureen O'Brien, Lisa Peters, Karen Quinn, Ken Ratner, Eliza Rathbone, Sonja P. Reid, Inga Reist, Rona Roob, Deborah Rebuck, Isabelle von Rundstedt, Debora Ryan, Bart Ryckbosch, Jorge Santis, Barbara Schaefer, Nancy Shawcross, Christopher Shields, Dione J. Simmons, Stacy Slavichak, Barbi Spieler, Lauren Stark, Jost Stephan, Joanthan Stuhlman, Tom Styron, Susana Tejada, Diane Tepfer, Gary Tinterow, James W. Tottis, Carol Troyen, Roger Ward, Deborah Webb, Barbara Weinberg, Robert Workman, Rebecca Withers, Melissa Wolfe, Judith Zilczer, Margaret Zoller, Jacqueline Zorn, and Sylvia Yount.

This exhibition would not have been possible without magnanimous, supportive lenders and funders, who are listed separately. We are deeply appreciative of their great generosity.

— Gail Stavitsky   — Laurette E. McCarthy

LIST OF LENDERS

Archives of American Art, Smithsonian Institution

The Angerman Collection

Carnegie Museum of Art

Corcoran Gallery of Art

Delaware Museum of Art

Barry and Helene Downes

Greenville County Museum of Art

Mr. and Mrs. Hurdle Lea

Mint Museum of Art

Museum of the City of New York

Naples Museum of Art

Francis M. Naumann Fine Art

Norton Museum of Art

Private Collection

Smithsonian American Art Museum

Staten Island Museum

Virginia Museum of Fine Arts

Arthur A. Anderson

Brooklyn Museum

Columbus Museum of Art

Earl Davis

Robert di Domizio/Stillwell Fine Art and Antiques

Everson Museum of Art

Hirshhorn Museum and Sculpture Garden

The Metropolitan Museum of Art

Museum of Art, Fort Lauderdale

The Museum of Modern Art

National Gallery of Art

Francis M. Naumann and Marie T. Keller

Parrish Art Museum

Harry Ransom Center, The University of Texas at Austin

Lazar Spasovic

Whitney Museum of American Art

Yale University Art Gallery

AMERICANS & THE ARMORY SHOW:
An Introduction by Gail Stavitsky

THE INTERNATIONAL EXHIBITION OF MODERN ART, better known as The Armory Show, comprised more than 1,200 works of art by American and European artists. During its original run in New York, Chicago, and Boston from mid-February to mid-May of 1913 and in the subsequent scholarship on the topic, most attention has centered on the avant-garde European artists, particularly Marcel Duchamp, Constantin Brancusi, and Henri Matisse, even though art by Americans composed two-thirds of the works on view in this legendary show. *The New Spirit: American Art in the Armory Show, 1913* is the first project to focus primarily on the contributions of American artists to this landmark exhibition. Previous scholarship is revised in the presentation of a variety of works that challenge the long-held view that the American art in the Armory Show was somewhat monolithic, pallidly provincial, and overshadowed by the uproar of critical and popular attention paid to the avant-garde Europeans. A pluralistic spectrum of stylistic options is presented, from Realism and Impressionism—as represented by such artists as Robert Henri, George Bellows, D. Putnam Brinley, Katherine Dreier, and Edward A. Kramer— to the au courant Modernism of Oscar Bluemner, Manierre Dawson, Arthur B. Carles, Patrick Henry Bruce, E. Ambrose Webster, Edward Middleton Manigault, and others. A necessary reappraisal is made of the conventional notion that American artists, in the words of co-organizer Jerome Myers, "in this swirling medley of art on parade,…had to take it on the chin."[1] While a profound debt to European art must be acknowledged, the inherent artistic quality and variety of American art on view in 1913 attests to its ongoing vitality.

The usual emphasis upon foreign art in the Armory Show can be linked to the pervasive notion that American art before 1940 has played only a marginal role in historical narratives, especially in relation to French art, which became the standard for modern art. Only with the rise of Abstract Expressionism after 1940 did American art finally achieve international significance, which afforded the opportunity "to shuck its affected provinciality and its feeling of inferiority to contemporary European movements."[2] The prevalent assumption about American art as a relative monolith of conservatism in the Armory Show has been reinforced by the lack of any extensive examination of its critical reception. Dismissed as either poorly received, or suffering from a lack of publicity, American art was in fact the subject of many articles that responded to its diversity in a variety of ways. This mixed, nuanced reception can be related to the proposal of JoAnne Mancini that the majority of the critics did not respond "as a monolithic screed against the new"; very few condemned the show outright.[3] Many critics believed that the Armory Show featured fine examples of both European and American art, pointing the way beyond what one of its illustrious visitors, Theodore Roosevelt, referred to as "simpering, self-satisfied conventionality."[4]

The origins of the Armory Show lie in the emergence of progressive groups and independent exhibitions in the early 20th century, with significant French precedents, which challenged the aesthetic ideals, exclusionary policies, and authority of the National Academy of Design, while expanding exhibition and sales opportunities, enhancing public knowledge, and enlarging audiences for contemporary art.[5] In 1904 renowned artist and teacher Robert Henri organized a loan exhibition of his work and that of his colleagues Arthur B. Davies,

William Glackens, George Luks, Maurice B. Prendergast, and John Sloan at the National Arts Club in New York. Advocating artistic freedom, individualism, authenticity, and contemporaneity, Henri subsequently organized the jury-free exhibition of "The Eight," which included the aforementioned artists, as well as Everett Shinn and Ernest Lawson, held at the Macbeth Galleries in 1908. This groundbreaking exhibition was an important precedent for the Armory Show. All of its members would be represented, with the exception of Shinn, and several would play key organizational roles, especially Davies, Glackens, and Prendergast. The exhibition of "The Eight" also attracted a significant audience, considerable publicity, and financial returns. Furthermore, a tour to six institutions was arranged for 1908-9.[6]

Weekly receptions were held in Henri's studio and attended by members of "The Eight," especially Sloan, as well as Henri's students Walter Pach and George Bellows. They were joined in the spring of 1908 by Walt Kuhn, a younger artist, whose newspaper work as a cartoonist and illustrator had served as an entrée into the Henri circle.[7] Likely a frequent topic of their encounters was their desire to expand exhibition opportunities for progressive artists. Kuhn likely learned from the adept members of "The Eight" the importance of manipulating the press and securing sufficient publicity, in order to entice the American public to attend art exhibitions—skills that he would build upon as future secretary of the Armory Show.

Henri and Sloan visualized a larger group of independent artists banding together to exhibit and in 1910 Kuhn had the opportunity to join forces with them. In a review of the April 1910 show of "The Independents," Henri praised the "rugged vigor" of Kuhn's painting and characterized him as among those "who contributed interest, time, and money to the organization of the exhibition," which he characterized as "an opportunity for experimenters."[8]

Held in opposition to the National Academy of Design's Spring exhibition, the *Exhibition of Independent Artists* has not been sufficiently recognized as a major precedent for the Armory Show. As Sloan later observed, the 1910 Independent Show provided the future Armory Show co-organizer Walt Kuhn with some vital experience in organizing a large exhibition.[9] Comprising over 400 paintings, drawings, and sculpture by 103 artists, it was the first large scale, nonjuried, artist-organized exhibition of contemporary American art in this country. This exhibition brought together the artists who would play the primary roles in the organization of the Armory Show—Arthur B. Davies, Kuhn, and Walter Pach, who organized the show with Henri and Sloan. Discussions about the exhibition progressed through various proposals, including the possibility of a small international exhibition, proposed by Jerome Myers.[10] In March 1910, Kuhn suggested to Henri a plan for a large show to be held during a short period of time and to be financed by contributions of $200 apiece by Henri, Sloan, Davies, and himself.[11] He played a key role in the arrangements to rent a vacant building on West 35th Street to house the show. A diverse list of progressive artists was devised by Henri, Sloan, and Kuhn to invite to exhibit, with the goal of rivaling the National Academy in size and importance. A significant number of these artists were students and associates of Henri; nearly 50 of them would exhibit their work in the Armory Show.[12]

Kuhn helped to compile the catalogue and witnessed Sloan's hectic activities as secretary-treasurer. He also took over the preparation and management of the exhibition gallery and served on the Hanging Committee, along with Davies.[13] An extensive publicity campaign was mounted; Kuhn's attempt as manager, however, to take over "the whole responsibility so far as newspapers went" was resisted by Henri.[14] Thus the seeds of a growing power struggle with Henri were planted, with the ultimate result of Henri's diminished role in the organization of the Armory Show.

On April 1, 1910, a record-setting gathering of 2,000 people jammed the opening of what Sloan referred to as "the best exhibition ever held on this continent (that is, composed of

American art exclusively.)"[15] Attracting a great deal of press and initial attendance, the exhibition did not, however, result in many sales. Nevertheless, the Independents show likely made its organizers more aware of modern art, as suggested in an article by artist-critic and participant Guy Pène Du Bois, stating that the exhibition committee had recognized American followers of the latest European developments—"There will be represented in the exhibition paintings by the realists, the impressionists, the men who, with Matisse, followed the theories of [Paul] Cézanne, the followers of the geometrical art of [Pablo] Picasso and by men whose art, purely personal, is directly connected with no concerted movement."[16] The range of artists from academicians to "confessed worshippers at the shrine of time" like Leon Dabo and "those whose are wearing the shoes of Cézanne" such as Prendergast and Morton L. Schamberg was also noted in reviews of the exhibition as the promise of a revitalized American art that was "not simply lagging in the footsteps of the Ecole des Beaux Arts."[17] Du Bois predicted that this "largest opposition exhibition" would "make art history in New York as the Salon des Refusés did in Paris."[18] Pach later observed that the "chief effect of the gesture of 1910 was to demonstrate the extent of progressive sentiment in America and to bring together the men who, in 1912, organized the Armory Show."[19]

During the planning of the exhibition, Sloan wrote in his diary that "Stieglitz of [the] Photo Secession [Gallery] is hot under the collar about our show…I imagine he thinks we have stolen his thunder in exhibiting 'independent' artists."[20] As the pioneering proprietor of the intimate "291" gallery known for its Fifth Avenue address, Alfred Stieglitz had already presented the first exhibitions of Matisse's work in America in 1908, as well as *The Younger American Painters*, just prior to the Independents exhibition. Stieglitz's landmark show of American art, co-organized with his colleague Edward Steichen, featured the work of D. Putnam Brinley, Arthur B. Carles, Marsden Hartley, John Marin, and Alfred Maurer, all of whom who would be represented in the Armory Show. Regarded as the first exhibition of American artists influenced by European modernism, it was largely an outgrowth of a short-lived, secessionist group—Steichen's New Society of American Artists in Paris.[21] Preferring to operate on a smaller scale, Stieglitz turned down many outside requests to organize contemporary, Post-Impressionist art exhibitions and publicly shared his belief in a letter to the editor late in 1911 that such an exhibition was the responsibility of larger institutions, specifically the Metropolitan Museum of Art.[22] Although Stieglitz was an inspiration for, as well as a lender, buyer, and supporter of the Armory Show, he would not come to play any significant organizational role, nor would any of the modernist artists in his circle. One of his early patrons, however, was Davies, who would be the only buyer of Cézanne's work at the master's American show in 1911 at 291.[23] Davies also participated in an exhibition of independent artists in March 1911, organized by Rockwell Kent, which combined works by artists in the Stieglitz circle—Marin and Hartley—with ex-Henri students Homer Boss, Glenn O. Coleman, Guy Pène du Bois, and Julius Golz, as well as Maurer, Prendergast, and Luks. All, with the exception of Kent, were later featured in the Armory Show.[24]

At the end of 1910, another progressive group of artists was formed for the purpose of exhibiting works in the medium of pastel—the Pastellists. Its founder was Elmer Livingston MacRae, who as secretary-treasurer would assume a similar role in the organization of the Armory Show. President Leon Dabo would also become involved; among other artists who exhibited with The Pastellists were Kuhn, Davies, Bellows, Glackens, Pach, Henri, and board member Jerome Myers. According to Myers, the Pastellists' membership and shows were a direct precedent for the formation of the larger organization that would assemble the Armory Show—the Association of American Painters and Sculptors (AAPS).[25] Kuhn allegedly asked Myers, "You…have done so well with your Pastellist's Society, why can't we get together on a scheme for a large exhibition?"[26] This conversation likely took place around the time of the second Pastellists show, which opened December 9, 1911, at Folsom Galleries and soon sparked the coalition of the AAPS.

Myers and Kuhn had also exhibited their work together in a two-man show in April 1911 at the first headquarters of the AAPS, the Madison Art Gallery, whose owner Clara Davidge and director Henry Fitch Taylor would play important roles in the organization of the Armory Show.[27] The Madison Art Gallery was also the site for Kuhn's first one-man exhibition in late 1911, during which he met, through the journalist Frederick Gregg, his most important patron, the lawyer and pioneering collector of modern art, John Quinn. Kuhn soon became a close friend of Quinn, who would come to play major roles in support of the Armory Show as legal advisor and patron.[28]

Kuhn's approach to Myers about an independent show may therefore have been prompted by a variety of events: the second Pastellists exhibition, his disappointment over the lack of sales during his first one-man show, or a preceding group show at the Madison Art Gallery in which he participated. In a letter dated December 9, 1911, to his wife, Vera, Kuhn provided what is likely his earliest comment on the origins of the AAPS. Complaining about the recently opened National Academy exhibition, he asserted, "I hear it's very rotten, worse than ever. It seems that …it only needs a match to set off the formation of a new society."[29] Observing that Clara Davidge and Taylor "realize that they've got to have our sort of stuff to make a hit," Kuhn stated in a letter of December 12 his desire to personally plan and launch a movement in the new year, independent of Henri's control.[30] Henri was, as noted by Kuhn, distracted with launching the MacDowell Club as a setting for small, progressive shows by self-selected American artists, many of whom would be represented in the Armory Show.[31]

Despite Kuhn's egotistical claims, the AAPS and its first meeting on December 14 emerged as a collaboration with MacRae, Myers, and Taylor. The minutes indicate that they met "to discuss the possibilities of organizing a society for the purpose of exhibiting the works of progressive and live painters, both American and foreign, favoring such work usually neglected by current shows and especially interesting and instructive to the public."[32] (cat. 50) Kuhn continued to build his ideas about his role as the power behind the throne, stating in a letter to Vera his preference for a minor office such as secretary, which would reap publicity, develop his reputation for liberality, and allow him to use his organizational skills.[33]

Grudgingly admitted by Kuhn into the new society, Henri was evidently not invited to the first official meeting on December 19, held at the Madison Art Gallery.[34] Davies, however, was present, along with 12 other artists—Brinley, Gutzon Borglum, John Mowbray-Clarke, Leon Dabo, Glackens, Kuhn, Lawson, Jonas Lie, Luks, MacRae, Myers, and Taylor.[35] A statement was made by Taylor as host, defining the goal of "an association of live and progressive men and women who shall lead the public taste in art rather than follow it. The National Academy of Design is not expected to lead the public taste. It never did and…never will."[36] The fundamental platform was defined as an organization, called The American Painters and Sculptors, "for the purpose of developing a broad interest in American art activities, by holding [nonjuried] exhibitions of the best contemporary work…representative of American and foreign art."[37] Not present but represented by proxy was the liberally inclined academician J. Alden Weir, who was elected president, likely as a figurehead of respectability. The well known academic sculptor Gutzon Borglum was elected vice-president, probably for similar reasons and because of his ability to garner attention in the press. Kuhn succeeded in his bid to become secretary; and MacRae was elected treasurer. Davies, Borglum, and Mowbray-Clarke, a sculptor and specialist in medals and animals, were elected to the Constitutional Committee to devise the constitution.

Henri was invited to attend the next meeting of the new society on January 2, 1912. Commenting that Davies was already "very active in it," Henri also observed that the officers had already been elected and that the draft of a constitution was read.[38] Noting that he "was not interested in this society except as it may be useful to check NAD," Henri felt that "it is too much of the old thing—judging others and not working to the opportunity for others to exhibit and judge themselves," as part of his MacDowell Club scheme.[39] Henri made a motion at the meeting to elect additional members, resulting in the election of several of his associates— Bellows, Prendergast, Du Bois, Sloan, and Shinn.[40]

On the evening of January 2, Kuhn provided a statement from the tentative constitution to newspaper reporters, which was quoted in the papers the following morning—"The society has been founded for the purpose of developing a broad interest in American art activities, by holding exhibitions of the best contemporary work that can be secured representative of American and foreign art."[41] Various newspaper articles promoted the new organization as "a society that will give the artists who are not members of the Academy, and in some cases heartily opposed to [its] methods, a chance to exhibit their work under conditions of as much dignity…as the Academicians now enjoy."[42] It was also noted that one of the goals of the AAPS "was to erect a building in New York, where exhibitions can be given…which will not be dominated by any school of art or artists. In this they are openly at war with the Academy…."[43] Gutzon Borglum was cited as the leader of those opposed to the Academy's previous efforts to secure a site in Central Park. The group was situated within the international history of "Separatist art bodies" such as the Viennese secession and it was also noted that a number of the new society's "insurgents" were in fact members and exhibitors at the Academy.[44] Also including "a proportion of men still young but already favorably known," the charter group of 25 AAPS members (see Appendix I) were commended as giving "promise of strength."[45]

The publicized anti-Academy stance of the AAPS prompted the immediate resignation of Weir from the presidency and membership in a letter dated January 3, in which he stated that he had "consented to serve…on the distinct understanding that no opposition to the National Academy of Design was intended."[46] Borglum called up Henri the following day, asking him if he would accept the presidency, which he declined. On the same day, Henri consented to the request of MacRae, who called him to ask if he would vote for Davies for President.[47]

There are differing accounts as to who ultimately persuaded Davies to assume this position. Kuhn later asserted that he "called alone" on Davies and "induced him to come to a meeting."[48] Kuhn implied his primary responsibility, observing that "at the resignation of Alden Weir… [Davies] was induced to take over that office."[49] Myers asserted that he and MacRae called on Davies at a time when "even the stout-hearted Walt Kuhn [was] becoming discouraged."[50] MacRae's January 5 diary entry read "Called on Davies consent for president."[51] John Sloan later recalled that MacRae and Myers were the ones who "interested Arthur B. Davies—who took the bit in his mouth and turned out to be a very effective administrator and money raiser…."[52] Thereafter Davies and Kuhn launched an enterprise that, with the critical involvement of Pach, would evolve from "a large American exhibition, with perhaps a few…radical things from abroad" into "the great showing of works" that, in the opinion of Myers, Sloan, and others, was carried out by a "supercouncil" employing secretive, dictatorial methods.[53]

At the January 9 meeting at which Davies was elected to replace Weir, the constitution was adopted, and a board of trustees was elected, as well as a committee to speak for the AAPS. Henry Fitch Taylor, as chairman, issued a statement of purpose and policy, which was reprinted at length in newspapers. The primary goal to hold annual, non-juried exhibitions was reaffirmed, as was the intent to make them "as interesting as they will be representative…of American and European art activities."[54] With regard to its American identity, it was noted that the society is "called American because we are an American organization beyond that we are not drawing the line of locality or nationality upon art."[55] Luks was referred to in one article as having stated that "the association would hold its first exhibition probably this spring.[56]

That the organization was originally founded to focus primarily on exhibitions of the work of the American members is suggested in Kuhn's extensive correspondence in late January with potential venues, in pursuit of national travel of the forthcoming show.[57] In his letter to the St. Paul Institute of Arts and Sciences, Kuhn stated that he was instructed by the board of the AAPS to inquire whether "your institution would be interested in exhibiting the work of members of this organization….We are prepared to show a collection of one or more works of each member, such an exhibition to comprise the work of active members of the society only."[58] He received receptive responses from the Cincinnati Museum Association and the Syracuse Museum of Fine Arts, stating that a number of the members had already shown at their institutions.[59]

By March 1912, there was a marked change in direction for plans of the first show of the AAPS. This is suggested by a letter of March 5 from Kuhn to Milton Matter, acting director of the John Herron Art Institute, Indianapolis, who was interested in receiving a show of the work of the AAPS in March-April 1912.[60] Kuhn replied that at a "recent meeting of the Society, extensive changes were made in the program for the ensuing year. All action pertaining to the giving of Exhibitions outside of New York has been postponed until after our first comprehensive show in this city."[61] Although no minutes for this meeting appear to exist, this policy shift is corroborated by a letter dated March 16 from Cornelia Sage, Director, Albright Art Gallery, Buffalo, to Kuhn, regarding his letter of February 20 requesting help in determining "the expense of a foreign exhibition, transportation, insurance, brokerage, etc." [62] Sage referred to the "French Exhibition," which she recently brought over, the exhibition of works by the Members of the Société Nouvelle of Paris, for which she would know costs in a few weeks when the bills came in. She recommended Lloyd's of London, with which Kuhn, Davies, and Pach eventually entered into an insurance agreement for the Armory Show.[63]

The exhibition of the Société Nouvelle had been publicized in *American Art News* at the end of 1911 as a lost opportunity by the MacDowell Club by a critic who hoped that it could secure this "admirable display…now on exhibition at the Albright Gallery."[64] This idea was presented in the context of "much talk in the studios [about] the seeming failure of the… MacDowell Club to have grasped…the 'psychological moment'…of the present season, to give the art public the chance to see and study the latest works exemplifying the art movements in Europe of the time…What Mr…Stieglitz has done…on a necessarily small and inadequate scale…the MacDowell Club could have performed in a larger and satisfying way…" [65] This controversy was continued in the January 6 issue of *American Art News*, which also featured an article on the formation of the AAPS.[66]

Considerable curiosity about what the *American Art News* critic called "the merits or defects of Matisse and his followers, the 'Cubists' and other 'faddists' in France" had been generated earlier in the year by Roger Fry's groundbreaking exhibition *Manet and the Post-Impressionists*, held at the Grafton Galleries in London.[67] The extensive press coverage of this exhibition had greatly stimulated public interest in Post-Impressionism and a book about the show was read by Quinn, who forwarded copies to the *Evening Sun* writer Gregg, who would become an important publicist for the Armory Show. Fascinated with the landmark show of Post-Impressionist and modern art held at the Grafton Galleries in London late in 1911, Quinn had expressed his interest in seeing Post-Impressionist pictures brought to America. Likely Kuhn and Davies became aware of the Grafton Show and Post-

Impressionism through their connections with Quinn and Gregg. In March 1912, Quinn bought two Matisse drawings from Stieglitz, and by spring of that year, Kuhn and Davies were having "many conversations debating some sort of program for the projected exhibition."[68]

These discussions coincided with the search for a suitable exhibition space. In May, successful negotiations were concluded for the rental of the 69th Regiment Armory on Lexington Avenue between 25th and 26th Streets, the training ground and meeting place of the New York National Guard.[69] By June 27, the exhibition's location and status was being promoted as the "largest exhibition of painting and sculpture and the first international one of its kind ever held in this city."[70] It was noted that Henri had been asked to help gather foreign works during his summer trip to Paris and that he "refused flatly…unless given full authority," which was not forthcoming.[71] Also provided was an initial listing of foreign exhibitors, which, with the exception of Cézanne, included such relatively conservative artists as as Henri Le Sidaner, Jean-François Raffaeli, and Albert Besnard, all of whom had exhibited in the Société Nouvelle show in Buffalo and were later dropped from the Armory Show roster.

During the summer of 1912, plans for the show progressed as some American artists, such as the Philadelphia-based modernist Morton Schamberg, began to receive invitations to exhibit, which likely were in the form of a circular.[72] It appears that Pach received this circular and then wrote notices in May and September 1912 in *L'art et les artistes* to promote the show.[73] Davies himself was evidently preoccupied with transforming the rather tame list of foreign exhibitors. According to Pach, Davies had for years been browsing in shops, acquiring foreign books and magazines "and so had accumulated a most surprising fund of knowledge as to developments in Europe."[74] Since their meeting around 1909, Pach had translated articles on modern art for Davies and shared his own writings, including essays on Cézanne and Matisse, thereby playing a significant role in his friend's growing knowledge.[75]

Among the various art publications Davies perused at this time was the catalogue for the *Sonderbund Exhibition*, the first truly comprehensive show of modern art, on view in Cologne, Germany. On September 2 he sent a letter with the catalogue to Kuhn, who was vacationing in Nova Scotia, urging him to see this exhibition before it closed on September 30—"I wish we could have as good a show as the Cologne Sonderbund…."[76] (cat. 60) The decision to go abroad was made; Vera noted in her diary that the morning of September 5 was "spent in letter writing and talking about Davies and Europe."[77] By September 25, Kuhn was "mid ocean," writing that, "It's up to me to get a bunch of fine things and if it can be done within the money on tap, I am going to do it. I only hope that I'm not too woozy next Monday—that Cologne show is important."[78]

Organized to provide "an overview of the state of the latest movement in painting," the Sonderbund Exhibition featured almost 650 works on view by 173 artists, including Matisse, Picasso and the Post Impressionist pioneers Cézanne, Paul Gauguin, Edvard Munch, and especially Vincent van Gogh, who was represented by over 120 paintings and drawings.[79] This grouping of avant-garde Fauves, Cubists, and Expressionists with 19th century antecedents was an important role model for the Armory Show. Furthermore, the well publicized exhibition was a commercial success, promoted by modern advertising strategies.[80]

Greatly impressed with the *Sonderbund Exhibition*, Kuhn wrote to Vera about his enthusiasm for the work of van Gogh and Gauguin, adding that although Cézanne's landscapes were "still Greek to him," he would understand them before his return home.[81] Studying the show closely as "a key to future actions," Kuhn also met Munch, admiring the Norwegian's "big, wild figure things, very crude but extremely powerful."[82] Kuhn's subsequent brief sojourn in Holland from October 5-7 was especially fruitful. In The Hague, he forged a

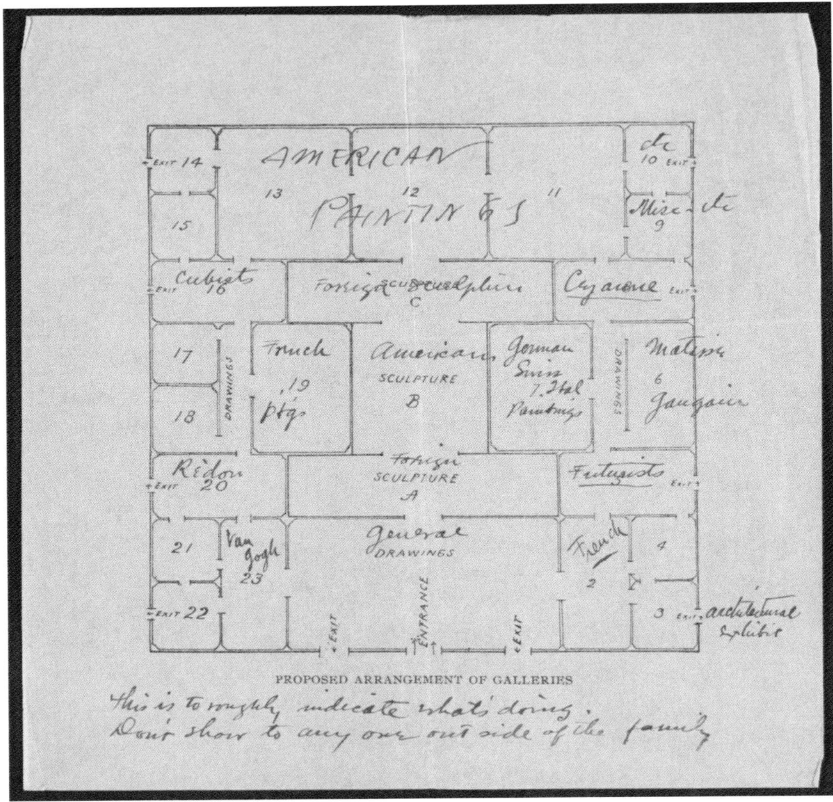

Cat. 61.
Arthur B. Davies letter to Walt Kuhn, October 1912: handwritten, ill. 2 p., letter and floorplan
10 x 8 in.
Floorplan: 7 1/4 x 7 2/3 in.
Walt Kuhn, Kuhn Family Papers, and Armory Show Records, 1859-1978, bulk 1900-1949, Archives of American Art, Smithsonian Institution

productive relationship with the art dealer J.H. de Bois, who was preparing a one-man show for the Symbolist Odilon Redon and ultimately lent 12 works by this "big Frenchman hardly known at home…already 72 years old and somewhat like Davies, perhaps a trifle more eccentric," whom he correctly predicted "will make a hit in the show."[83] After a brief stopover on October 7 in Amsterdam, where he could have seen the first Moderne Kunst Kring exhibition with works by Pablo Picasso and Georges Braque, Kuhn arrived in Berlin the next day.[84] On October 9 he was still tied up in Berlin, complaining to Vera that there was no good art being made in Germany and that he was anxious to move on to Paris.[85] Kuhn was in regular contact with Davies, who provided various instructions and ideas, asserting, for example, in an undated letter in which he enclosed an initial plan for the show: "Don't forget we want a roomful of Futurists and another of Cubists."[86] (cat. 61) Davies also informed Kuhn that he intended to write to Roger Fry, who "is to have another show [of modern art] in London immediately [and] you can certainly make use of those fine things he will have in this year's show and those of last year yet attainable."[87] Davies additionally observed that a second circular to artists was going to be drafted (to be sent out after Kuhn's return) and that Pach had an article in *L'art et les artistes* "on the coming exhibition (evidently suggested by the circular sent with invitation card)."[88]

Kuhn's disappointment with German art continued in Munich, where he nevertheless conducted a lot of business from October 15 to 24. He appears to have connected with the dealer and future lender Hans Goltz, who was showing works by Braque, Cézanne, Robert Delaunay, André Derain, Gauguin, Ernst Ludwig Kirchner, Wassily Kandinsky, Matisse, Picasso, van Gogh, and Maurice Vlaminck in the *Neue Kunst* exhibition. This may account for why Kirchner and Kandinsky were the only German expressionists represented in the Armory Show. Kuhn's knowledge of German from his Munich school days was useful in the preparation of a printed circular listing conditions for exhibiting artists.[89]

In mid-October, Kuhn observed that "Munich is absolutely dead as an art city.…[full of] 'pot-boiler'…sentimentalism.…The more I get about the more I feel that New York is the coming place for art and anything else—It's a fine thing that we are in at the start."[90] When Kuhn arrived in Paris on October 25, he soon sought the assistance of American artists who had a much greater knowledge of the contemporary art scene—the sculptor Jo Davidson, Fauve pioneer Alfred Maurer, who introduced him to the dealer Ambroise Vollard, and especially Pach, who, as one of the earliest and most articulate promoters of modern art, would become primarily responsible for the assembling of almost all the avant-garde Parisian art in the Armory Show.[91] Davies had requested Pach's help the month before, expressing his confidence in Kuhn's "healthy outlook, honesty of purpose and gameness in putting through anything he is fairly up against."[92]

On October 28 Kuhn wrote about his visit to the Salon d'Automne, which would be a fruitful source for some of the more notorious Cubist loans to the Armory Show, including Francis Picabia's *Dances at the Spring* (see cat. 76) and Albert Gleizes' *Man on a Balcony* (both 1912, Philadelphia Museum of Art), as well as Alexander Archipenko's sculpture *Family Life* (destroyed):

> *So far everything grand* success! *Saw the autumn salon yesterday, immense and fine show, but not as choice as the Sonderbund….Have not seen the futurists as yet and the cubists I must first digest….I have made tremendous progress in my sense of good things and will probably be jumped on for bringing over things which they will at first consider too wild but I have been inspired by the possibilities and… we will show NY something they never dreamed of.* [93]

Kuhn further commented that Paris is "still the same wonderful city, nothing like it on earth- but no place to stay for us. We've got a healthy American germ, that is personal and the art of the future. America in the spirit of its newness is destined to be the coming centre….When I get back we begin a new epoch!"[94] This concept of a new spirit would become the tagline of the Armory Show. It is possible that Pach and Kuhn also visited at this time the important *Salon de "La Section d'Or"* at the Galerie la Boetie, which featured paintings and sculptures by the Duchamp brothers, especially Duchamp's *Nude Descending a Staircase , No. 2* (see cats. 51,79).[95]

With Davies's arrival on November 5, Kuhn must have felt great relief; he wrote to Vera that only recently had the "full size" of the project dawned on him.[96] Pach played an essential role during their hectic ten-day sojourn, taking them around Paris to locate the best and most advanced art, including examples in the Stein collections, such as Matisse's *Blue Nude (Souvenir of Biskra)* (1907, Baltimore Museum of Art) and *Red Madras Headdress (Le Madras rouge),* (1907, Barnes Foundation. See cat. 74)—one of the most controversial works in the Armory Show.[97] Dovetailing with Pach's and Davies's personal tastes was the growing importance of French art for Kuhn as well; thus it is not surprising that it became a primary aspect of the Armory Show. Most accounts emphasize the European artists who were visited, especially Redon, the Duchamp-Villons, and Constantin Brancusi, (about whom Davies declared "That's the kind of man I'm giving the show for!").[98] The assistance of key dealers was also secured, including Vollard, Bernheim-Jeune, Daniel-Henry Kahnweiler, and especially the Galerie Emile Druet, from which the largest loan of Post-Impressionist and modern works would come.[99]

Nevertheless, although French artists, dealers, and collectors were the focus of their whirlwind expedition, American artists living in Paris, such as Davidson and Maurer, as well as Patrick Henry Bruce, a student of Matisse, and modernist painter Morgan Russell, were also likely solicited at this time.[100]

With a survey of 19th-century paintings marking its 10th anniversary, the Salon d'Automne—a possible model for the Armory Show—also featured the work of some American artists, including Bruce, Carles, James McNeill Whistler, as well as Maurer, whose still life painting was deemed "very nice" by the modernist painter Marsden Hartley.[101] Davies and Kuhn visited Hartley, who had on August 19 received the official AAPS invitation/circular, sent

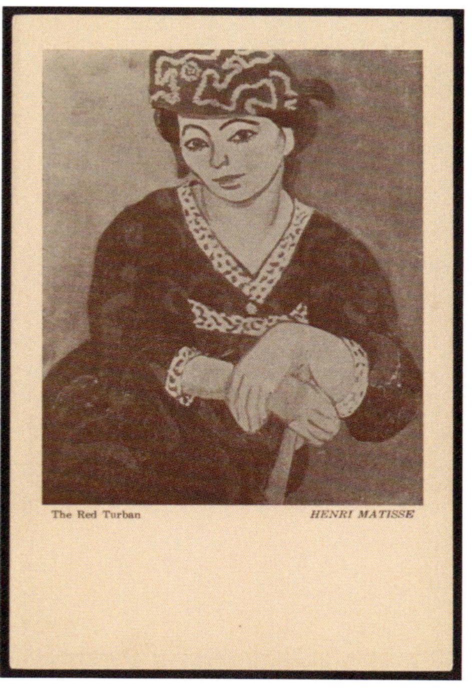

Cat. 74.
The Red Turban by Henri Matisse
International Exhibition of Modern Art postcards, Association of American Painters and Sculptors (New York, N.Y.)
1913
5½ x 3½ in.
Walt Kuhn, Kuhn Family Papers, and Armory Show Records, 1859-1978, bulk 1900-1949, Archives of American Art, Smithsonian Institution

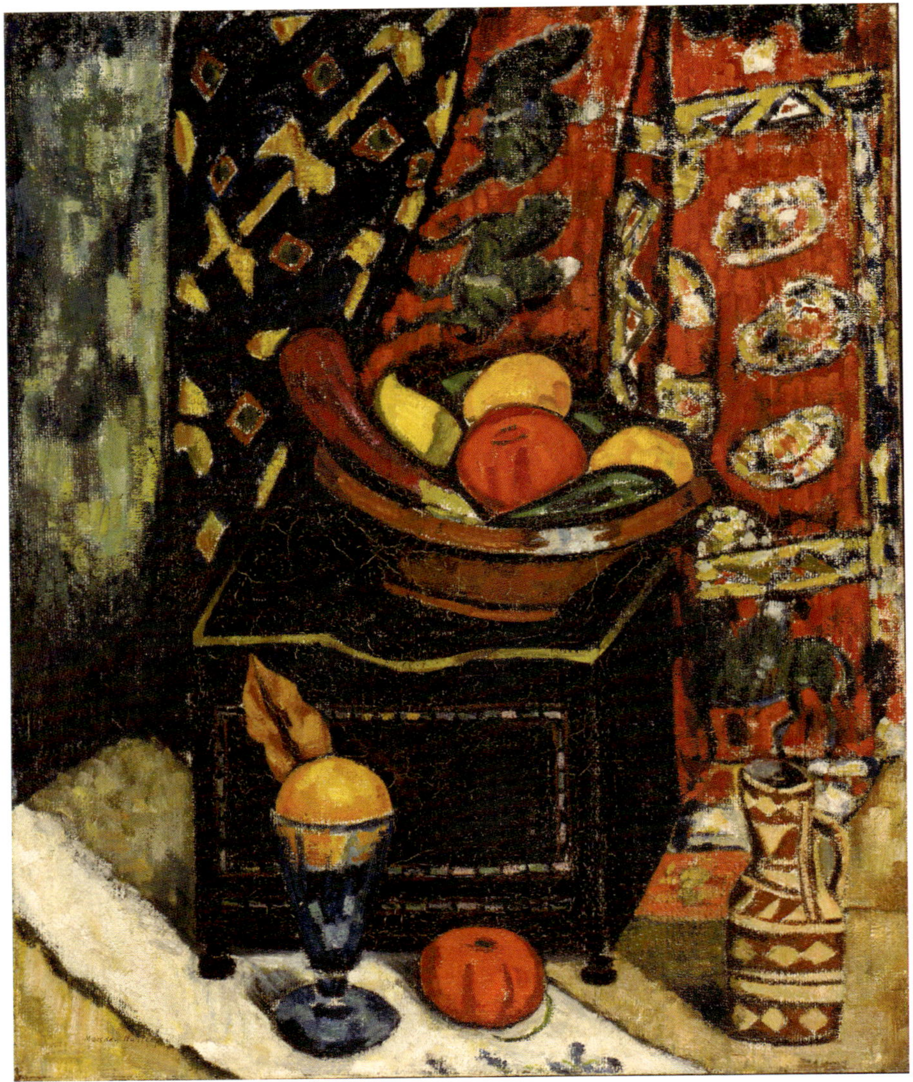

Cat. 16.
Marsden Hartley
Still Life No. 1, 1912, oil on
canvas, Columbus
Museum of
Art, Ohio; Gift of
Ferdinand Howald,
1931.184

to him by Stieglitz. He was excited that there would be "at last something of worth on a decent scale in America."[102] In early November he reported to Stieglitz that he "was wholly amazed…with a call from…Davies and…Kuhn who… are over here getting stuff for the show in February which from all accounts bids fair to be an electric show in America—really most encouraging to us Americans….I truly believe it will be a most excellent thing—and will wake America up terrifically as the two Grafton shows have aroused the English."[103] Kuhn reported on the Post-Impressionist art he had secured from Germany and Holland and Davies selected two still lifes (cat. 16). Hartley noted that he would not have chosen them himself, being "so interested at this time in the directly abstract thing but Davies says that no American has done this kind of thing—and they would serve me and the exhibition best at this time."[104] He was apparently allowed more flexibility with his submission of six drawings—"these will be the abstract thing of the present time."[105] In another letter, Hartley restated Davies' priority in selecting his works for the Armory Show:

> *It was Davies who chose the still lifes—he said—you can send whatever you like but I would advise sending these two—as I think it would do you good to send them and there will be nothing just like them. I had a feeling that "do you good" meant being good for me financially—which is most necessary. I am rather hoping…on a sale of one of these two pictures through Davies.*[106]

By the time of their departure for London on November 12, Kuhn confidently proclaimed that their exhibition "is going to be fully as good as the one at Cologne."[107] In London, Kuhn admitted that "the work to do still looks insurmountable," given that their "plans were entirely changed owing to a fine deal we made with the Insurance Co. allowing us to double on the quantity of pictures….I am simply overwhelmed by the big-ness of the whole thing."[108] Although they had stopped there specifically to see the Grafton Gallery exhibition of Post-Impressionist art, which proved to be a fruitful source of loans, especially of Matisse's work, Kuhn proclaimed the superiority of the forthcoming Armory Show. Steeped in his exposure to foreign modern art, he commented that the "American annex, of course, will be a sad affair…"[109]

Kuhn also continued to promote the show with his various German contacts, including the Berlin critic Paul Mahlberg, writing to him about their progress, including plans for a "room showing the highest cubistic direction by the brothers Duchamp-Villon and the balance of the show besides embracing the futurists and young post-impressionists will be of equally extreme importance…."bahn brechend" [groundbreaking] for the great new movement in Art…."[110] Kuhn and Davies departed London on November 21, having arranged for the loan of about 430 examples of European art and leaving Pach in charge. In a final letter, Kuhn provided detailed instructions to Pach, expressed his surprising conviction that there was "not a thing doing here in the way of art" and advised him regarding "Grafton show, take all you can get. ….*Matisse* is most important….Anxious to have Braque and Derain but must leave Kahnweiler to you…. Make it clear to him that every first-class dealer in Europe is participating."[111]

As part of the build up of anticipation of the Armory Show, there was considerable newspaper coverage of the trip abroad and the emerging exhibition plans, as summarized in the headline "Davies and Kuhn Collect Works in Europe" where "they obtained the right to exhibit some four hundred examples of foreign art."[112] This may be due to Davies' and Kuhn's activities on board the SS *Celtic* to America, during which they planned publicity and publications. Kuhn translated the text for Gauguin's Tahitian journal, *Noa Noa*, published as a pamphlet for the Armory Show, as well as a group of van Gogh's letters, which he dictated to Davies.[113] One of the translated letters was eventually published as an essay by van Gogh entitled "The Spirit of Modern Art" in the special Armory Show issue of *Arts and Decoration*.[114]

While Kuhn and Davies were abroad, an article in *The Sun* announced that "plans will be perfected for the American division of the exhibition…to be done mainly by invitation" by the time of their return at the end of November.[115] It was noted that the "scope of the new society's display has widened considerably since the organization of the movement not quite a year ago" to include works from abroad and the categories "Classicists, Romanticists, Impressionists, Post-Impressionists, Cubists, Futurists"— quoted from the "advance circular" co-signed by Davies and Kuhn.[116] The new society's interest in unconventional media such as wood carving, pottery, and needlework was also emphasized and seems related to what was likely a second circular inviting artists' submissions by January 1 (cat. 48), co-signed by Davies and Mowbray-Clarke, which stipulated that artists "will not be limited to any particular medium of expression….[to] encourage non-professional as well as professional artists to exhibit the result of any self-expression…that may come most naturally to the individual," providing woodcarving as an example.[117]

Back in the United States, Kuhn and Davies became thoroughly engaged in the many remaining details of planning the Armory Show, and were perceived by Henri, Sloan and others as part of an inner circle in control. Sloan later observed that suddenly "we found that an inner clique in the Association was making plans to hire an Armory with funds from no one knew where and we were going to import from Europe a tremendous exhibition of painting and sculpture. Henri and the rest of the group around him were rebuffed whenever they asked questions and I was so wrapped up in *The Masses* that I had little to do with the plans or meetings."[118] As one of the members of this inner circle, MacRae later commented that:

> *Many committees were formed, many members, and soon it got down to about six who ran it to the finish. Four or three worked together in an office, side by side for a year, no painting, just clerical work…Walt Kuhn, Davies + myself were the happy slavies.*[119]

By late November, the process of selecting the American art was still being promoted on the one hand as nonjuried and on the other as by invitation. When the AAPS met on December 17, a Committee of Domestic Exhibits was formed, with Glackens as Chairman and Borglum, Brinley, Clarke, Fry, Nankivell, Prendergast, Taylor, and Tucker as members.[120] Kuhn observed that "Glack has come out strong and determined to keep the standard of American stuff way up."[121]

The Domestic Art Committee Record Book (cat. 53)—in which accepted and rejected works were noted—provides a fascinating, if incomplete, glimpse into the complex selection process. Notable absences included William Merritt Chase and John Singer Sargent, whose conventional success, academic affiliations, and negative opinions of modern art likely resulted in their exclusion. Various modernists, however, were, for unknown reasons, also not represented, including the pioneering Arthur Dove, as well as A.S. Baylinson, Jerome Blum, Charles Demuth, and B.J.O. Nordfeldt.[122]

Davies and Kuhn had already played important roles in the selection of American art and would continue to do so. Katherine Dreier (cat. 13) wrote that she was "thrilled to think that…Davies liked my work sufficiently to invite me."[123] Kuhn wrote to his illustrator friend Arthur Young that he was instructed by the committee to invite him to exhibit six drawings, later urging the tardy artist not to "disappoint me in this as it was upon my suggestion that you were invited." [124] Similarly, he wrote to the modernist painter Henry Keller in Cleveland, responding to his question of whether he would "have any chance with the jury," exclaiming "why man you are invited and can send anything you please."[125] Kuhn also asked Keller to do some advertising by distributing poster-window cards.

By mid-December, Kuhn had launched a nationwide publicity campaign, positioning the show as "a logical sequel to the modern exhibitions at Cologne…and the two Post-Impressionist Exhibitions in London," sending buttons and posters to Prendergast in Boston, Schamberg in Philadelphia, and James Lamb in Washington D.C., among others.[126] In a letter of December 12 to Pach, Kuhn referred to a list he had given papers of the "European stuff which we know of definitely," which "will be like a bombshell."[127] Asking Pach for thumbnail bios and portrait photos of the artists, Kuhn exclaimed, "Don't disappoint me on this—our show must be talked about all over the US before the doors open….We want this old show of ours to mark the starting point of the *new spirit* in art, at least as far as America is concerned."[128] A Subcommittee released the names of many of the prominent foreign artists, ranging from Jean-Dominique Ingres, to Cézanne, Gauguin, van Gogh, Redon, Matisse, Picasso, and others. It was noted that a list of works by Americans "is in progress and the result will be announced later."[129]

Kuhn claimed credit at this time for devising the uprooted pine tree emblem for the show, adapted from the Massachusetts flag carried into battle during the Revolutionary War,

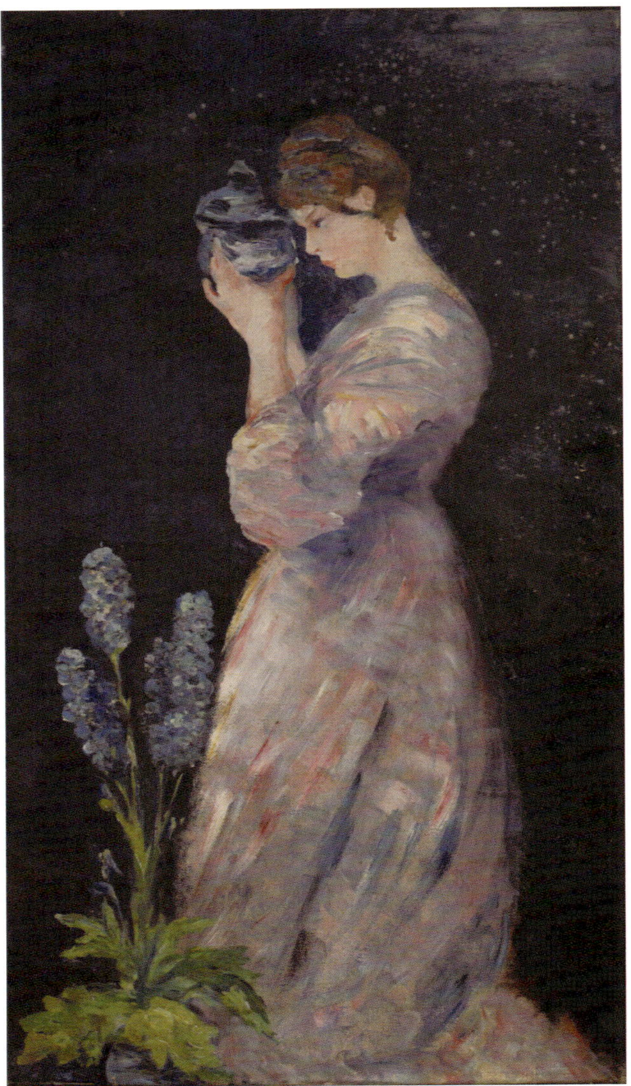

Cat. 13.
Katherine Dreier, *The Blue Bowl*, 1911, oil on canvas, Yale University Art Gallery, Gift of Barbara B. and Theodore Dreier, Jr., in honor of the Katherine S. Dreier Bequest

in a letter to Vera on December 14 (cat. 63).[130] He noted that Davies made the drawing and that it would be used for all printed materials, including thousands of "campaign buttons" to distribute "to anybody—from bums to preachers."[131] Kuhn's student Wood Gaylor was among those recruited to publicize and talk about the exhibition of new art: "Walt wanted to make sure that this thing was an intensely popular sort of show and his instructions to us when we were distributing posters was to put them in every gin mill on Second, Third and Ninth Avenues and to cover not only the part of the town that would normally be interested but to get into the parts of the town that would not ordinarily think in terms of art exhibitions."[132]

Inquiring about the costs of an electric sign on Broadway, Kuhn also wrote extensively to newspapers, including the *Kansas City Post*. Kuhn noted that he was looking at the press book (cat. 47) and realized that "you might be able to use some stuff…The papers all over the country have already given us 62 columns of articles, many of them illustrated with photographs…. We are doing this according to American methods and have already spent a good deal of money on advertising."[133]

At the end of 1912, it was observed that the "new movement in art" guided by the AAPS 'has at last got past the stage of simple news."[134] The list of artists, from Ingres to the Italian Futurists, was "no surprise [for the] the classics of modern times are hand in hand with the revolutionists."[135] Projecting about 500 foreign and 1,500 American works, presented in 27 temporary rooms, the AAPS was credited with organizing what "is going to be the greatest art exhibition ever held in this country….as catholic as the widest definition of that word."[136] The educational focus of exposing the American public and artists to modern art was emphasized in an official statement released by Davies and elaborated upon by Gutzon Borglum.[137] Furthermore, Borglum reported that some of his fellow AAPS artists, looking at the list of foreign paintings, had exclaimed, "'It will take the best that's in us to stand up against this.'"[138] By January 6, Quinn was referring to the project as "this show of Davies and Kuhn," and less than a month before the opening of the show, Davies' plan for the installation— arranged chronologically to encourage the public to apprehend the advanced European at the end of a continuous evolution—was officially accepted at the AAPS meeting of January 22.[139]

In the beginning of the new year, the publicity for the forthcoming show projected 2,000 works representative of all the various phases of modern art, especially in France, with separate rooms devoted to Cézanne, van Gogh, Gauguin, Matisse, and Redon. The list of artists' names and numbers of works did not yet include any Americans. It was noted, however, that "the revolutionaries to be present in this exhibition are by no means confined to Europe" for "there are a considerable number in our own country, of which…Davies is a distinguished example."[140]

Referring to the previous Independent exhibitions of 1910 and 1911, Arthur Hoeber commented that the forthcoming show "promises far more excitement, interest and, enter-

Cat. 63
Walt Kuhn, New York, NY. letter to Vera Kuhn, 4 p. handwritten, illustrated, December 14, 1912
Walt Kuhn, Kuhn Family Papers and Armory Show Records, 1859-1978, bulk 1900-1949, Archives of American Art, Smithsonian Institution

tainment…"[141] Another critic observed that the prominent and upcoming AAPS members and organizers of the show were not a group of "'refused' [artists] looking for an opportunity to show their work," but rather aimed "to encourage the modern artists of Europe and America, whether or not their art has been acceptable with those who have largely controlled the exhibits heretofore."[142] Finally, on January 26, with most of the domestic works received, a partial list was released, with a separate mention of the specialist in painted screens, Robert Chanler, as most "impressive of the American work that has felt the influence of this movement in Europe."[143] One of his decorative panels was illustrated along with works by Brancusi, Redon, and Matisse's *Red Madras Headdress* (*Le Madras Rouge*, see cat. 74). Although the projected 1,500 works by native artists was going to be "the largest number ever assembled at one time in this city," it was noted that "the main interest …lies in the display of 400 works from abroad…."[144] Promoting the Armory Show in an advance interview, Stieglitz placed Marin on an equal footing with Matisse, Picasso, Braque, and Gleizes as "emancipated artists" who would all "froth at the mouth" if pigeonholed and labeled "down the line of alleged 'Futurist' descent."[145]

On February 6, in the midst of the final preparations for the opening of the show, Borglum bitterly resigned from the AAPS, charging that the selection process for American sculpture was compromised by favoritism on the part of Davies and Mowbray-Clarke, fellow members of the sculpture committee who had allegedly ignored the work of Daniel Chester French and others. The flurry of publicity generated little sympathy for Borglum but greater excitement about the monumental undertaking.[146] Adding to the excitement had been a delay in the first shipment of art works from abroad due to heavy storms at sea.[147] By February 13, the exhibition was ready for the installation of nearly 1,200 works of art by the Hanging Committee in record time within several days, which was lauded as an epic feat reflecting "American business methods on a scale and of a kind not before applied to such problems as this."[148]

On Sunday, February 16, the successful viewing for the press was held. The formal opening of the International Exhibition of Modern Art was held on Monday afternoon and evening, February 17, with around 4,000 guests present—as Kuhn observed, "all society was there, all the art public," mostly viewing the new, seemingly incomprehensible works of the European moderns.[149] (cat. 56) Art students (such as Wood Gaylor) sold catalogues and handed out free buttons with the pine tree emblem and the words "The New Spirit" emblazoned in red below. (cat. 65) Quinn formally opened the exhibition with the pronouncement of the show as "the most complete art exhibition that has been held anywhere in the world during the last quarter of a century."[150] Extending special thanks to Davies and Kuhn, he asserted that "American artists…do not dread the ideas of the culture of Europe."[151]

The concept of "The New Spirit" as a promotional tagline for the exhibition may be related to an article with the same title by Hutchins Hapgood, published prior to the opening. An anarchist, believer in progressive socialism, associate of Stieglitz, and editorial writer for various New York newspapers, Hapgood linked the new "spirit of self-expression in art" with "that of industry."[152] Both were "two manifestations of the new social spirit….the new spirit of democracy working against self-righteous authority and oppressive overlordship," as well as the corruption of Tammany Hall politics.[153] Hapgood also quoted his conversation with Mowbray-Clarke, "who talked enthusiastically of the new spirit underlying the organization" of the AAPS."[154] Discussing plans for the forthcoming Armory Show, Mowbray-Clarke

Cat. 65

asserted that "our impulse is to follow the spirit that does not accept authority."[155] Hapgood reprised these themes in articles at the opening and closing of the Armory Show, which he characterized as "a vital, restless attempt to bring art back to life, to instinct, to feeling, to expression, to personality."[156]

The exact number of works on view in the Armory Show remains unknown. Pach set the total as high as 1,600 works, "though the catalogue (cat. 57) [listing 1046 works] …listed far less than that number, whole sets of lithographs or etching being set down as a single item, and many things arriving too late to be included even in [the] supplement [bringing the total to 1112]."[157] As mysteriously noted by the critic Frank Jewett Mather, the exhibition "shifts bewilderingly day by day through changes of hanging and admission of new pictures."[158] The Armory Show was partitioned into 18 burlap-covered, octagonal rooms, referred to as "a cubist ground plan" and lettered from A to R in chronological order, ranging from French neo-classicists to Fauves and Cubists, with an inter-mixing of old and new.[159] The public was thereby encouraged to apprehend the advanced European

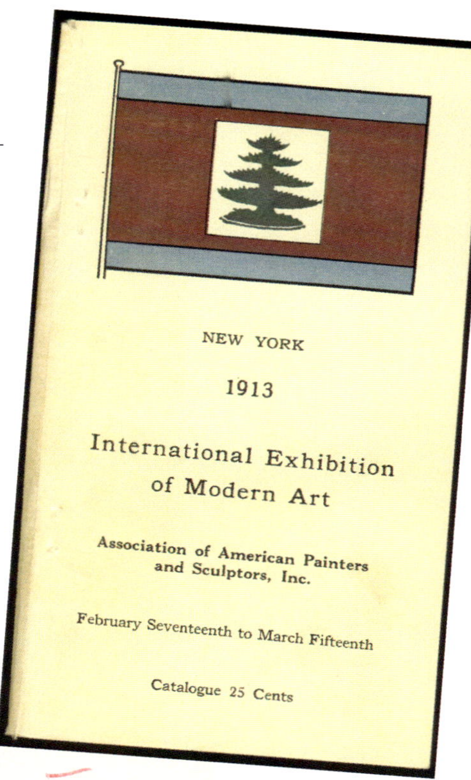

Cat. 57

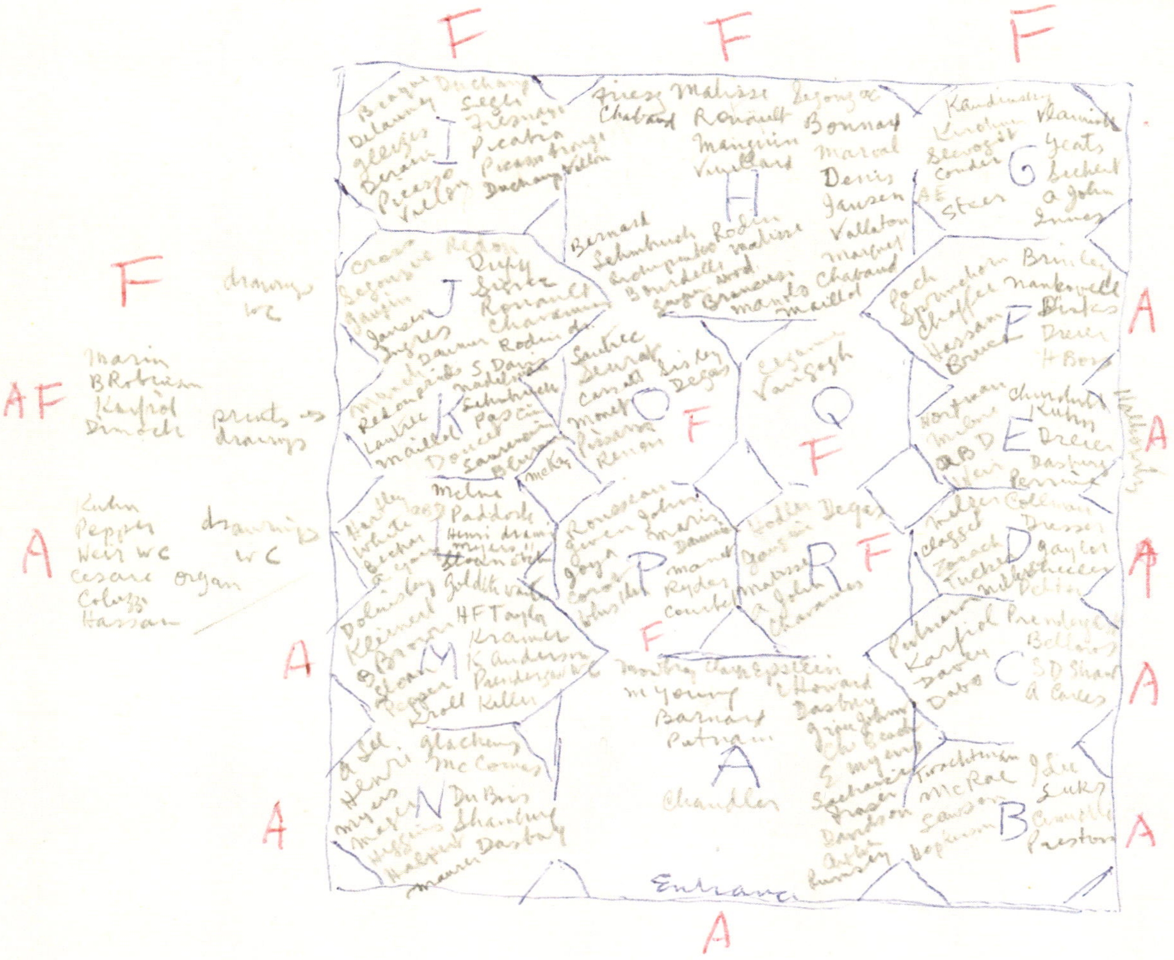

Fig. 1
Carl Zigrosser's diagram
of the Armory Show, n.d.,
Carl Zigrosser Papers,
Rare Book & Manuscript
Library, University of
Pennsylvania

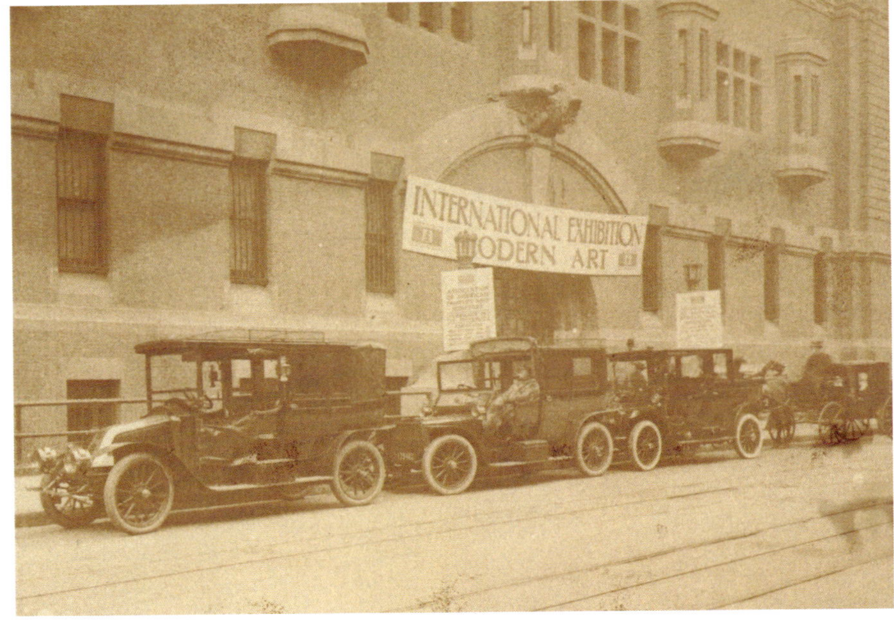

Fig. 2
Exterior view of 69th
Regiment Armory
Building, 1913, Archives
of American Art,
Smithsonian Institution

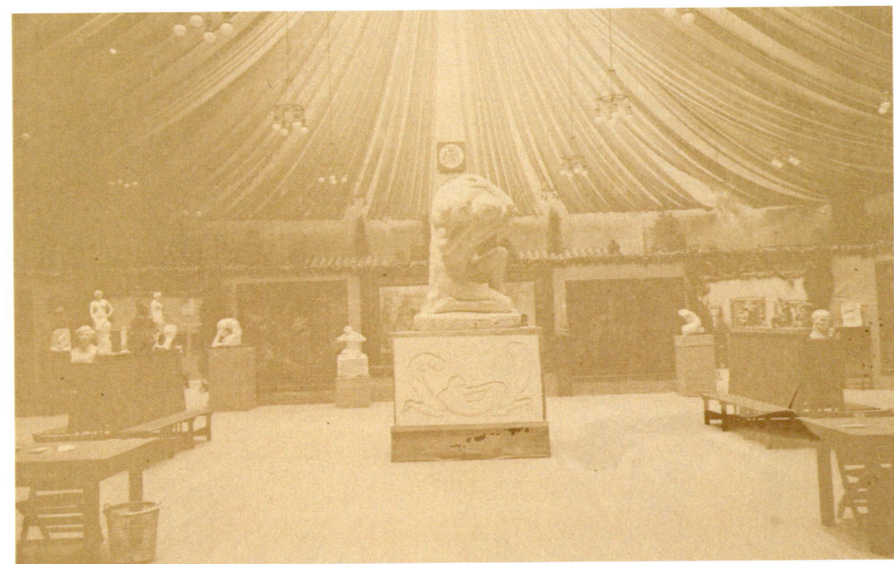

Fig. 4
Armory Show installation
view featuring Gallery A,
Archives of American Art,
Smithsonian Institution

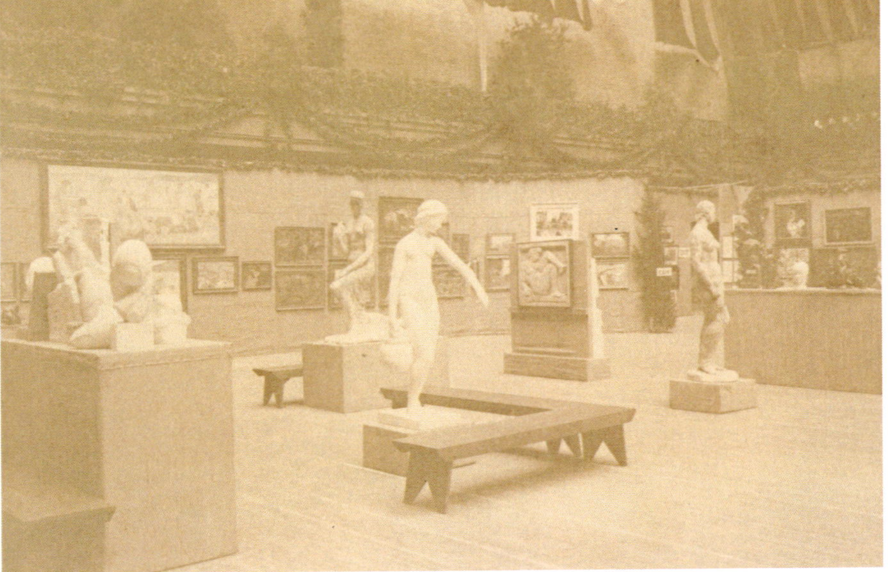

Fig. 5
Armory Show installation
view featuring Gallery H
Archives of American Art,
Smithsonian Institution

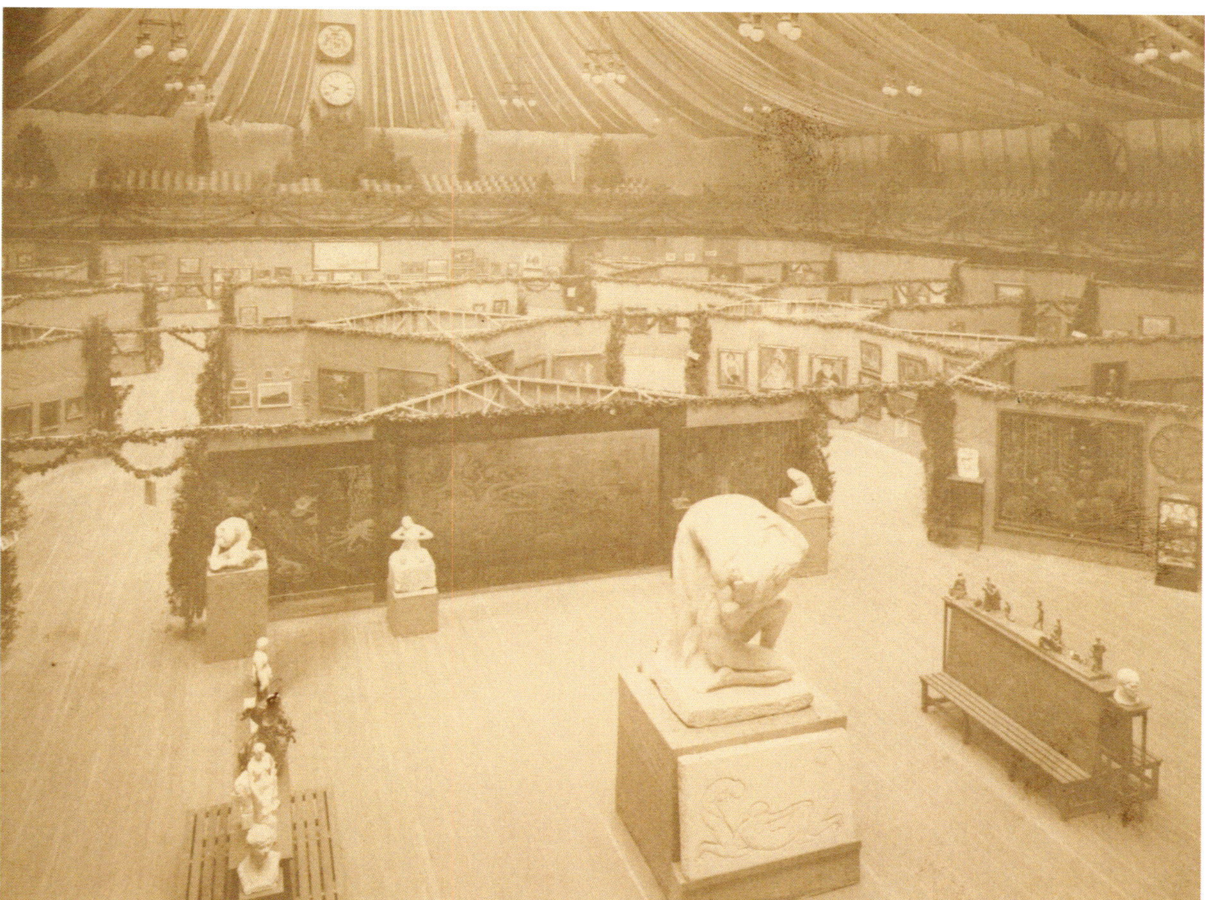

art at the end of a continuous historical and stylistic evolution. The military drill hall was further transformed into an art gallery by swags of greenery, including smilax and laurel, which were hung from the Armory balcony; evergreen trees were rhythmically placed behind them, unifying the entire installation visually and symbolically. Equated with the uprooted pine tree emblem of the AAPS, the greens were interpreted as representative of "artistic upheaval" and "the independent movement in contemporary art."[160] Bright yellow streamers, suspended from the ceiling and crowned by a monumental flag bearing a white pine tree, formed a canopy over the partitions, which were themselves decorated with garlands of laurel, evergreen, and smilax. [161]

Among the many visitors to the Armory Show was Carl Zigrosser, a young librarian and research cataloguer employed at the print gallery Keppel and Company. Later Curator of Prints at the Philadelphia Museum of Art, Zigrosser published an article about his experience of visiting the show. He also drew a little known diagram of the layout of the exhibition. (fig. 1) Zigrosser seems to have correctly identified the locations of many of the artists' works and described which galleries were devoted to American or foreign art or a combination. According to Zigrosser, the Armory Show "was really two exhibitions in one…a show of American paintings and sculpture by the young Independents and by a few sympathetic Academicians" and the European works.[162] Unfamiliar with many of the Americans, Zigrosser attempted to arrange them in groups in his notes, allying, for example, Ryder, Howard Coluzzi, Agnes Pelton, and Van Dearing Perrine with Davies.[163]

Entering the gallery from Lexington Avenue (fig. 2) through the pine-tree flanked entrance, a large central room (Gallery A) featured American sculpture and decorative arts, including Grace Mott Johnson's *Greyhound Pup #2* (cat. 20) and Ethel Myers's *The Gambler, Joe Johnson* (cat. 27, p.39). This gallery was dominated by George Gray Barnard's monumental sculpture influenced by Rodin, *The Prodigal Son and His Father* (1904, J.B. Speed Museum).[164] Jo Davidson's Rodinesque *Seated Female Nude (Study in Repose)* (cat. 9) and his relief sculpture of three abstracted nudes, located on the base below, represented a more modernist direction, thereby suggesting the range of works that would be encountered. Robert Chanler's universally praised, large, decorative screen paintings were also featured. (figs. 3,4)

Turning to the right toward 26th Street, the visitor entered a row of galleries, B-F, primarily featuring American paintings and some sculptures, including, in Gallery B, Chester Beach's allegorical *Unveiling of Dawn* (cat. 2, p.122), inspired by Rodin. MacRae's *Fairy Stories* (cat. 22, p. 90) and Lie's *The Black Teapot* (cat. 21, p.133), also on view in Gallery B,

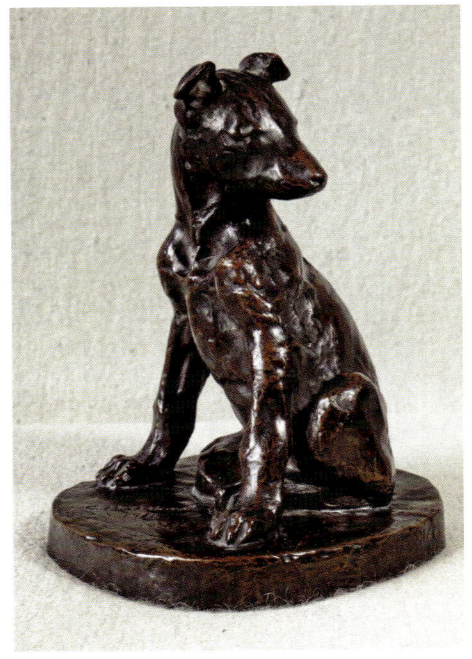

Cat. 20.
Grace Mott Johnson,
Greyhound Pup #2, 1911,
bronze, Collection of
Arthur A. Anderson

represented Impressionist and Post-Impressionist tendencies in American art on the part of two AAPS members. Paintings by Bellows, Prendergast, Hartley, Dabo (cat. 8, p. 126), Carles (cat. 6, p. 124), Webster (cat. 38, p. 138), and other Americans were shown in Gallery C. Hartley's other still life (cat.16, p. 16) was on view in Gallery D, which included modernist works by Charles Sheeler (cat. 32), Allen Tucker (cat. 36,p. 84), and former Henri pupil Kathleen McEnery, whose striking, large scale *Going to the Bath* (cat. 25, p. 135) greeted visitors with its strong colors, simplified forms, and flattened perspective.[165] The work of the show's primary organizers, Davies (cat. 10, p.127) and Kuhn (see cat. 72, p. 155), was featured in Gallery E, along with Henri pupil Florence Howell Barkley's vivid *Jerome Avenue Bridge* (cat. 1, p. 121), Van Dearing Perrine's abstract, tonalist painting, *The Ice Floes* (cat. 30, p. 136), and works by Gustave Cimiotti (cat. 7, p. 125), J. Alden Weir, and others. AAPS member Brinley's Post-Impressionist landscape *The Peony Garden* (cat. 4, p. 83), Bruce's Cézannesque *Still Life (with Dish of Fruit)* (cat. 5, p. 26), Edward Middleton Manigault's Expressionist *Adagio* (cat. 23, p. 29), Pach's

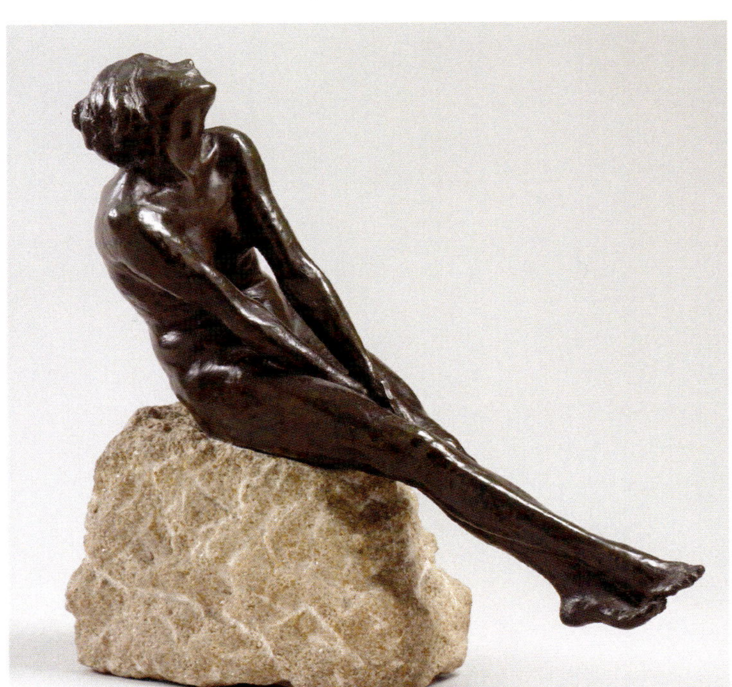

Cat. 9.
Jo Davidson,*Seated Female Nude (Study in Repose)*, 1913, bronze, The Angerman Collection

Cat. 32.
Charles Sheeler,
Chrysanthemums, 1912, oil on canvas, Whitney Museum of American Art, New York, Gift of the artist, 55.24

simplified, colorful *The Wall of the City* (cat. 29, p. 80), and Dreier's Impressionist painting, *The Blue Bowl* (cat. 13, p.18) were located in gallery F, the last space in this sequence. There was no exit, except by going back or forward to Gallery G, which featured English, Irish, and German painting, including Kandinsky's *Improvisation #27, Garden of Love* (1912, Metropolitan Museum of Art, see cat. 81, p. 157), which would be purchased by Stieglitz.[166]

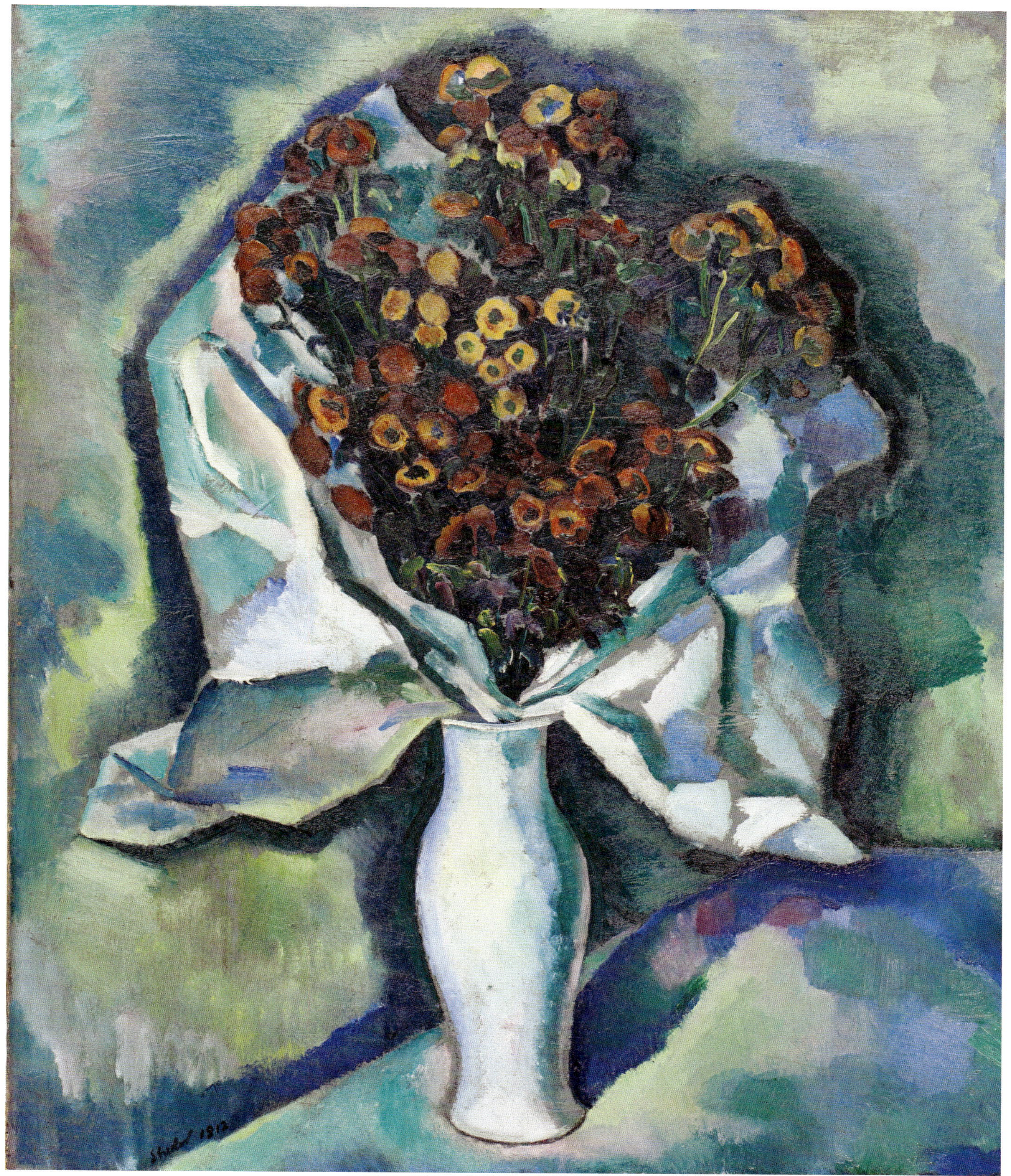

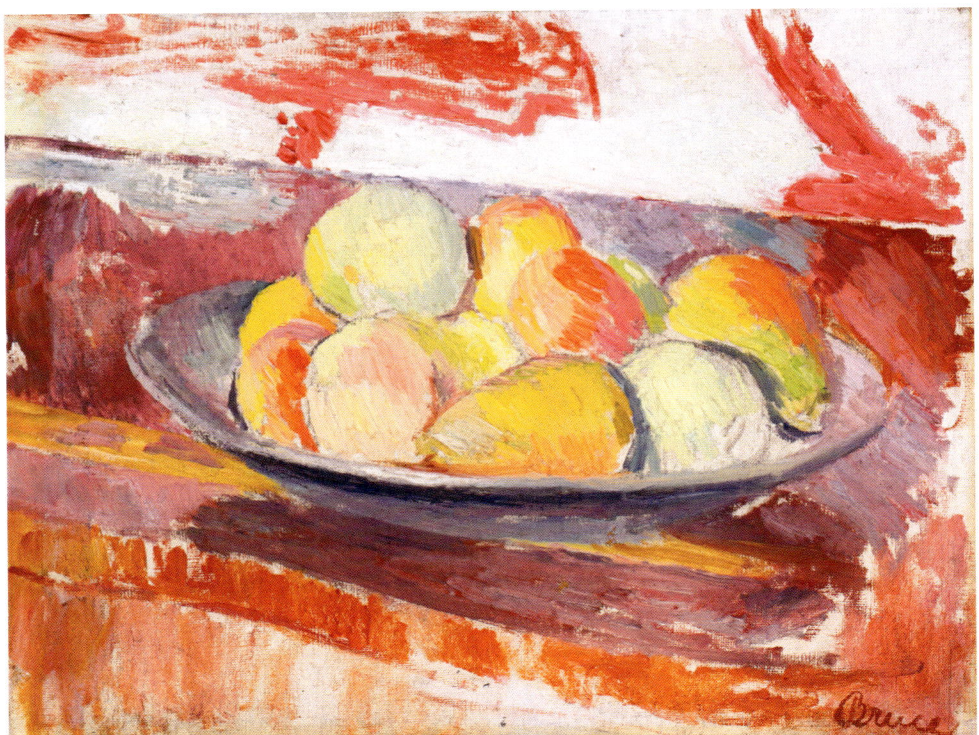

Cat. 5.
Patrick Henry Bruce, *Still Life (with Dish of Fruit)*, 1911, oil on canvas, Greenville County Museum of Art, Museum purchase from the Arthur and Holly Magill Fund

Continuing to the left, the visitor entered the largest gallery in the show, Gallery H (fig. 5), which featured a large group of French paintings and sculpture. Critics accorded ridicule and praise to the work of two artists in this gallery, Constantin Brancusi's abstract sculptures and Matisse's paintings, including the bold, colorful, Fauve study of a *Nude in a Wood* (cat. 40), which had been exhibited in the artist's first show in America at "291" in 1908. The next gallery, I, known as the "Chamber of Horrors," became the main attraction, featuring the *succès de scandale*, Marcel Duchamp's *Nude Descending a Staircase , No. 2* (1912, Philadelphia Museum of Art), subject of many parodies (see cat. 79, p. 156). Also featuring paintings by Picasso and Francis Picabia, this gallery of French paintings and sculpture soon became known as The Cubist Room, attracting the greatest numbers of visitors.

Going back toward Lexington Avenue, the next galleries, J and K, were dominated by the well-received symbolist figures and landscapes of Redon, complemented by Ingres's drawings (Gallery J) and Munch's prints (Gallery K). Gallery K, featuring French and American works on paper, included modernist watercolors and *Hackensack River* (cat. 3, p. 123) by Oscar Bluemner, as well as Stuart Davis's *Romance/The Doctor* (cat. 11, p. 128), and Hilda Ward's vibrant pastel *The Kennels* (cat. 37, p. 85), both former Henri students. Among the other highlights was Marin's modernist watercolor *St. Paul's, Lower Manhattan,* (cat. 24, p. 134), related to his series of the recently completed Woolworth Building, which were also on view and interpreted as futurist renditions of the metropolis. Gallery L featured a comprehensive group of American works on paper, including Prendergast's Post-Impressionist *Study* (cat. 31, p. 137), Sloan's Ashcan School etchings of contemporary life, *Night Windows, The Picture Buyer,* and *Anschutz Talk on Anatomy* (cats. 33-35, p. 28). Pastels by Davies and MacRae were also featured, as well as Henri's ink drawing *Where We Dined in the Latin Quarter, Paris, in 1896* (cat. 18, p. 42). Gallery M represented the range of American styles in painting, from the well-received realist cityscape *Terminal Yards* of Leon Kroll (fig. 6, p. 31), to the Impressionist paintings of Karl Anderson and G. Ruger Donoho, to works variously inspired by Cézanne, including Henry G. Keller's allegorical nudes, *Wisdom and Destiny* (1911, Cleveland Museum of Art) and Anne Goldthwaite's *House on the Hill* (1910-11, location unknown). Another highlight of this gallery was Hopper's boldly simplified *Sailing (The Sailboat)* (cat. 19, p. 132), his one entry in the show and first sale.[167]

Gallery N, to the left of the entrance of Gallery A, was devoted to American painting and sculpture, with works by pioneer Ashcan School sculptor Abastenia St. Leger Eberle (cat. 14,

Cat. 40.
Henri Matisse, *Nude in a Wood (Nu dans la forêt; Nu assis dans le bois)*, 1906, oil on board mounted on panel, Brooklyn Museum, Gift of George F. Of 52.150

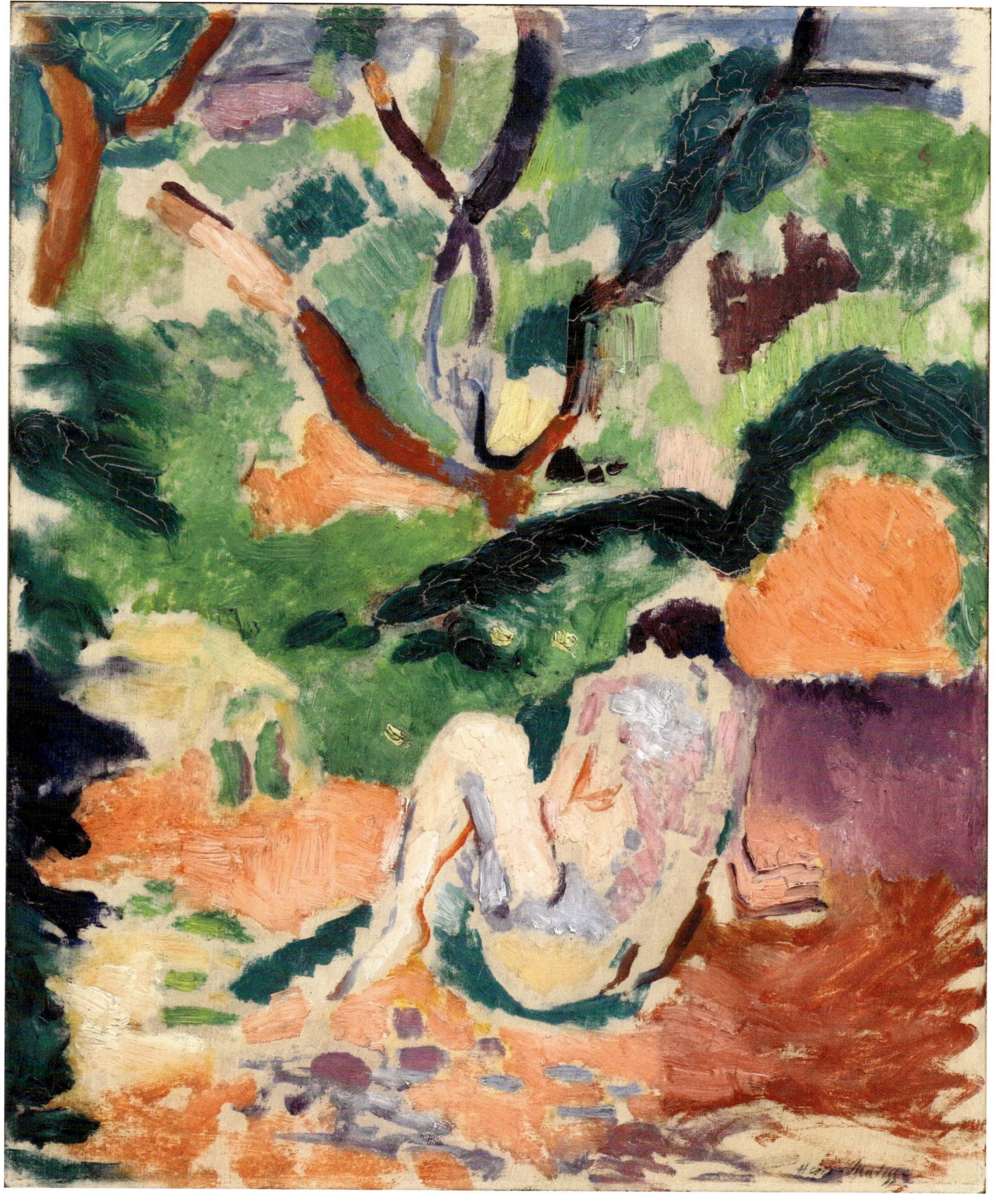

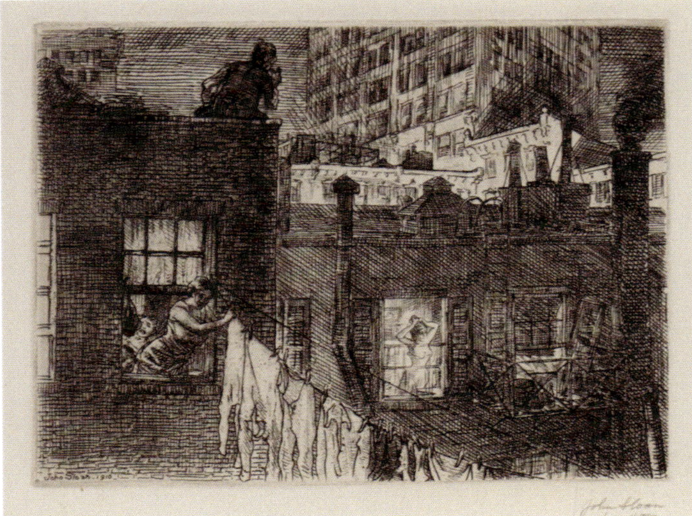

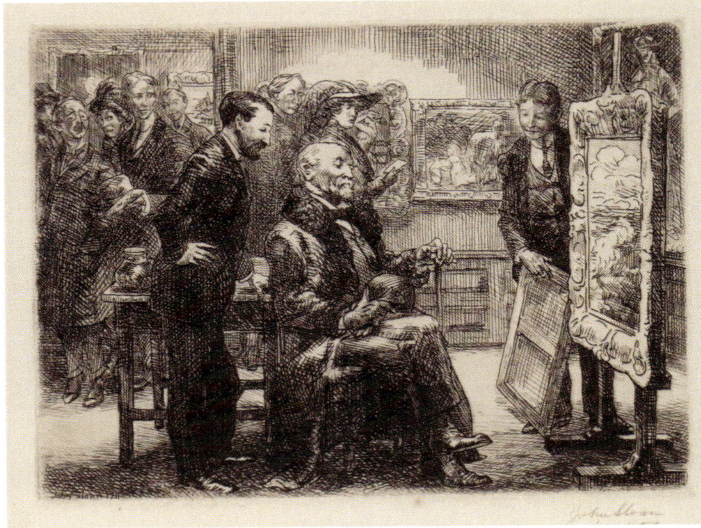

Cat. 33.
John Sloan, *Night Windows*, 1910, etching on paper, Montclair Art Museum, Gift of an anonymous donor, 1982.23

Cat. 34.
John Sloan, *The Picture Buyer*, 1911, etching on paper, Montclair Art Museum, Gift of an anonymous donor, 1982.24

Cat. 35.
John Sloan, *Anshutz on Anatomy*, 1912, etching on paper, Delaware Art Museum, Gift of Helen Farr Sloan, 1963

p. 30), Jerome Myers's *End of the Walk* (cat. 27, p.89), and Robert Henri's *The Spanish Gypsy* (cat. 17, p. 131), praised for its naturalism when it was purchased the following year for the Metropolitan Museum of Art .[168] Also featured were works by Du Bois, Maurer, Mowbray-Clarke, Schamberg, and Glackens's monumental, well-received *Family Group,* reflecting the influence of Auguste Renoir (cat. 15, p. 130).

The work of Renoir himself, along with his fellow French Impressionists Claude Monet, Edouard Manet, Edgar Degas, Camille Pissarro, and Alfred Sisley, were featured in Gallery O, which formed part of a quartet of galleries in the center of the show, devoted to the historical sources of modern art. To access this gallery, the visitor had either to pass through the entrance space (A) or to enter it from the "Cubist Room" (H). Cassatt was grouped with the Impressionists, likely without her knowledge or permission.[169] The work of Post-Impressionists Georges Seurat and Henri Toulouse-Lautrec was also exhibited here, as well as in Gallery P, which included a striking group of works by Henri Rousseau, lent by pioneering modernist Max Weber, who had withdrawn his own works from the show because only two had been accepted.[170] This gallery also included the work of pre-Impressionists Francisco Goya, Gustave Courbet, Honoré Daumier, Eugène Delacroix, and the historical American contingent, Theodore Robinson, John H. Twachtman, James McNeill Whistler, and especially a group of 10 evocative landscapes, luminescent seascapes, and figure paintings by Albert Pinkham Ryder, whose works outnumbered any of the French Impressionists.

To access the final two historical spaces of the show, Q and R, one had either to return to the entry gallery or access them from the "Chamber of Horrors" (H). Gallery Q featured the paintings of Cézanne and van Gogh. Gallery R was a mixed array, including historical works by Gauguin and the symbolist painter Pierre Puvis de Chavannes, as well as Matisse, Picasso, and Augustus John, the primary representative of English Post-Impressionism.

Given the complexity of these arrangements, the presence of special attendants wearing information buttons (cat. 41, see front cover) to direct visitors must have been very helpful, as commented upon in the press.[171] Their assistance was all the more vital since the original goal of separate rooms—setting apart "the work of one man or a group of kindred spirits, so that what they say will not interfere with the messages of their neighbors"—had not been achieved.[172] The availability of the catalogue,5 pamphlets on European art, and 57 half-tone postcards of American and foreign art for purchase (cats. 57, 72-82, pp. 152, 155-7) further augmented the educational functions of the show.[173] In the catalogue preface, Davies empha-sized the European section of the show "to give the public here the opportunity to see for themselves the results of new influences at work in other countries in an art way."[174] Gregg

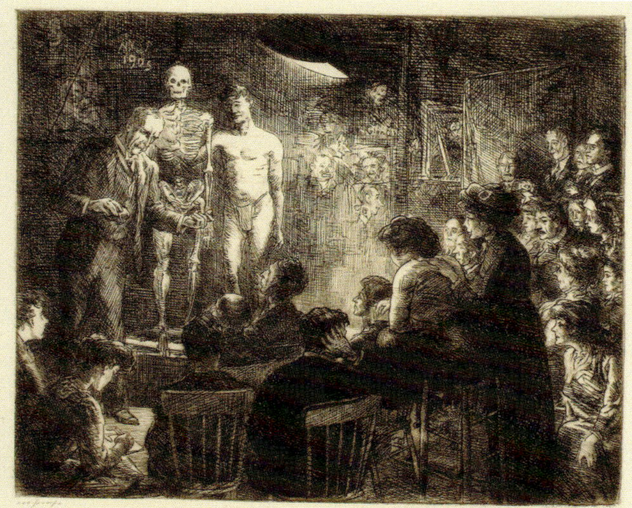

also stressed the importance of the foreign art for American artists who may "have fallen behind through escaping…through distance and for other reasons…the forces that have manifested themselves on the other side of the Atlantic" and "cannot be ignored because they have had results."[175] Proclaiming the AAPS to be "against cowardice," Gregg asserted that "art is a sign of life" and that "there can be no life…no development without change" and a willingness to confront the unfamiliar.[176]

While the initial attendance at the Armory Show was disappointing, by the second Saturday, March 1, "the storm broke…and controversy raged." [177]

Fueling the mounting attendance was an avalanche of publicity at a time when daily newspapers in New York had begun to expand their reporting on and criticism of the arts.[178] (cat. 47) The primary focus of publications on the Armory Show was European art, especially the work of Duchamp, Brancusi, Picabia, and Matisse. Deemed "a puzzle of the cubist variety," or "an academic painting of an artichoke," Duchamp's *Nude Descending a Staircase, No. 2* generated the most written and visual commentary.[179] As "the conundrum of the season," it was described, in only one of many instances, as "having the effect to the vulgar minded of a sliding of all the weather-beaten shingles off from the roof of a house."[180] Picabia was "the latest and most daring cubist" who "shows mathematical shapes of which Euclid would have never dreamed."[181] Brancusi's sculpture *Mademoiselle Pogany* was described as "a kid's glass marble placed on a cracker."[182] (see cat. 50, p. 157) The work of Matisse, "the young idol of Paris," was typically characterized as "monstrous things…fantastic in drawing, crude in color, absurd and unintelli-

gible."[183] Receiving more positive critical attention were the older masters, such as Redon, Puvis de Chavannes, noted for his "serene majesty," and Cézanne (see cat. 39, p. 157), who "reigns as king of the new Art."[184]

Given that the Armory Show was composed primarily of American art, it is not surprising to discover, upon closer examination of the publicity, that considerable coverage was also devoted to the contributions of native artists. The earlier European artists were at times grouped with such older American artists as Ryder, Weir, Twachtman, and Whistler as "sane and serious men…whose art only shines the more by its close proximity to this vaudevillian collection."[185] The show was widely acclaimed for its goal of stimulating "our American artists by showing what the rest of the advanced world is about" in presenting a

Cat. 23.
Edward Middleton Manigault, *Adagio*, 1912, oil on canvas, Collection of the Mint Museum, Charlotte, North Carolina.
Museum Purchase with exchange funds from various donors; 2010.66

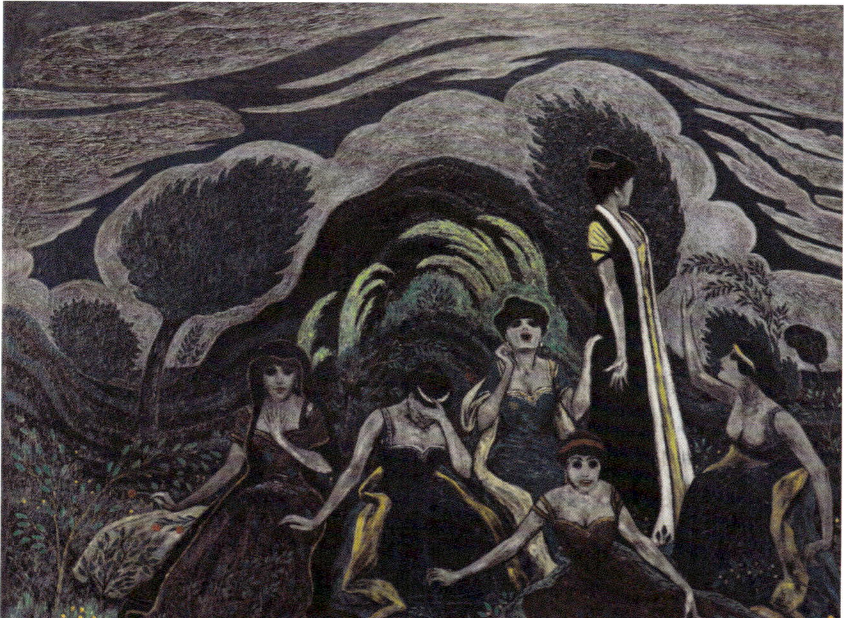

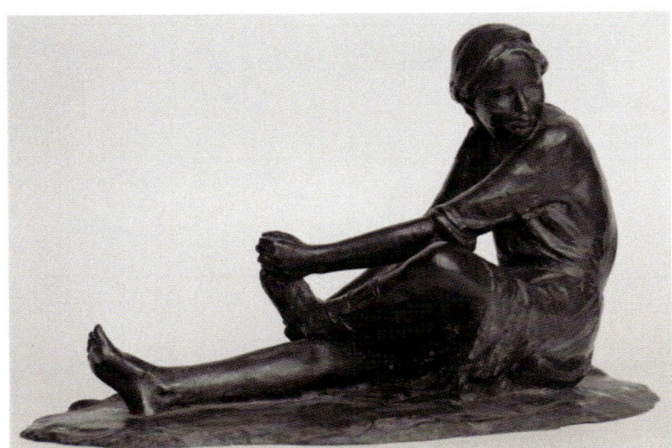
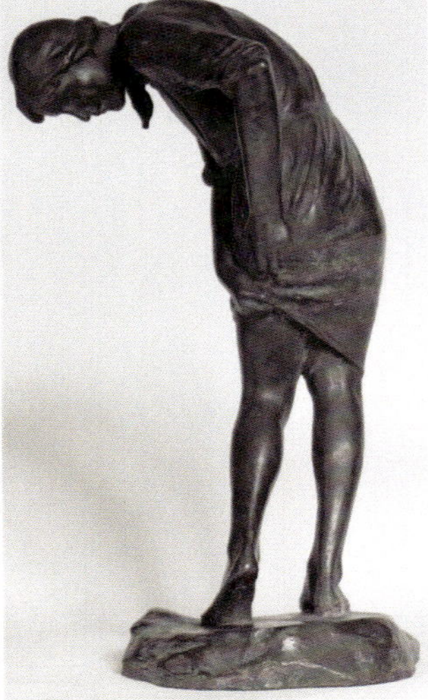
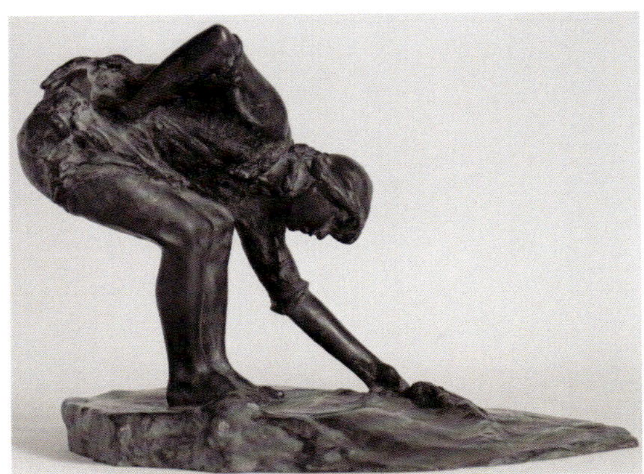

Cat. 14.
Abastenia St. Leger Eberle, three bronze sculptures from the *Wading Series* exhibited as a group: *Girl Seated*, *Girl Standing*, *Sea Treasures*, modeled 1911, cast in 1913 or later, Corcoran Gallery of Art, Washington, DC, Museum Purchase, Special Authority of the Director

much larger scope of modern foreign art than the international exhibitions at the Carnegie Institute in Pittsburgh and elsewhere.[186] The AAPS, and often specifically Davies and Kuhn, was thanked for providing "these shocks to our aesthetic sense" which "will clear away some of the cobwebs…"[187] Therefore, "a careful student may trace the connection between the men of today, who express themselves in the language of Post-Impressionism, back to the earlier revolutionists Ingres, Courbet, and Delacroix, and later Puvis de Chavannes, Daumier, and Manet."[188] Referring to the American art on view as "a somewhat gorgeous family affair," based on "the old 'Eight,' with those whom they have encouraged to contribute," critic Frank Jewett Mather praised the "distinctly self-sacrificing and public-spirited willingness [of the AAPS] to centre the interest of the show in the foreign exhibits."[189] In sequels, he discussed the American contributions in greater depth, praising Jo Davidson's "adroit and charming sculpture," as well as the figurines of St. Eberle and Ethel Myers (cats. 14,27, p. 39).[190] He also observed that "Weir and Hassam, both well represented by retrospective groups, shine with old masterly serenity amid the strident new work;" except for Ryder, whose nocturnes "represent about the best America has produced in purely imaginative painting," they were "the only older Americans honored by a group exhibition."[191] Henri's "intensely conceived" *Spanish Gypsy* was regarded by Mather as "one of [his] best."[192] (cat. 17, p. 131)

One of the most common themes of the publicity was the relative sanity of American art, as proclaimed soon after the opening by one critic who noted that among "the types of work to be seen outside the Post-Impressionist lot there are works by a goodly sprinkling of American painters of achieved position, like Henri and Davies….so welcome to the eye that the very presence of the freak canvases gives the rest an enviable general air of conservative worth and good old fashioned charm."[193] This notion was also articulated by James B. Townsend, who asserted that, in comparison with Cézanne, Gauguin, van Gogh, and especially Matisse, such Americans as Weir, Hassam, Brinley, Lawson, Bellows, Cassatt, Glackens, Cimiotti,"and even Arthur Davies seem almost academic."[194] Another critic complained about the tendency of visitors to throng the rooms of European modernist art while ignoring the more conventional displays of American art:

We would call the attention of our readers to the fact that, entirely apart from the weird output of the "Eccentrics," there is on at the Armory an unusually good display of the work of… such sterling American painters as…Henri…Glackens…Myers… Davies… Kuhn…Brinley…MacRae[and others.] Yet this fine and exceptional display

Cat. 26.
John Mowbray-Clarke, *The Tree*, ca. 1912, plaster medallion, Harry Ransom Center, The University of Texas at Austin, The Sunwise Turn Bookshop Collection

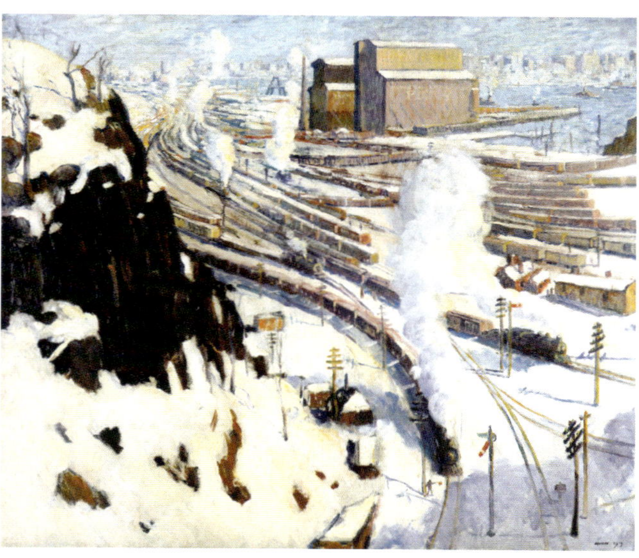

Fig. 6
Leon Kroll, *Terminal Yards*, 1913, oil on canvas Collection of the Flint Institute of Arts, Michigan, Gift of Mrs. Arthur Jerome Eddy, 1931

has been and is being neglected while curious New York runs in to the Armory '"to see the freaks"...[195]

Observing that the "merely eccentric artists occupy a comparatively subordinate position," Royal Cortissoz commented that it was "to the credit of our countrymen that their indulgences in egotistical fatuity has as yet been slight," with only a few exceptions of those "making portentous use of the new found 'independence.'"[196] Recently rediscovered by Laurette E. McCarthy, this article also featured what may well have been the first images revealing exactly how Duchamp's infamous *Nude Descending a Staircase, No. 2*, Gleize's Cubist *Man on a Balcony*, and several of Matisse's notorious paintings were presented in the Armory Show.[197] (fig. 7, p. 33)

Progressive critic Charles Caffin viewed the show as "a two-ringed circus...of conflicting impressions;" however, he was hopeful that "when we have digested this exhibition we shall be less stolidly complacent over the achievements of our painters," noted for their "rank materialism and mild sentimentality," and for being "at least a quarter of a century behind Europe."[198] In a later review, Caffin characterized "the bulk of the American exhibits" as sharing the motive of "naturalistic, or impressionistic representation," as distinguished from "the spirit of the new [European] movement, interpreted as an expression of the effort to intellectualize the emotions and sensations."[199] Referring primarily to the Eight, Caffin also noted landscapes by Lawson, Brinley, Kuhn, Tucker, and others, which "vary the routine of naturalism by the quality of invention displayed," singling out works by Hartley, Sheeler, and Schamberg as by those "who are feeling the influence of the foreign movement."[200]

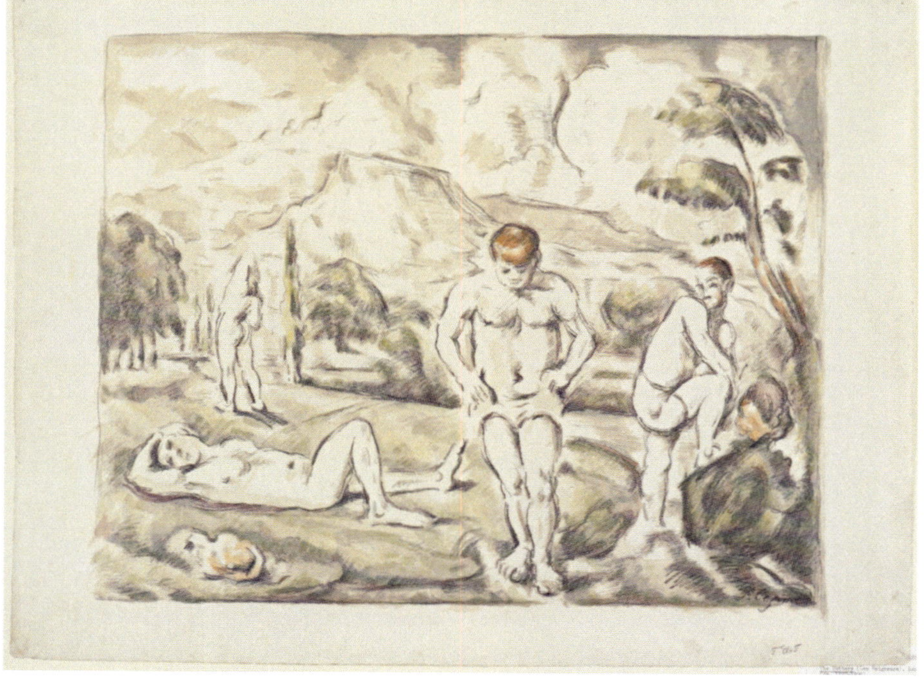

Cat. 39.
Paul Cézanne, *The Bathers*, large plate (Les baigneurs, grand planche), 1896-97, lithograph, The Museum of Modern Art, Lillie P. Bliss Collection, 1934

Others, however, equated some of the American work with the European avant-garde, as seen in a group of caricatures, "Art at the Armory Show by Powers, Futurist," in the *New York American*, (fig. 8). Among the works featured were Kuhn's painting inspired by van Gogh, *Morning* (see cat. 72, p. 35), with the caption "4th of July in Egypt, The Mexican Revolution has nothing on this painting" and in which the artist himself was mistakenly designated as a Cubist.[201] Other Americans represented alongside caricatures of works by Duchamp and

31

Brancusi were Luks, Davidson, and Marin, with one of his watercolors from the Woolworth building series, which had already received considerable attention in the press when exhibited at 291 just prior to the opening of the Armory Show.[202] Regarded by Harriet Monroe as "one of the most poetic of our radicals," Marin had received favorable notice for his watercolors from Caffin, who had observed that the Armory Show "will be an exhibition almost exclusively—certainly in its main interest—foreign. So it is pleasant in anticipation of this foreign invasion, to note an exhibition fully as independent, quite as conclusively one of artistic liberty, which, moreover, is thoroughly American."[203] The caricature of Marin's watercolor *Woolworth Building, No. 29* (fig. 9, p. 34) was accompanied by the caption "The Ten Cent Store with a Soul," which alluded to the new corporate headquarters of the Woolworth stores and to the verbiage of self-expression under critical attack in an accompanying satirical article by Aloysius P. Levy. Taking aim at "Joe" Davidson, "Maury" Prendergast, and "Bob" Henri, Levy reserved his most humorous ire for the American modernist Marguerite Zorach, in the company of "Paul Picasso" and Matisse, as among "the Cubists…Futurists… Post-Futurists…Post-Impressionists…Cabalists and the Post-Paranoics."[204] Her "extreme modernity" was also noted by another critic commenting on the diverse and "democratic arrangement" of the American art galleries.[205]

One of Pach's paintings, *Casentino Mountains*, would later, during the show's run in Chicago, be mysteriously illustrated in a newspaper article with Matisse's *Le Madras rouge*, along with the headline "Futurist Pictures-Two of them from Dunning. Which are Which?," comparing the two pictures to works by patients at the local mental health institution.[206] Similarly Marin was grouped as an extremist/Post-Impressionist in an article entitled "The New Delirium" (fig. 10, p. 37), which featured a caricature of his *Woolworth Building No. 32* (1912, National Gallery of Art), alongside parodies of Picabia's work.[207] Marin was also paired with Duchamp as a Futurist in an infamous article entitled "Nobody Who has Been Drinking Is Let In To See This Show."[208] Marin, Picabia and Maurer were castigated in another article as "unintelligible in their efforts to paint abstractions—such as motion, feeling, pure sensation, sound."[209] Marin's Woolworth building series, "suffering from severe indigestion," was combined by one critic in an article also parodying Duchamp's and Brancusi's work.[210] Maurer was accused of slinging "gobs of paint…in his spattered land-

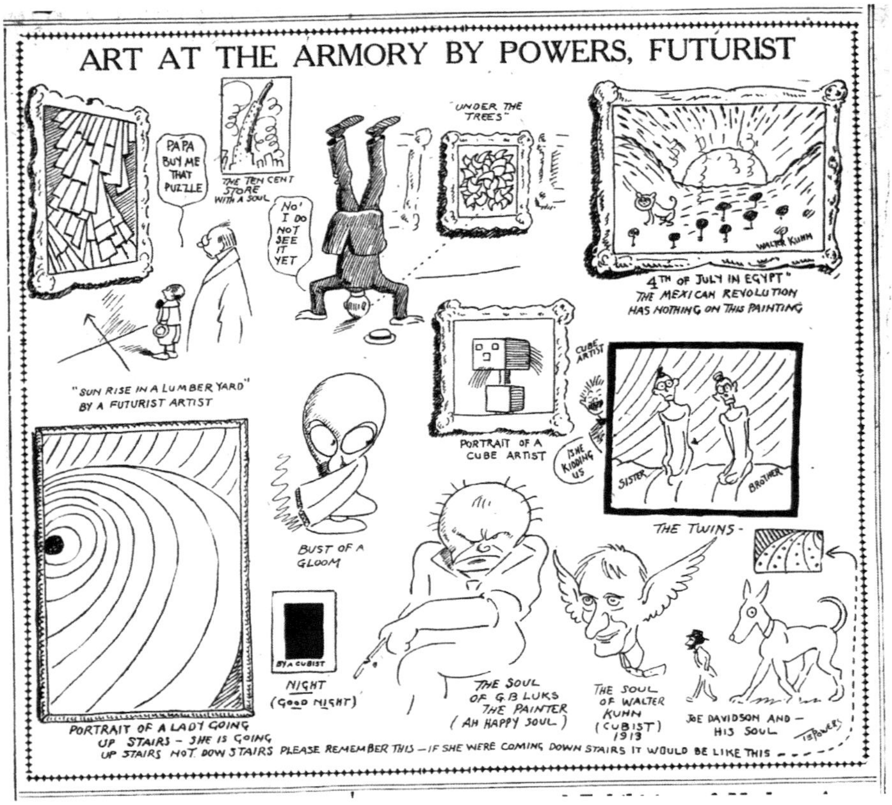

Fig. 8
"Art at the Armory Show by Powers, Futurist," *New York American*, February 22, 1913, Library of Congress, Washington D.C.

Fig. 7 (opposite)
[Royal Cortissoz], "'The Ism' Exhibition," *New York Tribune*, February 17, 1913, 7, with works by Matisse, Duchamp, and Gleizes. Library of Congress, Washington D.C.

NEW-YORK TRIBUNE. MONDAY, FEBRUARY 17. 1913.

THE "ISM" EXHIBITION

Painting and Sculpture at the 69th Regiment Armory.

INDEPENDENCE IN ART

A Remarkable Affair, Despite Some Freakish Absurdities.

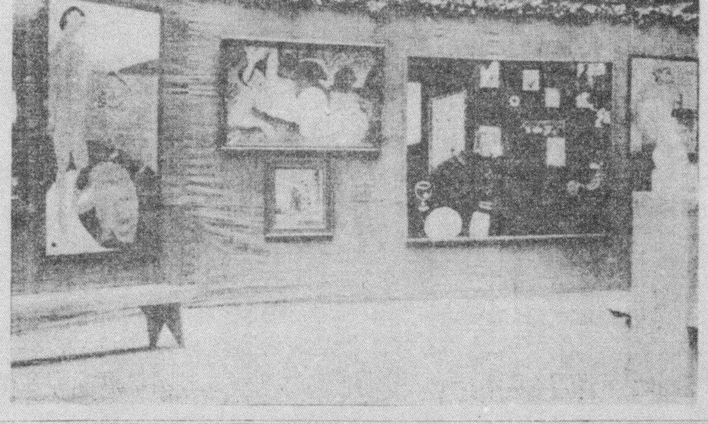

POST-IMPRESSIONISM AT THE INTERNATIONAL EXHIBITION OF MODERN ART.
Nudes by Matisse and an interior by the same painter.

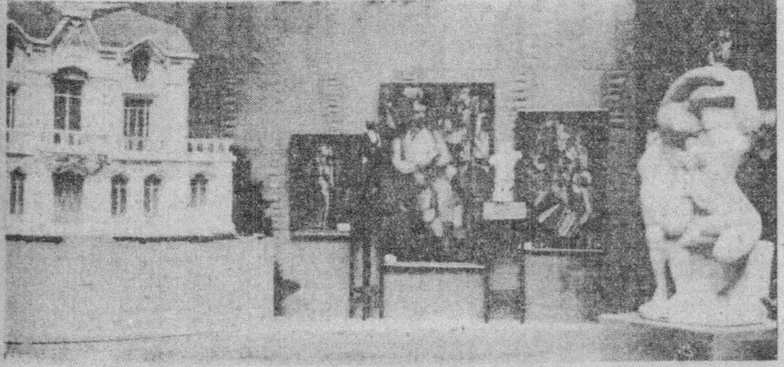

IN THE CUBIST ROOM AT THE MODERN ARTS SHOW.

Cubist facade by Duchamp-Villon on left; painting by Marcel Duchamp in centre, and "Family Life," a sculpture by Alexandre Orchifenko, on right.

DID NOT CRITICISE TAFT

Dr. Eliot Denies Attacking President's Appointments.

"THE GEISHA" TO BE REVIVED.

THE ROSE BOWL.

An Excursion Into Art.

"MOVIES" TO TALK TO-DAY.

LILLIAN RUSSELL TO LECTURE.

GEN. WOODFORD FUNERAL

Distinguished Gathering Attend Last Impressive Rites.

BIG ARMY DELEGATION

Veterans Accompany Cortege to House and Take Last Leave of Dead Comrade.

AID FOR ALL IN LIBRARY

Annual Report Sounds Key of Broader Policy.

NEW MOTTO FOR 1913

Great $12,000,000 Institution Will Try to Solve Every Sort of Problem.

TO AID CITY HISTORY CLUB

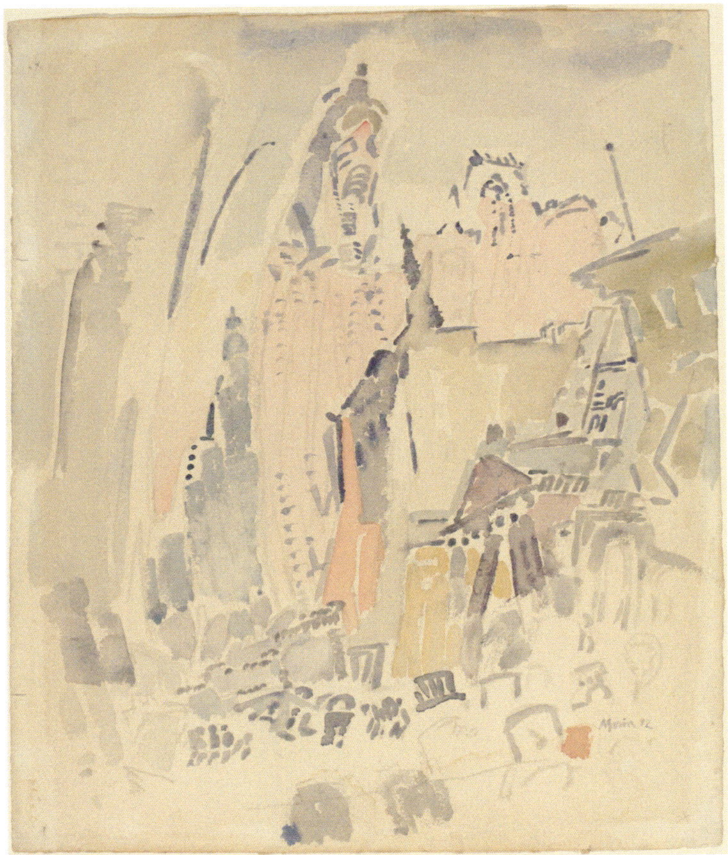

Fig. 9
John Marin, *Woolworth, No. 29*, 1912, watercolor, National Gallery of Art, Washington, Gift of Eugene and Agnes E. Meyer 1967.13.10

scapes."[211] Academician Kenyon Cox targeted Hartley as having "pushed the new doctrines to a conclusion in some respects more logical and complete than have any of the foreigners" by taking "the final step… to arrange his lines and spots purely for their own sake, abandoning all pretense of representation or even suggestion," constituting "the real meaning of the Cubist movement…the total destruction of the art of painting."[212]

Another critic noted approvingly "the manner in which some of the American artists have played a sort of color music of their own, a music that is understandable and appeals to the common man."[213] Referring to the work of Brinley, Lie, Hassam, and Karl Anderson in this context, the critic cited the incomprehensibility of Picabia's approach to color and form. Davies, Henri, Prendergast, and the other members of the Eight were singled out by another critic as "the group which has already assimilated and practiced foreign innovations with American improvements."[214] It was also observed by another writer that "beneath the superficial resemblances" of many examples of American art to "the modern foreign schools…lies…that spirit of moral reticence which is peculiar to America."[215] The "deep reserve [and] rich delicacy" of Davies' paintings was cited, along with the work of Kuhn, Marin, McEnery, and Glackens' *Family Group* (cat. 15, p. 130) as proof of this "National trait…of instinctive refinement modifying the influences that come from France." [216]

This theme of Americans holding their own amidst the European art was adopted by several writers. Chicago critic Harriet Monroe defined the American contributions, which "hold their own with complete assurance," as progressive, stating that "the radicals are in control and there are new voices in the chorus," while praising the work of Davies, Bellows, and Glackens.[217] In another article, she declared that the "various loud voices from Paris… have not as yet persuaded the Americans to any dangerous degree," with the exception of a few, "like Alfred Maurer [who] are imitating Matisse, and one may trace a milder sort of Cubism in a few inconspicuous exhibitors."[218] Although the Americans had not entirely abandoned familiar subjects to explore "the uncharted realm of abstract emotion," Monroe observed that the AAPS had offered "their more daring experiments, pictures beyond the pale of the ordinary exhibitions," which accounted for "the independence and free-spirited vitality one feels in this exhibition." [219] Referring in another article to Marin "as one of the most poetic of our radicals" and Glackens as having "taken a lesson or two from Renoir" in his successful *Family Group* (cat. 15, p. 130), Monroe commented that the Americans "have their full share of vitality." [220] Another critic, the American painter James Britton, observed that the "characterizing power, both with line and color, of Henri and Luks, the imaginative versatility of Davies, the tonal ingenuousness and technical fluency of Bellows, are qualities undimmed in the international maze." [221]

Monroe's observations and those of other critics indicate the breadth of interpretation and range of what was considered to be new, progressive art at that time. Adding to the general confusion was the use of the term "futurist" indiscriminately applied to such European modernists as Picabia and Villon, whereas the Italian Futurists were not actually represented in the exhibition, due to conflicting commitments abroad.[222] One critic grouped the disparate work of Pach, (cat. 29, p. 80), Prendergast (cat. 31, p. 137), and Zorach as creations of "American 'extremists.' "[223] Royal Cortissoz, in an article on the American section of the exhibition, observed that the artists in the Henri circle, "working in the van[guard]," had no place "in any sequence of artistic events…stand[ing] for a sharp…break with the existing order of things."[224] Discussing Luks, Bellows, Sloan, Myers, and Henri as well, with a brief reference to Marin, Mather noted that the Armory Show featured "only the extreme left of our art."[225] Artist-critic Anna Page Scott referred to Kuhn, Henri, Lawson, Myers, Bellows, Prendergast, and "a host of others" as "stirred by the new influence" of modernism.[226] Therefore, whether discussing American or European avant-garde or progressive art, many writers often used the terms "Cubists," "Futurists," "Post-Impressionists," and "Extremists" interchangeably.[227] This tendency was ingeniously exemplified by a little-known publication, *The Cubies' ABC* (cat. 46, p. 38), designed as a grade-school primer. The Cubies, who are children with geometric forms, frolic in alphabetical order with the work of Brancusi, Duchamp, Matisse, Picasso, and Marin's "Woolworth, the building so stable…Which Cubies paint writhing from cellar to gable [d]istinctly resembling the Tower of Babel."[228]

MORNING   By Walt Kuhn

Cat. 72
Morning by Walt Kuhn
International Exhibition of Modern Art postcards, Association of American Painters and Sculptors (New York, N.Y.)
1913
5 ½ x 3 ½ in.
Walt Kuhn, Kuhn Family Papers, and Armory Show Records, 1859-1978, bulk 1900-1949, Archives of American Art, Smithsonian Institution

Having reviewed the foreign works in the show, several critics also wrote focused articles on the range of American art on view. Commenting that the American artists are "by no means unworthy to appear in the company of the European men," Joseph Edgar Chamberlain noted the vitality and individuality of the native contributions, citing, as examples, Barnard's *Prodigal Son*, "as fully in the modern movement as the work of Rodin," Eberle's sculpture (cat. 14, p. 30), Ethel Meyer's "free and humorous city studies," (cat. 27, p. 39), as well as Brinley's work—"Impressionist to the verge of the 'post.'"[229] (cat. 4, p. 83) Glackens was praised as coming out "strong with his 'Family Group'—a scream of color."[230] (cat. 15, p. 130) McEnery's *Going to the Bath* (cat. 25, p. 135) was deemed "as full of light and vibration as a picture can be."[231] Commenting on the "extremely creditable" and "progressive" display of American art, Charles Henry Dorr characterized the range of works, from "the evanescent Whistlerian poems of Dabo to the explosive examples of…Bellows" to Van Dearing Perrine's *The Ice Floes* (cat. 30, p. 136), "imbued with the solitude of the Palisades at nightfall."[232] Adding to the perception of variety was the inclusion of so-called secondary mediums (watercolor, pastel, drawings, prints) and the contributions of many relatively unknown American artists "who have the flavor of novelty and the enthusiasm of youth."[233] It was observed that "the stimulating effect" of the show was "by no means entirely due to the contributions of the foreign artists," given that the native artists covered a "very broad field of artistic endeavor" from "conventionality" to "the last affectation which the most enthusiastic young American, alone in Paris…could possibly hope to attain."[234] Robert Henri was praised for his "picture of a Gypsy woman" (cat. 17, p. 131), which "glows with smouldering color."[235] It was noted that Kroll's *Terminal Yards* (fig. 6, p. 31) "made such a good impression when seen at the

MacDowell Club where, thanks to the artistically democratic policy of its galleries, much of the freshest work in the present exhibition has been seen."[236] Indeed other submissions such as Henry Glintenkamp's painting *The Village Cemetary* and, most notably, Edward Hopper's *Sailing* (cat. 19, p. 132) had been seen in MacDowell Club exhibitions and solicited afterwards, during the rush to invite domestic submissions.[237]

The role of American art was also addressed in the March issue of *Arts and Decoration*, offered for sale at the Armory Show in a special booth.[238] Davies's explanatory statement emphasizing the goal of the show as assembling "the works of the European moderns…on exhibition so that the intelligent may judge for themselves" was followed by his chronological chart showing the development of modern art from Ingres to Picasso.[239] Guy Pène du Bois, editor of the magazine and AAPS member, observed that "America should find in this exhibition a new stimulus…as great as the declaration of our political independence."[240] Stating that Americans have been "but a foundling on the shore of art," du Bois affirmed "that the hub of the wheel of modern art is France, the

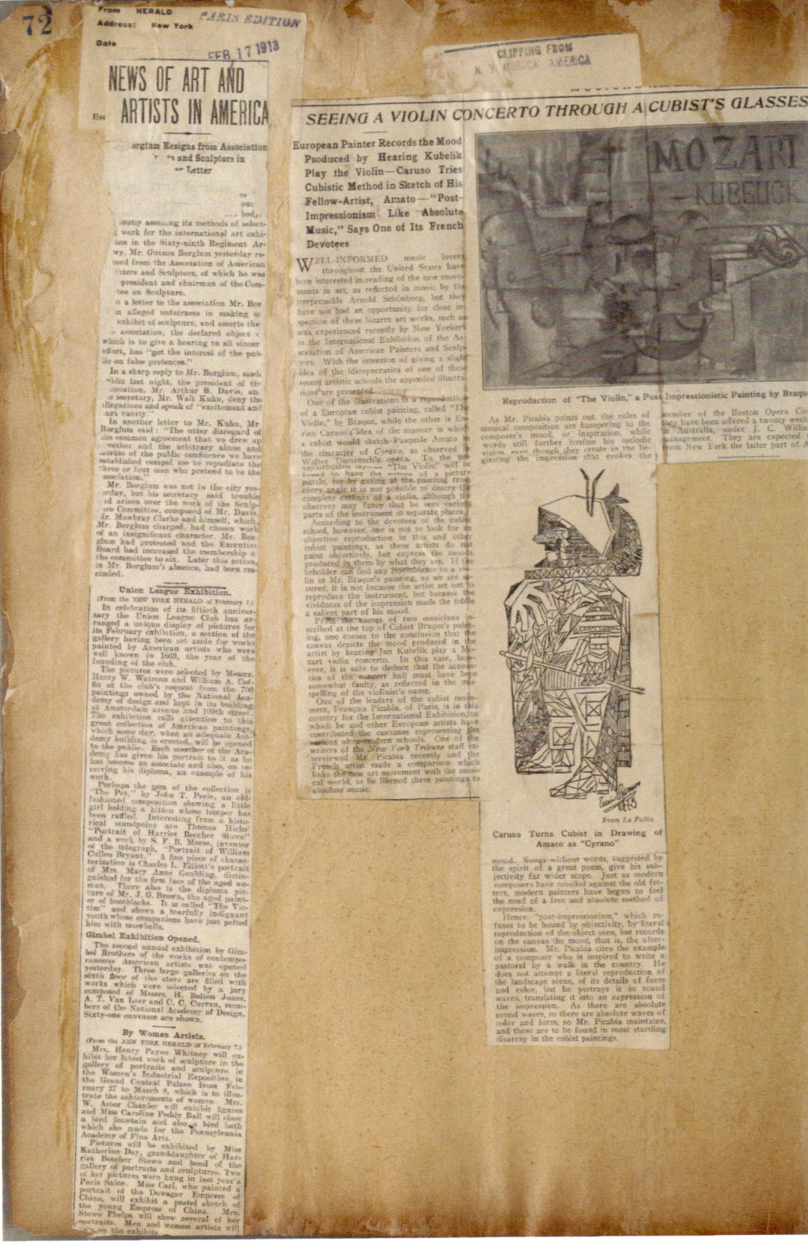

Fig. 10
"The New Delirium," unidentified press clipping from Kansas City, Missouri, February 23, 1913. Scrapbooks: Press II, Part I, Armory Show Records, Archives of American Art, Smithsonian Institution

leader in this return to spiritual independence."[241] In his essay on modern art from a layman's point of view, Quinn also concluded that "American art needs the shock that the work of some of these men will give."[242] His conception of American art as "too long vegetating" was affirmed by Glackens as chairman of the Domestic Committee.[243] Ghostwritten by Du Bois, on the basis of an interview with Glackens, this article on the American section of the show noted that the technical fluency of American artists was "limited by a lack of bravery…a skill enslaved by academies."[244] Stating that "we have had no innovators here," Glackens asserted that "everything worth while in our art is due to the influence of French art."[245] Decrying American art as "arid and bloodless," Glackens shared his fear "that the American section of this exhibition will seem very tame besides the foreign section."[246] Noting the "promise of a renaissance in American art," Glackens referred to Robinson, Hassam, Weir, and Twachtman as the first artists influenced by Impressionism and praised Davies as "the most important man….a symbolist, a painter of ideas" who has "felt the influence of the modern Frenchmen."[247]

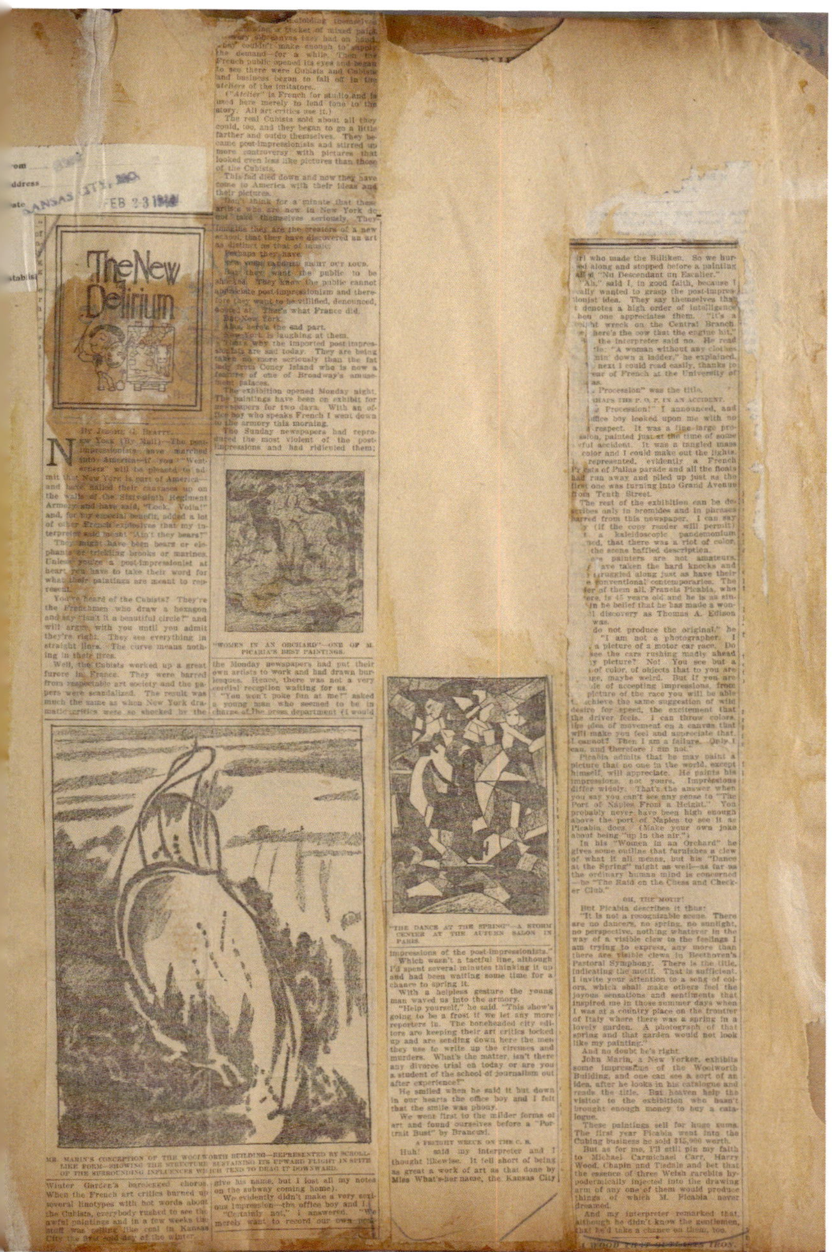

In his contribution to *Arts and Decoration*, Gregg similarly observed that conventional "American art…is deadly dull and suggests decay instead of growth." [248] He observed that it was "possible that, when the affair is over, the verdict will be that the vast mass of the American works exhibited represented simply arrested development….while, in the work brought here from Europe, and in that of the few Americans who…are struggling after something better was to be found all that was worth any serious attention."[249] Gregg believed, however, that this "risk of the deadly comparison" could be "the clinching argument that the enterprise was necessary if the lethargy into which our painters and sculptors had fallen was to be put an end to." [250] He concluded that "even if the American work in these rooms represents no such vigor as the European work, nothing was accepted or asked for which did not…show a susceptibility on the part of the artist to the vital influences of his period."[251] For Gregg and his associates, "the main thing was to get the foreign paintings and sculptures here, and each man made the question of how his own work would look under such trying circumstances quite a secondary considera-

tion." [252] He quoted one notable American painter as stating, "I am just as anxious as you fellows are to see how bad my pictures look."[253] Writing about the American sculpture in the exhibition, William Murrell Fisher referred to the younger generation of native sculptors as "in embryo," observing that the "foreign stimulus is evident in the work of such men as Lee, Davidson, and Dasburg."[254] Davidson was interviewed about the "theory of the new modernist painters and sculptors…against representation" and modernist art patron/salon hostess Mabel Dodge Luhan's speculations on Post-Impressionism affirmed the notions of the new spirit and vitality in relation to French philosopher Henri Bergson's theory of intuition and the *élan vital*.[255]

Reacting to the negative verbiage of the *Arts and Decoration* issue, critic William B. McCormick was "forcefully impressed by the vitality of our native pictures" as he walked about the rooms "from which the post impressionist and other modern horrors are barred by the scheme of arrangement."[256] He praised a range of work, including Brinley's "poetry in paint" and McEnery's nudes. (cats. 4.25, pp. 83,135) and also addressed the modernist work of Manigault, Zorach, Carles, and Dasburg.[257]

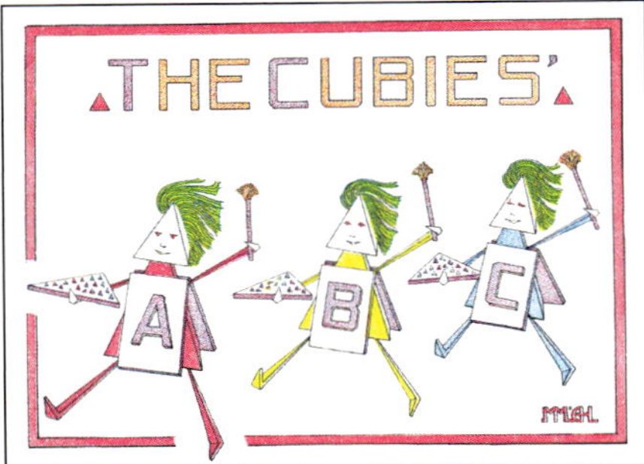

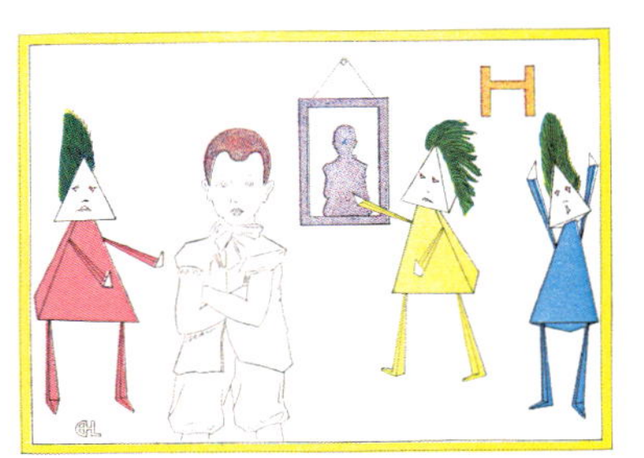

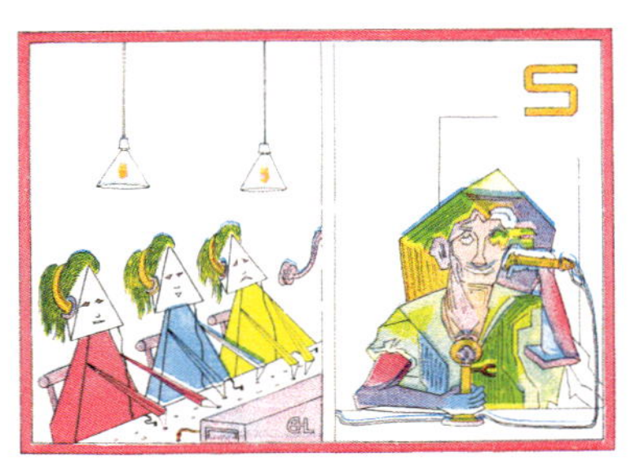

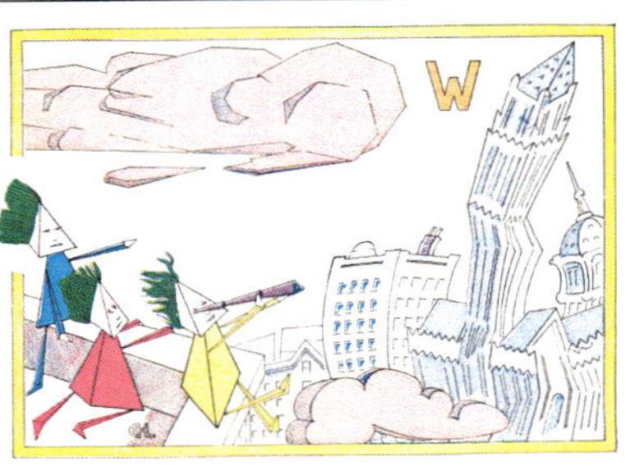

Cat. 46.
Mary Mills Lyall, author and Earl Harvey Lyall, illustrator, *The Cubies' ABC* (New York and London: G.P. Putnam's Sons, 1913), Francis M. Naumann and Marie T. Keller, Yorktown Heights, NY

On March 4, a very distinguished visitor, former president Theodore Roosevelt, toured the Armory Show, later that month publishing an article on his layman perspective. Comparing the sensational draw of "the European extremists" to P.T. Barnum's "faked mermaid," Roosevelt felt that "it is the work of the American painters and sculptors which is of most interest…and a glance at this work must convince anyone of the real good that is coming out of the new movements."[258] Among the Americans doing original and serious work, he cited Kroll, Davies, Chanler, Dabo, Sloan, Luks, Ethel Myers, and others.

To celebrate the Armory Show's success, the Press Committee of the AAPS hosted a beefsteak dinner for "friends and enemies of the press" (Fig. 17, p. 117) at the restaurant Healy's on March 8. Accompanied by singing and dancing, especially that of Brinley, winner of the high-kicking contest, Quinn announced to a group of artists and representatives from almost every metropolitan daily paper, that nearly 50,000 people had attended the Armory Show since its opening 19 days ago and that over 100 works had been sold.[259] As reported in an article on the visit of the opera tenor Enrico Caruso, "artists, literary people, engineers, everybody found their way to the armory."[260] The critic Forbes Watson, who attended on a daily basis, later recalled that the "American artists did not so much visit the exhibition as live at it. For six weeks it was impossible to find an artist (not an Academician) in his studio."[261]

Kuhn had played a vital role in encouraging this record-breaking attendance by giving out thousands of free admission tickets to schools and societies, as recorded in his correspondence.[262] He had also reached out to New York University and other local institutions, as well as out-of-state locations, offering posters and observing to the Washington-based artist James Lamb that the "show will mean more than a two months trip to Europe to anyone."[263] Kuhn also launched a letter-writing campaign to museums to encourage purchases.[264]

On the last day of the Armory Show's run in New York, March 15, around 10,000 thronged the galleries. During the closing night celebration, the AAPS formed a procession with Brinley as drum major.[265] In total, around 100,000 were estimated to have seen the exhibi-

tion and over 230 works of art had been sold,
among them Cézanne's *View of the Domaine Saint-Joseph* (1888-90), sold to the Metropolitan Museum
of Art as the first work by this master to enter an
American public collection.[266] Hailed as "the most
stimulating episode in this city's art history up to
the present time," one critic observed that "while
there is no doubt the sensational performances of
some of the advanced Frenchmen" drew crowds, "it
is safe to say that the vitality and energy…among
the remaining pictures and sculpture would have
secured [the] record breaking attendance."[267]
According to Kuhn, the up-to-date publicity, "keen
business sense…artistic daring," and sound
management of the Armory Show had ensured its
record attendance and sales.[268]

As plans for the travel of the show to the Art
Institute of Chicago (AIC) progressed, Andrew
Dasburg, a frequent visitor to the show who also
may have served as a guide or part of the
"committee on hand daily to explain the art," wrote
to his wife, the sculptor Grace Mott Johnson, about
his dissatisfaction with the decision that none of
the American sculpture would travel, complaining
that "the members of the Association seem to be
prejudiced against anything that smakes [sic] of
American Post-Impressionism."[269] Kuhn had
corresponded with AIC director William French
about choosing part of the show—a "very fine" and

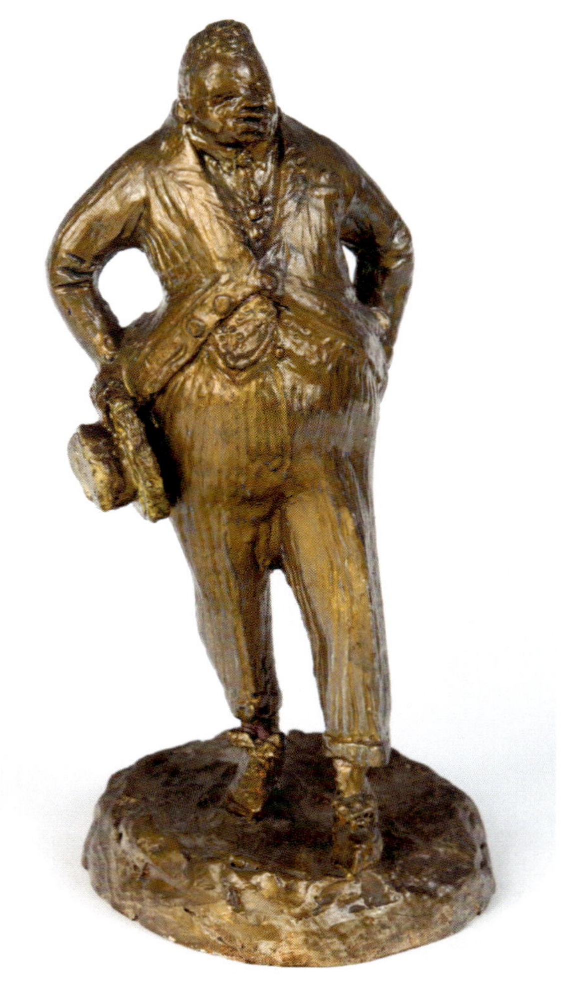

Cat. 27.
Ethel Myers, *The Gambler,
Joe Johnson*, 1912, painted
plaster, Collection of
Barry and Helene Downes

"representative" selection-—since the designated space could not accommodate all of it.[270]
French indicated to Davies his preference for "the more novel part of the exhibition…from
Europe," suggesting that they "limit the American exhibitors to one work apiece" because
some were represented in the AIC's collection.[271] Kuhn and Pach were in charge of the
hanging of the show of around 634 works, which occurred in one day on March 22, directed
by Kuhn, Gregg, and Pach.[272] (cat. 58, p. 40)

Complaining that the Chicago "so called intelligent class are a lot of self advertisers and
ignoramuses," Kuhn soon observed that the newspapers "print anything you tell 'em.…I have
to pass myself from one official to another as well as reporters to give information."[273] He was
quoted as affirming the educational purpose of the show for American artists who "will have
to consider whether painters and sculptors here have fallen behind, …through distance and
for other reasons, the [modernist] forces that have manifested themselves on the other side of
the Atlantic.…forces which can not be ignored because they have had results."[274] The smaller
selection of work on view by American artists such as Ryder, Glackens, Kuhn, McEnery,
Prendergast, and others "representing the modern movement in this country," received a
"comparatively smaller number" of visitors than "the sensational aspect[s] of the show."[275]

The critic Harriet Monroe observed that "the American section is full of surprises.…there
is a large troop of clever Americans [who are] intensely individual and original—without being
in the least incomprehensible."[276] In another article, she reprised the refrain of American art as

39

"under conservative management, getting too pallid, nerveless…photographic."[277] Monroe noted elsewhere that "the special treasure" of the large southeast gallery devoted to American art was the work of Ryder.[278] Another critic commented that the room of Cubists or "Gallery of Mirth" was the center of attention, incorrectly noting that "many of the Americans are not here because they are represented in various exhibitions which come annually."[279] An art history professor, George Zug, complained that all of the great historical masters had been omitted, as well as "room after room [of] the vigorous work of progressive Americans, many of whom were represented by whole groups of paintings whereas in Chicago some of these men are represented by only one painting and some, like…Weir and Whistler are entirely missing."[280] He stated in a later review that if "the exhibition of paintings by progressive Americans…in room 25 (fig. 11) had come to us at any other time it would have created a sensation."[281] Featuring works by acknowledged masters such as Ryder, Hassam, and Davies, the show also included works by those whom Zug regarded as "younger radicals" employing "gay color and dashing brushwork," such as Kroll, Brinley, Lawson, Luks, Glackens, and MacRae.[282] Artist-critic James William Pattison praised the works of Brinley, Lawson, and others in the gallery of American "Impressionistic pictures," observing that these "uncommonly attractive" paintings would have been condemned "as too sketchy and rude" a few years ago.[283]

Carles' abstract, colorful painting *Girl at the Piano* (1912, Baltimore Museum of Art) appears to have been the target of a satirical commentary as "an explosion in a shingle factory" who, if she "plays the piano at all, …can get a job in any 5-cent theater in Chicago."[284] Arthur Freund's *The Pig* (n.d., Property of Ginger H. and H. Richard Dietrich III) and Karl Anderson's *Woman Drinking Glass of Water* (location unknown) were subjects of a mock appreciation by Dr. Otto Nohn Behterr [his name being a play on the words "ought to have known better"] as examples of Post-Impressionist "vitality and vividness," along with works by Duchamp, Picabia, Picasso, Braque, and Brancusi—'Whatever is, is art.'"[285] Henri's *Figure in Motion* (1913, Terra Museum of American Art) featuring a nude standing woman and Charlotte Meltzer's *Loverine* (date and location unknown) were, along with Gauguin's *Spirit of Evil* (now known as *Words of the Devil*, 1892, National Gallery of Art, Washington D.C.), branded as immoral by the press, public, and several Art Institute of Chicago trustees.[286]

To address the more conservative, less balanced, lighter press coverage, and to provide more background material in response to many inquiries, Kuhn and Gregg issued the pamphlet *For and Against. Views on the International Exhibition Held in New York and Chicago.* (cat. 70) The educational emphasis of the exhibition was explained as portraying "the line of development from the early part of the last century until the present day…represent[ing] some definite breach with accepted authority and tradition, from Ingres…to the 'Cubists.'"[287] In one of the essays "against" the new art, Mather observed that "Ryder and Davies represent a similar mood [to that of Redon] with equal ability and perhaps with greater freedom from literary implication."[288] He regretted that "Mr. Davies's self-renouncing conception of his office as president of the Association has deprived us of a one-man show that would have furnished an excellent complement for the Redon gallery."[289] In essays "for" modernism by Gregg and Pach, a brief history of the New York and Chicago shows was provided, with references to the focus on French artists in the show and the absence of the Futurists.[290] In the report of the AAPS subcommittee in Chicago, it was observed that, as in New York, "the 'Cubist Room' attracts the biggest crowds" but "none of the rooms are neglected, and the Americans are holding their own very well, as far as visitors are concerned."[291]

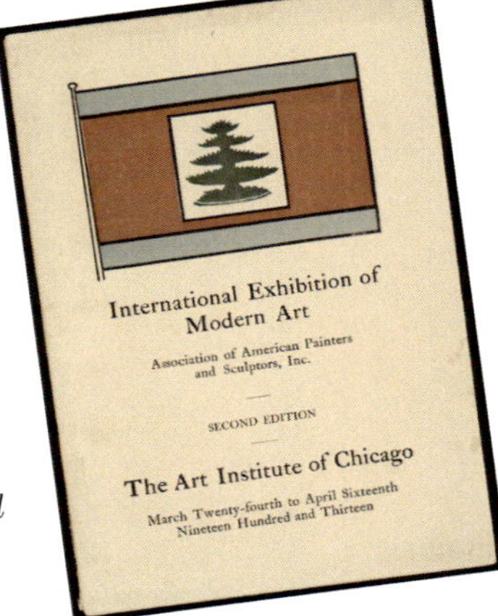

Cat. 58

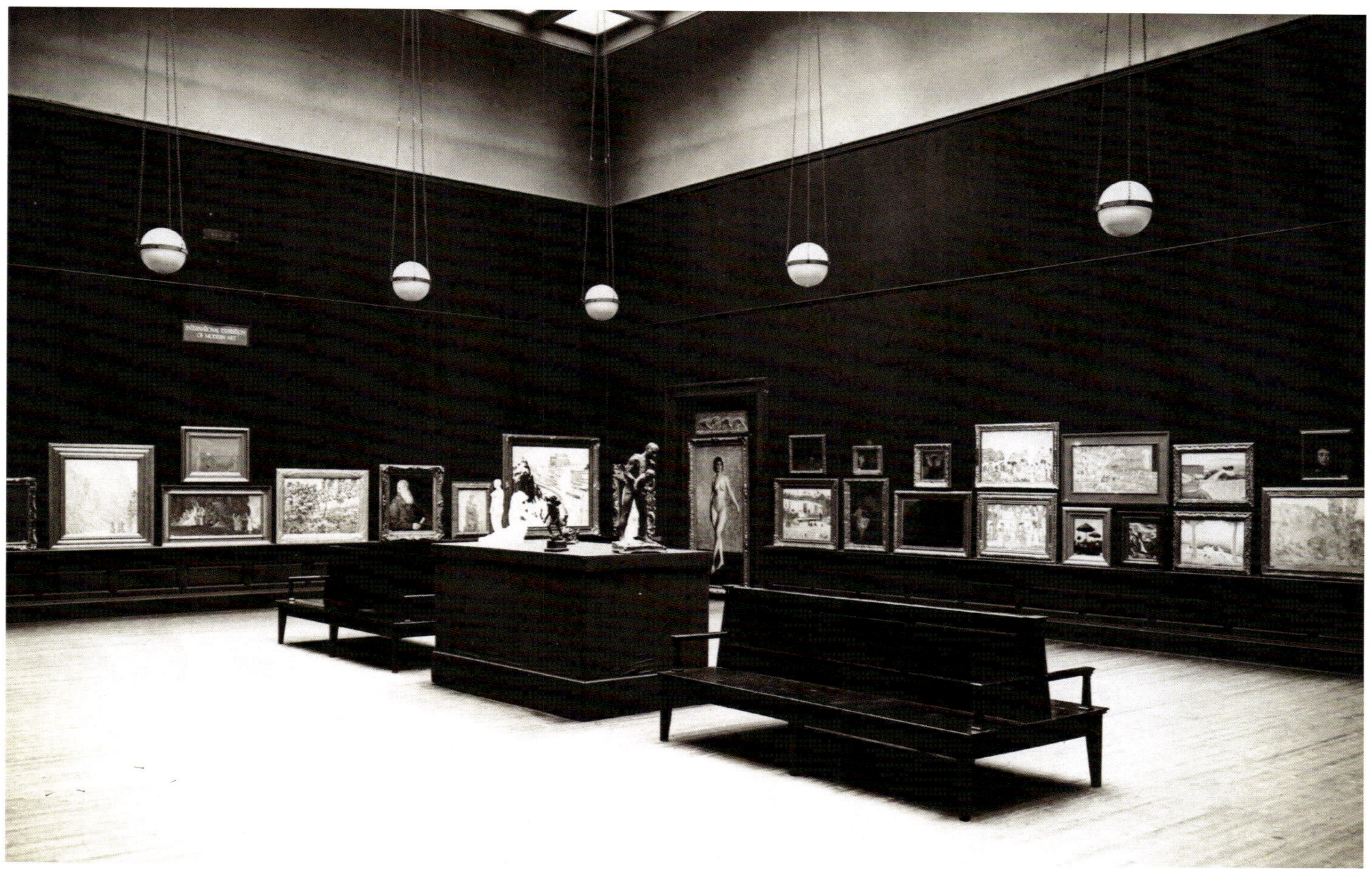

Fig. 11
Installation of American art in the Armory Show, Room 25, Art Institute of Chicago

Greatly inspired and aware of the "terrible misunderstanding" of the Chicago press in general, the pioneering modernist Manierre Dawson frequented the Armory Show, recording his impressions in his journal. Feeling affirmed by the advanced art on view, Dawson met Pach, who secretly added his *Wharf Under Mountain* (cat. 12, p. 129) to the American section in gallery 25. As the only abstraction by an American artist, it was likely the most progressive native contribution to the exhibition.[292]

Before the closing of the show, Gregg wrote an essay for the Buffalo Fine Arts Academy on the show's organization and goal to "afford a chance to our artists to see to what an extent they had been or had not been influenced by recent European, and especially by French, works."[293] Characterizing the show as "the record of a hundred years of struggle between the forces of conservatism and the forces of innovation of battles long ago," Gregg noted that the "Americans whose work flanked that of the foreigners held up gallantly under the strain." [294] For the Americans, "the interesting thing…as Maurice Prendergast put it in a remark to Walt Kuhn, was…'How is all this going to influence your painting and mine?'"[295] The article was accompanied by reproductions of works on view in New York by Gauguin, Redon, and Davies (fig. 12, p. 43), whose *Fording the Stream* was not listed in either the catalogue or supplement—evidently one of what may be many possible rediscoveries of works in the show.

Kuhn's correspondence continued to chronicle his disappointment with the visitors' and press's appetite for sensationalism, as well as the conservatism of the local artists and AIC faculty, as manifested in such incidents as the withdrawal of Gauguin's *Noa Noa* booklet and the burning of copies of paintings by Henry Hair Mattress (Matisse). [296] Aided by three free-admission days each week, the attendance reached a record of almost 200,000 visitors. Concluding that they had "made a big mistake by not being on hand here sooner," Kuhn

41

asserted that the "press had no idea of the importance of the show, they simply imagined it was a sort of circus. In the case of Boston we must not make this same mistake."[297]

Having received applications from various institutions in Kansas City, Milwaukee, and elsewhere, Kuhn was contacted by the Copley Society of Boston in January 1912 for the "exhibition of Futurists" to be held there April 28-May 19, 1913.[298] This request was clarified further in a later letter from Holker Abbot, President of the Copley Society, who was "very anxious…to have the French portion, especially the Post Impressionists.[299] Despite these assertions, the original intention was to include American works as well, as discussed during a meeting on March 14 when a delegation from Boston saw the Armory Show. In fact, Edward Warren of the Copley Society expressed concern in April that "the exhibition as a whole would be less complete and interesting" and "would not be an International Exhibition of Modern Art" if all of the American art were to be withdrawn.[300] Nevertheless, Kuhn reported that the AAPS directors had decided that it would be "impossible to discriminate" in making selections of American art for the more limited space.[301] The decision to omit the American art was explained by Gregg in an additional final paragraph to his essay which had appeared in both the New York and Chicago catalogues. Stating that the AAPS members preferred to withdraw their work rather than "make a choice" or "have themselves represented when other American exhibitors were not," Gregg reasserted the primary goal "to display the European section of the International Exhibition to the greatest possible advantage."[302] (cat. 59)

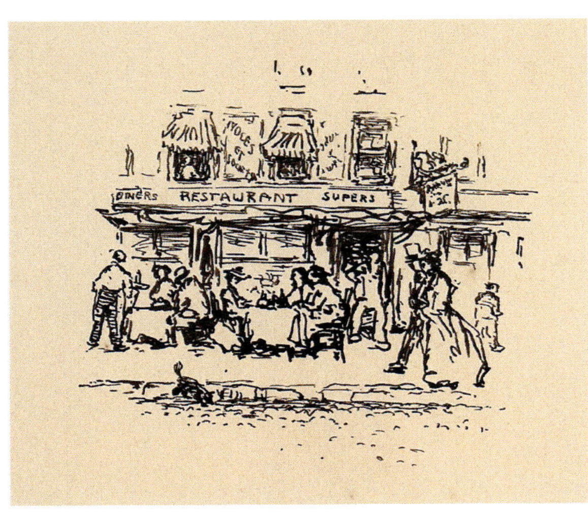

Cat. 18.
Robert Henri, *Where We Dined in the Latin Quarter,* Paris, in 1896, 1904, ink on paper, Delaware Art Museum, Gift of Helen Farr Sloan, 2011

With his characteristic spirit of boosterism, Kuhn declared that whereas the "New York show was a great demonstration…the Boston one," with its more concentrated focus on modernist French art, "excels as an art exhibition."[303] Kuhn also fielded many requests for extended travel of the show from venues all over the country and even Canada. Although he was quoted as allegedly declaring to "chop it off in Boston," Kuhn's replies indicate that some requests were considered; however, the overwhelmed association decided further travel would not be feasible.[304] At the end of the run in Boston, over 12,000 visitors attended the show of around 300 works, which, with no American art and almost none of the historical examples, caused such conservative critics as William H. Downes to complain that "the crazy element is allowed to predominate much more conspicuously."[305]

After the closing of the Armory Show, the progressive critic W.D. MacColl wrote about his impressions of experiencing "a quickened consciousness of the value and meaning of life itself" while encountering the work of Gauguin, Cézanne, Matisse, as well as Prendergast's "unexampled use" of color.[306] Dismissing Henri's "fleshly nude" and Glackens's *Family Group* (cat. 15, p. 130) as "a mannerism in the style of Renoir," MacColl indicated his preference for the Post-Impressionist Americans Maurer, Halpert, and Dasburg, whose works, "with poetry and force [convey] a spiritual quality….[they] make you touch the motions of their spirit before what they have seen, not simply its flesh."[307] Oscar Bluemner, one of the modernists who had been represented in the show (cat. 3, p. 123), wrote a lengthy commentary for Stieglitz's publication *Camera Work,* with only one brief reference to the American section, observing that "a great deal of the contemporaneous art, especially from America, is virtually foreign to the new intents and modes," evidently part of "the melée of antagonistic examples…arranged in a manner that could only add to the confusion of the public."[308]

At the time this article was published, AAPS members—especially Kuhn— were immersed in the complexities of the exhibition's aftermath, processing the return of loans and insurance claims, terminating leases, corresponding about any follow up exhibitions, and disseminating the remaining 40,000 postcards.[309] Kuhn informed the dealer Hans Goltz that "as soon as our business affairs have been put into good order, our various members will retire to their studios to exercise the benefits derived from this great European display."[310]

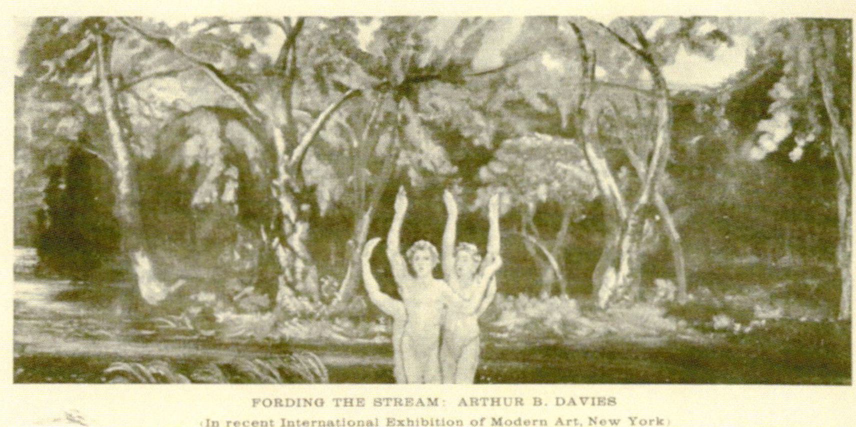

Fig. 12
Article by Frederick Gregg featuring Arthur B. Davies' *Fording the Stream* (location unknown), an uncatalogued work which had been on view in the Armory Show in New York. *Academy Notes*, April 1913, Vol. VIII, No. 2. Published by *The Buffalo Arts Academy*.

The influence of the Armory Show was noted in reviews of American art shows by the fall of 1913. The Montross gallery featured a show that included paintings by "the younger group of innovators, many of whom were represented last season at the Amory Show," including Brinley, Kramer, Perrine, Bellows, MacRae, Du Bois, and others.[311] Another critic was relieved to note that the painters "have not imitated any of the eccentrics of the International show...simply assimil[ating] the inspiration of an exhibition which contained more individual work, more character, more of the protein of the soul than any other picture show that New York ever saw."[312]

Kuhn joined forces with Davies and Pach in organizing an exhibition of their American artist-associates who had participated in the Armory Show. Like many others, all three artists had been experimenting with aspects of the Fauve and Cubist art that they had encountered on such a regular basis. Opening at the Carnegie Institute of Pittsburgh, their show traveled to venues in New York, Detroit, Cincinnati, and Baltimore from December 1913 to May 1914, and was one of the first exhibitions of modern American art in the country. Also featuring work by Dawson, Glackens, George Of, Prendergast, Schamberg, Sheeler, Joseph Stella, Taylor, and Tucker, the exhibition took place at New York's Montross Gallery in February 1914, during the first anniversary of the Armory Show.[313] The Montross show and a concurrent exhibition at the National Arts Club were declared "the most important since that epoch-making one at the armory, on account of the creative spirit which imbues them."[314] James Townsend referred to the exhibition as "a condensed reflection of the Armory Show," while Gallery owner N.E. Montross allegedly stated that "the exhibition will prove to be a natural sequel to the International Exhibition of Modern Art."[315] Well publicized and a modest commercial success, this exhibition revealed the impact of the Armory Show on certain AAPS members and focused interest on American modern art, helping to spread it to a broader audience.

In the summer of 1914, discussions about the prospect of another international exhibition organized by the AAPS were publicized in an article, which defined two factions within the group. Davies and the rest of "the controlling element in the management of the great show" thought that it would be "inexpedient" and not as successful, whereas "the Henri crowd" felt that a nonjuried show of progressive American art should be held that season.[316] This sentiment was in keeping with Henri's alleged remark made to Pach in the Armory Show, "If the Americans find that they've just been working for the French, they won't be prompted to do this again."[317] None of the artists associated with Henri had been selected for the Montross show. Kuhn had even accused "the Henri bunch" of manipulating the critics into writing negative reviews, asserting that "they are simply sore at the managers of the International show."[318] This schism within the AAPS was greatly exacerbated by financial disagreements over the settling of final accounts and an apparent lack of transparency in the process, which led to the group's dissolution. On May 18, during the first general meeting since the Armory Show, the Henri group, failing in its effort to unseat the incumbent board of directors, resigned from membership. Bellows was quoted as objecting to "the control of a self-perpetuating body of dictators," asserting that the resignations had taken place in protest of "the clique" and "bad financial management."[319] The resignations prompted a scorching reply from Davies, who stated that "a minority which had taken only a passive part in the preparation…displayed…a material resentment towards what makes their own work look old-fashioned and out-of-date" and were "only interested in what they had to sell themselves," rather than the educational goal of the show.[320] Du Bois's published response pertained to the resentment of the Henri faction's exclusion from the Montross show, which had created "the impression…that they [the Davies-Kuhn group] were the pick of the Armory Show" and were artists "who became Post-Impressionists overnight, when the time was ripe."[321] Although a new board of directors had been elected that reflected the continuing control of Davies' colleagues, the AAPS was effectively finished as an organization.[322]

The legacy of the AAPS's factionalism can be found in the organization of another exhibition at the Montross Gallery in 1915, and especially in the Forum Exhibition of modern American art in 1916. Davies, Kuhn, MacRae, and others of the "so-called 'Armory Group'" were joined by Man Ray, whose Cubist painting *War* (1914, Philadelphia Museum of Art) reflected the great impact of the International Exhibition upon this budding modernist.[323] The Forum Exhibition was planned in reaction to the Armory Show "to turn public attention for the moment away from European art and concentrate it on the excellent work being done in America."[324] As stated in the accompanying catalogue, the goal was "to present for the first time a comprehensive, critical selection" of "the more modern American art" because the Armory Show's "plethora of material selected at haphazard" had confused visitors.[325] Neither Kuhn nor Davies was included in this landmark show, for which Henri served on the selection committee.[326] The availability of a significant group of 50 "very modern American painters" exemplified the significant growth of advanced painters since the Armory Show.[327] Among the 17 artists ultimately chosen, 10 had been represented in the Armory Show, which still set the standard for exhibitions of modernism, as noted by Wright in his review of the Forum Exhibition. He observed that "next to the Armory Show, it is the most complete… exposition of the new school's work this country has ever had."[328]

Nevertheless, the notion of the American art scene as lagging behind the European avant-garde was perpetuated, especially in subsequent accounts of the Armory Show. Early in 1938, upon the occasion of the 25th anniversary, Kuhn self-published *The Story of The Armory Show*, which became the most commonly quoted source. This 28-page booklet was the first attempt at a detailed presentation of the objectives, plans, progress, and implementation of the Armory Show. Emphasizing the story of the European art on view, Kuhn asserted that the exhibition had developed from "the need of breaking down the stifling and smug condition of local art affairs" and that progressive American artists, with few exceptions, "had no place to show their wares."[329] Noting that the AAPS's "purpose was solely to show the American public what was going on abroad," Kuhn discussed the impact of the show from his vantage point in 1938, observing that its primary influence in America was on fashion, industry, decorative arts, and advertising, rather than the fine arts.[330]

Relatively overlooked has been Walter Pach's 1938 chapter on the Armory Show in *Queer*

Thing, Painting: Forty Years in the World of Art, which focused on "America's reaction to its first great contact with [French] modern art" and concluded that, while "we opened up a new business for the dealers…the essential effect of the big show was…on the work of the artists."[331] Noting that some went the "'easiest way,' becoming little Derains, Picassos, or Cézannes,… academic Post-Impressionists and Cubists," others such as John Sloan benefited more profoundly from their contact with modern art.[332] A decade earlier, in a briefer discussion of the Armory Show, Pach commented that American artists had "never asked to be protected from comparison with the artists of Europe;" in fact, "welcoming it," they had launched a successful campaign, with Quinn and members of the AAPS as the most actively engaged, to repeal the tariff on the importation of modern works of art, providing a great "stimulus [which] has served to make us develop all the more fully those elements which are purely our own."[333]

In 1940, Jerome Myers, in *An Artist in Manhattan*, firmly established the mythic conception of the Armory Show as complete anathema for American artists. Myers recalled a comment made by Dabo, that "this man Davies has started something. I'm afraid it may be more of a calamity than a blessing, though it's a damn good show." [334] Having approached Davies for the AAPS presidency, Myers felt "we had saved the day [yet] without knowing we had doomed American Art [to Davies's] fanatical idea of showing Europe's latest art moods to New York, to outmode our artists' work…."[335] When Myers saw the Armory Show for the first time, he felt that "Davies had unlocked the door to foreign art and thrown the key away."[336] Throwing America "wide open to foreign art, unrestricted and triumphant," the Armory Show presented the "French moderns…in all their pristine glory; and while the American artists were finally shown, in this swirling medley of art on parade, they had to take it on the chin." America "had become a colony; more than ever before, we had become provincials."[337]

During the Armory Show's 30th anniversary, Jerome Mellquist's account continued the pattern of emphasis upon the European avant-garde aspects of the exhibition, although he also recalled that various American painters such as Marin and Hartley, who had borne the critical incomprehension of Mather and Cox, continued to "push through the breach that had been made." [338] Curator Lloyd Goodrich, in his 1946 catalogue for the Whitney Museum's *Pioneers of Modern Art in America*, dismissed the American art in the Armory Show as "a great hodge-podge, ranging from modern to academic, with modernists in the minority, and mild, progressives predominating." [339] Quoting Glackens and Gregg as to the less advanced state of American art, he concluded that this "general sense of inferiority shows how heavily outnumbered the few progressive artists still felt."[340] In her master's thesis of 1950, Chloe Hamilton observed that the American artists had outnumbered the foreign ones, "but since they did not create the stir that the latter group did, this fact is often forgotten." [341] She commented that had "the American group been more carefully selected, the Association might have seen fit to include Inness, Eakins, and Homer; thus establishing a more valid comparison with the French."[342] Surprisingly, Hamilton also asserted that although the American artists constituted over half of the exhibitors, "considering the volume of publicity given to the foreign work, they might as well have not been included at all."[343]

The concept of the American contributions as predominantly conservative, provincial, and therefore relatively negligible was furthered by authors in the 1950s. In his survey of 1951, Brooklyn Museum curator John Baur stated that the pioneer American modernists' work on view "was almost lost in a flood of more conservative paintings, for the American section comprised roughly three quarters of the whole."[344] Basing much of his account on that of Kuhn, Rudi Blesh dismissed " the American work, the most radical of it—except for Stella and one or two others—pale and ineffectual, even its freshest paint badly dated."[345]

Only Ryder "shone with the timeless validity of the true mystic" amidst the "welter."[346] Milton W. Brown, in his classic study *American Painting from the Armory Show to the Depression* (1955), declared that in the years after the Armory Show, "the Americans, neophytes in modernism, could not successfully compete with their more famous French contemporaries."[347] Discussing the "backwardness of American painting and sculpture relative to Europe," Meyer Schapiro in his landmark analysis of the Armory Show in 1952, asserted that America's "provinciality" may account for its "minor place in modern art," adding that The Eight, "affirming in retarded form the living spectacle of modernity, made at least some part of the new European art accessible."[348]

The secondary status of American art was perpetuated on the occasion of the 45th anniversary in 1958 in a catalogue essay for *The 1913 Armory Show in Retrospect*, an exhibition held at Amherst College. Commenting on the challenge of trying to reassemble works from the original exhibition that are in limbo, lost, or destroyed, Professor Frank Anderson Trapp noted that, although "not all of the contemporaneous Europeans came off well…far fewer of the American artists…have survived the intervening years."[349] Next to the "dazzling if confusing array of European talent, the American offering must have seemed pallid….dull and mediocre."[350] Trapp believed that "the oblivion which has befallen much of its contributors was predicted by the initial reaction of the public itself," which thronged the European modernist rooms instead. [351]

Quoting Myers and Gregg to bolster his observations on the arrested state of development of American art, Trapp stated in a contemporaneous article that the Armory Show had helped to "create a more insidious force in fostering a public dedicated to the superiority of the modern European schools."[352] Aline Saarinen characterized the American paintings on view as "a pale rim around the blazing, dominant core of art from abroad."[353] Observing that "it's generally been forgotten that the largest part of the…show, given to American works, was conservative," Emily Genauer nevertheless singled out works by Hopper, Hartley, Davidson, Marin, Bellows, and Kuhn as "quick with life and force," reinforcing her belief that "vitality…must not necessarily be equated with novelty."[354]

The large-scale 50th anniversary exhibition presented a larger reconstitution with over 300 works from the Armory Show at the Munson-Williams-Proctor Institute and in its original location. In the accompanying catalogue, Institute director Edward Dwight characterized the American art as "so conservative," stating that if the European modernists had "not been invited to show in the Armory, it is doubtful that anyone would have wanted to do the show again."[355] Noting that only recently had much attention been paid to any of the American artists, such as Davies, he stated that perhaps in 1963 the Americans will be more recognized. In his essay for the 50th-anniversary catalogue, Milton W. Brown affirmed "the mythic guise" of Kuhn's "little pamphlet," which had "set down the heroic outlines of the epic story for all time," even with the recent discoveries of the Kuhn and MacRae Papers.[356] Discussing the exhibition itself, Brown concentrated on the European art, only briefly describing the American work as "a great, somewhat anomalous mass…what was considered progressive here had little relation to the revolutionary art of Europe."[357] Reducing the discussion of the American work to the critics' having "'thanked the Lord' for 'American sanity' and 'honest craftsmanship,'" Brown repeated the timeworn legend that "the Europeans stole the show."[358] Referring to "the plight of the American artist and the problems of exhibiting," Brown also reiterated the mistaken assumption that opportunities at the National Arts Club and elsewhere for American moderns to show their work generally postdated the Armory Show.[359]

Also featured in the catalogue were the reactions of several American exhibitors still alive in 1963. Stuart Davis referred to the Armory Show as "an amazing spastic convulsion in

American provincial art culture…a masochistic reception whereat the naïve hosts are trampled and stomped by the European guests at the buffet."[360] Davis characterized his "personal reaction to the rowdy occasion" as "an experience of Freedom….present in the mechanics of many of the foreign items on display."[361] Among the other artists quoted was William Zorach, who, in an earlier interview, had stated that American artists had "cut their own throats by bringing this over…all this modern French art."[362] When the importation tariff was removed, "the result was…this flood of French art and a diminishing of the values…the downward grading of all American art."[363]

The 50th-anniversary exhibition was the occasion for examination and perpetuation of the usual myths, with critic Frank Gettlein stating that "the European work is generally superior to the American," although "there is life even among the Americans."[364] Sidney Tillum commented on "the extreme unevenness that did much to undermine the case for American progressivism" and the exhibition's "deathblow to the Eight, whose ash-can realism seemed not so removed from the provincialism that issued from the American section as a whole."[365] For Tillum, the Armory Show was "a noble failure" that set the cause of the avant-garde "back twenty-five years, because it showed how far ahead…the Europeans were."[366] Trapp similarly declared that the Europeans "'stole' most of the publicity" and outsold the Americans more than two-to-one," exposing "on a vast scale" the relative provincialism of native art.[367] Harold Rosenberg observed that the "foes of modern art" praised the Americans "for refusing to budge from the Continental values being subverted on the continent," citing the criticism of Cox, who had discovered "one exception among the American innocents"— Hartley.[368] Having organized a complementary exhibition at the Whitney on *The Decade of the Armory Show*, Lloyd Goodrich observed that the American section was a "great hodge podge" with notable absences of work by Weber, Sterne, Dove, MacDonald-Wright, Man Ray, Demuth, Dickinson, Feininger, and others.[369] Citing Gregg, he stated that "to some intelligent sympathizers the effect was not impressive."[370]

The American section of the 50th-anniversary show was deemed by one critic to be "weak by the sheer number of indifferent works."[371] Another critic observed, however, that "if the show shattered Aschcan hopes of becoming the dominating force in U.S. art, those who called the U.S. provincial were obviously passing judgment too soon," and cited Davis as "now one of the world's best abstractionists" and Hopper, who "carries on the realist tradition at its best."[372] Davis himself was quoted as having asserted that the Armory Show "was the greatest single influence I have experienced in all my work."[373]

In 1963, the first edition of Milton W. Brown's classic study, *The Story of the Armory Show*, attracted reviews that highlighted the author's reliance on Kuhn's booklet as "providing the main body of information," augmented by the recent donation of his papers to the Archives of American Art.[374] Art historian Irma Jaffe took issue with Brown's emphasis on the uniquely backward nature of American aesthetics, stating that "Parisian criticism and taste were almost concurrently registering the same symptoms of indigestion" in response to avant-garde art.[375] Other studies in the 1960s, such as Barbara Rose's *American Art Since 1900*, continued to characterize the American section of the Armory Show as "tentative, plain, and underdeveloped," establishing "the hegemony of European art for another thirty years."[376]

In the 1970s and 80s, scholars such as Judith Zilczer began challenging the prevailing litany that "American artists and the public were unequal to the challenge of European modern art."[377] Scholars such as Roberta Tarbell, Carol Nathanson, and Charles C. Eldredge challenged the traditional conception of the Armory Show as "the initial skirmish in the battle for modern art in America," examining "the ample opportunities for American artists and critics [in New York] to familiarize themselves with the artistic revolution."[378] As noted by Zilczer, "the increasingly frequent exhibitions of American and European modern art from 1907 until 1913 would seem to indicate that new art had a more tangible impact on America than merely to stimulate debate within the Stieglitz and Mabel Dodge circles."[379] Over 60 modern art exhibitions held in New York from 1907 to 1913 were complemented by the expansion of art criticism in American periodicals, newspapers, and imported literature on new art, as well as reports from artists who had travelled abroad.[380] In the catalogue for the first exhibition devoted to North American Post-Impressionism, held in 1986, Zilczer observed that "on the eve of the Armory Show, American Post-Impressionsim had already been introduced in cities across the North American continent."[381] She also observed that both the French and American Post-Impressionist works were "almost overshadowed" by the focus on "the most advanced forms of modernism."[382] From 1913 to 1918, over 30 New York galleries, organizations, and clubs mounted around 250 exhibitions. The proliferation of galleries and collectors of vanguard art was also, as before 1913, accompanied by a more liberal definition of the term "modern" at that time, which ranged from Davies to Dove.[383] This more inclusive viewpoint has also been adopted in recent studies such as Erika Doss's *Twentieth Century Art* regarding "the tremendous diversity of early American modern art," which "refuses broad categorization and stylistic consistency."[384] Observing that "modern American art is not all, or simply, non-representational," Doss asserted that "both the Ashcan painters and those in Stieglitz's circle…were modern artists."[385]

Upon the occasion of the Armory Show's 75th Anniversary in 1988, an exhibition of the artist-organizers was presented at the Hirshhorn Museum. The works of Davies, Kuhn, MacRae, Myers, and Taylor were overshadowed by the usual recitations of information about the avant-garde European art on view. One critic observed that when "one remembers what they borrowed, it comes as something of a shock to walk into the Hirshhorn and see the sort of pictures, mild, unadventurous, that they produced themselves."[386] Another show at the New York offices of the Archives of American Art and accompanying publication of archival material provided further acknowledgment of this "most important single occasion in American art history."[387] Since Kuhn's personal correspondence was still unknown when Brown's book was published, its discovery prompted the art historian to write the ground-breaking article "Walt Kuhn's Armory Show" upon this occasion, published in a special issue of the *Archives of American Art Journal*, along with other relevant archival material. Surprised at the lack of advance publicity and projects associated with the 75th anniversary of the Armory Show, Brown asked whether its legendary appeal was fading and attributed the casting of its "mythic guise" to Kuhn's pamphlet.[388] Brown did not pursue much further the archival materials in the revised second edition of his book, also in 1988, except to provide "minor emendations."[389] Therefore, his few comments on American art and its reception remained couched in such generalizations as the critical applause for "the sanity of the American section in contrast to the wildness of the radical Europeans."[390]

Many subsequent publications have not challenged the litany of Kuhn's and Brown's accounts of the Armory Show.[391] A few art historians such as Laurette E. McCarthy have contributed new perspectives by examining the forgotten co-organizers, especially Walter Pach, whose role, if mentioned at all, has been largely relegated to European agent. Christine I. Oaklander has resurrected the contributions of the overshadowed Clara Davidge and Henry Fitch Taylor of the Madison Art Gallery, whereas Susan Larkin has referred to the unsung labors of Elmer MacRae.[392] Others have sidestepped the mythic narrative to focus on other aspects of the Armory Show, especially its critical reception, public reactions, shock value, its connections to the circus spectacles of Barnum, and associations with anarchism and revolutionary politics.[393] Referring to the familiarity of the Armory Show, J.M. Mancini has observed that it "is an event whose meaning has remained peculiarly impervious to serious reevaluation."[394] Revising the model of "coupling modernist revolt with a broad array of social and political transformations," Mancini observed that historians have allowed the highly publicized views of a few conservative critics such as Kenyon Cox to stand for all of critical opinion as a misleading, "monolithic screed against the new."[395] Examining the more nuanced responses to the show, however, Mancini focused on reactions to foreign art, although she commented that many critics believed "the show contained fine examples of both European and American art, providing important evidence of American's art's improvement over the preceding half-century…pointing the way beyond 'stereotyped and fossilized standards' and 'simpering, self-satisfied conventionality.'"[396] Emphasis was placed by Mancini on "critical willingness to embrace" the AAPS's "organizational contribution to the enlargement of the American art world" rather than their work and critical reactions to it.[397] In another variation on this theme of the self-sacrifice of the Americans to their educational goal of promoting foreign art, French scholar Charlotte Laubard commented that while "the Armory Show marked the decreasing influence of American art over the next two decades, it enabled the European avant-garde to gain active support on American soil in its strategic struggle to impose itself as the dominant aesthetic of the 20th century."[398]

The profound impact of the Armory Show has often been discussed in terms of the growth of the modern art market, collecting, galleries and organizations providing more lasting exhibition opportunities, amidst the decline of the Academy. Significant aspects of this legacy were the founding of the artist-run Society of Independents, as well as the Whitney Studio and Club in 1917 and 1918, established by patron, collector, sculptor, and Armory Show supporter Gertrude Vanderbilt Whitney.[399] Collections inspired by visits to the Armory include that of Lillie P. Bliss, which became an early core collection of the Museum of Modern Art, the Louise and Walter Arensberg collection of the Philadelphia Museum of Art, Katherine Dreier's collection of the Société Anonyme, now at Yale University, and the Arthur Jerome Eddy collection at the Art Institute of Chicago.[400] The founding of three museums of modern and contemporary art in New York were ultimately the most enduring offspring of the Armory Show— the Gallery of Living Art at New York University in 1927, the Museum of Modern Art in 1929, and the Whitney Museum of American Art in 1930—the first museum dedicated to the work of living American artists.

In 1963, at the time of the 50th-anniversary exhibition of the Armory Show, it was predicted that the work "of the lesser known Americans…will attract the eyes of many, not because these works are really refreshing, but because they have been almost completely neglected for the past fifty years."[401] It was therefore noted that "in all probability, in 1963 the Americans will reclaim some of the attention the Europeans won in 1913 at the expense and energy of the 25 American artists who staged the show."[402] Although this prediction was mostly unrealized, another has come to fruition: *Be back in 2013 to reconsider the whole thing.*"[403] Thus the centennial is the appropriate occasion for re-examining standard accounts and presenting the case for the diverse "New Spirit" of American art in the Armory Show.

FOOTNOTES

1. Jerome Myers, *Artist in Manhattan* (New York: American Artists Group, 1940), 36.
2. Barbara Groseclose and Jochen Wierich, *Internationalizing the History of American Art* (University Park: The Pennsylvania State University Press, 2009), 74. On the concept of American provincialism, see especially John O'Brien, ed., *Clement Greenberg The Collected Essays and Criticism* Vol. 2 (Chicago and London: The University of Chicago Press, 1986), 192-3, Vol. 3 (1993), 59, 161, 163 and Vol. 4 (1993), 115, 303-6.
3. JoAnne M. Mancini, "One Term is as Fatuous as Another," Responses to the Armory Show Reconsidered," *American Quarterly* 51 (December 1999): 837.
4. Theodore Roosevelt, "A Layman's Views of an Art Exhibition," *Outlook* 103 (March 29, 1913): 719.
5. See Avis Berman, "'As National as the National Biscuit Company'; The Academy, the Critics, and the Armory Show," *Rave Reviews American Art and Its Critics, 1826-1925* (New York: National Academy of Design, 2000), 131.
6. See Judith K. Zilczer: "The Eight on Tour, 1908-1909" *American Art Journal* 16 (Summer 1984): 20-48; Elizabeth Milroy, *Painters of a New Century: The Eight & American Art* (Milwaukee: Milwaukee Art Museum, 1991); Sarah Vure, *Independent American Artists: The Post-Armory Show Careers of Robert Henri and John Sloan* (Boston University, Ph.D. diss., 2002): 1-7, 107-117, passim; and Elizabeth Kennedy, ed., *The Eight and American Modernisms* (Chicago: The University of Chicago Press, 2009), 13-22. Vure discusses the decades of secessionist practice by the 19th century French avant-garde who had rebelled against the government-sponsored Academy and Salons (p. 108).
7. See William I. Homer, *Robert Henri and His Circle* (Ithaca and London: Cornell University Press, 1969), 148, 155. Kuhn was also friendly with Henri's future wife, the artist Marjorie Organ, who would be represented by six drawings in the Armory Show. See Marian Wardle, ed., *American Women Modernists The Legacy of Robert Henri 1910-1945* (Brigham Young University Art Museum in association with Rutgers University Press, 2005), 10, 127.
8. Robert Henri, "The New York Exhibitions of Independent Artists," *The Craftsman* XVIII (May 1910): 170, 172, also lists him as on the hanging committee.
9. Helen Farr Sloan, Introductory notes for an article on the Armory Show, based on verbatim statements by John Sloan from 1944-1951, p. 3, Delaware Art Museum Archives. Bennard B. Perlman, "Driven to Abstraction," *Artnews*, 107 (February 2008): 115, has asserted that the Association of the American Painters and Sculptors was "founded for the purpose of presenting an expanded version of the 1910 Independent exhibition." See also Bennard B. Perlman, *The Immortal Eight American Painting from Eakins to the Armory Show, 1870-1913* (Cincinnati: North Light Publishers, 1979), 191-5 and for a more recent account, Sarah Vure, *Independent American Artists*, (as in n. 6), 113-115. See also Alan Antliff, "The Culture of Revolt: Art and Anarchism in America, 1908-1920," Ph.D. diss., University of Delaware, 1998, 48-52.
10. See Bruce St. John, ed., *John Sloan's New York Scene from the diaries, notes and correspondence, 1906-1913* (New York: Harper & Row, Publishers, 1965), 384, February 7, 1910 diary entry: "J.M. talks of an exhibition, International, small group."
11. Homer, *Robert Henri* (as in n. 7), 152 and Bruce St. John, *The Fiftieth Anniversary of the Exhibition of Independent Artists in 1910* (Wilmington: Delaware Art Center, 1960), 8-9. For a reprint of the original catalogue for the show, see pp. 5-10.
12. Homer, *Robert Henri* (as in n. 7), 153, noted that the show comprised a mix of young unknown artists, progressively inclined academicians, and avant-garde artists who refused to submit to the annual Academy shows—similar to the eventual mix of the Armory Show. Mahonri Sharp Young, *The Realist Revolt in American Painting: The Eight* (New York: Watson-Guptill Publications, 1973), 36 states that at least 38 were Henri's students. For a list of the artists who would be represented in the Armory Show, see Appendix I.
13. St. John, *John Sloan's New York Scene* (as in n. 10), 404—according to Sloan's March 27, 1910 entry, Davies was too ill to attend a meeting to hang the show. In his March 28 entry, Sloan stated that Stuart Davis and especially Glenn Coleman assisted with the installation—both would also be represented in the Armory Show.
14. Ibid, 399—"After dinner up to Henri's, where I broached a subject suggested by Kuhn….The old idea that in going in to a show we are the 'tail of his kite.' I don't agree with this idea but since Kuhn mentioned it and we had decided to ask Henri if he could shift the whole responsibility so far as newspapers went to Kuhn as manager, I opened the subject. And then Henri grew hot under the collar and proceeded to show how this was an impossibility…If he said nothing there would be little notice taken of the show. And the reporters are bound to come to him on account of his record as Revolutionist."
15. Ibid, 403 (March 23, 1910 diary entry).
16. Guy Pene Du Bois, "Great Modern Display Here April 1," *New York American,* March 17, 1910, cited in Homer, *Robert Henri* (as in n. 7), 283n59. In Henri's overview of the show, Du Bois was listed as serving on the Hanging Committee and among those who contributed "interest, time, and money" to the organization of the show. Glackens and George Bellows were also listed on the hanging committee. See Robert Henri, "The New York Exhibition of Independents," *Craftsman* XVIII (May 1910): 172. See also St. John, Sloan, *John Sloan's New York Scene* (as in n. 10), 404, du Bois "is in the ex. Scheme."
17. Clipping, *New York Evening Post*, April 2, 1910, John Sloan Papers, Delaware Art Museum Archives.
18. Guy Pene Du Bois, "Great Modern Display Here April 1," *New York American* (as in n. 16), cited in Bennard Perlman, *The Immortal Eight* (as in n. 9), 192.
19. Walter Pach, *Queer Thing, Painting: Forty Years in the World of Art* (New York: Harper and Brothers, 1938), 178.

20. St. John, *John Sloan's New York Scene* (as in n. 10), 402.

21. William Innes Homer, *Alfred Stieglitz and the American Avant-Garde* (Boston: New York Graphic Society, 1977), 87, Anne McCauley, "Edward Steichen, Artist, Impresario, Friend," in Sarah Greenough et al , *Modern Art in America Alfred Stieglitz and His New York Galleries* (Washington: National Gallery of Art and Boston, London, New York: Bulfinch Press, 2000), 60-61, and Lisa Mintz Messinger, ed., *Stieglitz and His Artists Matisse to O'Keeffe* (New York: The Metropolitan Museum of Art, 2011), 7, 16-17, 154, 156, 159.

22. Alfred Stieglitz, "Post Impressionism in America," *The Evening Sun*, December 18, 1911, 14, quoted in Charles Brock, " The Armory Show 1913, A Diabolical Test," in Sarah Greenough, *Modern Art in America* (as in n. 21), 127.

23. Ibid, 41, 127-136 and Gail Stavitsky and Katherine Rothkopf, *Cézanne and American Modernism* (Montclair Art Museum and the Baltimore Museum of Art in association with Yale University Press, 2009), 32, 194.

24. On Kent's mysterious exclusion, see Kenneth Miller's letter to Rockwell Kent, March 23, 1913, published in *Archives of American Art Journal* Vol. 27 Number 2 (1987), 31. On Kent's show, see Judith Zilczer, *"The Noble Buyer:" John Quinn Patron of the Avant-Garde* (Washington D.C.: Smithsonian Institution Press, 1978), 22, William H. Gerdts and Jorge H. Santis, *William Glackens* (Museum of Art, Fort Lauderdale and Abbeville Press, 1996), 86, and Jake Wien, *Rockwell Kent: The Mythic and the Modern* (Manchester and New York: Hudson Hills Press, 2005), 20-21.

25. Doreen Bolger et al, *American Pastels in the Metropolitan Museum of Art* (New York: The Metropolitan Museum of Art, 1989), 20-21, 30-31. See also Susan G. Larkin, *On Home Ground: Elmer Livingston MacRae at the Holley House* (Greenwich, Connecticut: Bruce Museum, 1990), 35-37. Larkin asserts that MacRae was the founder, although in reviews of the first show, Myers was cited as a co-instigator. The overlap with the group of artists in the Independents was also noted. See "A New Artist Society," *New York Mail* January 15, 1911 and other clippings, Holley/MacRae Papers, Box 15, Folder 178, Greenwich Historical Society.

26. Jerome Myers, *An Artist in Manhattan* (as in n. 1), 34. On the Pastellists, see also Susan G. Larkin, *"A Regular Rendezvous for Impressionists"; The Cos Cob Art Colony 1882-1920* Ph.D. diss. (The City University of New York, 1996), 91-2, 112n72, n73.

27. See Christine Oaklander, "Clara Davidge's Madison Art Gallery: Sowing the Seed for The Armory Show," *Archives of American Art Journal* 36 (1996): 20-37 (list of shows). See "Meyers and Kuhn," *American Art News* IX (April 8, 1911): 2. Kuhn praised for his landscapes with "broad washes" of color and "strong effects." There was also a group show at the Madison Gallery in November 1911 with Allen Tucker, Elmer MacRae, Karl Anderson, D. Putnam Brinley and others who would all form the AAPS.

28. On Quinn and Kuhn, see B.L. Reid, *The Man from New York John Quinn and His Friends* (New York: Oxford University Press, 1968), 93, 142, 143, 146, 149, 150, 165, 191, 192, 198, 202, 207, 246-7, 253, 264, 270, 285, 289, 292, 294, 303, 393, 467, 468. See also Zilczer, *"The Noble Buyer* (as in n. 24), 28-32, 34, 36. Kuhn's letters to Vera of October 18, Oct. 31, November 1, 22, and December 9, 1911, Box 3, Folders 45-46, Walt Kuhn Family Papers, Archives of American Art, Smithsonian Institution (hereafter cited as Kuhn Papers, AAA), chronicle his hopes for his show, including doing business with Quinn. See Oaklander, "Clara Davidge " (as in n. 27), 35n72 who notes that Quinn purchased two paintings, the first works Kuhn ever sold. He received the assistance of Frederick James Gregg, art critic for the *Sun* who agreed to write about him as well (Nov. 19 letter).

29. Oaklander in "Clara Davidge (as in n. 27), 36n96 challenges Kuhn's egotistical claim that he initiated the meetings that developed into the AAPS in reaction to the dismal reception of his November 1911 Madison Gallery show which was well received. She asserts that the show that inspired the coalition was not Kuhn's but the group show with 14 artists, including Kuhn MacRae, Myers, and Taylor. Nevertheless the timing and much of the content of Kuhn's correspondence seems to be more linked to his own show.

30. Letter to Vera, December 12, 1911, Box 3, Folder 46, Kuhn Papers, AAA: "What we need now is *publicity*... Beginning the first of Jan. [1912], I am going to organize a new society....No one is in on it except Gregg. As soon as I have it thoroughly planned we are going to give it to all the papers, and they'll jump at it. Of course Henri and the rest will have to be let in but not until things are chained up so that they can't do any monkey business.....He's so wrapped up in the McDowell Club that he is off guard, and I'll put it over before he knows it, *and* in such a way that he can't make a single kick... now is the time , for the academy has been worse than ever....I'm going to take my time thinking out every detail." On Henri, the MacDowell Club, and AAPS, see Homer, *Robert Henri* (as in n. 7), 166-9.

31. See Milton W. Brown, *The Story of the Armory Show* (New York: Abbeville Press Publishers, 1988), 38,51. On the MacDowell Club, see "An Art Exhibition without a Jury System of Awards," *The New York Times,* May 14, 1911, Magazine Section, Part Five,2, and clipping in the *Evening Post,* January 6, 1912, Daniel Putnam Brinley and Kathrine Sanger Brinley Papers, Box 12, Folder 22, AAA, citing the May 1, 1911 original prospectus invitation specifically "to all American artists" to make the gallery "an open field for expression of the various movements in art, whether old or new." For Henri's involvement with the MacDowell Club, see also his diary, Robert Henri Papers, reel 886, AAA, frames 495, 499, 500, 502, 504, 512, 521, 523, 532, 535, 540, 566, 572, 574, 580, 588, 605, 615, 618.

32. Minutes 1911-1914, December 14, 1912, Box 3, Folder 5, AAPS Records, Kuhn Papers, AAA. See also "International Exhibition to be Held in New York," *The New York Sun,* November 10, 1912, 15, on the formation of the AAPS ,which "has not been told until now....The idea was suggested in the course of a little talk at the studio of Jerome Myers...the other artists present being Henry Fitch Taylor...Elmer MacRae, and Walt Kuhn." See also Myers, *Artist in Manhattan* (as in n. 26), 34 and Walt Kuhn, *The Story of the Armory Show* (New York: 1938), 5 and MacRae diary, 1912, entry for "National Association of Painters and Sculptors," Box

15, Folder 177, Holley/MacRae Family Papers, Greenwich Historical Society Library and Archives.

33 Letter to Vera, December 15, 1911, Box 3, Folder 46, Kuhn Papers, AAA.

34 Letter from Henri to Kuhn, December 26, 1911, Box 3, Folder 3, AAPS Records, AAA.

35 Minutes, Box 3, Folder 5, AAPS Records, AAA.

36 Ibid.

37 Ibid.

38 Minutes, Box 3, Folder 5, AAA, and Henri's diary (as in n.31), frame 596, December 23, 1911 ("The American Painters & Sculptors, recent notice of new art society announcement that have been elected charter member"), frame 605, entry for January 2, 1912 ("today my first appearance at meetings....AB Davies very active in it.")

39 Ibid.

40 Homer, *Robert Henri* (as in n. 7), 167.

41 "Artists in Revolt Form New Society," *The New York Times,* January 3, 1912, 2.

42 Ibid. See also "Art Insurgents Organize," *Evening Post,* January 3, 1912, "New Society Growing," *Tribune,* January 3, 1912, and "Form New Art Society," *New York Herald,* Januayr 3, 1912, D. Putnam Brinley Papers (as in n.31), Box 12, Folder 22, AAA.

43 "Artists in Revolt…" (as in n. 41), 2.

44 "Art Insurgents Organize," *Evening Post,* January 3, 1912, Brinley Papers, Box 12, Folder 22, AAA and "Separatist Art Bodies," *The Evening Post,* January 4, 1912, 8. Henri was a full National Academician, Glackens and Lawson were associates. Among the exhibitors at the Academy were Mowbray-Clarke, Lie, and Myers.

45 "Separatist Art Bodies," *The Evening Post,* January 4, 1912, 8.

46 Letter from Weir to Henry Fitch Taylor, January 3, 1912, Box 3, Folder 3, AAPS Records, AAA.

47 Henri Diary (as in n. 31), frame 605 (January 3, 1912—"hear that J.A. Weir has resigned from new society because it is declared antagonistic to NAD.") Frame 606, January 4, 1912—"Borglum..asked me if I wd accept presidency of society—answer no—wd accept presidency of nothing…was called up by MacRae who asked me if would vote for Davies as Pres.—certainly—but advised him to find out if AB wd accept before going further."

48 Kuhn, *The Story of the Armory Show* (as in n.32), 5-6.

49 Ibid, 6. Helen Farr Sloan wrote that "Kuhn says that he alone got Davies to be Pres. of the Ass[ociation.]" See Armory Exhibition Notes, March 1962, n.p., John Sloan Papers, Delaware Art Museum Library Archives. See also Bennard B. Perlman, *The Lives, Loves, and Art of Arthur B. Davies* (Albany: State University of New York Press, 1998) , 204, who stated that Kuhn approached Davies right after Weir's letter of resignation in *The New York Times.*

50 Myers, *An Artist in Manhattan* (as in n. 1), 35.

51 Elmer MacRae Diary, entry for January 5, 1912, Holley/MacRae Family Papers, Box 20, Folder 207, Greenwich Historical Society Library and Archives.

52 John Sloan, Manuscript for Autobiography, p. 43, John Sloan Manuscript Collection, Helen Farr Sloan Library, Delaware Art Museum, box 49, folder 5.

53 Kuhn, *The Story of the Armory Show* (as in n. 32), 6, Myers, *An Artist in Manhattan* (as in n. 1), 27, and John Sloan, "Manuscript for Autobiography," (as in n. 52), 43. See also Helen Farr Sloan, "Notes in Connection with the Armory Show," verbatim notes checked by John Sloan, 1944-1951, 31—"…we soon found that Kuhn and Davies and Quinn had taken it over."

54 "No 'Skied' Pictures in New Art Society," *The New York Times,* January 11, 1912, 4. For the January 9 meeting, see Elmer Livingston MacRae diary entry, Holley/MacRae Family Papers, Box 20, Folder 207, Greenwich Historical Society Archives.

55 Ibid.

56 "Succeeds J. Alden Weir," *New York Daily Tribune,* January 11, 1912, clippings, Elmer Livingston MacRae Papers (hereafter cited as MacRae Papers), Joseph P. Hirshhorn Foundation, Smithsonian Institution, reel 4132, frame numbers are only partially legible, see frame number [1026], AAA. On this roll on frames [1023-1028], see also "Proclamation of the Insurgents," *New York Sun,* January 11, 1912, "Art Not 'Anatogonistic,'" *Herald,* January 11, 1912, "Arthur B. Davies to be President," *Evening Sun,* January 11, 1912, "An Exhibiting Association," *Evening Sun,* January 12, 1912, and "Methods of 'Encouraging Art'," *Evening Sun,* January 15, 1912, and "Arthur B. Davies, the New Head of the New Artists' Association," *Evening Sun,* January 19, 1912.

57 See Kuhn's letter to the St. Paul Institute of Arts and Sciences, January 29, 1912, Box 3 Folder 2, AAPS Records, AAA, which mostly contains responses from institutions in New York (i.e. the Albright Art Gallery), Massachusetts, Minnesota, the Art Institute of Chicago, Ohio, Michigan, Indiana, Washington D.C., Georgia, Pennsylvania, South Carolina. For Kuhn's membership correspondence, see Box 3, Folder 3, including a letter of May 30, 1912, from John Quinn, accepting honorary membership.

58 Letter of January 29, 1912 (as in n. 57), AAA.

59 See, for example, a letter of January 30, 1912, from the Syracuse Museum of Fine Arts director Fernand Carter, potentially receptive to the request, states that five of the members have already been included in shows there—Henri, Bellows, Davies, Lie, Lawson. Box 3, Folder 2, AAPS records, AAA. A similar observation was made by J.H. Gest, Director, Cincinnati Museum Association, February 2, 1912, Box 3, Folder 2, "In looking at your list of members I find that ten or eleven of them have already contributed to our annual exhibitions…" Gest was receptive to receiving the show as part of a circuit with AIC, St. Louis, and other

similar museums.

60 See Matter's letter of February 5, 1912, Box 3, Folder 2, AAPS Records, AAA,. expressing interest in a show of the work of the American Painters and Sculptors, and asking it would be possible to receive it in March or the first week in April 1912.

61 Letter of March 5 from Kuhn to Milton Matter, Box 3, Folder 2, AAPS Records, AAA.

62 Letter of March 16, 1912 from Cornelia Bentley Sage to Kuhn, Box 3, Folder 2, AAPS Records, AAA.

63 Ibid. She also recommended P. Naves, as packer in Paris. See Kuhn's thank you reply of January 18, 1913, about how useful the information was while abroad in arranging matters for the coming International Exhibition." Box 2, Folder 3, Armory Show Records, (hereafter cited AS Records), AAA. For Lloyd's insurance correspondence, see Box 1, Folder 36.

64 "Club Loses Opportunity," *American Art News* X (December 23, 1911, 4.

65 Ibid.

66 "New Art Society Formed" and "Alexander's Criticisms," *American Art News* X (January 6, 1912), 3,4. I am grateful to Laurette E. McCarthy for bringing these articles to my attention.

67 "Club Loses Opportunity (as in n.64), 4. See Carol A. Nathanson, "The American Reaction to London's First Grafton Show," *Archives of American Art Journal* 25 (1985): 6-7.

68 Kuhn, *The Story of the Armory Show* (as in n. 32), 7. See also Zilczer, *"The Noble Buyer'..."* (as in n. 24), 23-24. See also pp. 25-26—through the journalist Frederick James Gregg, Quinn became involved with preparations for the Armory Show.

69 Kuhn served on the Armory Committee with Davies and Borglum to negotiate for the lease of the 69th Regiment Armory, which was approved at the July 31 meeting of the Directors, as indicated in the minutes of the meeting, Box 3, Folder 6, AAPS Records, AAA. See also Colonel Conley's letter to Kuhn, April 19, 1912, Box 1, Folder 45, Armory Show Records, detailing terms of rental of the drill hall, cloak room for men, dressing room for women, for $5,000, from Feb. 1 or 15 to March 1 or 15, the April 23 entry in MacRae diary, 1912 (as in n. 51), the Agreement to Lease, May 6, 1912, Box 1, Folder 45, and the bond agreement, August 14, 1912, MacRae Papers, AAA, Reel 4132, frames 73-77. On the finalization of the lease in October, see Davies' correspondence with Kuhn September 2, October 10, 1912, Box 1, Folder 1, and Kuhn to Vera Kuhn, October 31, 1912, Box 1, Folder 4, AS Records, AAA.

70 "'Progressives' in Art Counted Out by Reactionaries," *New York American,* June 27, 1912, 13.

71 Ibid. See also Kuhn's letter to "Dear Sir," May 17, 1912, MacRae Papers, AAA, reel 4131, frame 867, listing the French artists Edmond Aman Jean and Raffaelli as among those who received a majority of first choice votes; neither were eventually represented. The Americans Cassatt, Weir, the Prestons, and Schamberg were also listed as among the top choices.

72 Schamberg's letter is so far the only concrete evidence of invitations being extended at this time; it was originally quoted in Brown, *The Story of the Armory Show* (as in n. 31), 63-64.

73 Walter Pach, "Le movement artistique a l'étranger. Etats-Unis," *L'Art et Les Artistes* XV (May 1912): 92 and XV (September 1912): 281-2. I am grateful to Laurette E. McCarthy for these articles.

74 Walter Pach, *Queer Thing, Painting: Forty Years in the World of Art* (New York: Harper and Brothers, 1938), 178.

75 Laurette E. McCarthy, *Walter Pach (1883-1958) The Armory Show and the Untold Story of Modern Art in America* (University Park: The Pennsylvania State University Press, 2011), 38-40.

76 Letter of September 1, 1912, Box 1, Folder 1, Armory Show Records, AAA. Davies had purchased the catalogue from the dealer Martin Birnbaum who had written to John Quinn in July from Cologne about this "great Futurist show," as quoted in Zilczer, *The Noble Buyer* (as in n. 24), 26.

77 Vera Kuhn Nova Scotia diary, September 5, 1912, Box 19, Folder 19, Kuhn Papers, AAA On September 4 Vera had noted in her diary—"Letter from Davies wanting Walt to go to Europe now, upset everything."

78 Letter of September 25, 1912, to Vera Kuhn, Box 1, Folder 3, Armory Show Records, AAA

79 "Vortwort," catalogue for the *Sonderbund* exhibition, 3, translated by Barbara Schaefer in the prospectus for *1912-Mission Moderne: Die Jahrhundertschau Des Sonderbundes/The Centennial Retrospective of the Sonderbund Exhibition* (Cologne: Wallraf-Richartz-Museum, 2012). I am indebted to translator Shannon Connelly who perused the catalogue for the following citations pertaining to the Sonderbund as a model for the Armory Show: 16,21,125,165-7, 167n33,278,300,302.

80 Ibid, 5-6. See also Isabelle Overbeck, *The Cologne Sonderbund Exhibition 1912 Regionalism, Nationalism, and Internationalism* (London: Courtauld Institute, 2000), 25-48,54-5.) For the emphasis upon van Gogh in among modernist pioneers, see Carol M. Zemel, *The Formation of a Legend Van Gogh Criticism, 1890-1920* (Ann Arbor: UMI Research Press, 1980), 121-2.

81 Letters of September 30 and October 2, 1912, Box 1, Folder 3, AS Records, AAA.

82 Letter of October 2, 1912 (as in n. 81).

83 Letter to Vera Kuhn, October 8, 1912, Box 1, Folder 3, AS Records, AAA. The Redon show opened in November 1912 at Artz & De Bois and is listed in Alec Wildenstein, *Odilon Redon Catalogue Raisonné De L'Oeuvre Peint et Dessiné* II (Paris: Wildenstein Institute, 1994), 322. For his arrival in Holland ,see his postcard to Vera Kuhn, October 5, 1912, Box 1, Folder 3. The Nemzell exhibition took place from July-December 1912 and is listed in John Rewald... On his way he stopped in Dusseldorf to see "a fine exhibit...[with] some fine Cézannes," likely a reference to the exhibition *Sammlung Marczell von Nemes, Budapest,* at the Städtische Kunsthalle Düsseldorf 1912.

84 The show had opened Oct. 6. See Donald E. Gordon, *Modern Art Exhibitions 1900-1916*, vol. 2 (Munich: Prestel-Verlag, 1974), 627-30. There were also works on view by Derain, Vlaminck, Archipenko, Gauguin, Léger, and Picasso. Arriving in Berlin on October 8, Kuhn was still very focused on locating Post

Impressionist works during his visit with the dealer Paul Cassirer since he thought it would be difficult to get any in Paris. See his letter of October 8 to Vera Kuhn, Box 1, Folder 3, Armory Show Records, AAA. In Berlin at Cassirer Gallery in October- November 1912, Kuhn could have seen works by Beckmann, Cezanne, Degas, Lehmbruck, Munch, and Toulouse-Lautrec. See Gordon, *Modern Art Exhibitions*, 618-19. For the failure of the Cassirer connection, see Milton W. Brown, "Walt Kuhn's Armory Show," *Archives of American Art Journal* 27 (1987), 7.

[85] Letter to Vera Kuhn, October 9, 1912, Box 1, Folder 3, Armory Show Records, AAA.

[86] Letter from Davies to Kuhn, undated, October 1912, Box 1, Folder 1, Armory Show Records, AAA. See also another undated letter in the same box directing Kuhn to visit Auguste Pellerin to see Cezanne's work, "the most desirable of all places for a visit."

[87] Davies' letter to Kuhn, October 10, 1912, Box 1, Folder 1, Armory Show Records, AAA.

[88] Ibid-—"Clark [Mowbray-Clarke] has promised to work on the second circular but I am inclined to work with Glackens on it he has…more horse sense than any of the other fellows even with the shadow of the 'Blackest Henri" over him." On the second circular, see also Davies' subsequent undated letters to Kuhn, October 1912 and his letter of October 23, Box 1, Folder 1.

[89] "Bedingungen für ausstellende Künstler, " sheet annotated with "Circular used in Germany" -Box 2, Folder 38 and Box 1, Folder 21, Armory Show Records, AAA. The circular states that expenses will be assumed by the AAPS which takes 10 percent of the net price as commission, shipment will take place between December 1-15, 1912, and that the undersigned (Kuhn) is prepared to provide any further requested information. Kuhn was listed as "representative in Europe." For the *Neue Kunst* show, see Gordon, *Modern Art Exhibitions* (as in n.84), 613-16. For his arrival in Munich, see Kuhn's postcard to Vera, October 15, 1912, Box 1, Folder 3.

[90] Postcard and letter to Vera Kuhn, October 18, 1912, Box 1, Folder 3, Armory Show Records, AAA. In a letter to Vera dated, October 16, 1912, in the same box and folder, Kuhn also claimed that he wrote Davies two recent progress reports; hopefully this missing correspondence will be recovered some day. On Kuhn's lack of interest in German Expressionism, see his letter of January 11, 1913, to Erich Heckel (in response to the artist's letter of December 16), stating that they can not accept any more works from Europe as the shipment is already here. "We trust that at a later date we shall have the pleasure of including some of the work of your society [Die Brucke]." Box 1 Folders 25-26, Armory Show Records, AAA. See also letter to Sec. Neue Secession, January 28, 1913, Box 1, Folder 25—"Our general plan did not include representation of your society in a general sense although we believe that several artists who usually contribute to your exhibitions. will be represented in our coming show." See also Brown, "Walt Kuhn's Armory Show," *Archives of American Art Journal* 27 (1987): 7-9.

[91] See Kuhn, *Story of the Armory Show* (as in n. 32), 10 and Stacey Epstein, *Alfred H. Maurer, Aestheticism to Modernism* (New York: Hollis Taggart Galleries, 1999), 39. See also Kuhn's letters to Vera, October 26, October 29 and 31, 1912, Box 1, Folder 4, Armory Show Records, AAA. On October 29 Kuhn mentioned Pach's assistance and, grudgingly, that of Jo Davidson— "also willing but of course has an ax to grind."

[92] Letter from Davies to Pach, October 2, 1912, Reel 4217, frames 95-96, Walter Pach Papers, AAA. See also Kuhn's October 26 postcard, Box 1, Folder 4, AS Records, AAA, noting that he had arrived in Paris last night. In a letter to Vera of December 14, 1912, Box 1, Folder 4, Kuhn stated that Pach "deserves a lot of credit." On Pach and the Armory Show, see McCarthy, *Walter Pach* (as in n.75), 40-45 and her forthcoming essay in *The Armory Show at 100* published by the New-York Historical Society, New York City in association- with D Giles Limited, London, 2013.

[93] Letter to Vera Kuhn, October 28, 1912, Box 1, Folder 4, Armory Show Records, AAA. At the Salon d'Automne, Kuhn also saw works by Bruce, Bonnard, Carles, Courbet, Degas, Duchamp, Duchamp-Villon, Gauguin, Segonzac, Matisse, Maurer, Toulouse-Lautrec, Whistler, van Gogh, and Vuillard. See Gordon, *Modern Art Exhibitions* (as in n. 84), 619-624.

[94] Ibid.

[95] See Gordon, *Modern Art Exhibitions* (as in n. 84), 630-31.

[96] Postcard to Vera Kuhn, November 6, 1912, Box 1, Folder 4, AS Records, AAA.

[97] On November 7, Kuhn wrote to Leo Stein informing him that "Davies and myself will take the liberty of calling today at about 3 pm." Series II, Box 113, Folder 2341, Gertrude Stein and Alice B. Toklas Papers, Beinecke Library, Yale University. For this visit and also to the home of Michael and Gertrude Stein, both evidently made with Pach as well, see Janet Bishop, ed. *The Steins Collect* (San Fransciso Museum of Modern Art, in association with Yale University Press, 2011), 138-9.

[98] Quoted in Pach, *Queer Painting* (as in n. 74), 178.

[99] See Brown, *The Story of the Armory Show* (as in n. 31), 72 and McCarthy, *Walter Pach* (as in n. 75), 42.

[100] Brown, *The Story of the Armory Show* (as in n. 31), 70 and McCarthy, *Walter Pach* (as in n. 75), 42, states that Pach revisited Russell's studio. On Russell, see Marilyn Kushner's forthcoming essay in *The New Spirit: The Armory Show at 100* (as in n. 92).

[101] James Timothy Voorhies , ed., *My Dear Stieglitz: Letters of Marsden Hartley and Alfred Stieglitz, 1912-1915* (Columbia: University of South Carolina Press, 2002), 33, see also 41. On the Salon d'Automne as a likely model for the Armory Show, see Bennard B. Perlman, "Explosion of a Shingle Factory," *Art & Antiques* XI (January 1988): 56.

[102] Ibid, 25.

[103] Ibid, 39-40.

[104] Ibid, 40. See also p. 57 and Hartley's expression of regret that Kuhn did not secure more German art for the

Armory Show, especially Kandinsky. While in Paris, Kuhn had been able to write to dealers whom he had met in Germany to update them and to secure loans. Writing, for example, in German to de Bois, Kuhn proclaimed with his characteristic hubris:

Presumably you have learned much since my visit about our exhibition in New York. I have been in Paris for two weeks and based on my efforts here, it will be an extraordinary exhibition of colossal significance for the new direction in art. ...Davies arrived yesterday...to assist me in all aspects of our affairs. I told him of my conversation with you and he was very interested to hear my report on Redon. ....Attached is a plan of our exhibition spaces. After brief consultation we are prepared to report that if it is amenable to you, we will make available an entire gallery for works by Redon....This is the finest and largest opportunity to introduce such an important yet still unknown figure in a new country....We would be most grateful for your perspective on these matters. And of course you will also write me about which Van Goghs you can secure for us....To avoid any hesitation on your part, I should also mention that many art dealers here in Paris will participate. Durand Ruel is in any case ready to assist us, and Mr. Feinhals in Cologne has also made himself available...

Letter to J.H. de Bois, November 7, 1912, Box 1, Folder 17, Armory Show Records, AAA. Translated from German by Shannon Connelly. Similarly he wrote to Hans Goltz that "first-rate Paris art dealers are prepared to vouch for us...Among the collectors is also included the well known Stein Family....A tremendous artistic and commercial success is certain and I am of the firm belief that the exhibition will be groundbreaking for the overall direction of modernism." November 8, 1912, Box 1, Folder 24, see also his letter of November 16, 1912, to Goltz, noting that he completed an insurance agreement with Lloyds, reached firm agreements with Bernheim Jeune, Vollard, Druet, Michael Stein, Leo Stein, and others—"we have already personally confirmed participation with the very best artists." Thannhauser wrote to Kuhn on November 23, 1912—"I hope that your exhibition will have great success and will achieve what we wish: the introduction of good modern art in America." See also Kuhn's letter of November 8, 1912, to "Herrn Romer, Moderne Gallerie, Munich with updates about the show including that the Stein family is "most interested." Box 1 Folder 27.

[105] Voorhies, *My Dear Stieglitz...*(as in n. 101), see also p. 58 about the drawings.

[106] Ibid, 58. For more of his thoughts on the Armory Show, see 64-65, 67.

[107] Letter to Vera Kuhn, November 11, 1912, Box 1 Folder 4, Armory Show Records, AAA. "We already have a better Cezanne and Gauguin collection than Cologne only in Van Gogh's they beat us. Our run of other material is much better..."

[108] Letter to Vera Kuhn, November 17, 1912, Box 1, Folder 4, Armory Show Records, AAA.

[109] Letter to Vera Kuhn, November 11, 1912, Box 1 Folder 4, Armory Show Records, AAA. Regarding the superiority of the forthcoming Armory Show and the Grafton Show as a fruitful source of loans, see Kuhn's undated letter to Pach, Box 1, Folder 7. He also noted, "The two Cezannes of Vollard were head and shoulders over anything else...You remember that M. Stein is to confer with Matisse regarding the London pictures." See also Gordon, *Modern Art Exhibitions* (as in n. 84), 624-27.

[110] Letter to Paul Mahlberg, November 16, 1912, Box 1 Folder 56, Armory Show Records, AAA. Kuhn also mentioned rooms of work by "Sezanne, [sic] Gogian, [sic]Van Goghe, Matisse, Picasso," which would not be realized.

[111] Letter to Pach, November 19, 1912, Box 1 Folder 7, Armory Show Records, AAA. Kuhn also wrote to dealers such as Alfred Flechtheim designating Pach as "charged with administering all unfinished affairs of the New York Exhibition," November. 20, 1912, Box 1, Folder 23.

[112] "To Show All Modern Art," *The Evening Post*, December 31, 1912, 14. See also "International Art Show to be Held in New York," *The New York Sun*, November 10, 1912, 15, which mistakenly mentioned that Davies joined Kuhn "who has been visiting French, German, and English cities for some time."

[113] The *Noa Noa* excerpts are in Box 2, Folder 16, Armory Show Records, AAA and the translated letters are in Box 2, Folder 17. They are accompanied by the notation, "Some of the letters of Vincent Van Gogh Walt Kuhn dictated to Arthur B. Davies and written in his hand on board S.S. Celtic Nov. 1912 homeward bound after collecting works abroad for the Armory Show NY 1913, not published." It is curious that these letters were not published; they may well have been among the first English translations of some of Van Gogh's correspondence with his brother Theo and artist friend Emile Bernard. In 1912 Anthony Ludovici's English translation *Letters of a Post Impressionist* was published in London. The following year, Davies contributed a foreword to Elizabeth Du Quesne Van Gogh's *Personal Recollections of Vincent Van Gogh,* translated by Katherine Dreier. The letters that Kuhn translated address a range of topics that likely fascinated him, from Van Gogh's techniques to his feelings about the act of creation and forging a personal, non-academic style—all of which enhanced his acclaim as " an impassioned and tragic figure who was dedicated, heroic, and martyred in the cause of his art."Carol M. Zemel, *The Formation of a Legend Van Gogh Criticism, 1890-1920* (Ann Arbor: UMI Research Press, 1980), 11. The following quotations were likely most pertinent for Kuhn: "I feel that things appear before me while painting in colors which I did not formerly see. Things full of Breadth and strength....there are now more means at my disposal to express it with greater force.... (first typed letter in Box 2, Folder 17, corresponds to letter to Theo, August 15, 1882, no. 225, *The Complete Letters of Vincent Van Gogh* (Boston: New York Graphic Society, 1978), 438.) I want to bring it so far that one will say of my work—'the man feels deeply....in the moderns lies something more personal more intimate which appeals more to us today. (typescript letter 2d to Theo, compare to Anthony M. Ludovici, *The Letters of a Post-Impressionist* (Boston and New York: Houghton Mifflin Company, 1913), 4-5) ....I find in my work an echo of that which gripped me. I know that nature has told me something...and that I wrote it down in shorthand....I put myself with all strength into painting, I sink myself into the color...."(5th typescript

letter, corresponds to *The Complete Letters of Vincent Van Gogh*, letter 228, p. 447).

[114] Typescript letter no. 53, which corresponds to Letter 489, *The Complete Letters* (as in. n. 112), 570), published in *Arts and Decoration* 3 (March 1913): 148. See Kuhn to Thomas E. Ashwell, December 19, 1912, Box 1, Folder 43, Armory Show Records, AAA, regarding the sale of this issue in a special booth.

[115] "International Art Show To Be Held in New York," *The Sun*, November 10, 1912, 15.

[116] Ibid. The circular is in the MacRae Papers, reel 4131, frames 836-7.

[117] Quoted from Cat. 48 (p. 150). The article in *The Sun*, November 10, 1912 (as in n. 115) also provided information on the formation of the AAPS, expenses, fundraising, and details of the projected installation. See also "International Art Show," *Evening Transcript*, November 11, 1912, D.Putnam Brinley Papers, Box 12, Folder 22, AAA and "Coming Internat'l Show," *American Art News* XI (November 16, 1912): 3. See also Davies' undated letter to Kuhn, October 1912, Box 1, Folder 1, (as in n. 113), stating that it had been decided to send the second circular after Kuhn's return, therefore, it would go out by November 25th or December 1.

[118] Manuscript for Autobiography, (as in n 52), 42-3.

[119] Elmer MacRae, letter to Virginia Teague, February 16, 1951, Virginia Teague Papers, AAA. See also MacRae to Beaumont Newhall, Holley/MacRae Family Papers, Box 17, Folder 187, Greenwich Historical Society Library and Archives—"Kuhn and Davies went to Paris and met Pach there…he knew the moderns-and they together picked out the pictures which…made the Armory Show memorable…All working committees dwindled down to a few willing…workers—-Davies, Kuhn, Pach, Gregg & myself gave up a whole year—Taylor and Tucker [were] part of this time."

[120] Letter from Kuhn, addressed "Dear Sir," December 20, 1912, Jerome Myers Papers, Box 7, Folder 1, Helen Farr Sloan Library, Delaware Art Museum. See also Kuhn's letter of Dec. 24, 1912 to Martha Walter about this committee, Box 1, Folder 16, Armory Show Records, AAA.

[121] Letter to Vera, December 20, 1912, Box 1 Folder 4, Armory Show Records, AAA. This letter and that of December 12 provide fascinating glimpses of the hectic activities, hubris, and factions at this time: "I have charge of the Press and all photos etc for reproduction besides being the business manager…..all interviews pass through me. Buttons will be ready and issued by end of next week. They are very artistic and ought to make a hit.…Everybody is awed by the enormity of the undertaking—even Lawson told Gregg that Davies and I were the only combination- With the exception of about 2 men we are a solid phalanx…" See also Kuhn's December 31 letter to Prendergast Box 1 Folder 13 - "Davies and I have had a great time abroad, in fact a regular orgie of art. It is hardly possible to grasp the enormity of this undertaking, and we feel that it will be many years before a show of like import will be gotten together…we are taking hold of this thing in a rather modern way, which we trust will aid in bringing the people into the building."

[122] Domestic Art Committee Record Book, Box 1, Folder 75-76, Armory Show Records, AAA (cat. 53). In the front of the book, there is a notice dated January 18, 1913, to send several works for inspection to the committee and a handwritten note by Kuhn that "it was intended to show only invited work but owing to the great demand by the uninvited a committee has formed to select from submitted work. The Committee's record of Rejection and Selection is contained herein." Not all works are marked, however. See section "B" for Baylinson's rejections. On Sargent and modern art, see Trevor Fairbrother, *John Singer Sargent*, (New York: Harry N. Abrams, 1994), 131-3. On Chase and the Armory Show, see Myers, *An Artist in Manhattan* (as in n. 1), and John Rewald, *Cézanne and America Dealers, Collectors, Artists and Critics* (Princeton: Princeton University Press, 1989), 188-190. See also Lloyd Goodrich, *The Decade of the Armory Show* (New York: Whitney Museum of Art, 1946), 61, who cites Weber, Sterne, Dove, Macdonald-Wright, Man Ray, Demuth, and Preston Dickinson as among the notable absences. See also Abraham A.Davidson, *Early American Modernist Painting 1910-1935* (New York: Harper & Row, Publishers, 1981), 165-167. Ann Lee Morgan has speculated that Dove may have declined to participate because Stieglitz was not one of the organizers; see her *Arthur Dove Life* (Newark: University of Delaware Press, 1984), 18. Robert Crunden stated that Dove was apparently not even asked to participate. See his *American Salons Encounters with European Modernism 1885-1917* (Oxford: Oxford University Press, 1993), 370 and on the Armory Show, 357-373.

[123] Katherine Dreier to her sister Dorothea Dreier, February 9, 1913, Box 1, Folder 39, Dorthea A. Dreier Papers, AAA. See also Harriet Monroe, "New York Has at Last Achieved a Cosmopolitan Modern Exhibit, *Chicago Daily Tribune* February 23, 1913, 6, referring to Davies' "enlightened despotism" and that "the committee of selection in America was infused with his ideas." See also Bartlett Cowdrey's oral history interview with Charles Sheeler, December 9, 1958, transcript, p. 4, AAA and Martin Friedman's interview with Sheeler, June 18, 1959, p. 9, crediting Davies with selecting his work and that of Schamberg for the Armory Show.

[124] Letter of February 10, 1913, Box 1, Folder 16, AS Records, AAA. See also Kuhn's letter to Charlotte Meltzer, January 4, 1913, Box 1, Folder 13.

[125] Letter from Kuhn to Keller, December 20, 1912, Box 1, Folder 12, AS Records, AAA—"If, as you say, you are being influenced by Cezanne—all the more reason why your stuff should please the committee.…only back up my judgment by sending the most serious and noncommercial things you may have."

[126] Undated letter addressed "Dear Sir," MacRae Papers, AAA, reel 4131, frame 843 and Letter of December 14, 1912, Box 1, Folder 4, AS Records, AAA.

[127] Letter to Pach, December 12, 1912, Box 1, Folder 7, AS Records, AAA.

[128] Ibid. Kuhn also mentioned plans for a cheap catalogue without illustrations and a de Luxe catalogue (never realized).)

[129] "Painters-Sculptors Show," *American Art News* XI (December 21): 3. See also "Show of Advanced Art

Promises a Sensation," *Sun*, December 14, 1912, MacRae Papers, AAA, reel 4132, frame [1029] and the Subcommittee's list, reel 4131, frames 839-842.

[130] Letter of December 14, 1912, Box 1, Folder 4, AS Records, AAA (cat. 63). On the pine tree emblem as based on an uprooted pine tree taken from the Massachusetts flag carried into battle during the Revolutionary War, see Eleonora Dragomir, "Destruction and Reconstruction in Modernist Art," *Ovidus University Annals of Philology* XVI (2005): 294.

[131] Ibid.

[132] Untitled manuscript, August 10, 1953, p. 3, Gaylor Papers, AAA.

[133] Letter to Ed Goewey, *Kansas City Post,* January 21, 1913, Box 1, Folder 51, AS Records, AAA. On the modern methods of marketing the Armory Show, see Dennis Raverty, "Marketing Modernism," *Prospects* 27 (October 2002): 359-374. Kuhn ordered 25,000 buttons as per a letter of December 21,1912 from W.L. Loweree, Box 1 Folder 54, AS Records, AAA. For the sign, see a letter of December 28, 1912 from [illegible signature], Box 1 Folder 43. For an example of correspondence with foreign media, see Kuhn's letter to the Editor of the Staats Zeitung, Jan. 3, 1913, Box 1, Folder 59, regarding reproductions of important old master paintings—"There will be no reproductions…the 400 foreign works will all be original….It is only necessary to read down the catalogue of the Moderns Exhibition of Cologne…and compare it with the list of paintings and sculpture which we have brought to this country,…to see that the New York Exhibition will be more representative of the modern school than any other ever held.

[134] "News and Notes of the Art World," *The New York Times,* December 29, 1912, 51.

[135] Ibid.

[136] Ibid.

[137] Quoted in "To Show All Modern Art," *The Evening Post,* December 31, 1912, 14.

[138] Ibid.

[139] Letter of Jan. 1, 1913 from Quinn to Kuhn, John Quinn Papers, New York Public Library Minutes of the Board Meeting, January 18, 1913, MacRae Papers, Roll 4131, Frame 845 (motion by Kuhn that Davie's floor plans be accepted), and Minutes, Special Meeting of Members, January 22, 1913, Box 3, Folder 6, AAPS Records, AAA—"Motion…that improved plan of arrangement…as well as Mr. Davies policy regarding the distribution of works be approved." See also January 18 Board Meeting minutes, Holley/MacRae Family Papers, Box 15, Folder 168, Greenwich Historical Society Library and Archives.

[140] Arthur Hoeber, "Revolution in Art to Sound Its Note here in February," *The Globe and Commercial Advertiser,* January 15, 1912, MacRae Papers, AAA, reel 4132, frame [1034]. See also "Modern Art Exhibition," *The New York Times,* January 2, 1913, 8 and "Advanced Paintings to be Shown," *The Sun,* January 5, 1913, 15.

[141] Ibid.

[142] "International Art Exhibition," clipping dated January 17, 1913, MacRae Papers, AAA, reel 4132, frame [1036].

[143] "Odd Paintings and Sculptures At American Art Exhibition," *New York Press,* January 26, 1913, 10.

[144] Ibid. See also "What is Happening of Importance in the World of Art Today," *New York Times,* February 2, 1913, SM14.

[145] Alfred Stieglitz, "The First Great 'Clinic to Revitalize Art,'" *New York American,* January 26, 1913, 5.

[146] See "Borglum Starts Strife of Artists, *New York Press,* February 3, 1913, "Borglum, in Huff Quits Art Circle," *Sun,* February 7, 1913; "Gutzon Borglum Resigns," *Evening Post,* February 6, 1913, "Mr. Gutzon Borglum Resigns from Art Body in Bitter Letter," *New York Herald,* Feburary 7, 1913, "Mr. Borglum in Action," *Globe,* February 8, 1913, and "Mr. Borglum's Resignation," *The Evening Sun,* February 8, 1913, all in MacRae Papers, AAA, reel 4132, frames [1042-1045, 1047-1052]. See Minutes of the February 7 AAPS Members meeting for the acceptance of his resignation, Virginia Teague Papers, AAA.

[147] See Kuhn, *Story of the Armory Show,* (as in n.32), 16, and Brown, *Story of the Armory Show,* (as in n.31), 95.

[148] "A Great Painter's Final Works," *The Sun,* January 26, 1913, 7. See also "International Art Show a Sensation," *The Sun,* February 18, 1913, 7 and MacRae diary entry on February 14, "Hanging pretty much finished." MacRae Papers, Roll 4131, frame 813. The article in *The Sun* stated that at least 150 men including AAPS members, carpenters, and electricians were "engaged in the task of doing in a few days the work that is usually spread over long periods." A temporary wall mounted on casters, wheeled over the armory floor was used to determine lighting conditions. There was over 24,000 running feet of line space and it was reported that the diffused radiance of white arc lights insured good illumination. Other details were provided about the catalogue and the never realized, illustrated deluxe edition, the stationing of attendants who will have learned the contents of the catalogue and could direct visitors., and souvenir postcards for sale.

[149] Kuhn, *The Story of the Armory Show* (as in n. 32), 16. Entry in Macrae Diary, February 16, 1913 (as in n. 148), press preview—"a great success."

[150] "2000 At Art Exhibit," *New York Tribune,* February 18, 1913, 6.

[151] Ibid. See also Brown, *The Story of the Armory Show* (as in n. 31), 110 and the clipping "Extreme Art Draws Crowd at Opening," reproduced in *1913 Armory Show 50th Anniversary Exhibition 1963* (Utica: Munson-Williams-Proctor Institute, 1963), 173, which states that four thousand guests of the AAPS thronged the galleries devoted to the "Cubists, the Futurists, and the Post Impressionists so Few can see Latest in Freak Art."

[152] Hutchins Hapgood, "The New Spirit," undated clipping, probably around February 13, 1913, MacRae Papers, AAA, reel 4132, frame [1013].

[153] Ibid. On Hapgood, see the Hapgood Family Papers, Yale Collection of American Literature, Beinecke Rare Book and Manuscript Library and Hutchins Hapgood, *A Victorian in the Modern World* (Seattle and

Washington: University of Washington Press, 1972, originally published in 1939), 340-41 (for his comments on writing about the "vitality" of the Armory Show).

[154] Ibid.

[155] Ibid. Perhaps Mowbray-Clarke made these comments in relation to the lecture that he gave on February 13 for the alumnae of the Young Women's Christian Association School of Art in New York. See "The New Freedom in Art" article reprinting highlights from his talk, MacRae Papers, AAA, reel 4132, frame 1041.

[156] Hutchins Hapgood, "The Picture Show, *Globe and Commercial Advertiser*, undated clipping, around March 16, 1913, Henry Fitch Taylor Papers, AAA, reel N738, frame 504. Hapgood also referred to his article written soon after the opening "Life at the Armory" about "the vitality of the thing as a whole," and the lively public response, which made "one trust democracy and realize that the people will take even the best, if there is life in it." For discussions of these ideas and the new spirit in relation to radical politics, feminism, and other social currents, see Adele Heller and Lois Rudnick, *1915, The Cultural Moment The New Politics, The New Woman, The New Psychology, the New Art & the New Theatre in America* (New Brunswick: Rutgers University Press, 1991), 3 and passim, as well as Alan Antliff, *The Culture of Revolt: Art and Anarchism in America* , University of Delaware, Ph.D. diss., 82-86. For the origins of the new spirit terminology in the 17th century German phrase "neue Zeit," and its relationship to modernity, including Guillaume Apollinaire's "The New Spirit and the Poets" (1917), see Edward Cutler, "News and the 'New Spirit' in Art: Mass Media Roots of the Temporal Aesthetic," *Communication Review* 3 (1999): 251-286.

[157] Pach, *Queer Thing* (as in n. 74), 192. See also Brown, *The Story of the Armory Show* (as in n. 31) ,110 and *Supplement to Catalogue Containing Additions, Errata, and Exhibits catalogued but not received* (New York: International Exhibition of Modern Art, 1913), Box 2, Folder 3, AS Records, AAA. See also Kuhn's letter to Leona Robbins, June 13, 1913, Box 1, Folder 57, explaining that an illustrated Catalogue DeLuxe had been planned but abandoned because "there [has] been so much discussion in the press."

[158] Frank Jewett Mather, Jr., "Art The Armory Exhibition II," *The Nation* 96 (March 13, 1913): 267.

[159] "Art Invisible At Last on View," *The Evening Sun*, February 18, 1913, Scrapbook, Macbeth Gallery Papers, AAA, reel Mc4, frame 64.

[160] Charles Henry Dorr, "Cubists and Futurists Have Reached America," *The World*, February. 23, 1913, Second News Section, p. 2. See also "Painters and Sculptors Show," *American Art News* XI (February 1, 1913): 3 (mentions smilax).

[161] See Evelyn Carol Hankins, *Homes for the Modern: En/Gendering Modern Art Display in New York City, 1913-1939* (Stanford University, Ph.D. diss., 1999), 25-31, for a detailed discussion of the Armory Show building and installation. Hankins discusses the modest banner on the exterior above the entrance and two small signs hung from adjacent lampposts, the framing of the interior entrance by two large white evergreens, and the intimacy of the 18 small octagonal galleries, in contrast to large salon-style public exhibitions of the past and reflecting the influence of the Viennese Secession. On the installation, see the agreements with the carpenter David Morison, January 6, 1913, MacRae Papers, AAA, reel 4132, frames 85-87 and January 10, 1913 contract, Box 1, Folder 56, AS Records, AAA.

[162] Carl Zigrosser, "My Catalogue," *Art in America* Number One (1963): 45. For Zigrosser's drafts of this article and his diagram which was not published in this article, see the Carl Zigrosser Papers, microfilm 4662, frames 86, 94-109 (following frame 476 at which point the numbering system starts over), AAA. In emails of May 8 and October 12, 2012, Nancy Shawcross, Curator of Manuscripts, Rare Book & Manuscripts, University of Pennsylvania where the original papers are housed, stated that she believes Zigrosser created the diagram years later when he was preparing his essay of reminiscences and that she has no recollection of approving a publication request for this item in 10 or more years.

[163] Ibid, 45 and microfilm 4662 (as in n. 162), frames 87-93.

[164] This description of the installation is based on the *Supplement to Catalogue*, New York, 1913, Box 2, Folder 3, Armory Show Records, AAA, which has an index of locations. Also used was the website created by Shelley Staples for the American Studies Program at the University of Virginia May 2001, http://xroads.virginia.edu/~MUSEUM/Armory/armoryshow.html . For her sources, see the "Bibliography" on the website. See also "Modern Art, *The Evening Post*, February 17, 1913, 9, "Art Notes," *The New York Times,* February 17, 1913, clipping in Holley/MacRae Papers, Box 17, Folder 188, Greenwich Historical Society Archives and Brown, *The Story of the Armory Show* (as in n. 31), 114-17.

[165] On McEnery and women artists in the Armory Show, see Marian Wardle, ed., *American Women Modernists* (Salt Lake: Brigham Young University Museum of Art, 2005), 125-7,191.

[166] Charles Brock, "The Armory Show, 1913—A Diabolical Test," (as in n. 22), 128.

[167] Diana Strazdes, *American Paintings and Sculpture in the Carnegie Museum of Art* (New York: Hudson Hills Press in association with The Carnegie Museum of Art, 1992), 268.

[168] "Art Museum Acquisitions," *The New York Times,* July 9, 1914, 6.

[169] See the University of Virginia website, (as in n. 164), http://xroads.virginia.edu/~MUSEUM/Armory/galleryO/tour.o.html.

[170] See Davies' letters to Weber, January 1,7, 27, 1913, Microfilm N69-83, frames 60-63, Max Weber Papers, AAA and Brown, *The Story of the Armory Show* (as in n. 31), 89, 148.

[171] "A Great Painter's Final Works," (as in n.148). The availability of special attendants to provide information as to galleries, and locations of works was noted in the front of the exhibition catalogue, *New York 1913 International Exhibition of Modern Art*, n.p.

[172] Ibid.

[173] Brown, *The Story of the Armory Show* (as in n. 31), 93. The pamphlets were Pach's *Odilon Redon* and *A*

Sculptor's Architecture about Duchamp-Villon's Cubist house façade, Elie Faure's *Cézanne,* translated by Pach, and excerpts from Gauguin's Tahitian journal *Noa Noa,* translated by Kuhn. There was also a pamphlet that was a translation by Pach of a piece written by Faure on Gauguin. See Laurette E.McCarthy, "The 'Truths' about the Armory Show: Walter Pach's Side of the Story," *Archives of American Art Journal* 44 (2004): 8, 13n85.

[174] "Preface," *New York 1913 International Exhibition of Modern Art,* n.p. It is noted that this is a reprint of Davies' statement of purpose made in December 1912.

[175] Gregg's statement is also part of the catalogue preface.

[176] Ibid.

[177] Kuhn, *The Story of the Armory Show* (as in n. 32), 17.

[178] See Steven Watson and Catherine Morris, *An Eye on the Modern Century Selected Letters of Henry McBride* (New Haven and London: Yale Unversity Press, 2000), 83 and passim.

[179] Charles Dorr, ""Cubists and Futurists Have Reached America," *The World,* February. 23, 1913 (as in n. 160)and C. Owen Lublin, "Through the Galleries, *Town and Country* (March 1, 1913): 24. On the notoriety of Duchamp's *Nude Descending the Staircase* in the Armory Show, see Michael Leja, *Looking Askance Skepticism and American Art from Eakins to Duchamp* (Berkeley and Los Angeles: University of California Press, 2004), 222-247.

[180] "A Bomb from the Blue," *American Art News,* February 22, 1913 and "Unmindful of the present," *Boston Globe,* March 6, 1913 (like "an explosion in a shingle factory"), clippings, Scrapbooks, Press II, Part 1, 1913, Box 2, Folder 34, Armory Show Records, AAA. See also "Modern Art Show at Armory Exhibit," *Brooklyn Daily Eagle,* February 17, 1913, 10.

[181] "Modern Art Show at Armory Exhibit," *Brooklyn Daily Eagle,* February17, 1913, 10.

[182] "At the Art Exhibit," *New York American* March 2, 1913, Section 4, 3.

[183] C. Owen Lublin, "Through the Galleries, " *Town and Country* (March 1, 1913), 24. On Matisse and the Armory Show, see John Caumann, *Matisse and America, 1905-1933,* Ph. D. diss., (The City University of New York, 200), 190-234, 288-307.

[184] James Britton, " 'The Open Eye,' "*American Art News* XI (March 8, 1913): 3 and C. Owen Lublin, "Through the Galleries," *Town and Country,* March 1, 1913 (as in. 183) . On Redon see, for example, "Art at Home and Abroad," *The New York Times,* March 2, 1913, SM15. On Cézanne and the Armory Show, see Gail Stavitsky and Katherine Rothkopf, *Cézanne and American Modernism* (Montclair Art Museum and The Baltimore Museum of Art in association with Yale University Press, 2009), 32-7.

[185] L. Merrick, "Exhibitions Now On," *American Art News,* XI (March 1, 1913), 2.

[186] "Notable International," *The Sun,*February 16, 1913, 15.

[187] C. Owen Lublin, "Through the Galleries, " *Town and Country* (March 1, 1913), 24.

[188] "Exhilaration of Modernism," *Rochester Post Express,* March 8, 1913, Scrapbook: Press II, Part 1, 1913, p. 65, Box 2, Folder 24, Armory Show Records, AAA.

[189] Frank Jewett Mather, Jr., "The Exhibition Again," *The Evening Post,* March 12, 1913, 9 and "Art," *The Nation* 96 (March 6, 1913): 241,

[190] Frank Jewett Mather, Jr., "Art—The Armory Exhibition-II, *The Nation,* 96 (March 13, 1913): 267.

[191] Ibid.

[192] Ibid, 268.

[193] "Art Invisible At Last on View," *The Evening Sun,* February 18, 1913, 7. See also "An Art Awakening," *American Art News* XI (March 15, 1913): 4.

[194] "A Bomb From the Blue," *American Art News,* February 22, 1913 (as in n. 179). See also an untitled clipping, *Philadelphia Review,* February 23, 1913, Scrapbook, Press II, Part I, Box 2, Folder 34, p. 29,—"There is lots of good work…which conforms more to the usual American ideals of a picture," referring to Henri, Luks, Chanler, Whistler, and others.

[195] "The Armory Exhibition," *American Art News* XI (March 1, 1913): 4. The other artists listed were Lawson, Homer Boss, Luks, Dabo, Hassam, Weir, Gifford Beal, Bolton Brown, Bellows, Cassatt, Chanler, Cimiotti, Ruger Donoho, Kenneth Frazier, Arhtur Lee, H. Dudley Murphy, Van Dearing Perrine, James and May Wilson Preston, Thodore Robinson, Ryder, Sloan, Tucker, Twachtman, and Whistler.

[196] "The 'Ism' Exhibition," *New York Tribune,* February 17, 1913, 7.

[197] Laurette E. McCarthy, "The Armory Show: New Perspectives and Recent Rediscoveries" *Archives of American Art Journal,* Vol. 51, nos. 3-4 (2012).

[198] Charles H. Caffin, "International Exhibition of Modern Art Opens Tuesday," *New York American,* February 17, 1913, clipping in Henry Fitch Taylor Papers, Microfilm N738, Frame 503, AAA.

[199] Charles H. Caffin, "International Still Stirs the Public," *New York American,* March 10, 1913, 8.

[200] Ibid.

[201] In emails of August 8 and 13, 2012, Laurette McCarthy identified other works and provided a biography of the political and satirical cartoonist, Thomas E. Powers. McCarthy noted that the "4th of July in Egypt" caricature might also refer to Theodore Butler's painting *Fourteenth of July, Paris* which she believes to be unlocated. The image "Under the Trees" might be a reference to Prendergast's watercolor with that title.

[202] Brock, "The Armory Show, 1913…," (as in n. 22), 128-131. Duchamp's *Nude Descending the Staircase* and Brancusi's *Mlle. Pogany* are also satirized.

[203] Harriet Monroe, "New York Has at Last Achieved a Cosmopolitan Modern Exhibit," *Chicago Sunday Tribune* February 23, 1913, 6 and Charles H. Caffin, "Chance to See Paintings by Marin," *New York American,* January 27, 1913, quoted by Brock, "The Armory Show…," (as in n. 22), 500n17.

204 Aloysius P. Levy (likely a pseudonym), "The International Exhibition of Modern Art," *New York American*, February 22, 1913. 18.

205 "Art Notes," *Times*, February 17, 1913, D.P. Brinley Papers, Box 12, Folder 23, AAA.

206 "Futurist Pictures—Two of them from Dunning, Which are Which?," *Chicago Sunday Tribune* (March 28, 1913), 3, as discovered by Laurette E. McCarthy and cited in her article "The 'Truths' about the Armory Show," *Archives of American Art Journal* (as in n. 173): 8 and her forthcoming essay on Pach for *The Armory Show at 100* (as in n. 92).

207 "The New Delirium," unidentified clipping from Kansas City, Missouri, dated February 23, 1913, Scrapbooks: Press II, Part I, 1913, Box 2, Folder 34, Armory Show Records, AAA—-"Marin exhibits some impressions of the Woolworth Building….heaven help the visitor…who hasn't brought enough money to buy a catalogue" and read the title.

208 "No One Who Has Been Drinking Is Let In To See This Show," *The World*, February 17, 1913, reprinted in *Art in America*, 1963 (as in n. 162), 35.

209 "Among the Art Galleries, *Evening News Newark, N.J.* March 1, 1913, Scrapbooks: Press II, Part I, 1913, p. 113, Armory Show Records, AAA.

210 "At the Art Exhibit, *New York American*, March 2 (as in n. 182). See also "Notes on the Futurists' Exhibit," *New York American*, March 9, 1913, 4 for a satire of what appears to have been Arthur B. Carles' *Woman Playing Piano/Interior* (1912, The Baltimore Museum of Art).

211 "Calls Futurist and Cubist Art Brain Vagaries," *New York American*, March 10, 1913, Scrapbooks: Press II, Part 1, 1913, Box 2, Folder 34, Armory Show Records, AAA.

212 Kenyon Cox, "The Modern Spirit in Art," *Harper's Weekly* 57 (March 15, 1913): 10, referring especially to Hartley's drawings in the Armory Show.

213 "Art Extremists in Broadsides of Lurid Color Invade New York and Capture an Armory," *New York Herald*, February 17, 1913, 10.

214 "Palette and Brush, Stray Reflections Anent the International Exhibition," *Palette and Brush*, 69 (February 27, 1913): 20.

215 "Art at Home and Abroad," *New York Times* , March 2, 1913, SM15.

216 Ibid.

217 Harriet Monroe, "Art Show Open to Freaks," *Chicago Daily Tribune*, February 17, 1913, 5.

218 Harriet Monroe, "Critics of All Kinds at Freak Art Exhibition, *Chicago Daily Tribune*, February 20, 1913, Scrapbooks: Press II, part 1, 1913, Box 2, Folder 34, Armory Show Records, AAA.

219 Ibid.

220 Harriet Monroe, "New York Has At Last Achieved a Cosmopolitan Modern Exhibition," *Chicago Tribune*, February 23, 1913, B6.

221 James Britton, " 'The Open Eye,' " *American Art News* XI (March 8, 1913): 3.

222 See for example Count Mourik De Beaufort, "Futurist Pictures Puzzle Visitors," *New York American*, February 20, 1913, 9, discussing work by Picabia, Duchamp, and Matisse. On the absence of the futurists, see McCarthy, *Walter Pach* (as in n. 75), 44. See also Kuhn to Roland Knoedler, February 1, 1913, Box 1, Folder 55, Armory Show Records, AAA, in which Kuhn states that the "fact that some of the work of the Futurists is shown does not signify that the Association is in sympathy with them…Aside from the foreign section there will be about 1500 examples by American painters…such…as…Weir,…Hassam, and others who are accepted leaders of American art, no discrimination being shown against any one school."

223 "Art Productions of Many Sorts Shown in International Exhibition," *The Christian Science Monitor*, February 21, 1913, 15.

224 Royal Cortissoz, "American Work in the Independent Salon," *New York Tribune*, March 2, 1913, II, 6, quoted in Virginia McCord Mecklenberg, *American Aesthetic Theory, 1908-1917; Issues in Conservative and Avant-Garde Thought* (Ph.D. Diss., University of Maryland), 1983, 17.

225 Mather, "Art—The Armory Exhibition," (as in n. 158), 268.

226 Anna Page Scott, "Exhilaration of Modernism," *Rochester Post Express*, March 8, 1913, Scrapbooks: Press II, Part I, 1913, Box 2, Folder 34, AAA.

227 See Mecklenberg, *American Aesthetic Theory* (as in n.224), 10 and Judith Zilczer, *The Aesthetic Struggle in America, 1913-1918: Abstract Art and Theory in the Stieglitz Circle* (Ph.D. diss., University of Delaware, 1975), 29-30.

228 Mary Mills Lyall, author and Earl Harvey Lyall, illustrator, *The Cubies' ABC* (New York and London: G.P. Putnam's Sons, 1913), 50. See also p. 42, "S is for Schamberg's fair dame at her 'phone." I would like to thank Francis M. Naumann for bringing this work to our attention. See also his introduction to the reprint (New York: Readymade Press, 2010). This book is quoted in Steven Watson's chapter on the Armory Show in *Strange Bedfellows The First American Avant-Garde* (New York: Abbeville Press, 1991), 178 and also referred to in Samuel Sachs, "Reconstructing the 'whirlwind of 26th Street,'" *Artnews* 61 (February 1963): 28.

229 Joseph Edgar Chamberlain, "More of the International Exhibition, *Evening Mail* February 1913 (date obscured), clipping in MacRae papers, Roll 4132, frame [1062].

231 Ibid.

231 Ibid.

232 Dorr, "Cubists and Futurists Have Reached America," *The World*, Feb. 23, 1913 (as in n. 160).

233 "International Art," *The Evening Post* February 22, 1913, 5.

234 Ibid. The work of Davies and Chanler is cited as attracting the most attention. Also discussed are works by

Whistler, Ryder, Twachtman, Robinson, Tucker, Glackens, Hassam, Weir, Brinley, Lawson, Prendergast, Bellows, Luks, Lie, Sloan, Ethel and Jerome, Myers, MacRae, Kramer, Marin, Hilda Ward, Boardman Robinson, Chester Beach, Anderson, Kuhn, McEnery, and others.

235 Ibid.

236 Ibid.

237 See Kuhn's letter to Glintenkamp, January 17, 1913, Box 1, Folder 10, Armory Show Records, AAA—The "Domestic Committee of the International Exhibition invites your picture 'The Village Cemetary," #11, recently exhibited at the MacDowell Club." On Hopper, see the entry for *Sailing* (c. 1911) in Strazdes, *American Paintings and Sculpture in the Carnegie Museum of Art* (as in n. 167), 268-9.

238 See Kuhn's letter of Dec. 19, 1912 to Thomas E. Ashwell, Editor of *Arts and Decoration.*, Box 1, Folder 43, Armory Show Records, AAA.

239 Arthur B. Davies, "Explanatory Statement" and "Chronological Chart Made by Arthur B. Davies Showing The Growth of Modern Art," *Arts and Decoration* Special Number 3 (March 1913): 149-150.

240 Guy Pène du Bois, "The Spirit and the Chronology of the Modern Movement," *Arts and Decoration* (March 1913), 178.

241 Ibid.

242 John Quinn, "Modern Art from a Layman's Point of View," *Arts and Decoration* (March 1913) , 176.

243 Ibid.

244 William J. Glackens, "The American Section—The National Art—An Interview," *Arts and Decoration* (March 1913), 159. On Du Bois ghostwriting this article, see Guy Pène Du Bois, *Artists Say the Silliest Things* (New York: American Artists Group, Inc., 1940), 174-5 and Ira Glackens, *Wiliam Glackens and The Eight* (New York: Horizon Press, 1957), 181.

245 Ibid.

246 Ibid, 160, 162.

247 Ibid, 162, 164. See also the comments about Kuhn, McRae, Preston, Henri, Lawson, Luks, Prendergast, Sloan, Myers, and Chanler.

248 Frederick James Gregg, "The Attitude of the Americans," *Arts and Decoration* (March 1913) (as in n.113), 166.

249 Ibid.

250 Ibid, 165, 166.

251 Ibid, 167.

252 Ibid.

253 Ibid.

254 William Murrell Fisher, "Sculpture at the Exhibition," *Arts and Decoration* (March 1913) , 168.

255 Jo Davidson, "The Extremists—An Interview" and Mabel Dodge, "Speculations or Post Impressionism in Prose," *Arts and Decoration* (March 1913), 170, 172. On Bergson, the *élan vital* and modern art, see Mark Antliff, *Inventing Bergson: Cultural Politics and the Parisian Avant-garde* (Princeton University Press, 1993), 11-12, passim. On Mabel Dodge and the Armory Show, see Linda Dalrymple Henderson, *The Fourth Dimension and Euclidean Geometry* (Princeton University Press, 1983), 201-210.

256 William B. M'Cormick, "Success of International Disproves Statements that Art is Dead," *The New York Press*, March 2, 1913, Section 2, 6.

257 Ibid.

258 Theodore Roosevelt, "A Layman's Views of An Art Exhibition," *The Outlook* (March 29, 1913): 718-19.

259 "50,000 Visit Art Show," *The New York Times* March 9, 1913, 32 and "Art Dinner," *New York Globe and Commercial Advertiser* March 10, 1913, 8. See also "125 Works Sold," *The Sun* March 6, 1913, 9; "Art Exhibition Succeeds, Press Agents Eat Steak," *New York Press* March 9, 1913, "Art Dinner," *Globe,* March 10, 1913; "Cubist Art Eugenists," March 9, 1913; "Insurgent Art Men Rejoice at Banquet," *New York Herald,* March 9, 1913, "55,000 See the New Art, " *New York Sun,* March 12, 1913, clippings, Scrapbook: Press II, Part 1, 1913, Box 2, Folders 34, 40, 48, AS Records, AAA. Box 2, Folder 34 also includes a series of humorous imaginary telegrams from Gertrude Stein and others, read at the press dinner. See also "Art-Beefsteak Dinner," *American Art News* XI (March 15, 1913): 3—Tall Brinley danced the Turkey Trot, Tango and Can Can with short Davidson.

260 "Caruso, "A Cubist at International," *The Sun* March 2, 1913, 11.

261 Forbes Watson, "Introduction," typescript re: Exhibition of American Art, n.d., 7, Box 9, Folder 82, Forbes Watson Papers, AAA. See also Watson's notes on the Armory Show, 1946, Box 9, Folder 53.

262 See for example his letter to Marjorie Kneeland, n.d. Music School Settlement, NY, Box 1 Folder 55, Armory Show Records, AAA. By March 12 the AAPS had to discontinue this practice because many thousands had already been given out and the "paid attendance has been so great that it would be a mistake to admit any more visitors on complimentary tickets" as per Kuhn's letter to Manuel Kormoff, March 12, 1913, Box 1, Folder 55. See also correspondence in Folders 56-57, such as Feb. 20, 1913 from Florence Levy, American Art Annual, thanking Kuhn for the season card. On Kuhn's "masterly job" in publicity, see also Forbes Watson, "1913-1923," typescript, n.d., 1, Box 9, Folder 59, Forbes Watson Papers, AAA.

263 Letter to James Lamb, January 18, 1913, Box 1 Folder 53, AS Records, AAA. For Kuhn's letters to New York University, Columbia University, and other local institutions, Box 1, Folders 43,48, 56,59. On the success of the Armory Show, see Kuhn's letter to Rudolph Dirks, March 3, 1913, Box 1 Folder 21-22.

264 See his form letter, February 1, 1913, Box 1, Folder 43, AS Records, AAA, stating that "should your institution desire to make any purchases, a properly accredited agent should be on hand as early after the

opening date as possible." See also letter from Cornelia Sage, Director, The Buffalo Fine Arts Academy, Albright Art Gallery, Feb. 3, 1913, Box 1 Folder 59, thanking Kuhn for writing to her about purchasing works.

[265] "Armory Show Echoes," *American Art News*, XI (March 22, 1913), 3. See also Frederick James Gregg, ed., *For and Against Views on the International Exhibition of Modern Art Held in New York and Chicago* (New York: AAPS, 1913), 15, regarding the total attendance figure of 100,00, of which the last day comprised 10,000, also sales of over 230 works. For eyewitness accounts of the closing night, see Kuhn, *The Story of the Armory Show* (as in n. 32), 19-20, Myers, *An Artist in Manhattan* (as in n.1), 37-8, and Pach, *Queer Thing, Painting* (as in n. 74), 203.

[266] Stavitsky and Rothkopf, *Cézanne and American Modernism* (as in n. 23), 36.

[267] "International Exhibition Just Ended Remembered as Most Stimulating Episode in City's Art Life," *The Sun*, March 16, 1913, Section 8, 4.

[268] "New Art a Big Success," unidentified clipping, Box 20, Folder 9, Kuhn Papers, AAA. See also his March 14, 1913, cable to Burlington Magazine, "can you use three hundred word official article International exhibition New York unprecedented success." Box 1,Folder 43, AS Records, AAA..

[269] Letter from Andrew Dasburg to Grace Mott Johnson, March 13, 1913, Box 2, Folder 5, Andrew Dasburg Papers, AAA.

[270] Kuhn to W.R. French, February 6, 1913, Box 1, Folder 61, Armory Show Records, AAA.

[271] French to Davies, March 6, 1913, quoted in Andrew Martinez, "A Mixed Reception for Modernism: The 1913 Armory Show at the Art Institute of Chicago," *Art Institute of Chicago Museum Studies* 19 (1993): 40, 103n38.

[272] Ibid, 46. See also *The First Week of the International Exhibition of Modern Art in Chicago*, report from the Sub-Committee of the AAPS in Chicago, April 1, 1913, 4, MacRae Papers, AAA, reel 4131, frames 1067-1070 and "Chicago," *American Art News* XI (March 29, 1913): 10 (states that there were 1000 pictures).

[273] Letter to Vera Kuhn, March 25, 1912, Box 1, Folder 5, AS Records, AAA.

[274] "Explain Cubist Array as Move to Teach City," *Chicago Examiner* March 25, 1913, Scrapbooks: Press II, Part 1, Box 2, Folder 34, AS Records, AAA. See also "Cubist Art Baffles Crowd," *Chicago Daily Tribune*, March 25, 1913,

[275] "Chicago," *American Art News* XI (April 12, 1913), 9.

[276] Harriet Monroe, "Davidson Sculpture Proves that Artist has Ideas," *Chicago Daily Tribune*, March 23, 1913, clipping, Art Institute of Chicago Library.,

[277] "Cubist Art a Protest Against Narrow Conservatism," *Chicago Daily Tribune*, April 6, 1913, clipping, Art Institute of Chicago Library. notes that "Glackens did not send his admirable "Family Group" (cat. 15, p. 130).

[278] Harriet Monroe, "Art Exhibition Opens in Chicago," March 25, 1913, 7.

[279] "Chicago," *American Art News* XI (April 5), 8.

[280] Untitled clipping, *Chicago Inter Ocean* March 30, 1913, Art Institute of Chicago Library.

[281] Untitled clipping, *Chicago Inter Ocean*, April 6, 1913, Art Institute of Chicago Library.

[282] Ibid.

[283] James William Pattison, "Art in an Unknown Tongue," *Fine Arts Journal* 28 (May 1913): 303. For his negative comments on Manigault and Maurer, see 299,303.

[284] "Cubist Critic Sees It, Raves," *Chicago American* March 20, 1913, Art Institute of Chicago Library.

[285] Otto Nohn Behterr, "An Attentive Survey of the Cubists," *Chicago Record Herald*, March 30, 1913, AIC Library. See also Martinez, "A Mixed Reception...," (as in n. 271), 48.

[286] Martinez, " A Mixed Reception....," (as in n. 271), 45, 46-7, 50, 51. See also Subcommittee report (as in n. 272), 3 and Kuhn's letter to Vera, n.d., March 1913, Box 1 Folder 5, AS Records, AAA.

[287] Frederick James Gregg, ed., *For and Against* (New York: Association of American Painters and Sculptors, Inc., 1913), 13. See also Subcommittee Report (as in n. 272), 1-2 (noting that the catalogue had already gone into a second edition) and clipping "Art" *Call* April 7, 1913, Scrapbooks, Press II, Part I, Box 2, Folder 34, 100, AS Records, AAA.

[288] Frank Jewett Mather, Jr., "Old and New Art," *For and Against* (as in n. 287), 56. This essay was reprinted from *The Nation*, 96 (March 6, 1913): 240-43.

[289] Ibid.

[290] Frederick James Gregg, "Letting in the Light," *For and Against* (as in n. 287), 17-25 and "As to Futurists," 49. In his essay "The Cubist Room," 51, Pach characterized himself as "European representative of the organization and.as the one who has probably come into most direct contact with the visitors," See also *Documents of the 1913 Armory Show: The Electrifying Moment of Modern Art's American Debut* (Tucson, Arizona: Hol Art Books 2009), 167.

[291] Subcommittee Report (as in n. 272), 4.

[292] Martinez, "A Mixed Reception..." (as in n. 271), 51 and McCarthy *Walter Pach* (as in n. 75), 48. See also Sue Ann Prince, ed., *The Old Guard and the Avant-Garde Modernism in Chicago, 1910-1940* (Chicago: The University of Chicago Press, 1990), 16-17,198-9 and Judith A. Barter, *American Modernism in the Institute of Chicago* (The Art Institute of Chicago and Yale University Press, 2009), 11-12.

[293] Frederick James Gregg, "The International Exhibition of Modern Art," *Academy Notes* VIII (April 1913): 54.

[294] Ibid, 54-55.

[295] Ibid, 55.

[296] Martinez, "Mixed Reception," (as in n. 271), 48, 53, McCarthy, *Walter Pach* (as in n. 75), 48, "New Art Shocks Chicago," *The New York Times*, April 3, X and "Cubist Exhibit Faces Illinois Vice Inquiry," *New York American*, April 3, 1913, Box 2, Folder 34 (as in n. 287), 104, AS Records, AAA.

[297] Letter to Vera Kuhn, March 30, 1913, Box 1, Folder 5, Armory Show Records, AAA. Martinez, "Mixed Reception," (as in n. 271),53, cites the attendance as 188,650 visitors. See also typewritten "Statement of Attendance," Box 1, Folder 87, Armory Show Records, AAA.

[298] Letter from J.F. Coolidge, January 27, 1912, Box 1, Folder 61, Armory Show Records, AAA and Garnet McCoy, "The Post Impressionist Bomb," *Archives of American Art Journal* 20 (1980), 13.

[299] Letter to Kuhn from Holker Abbott, February 19, 1913, Virginia Teague Papers, AAA.

[300] Letter to Kuhn from Edward Warren, April 12, 1913, Virginia Teague Papers, AAA. See also McCoy, "The Post Impressionist Bomb" (as in n. 298), 14, 15, 17n7 and the Copley Society treasurer Desmond Fitzgerald's diary, Desmond Fitzgerald Papers, AAA, entry for March 14, and entries from April 11-May 19, 1913.

[301] Kuhn's letter to Edward Warren, April 14, 1913, Virginia Teague Papers, AAA.

[302] "Preface," *International Exhibition of Modern Art* (Boston: Copley Hall, 1913), n.p.

[303] Letter to Arthur Young, May 2, 1913, Box 1, Folder 16, Armory Show Records, AAA. See also his letter to Vera, April 27, 1913, Box 1, Folder 5.

[304] Quoted in Brown, *The Story of the Armory Show,* (as in n. 31), 218. See letter of May 2, 1913 to R. Koehler, Minneapolis Society of Arts, Box 1, Folder 52, Armory Show Records, AAA: "We have had dozens of applications from various institutions and individuals desiring larger or smaller sections of the International Exhibition. After carefully weighing the various points of the question at a recent consultation of the officers of the association, we have arrived at the following conclusion: That the Boston exhibition should conclude all further exhibiting of the works as far as the association is concerned..." Kuhn corresponded with institutions in St. Louis, Milwaukee, Kansas City, Los Angeles, Pittsburgh, Montreal, Atlanta, Cleveland, and Canada. See, for example, to Alice Putnam, Carnegie Institute, June 16, 1913, Box 1, Folder 57; March 18, 1913 letter to John W. Beatty, originally intended to possibly send the show to Pittsburgh, Box 1, Folder 42; Box 1 Folder 43 The Art Association of Montreal, March 26, 1913, J.B. Abbott; to C.B. Bidwell, Atlanta Art Association, July 1, 1912, Box 1, Folder 43; to Anna Cobb, May 2, 1912, Board of Ed, Cleveland, Box 1Folder 44; to R. A. Holland, Director City Art Museum, St Louis, April 9, 1913, Box 1,Folder 49.

[305] William H. Downes, review in the *Boston Evening Transcript,* quoted in McCoy, "The Post Impressionist Bomb" (as in n. 298),16. For the attendance, as well as information (likely not entirely correct) on sales, see also Kuhn's handwritten notes with the header "Total Attendance," Box 1, Folder 87, Armory Show Records, AAA and notes in the MacRae Papers, AAA, reel 4132, frames 67-69.

[306] W.D. MacColl, "The International Exhibition of Modern Art," *Forum* L (July 1913): 28.

[307] Ibid, 29-30.

[308] Oscar Bluemner, "Audiator et Altera Pars: Some Plain Sense on the Modern Art Movement," *Camera Work* special number (June 1913): 31.

[309] See the correspondence in Box 1 Folders 21-22,48, 55, 57, Armory Show Records, AAA. See also Kuhn's letter to J.H. De Bois, June 14, 1913, Box 1, Folder 67, stating that another "thing of which we are very proud, is the fact that the Metropolitan Museum, has bought and now has on exhibition, the first Cezanne ever purchased by a public museum in America." Box 1, Folder 70, Kuhn to Burroughs, thanking him on behalf of AAPS— "We believe it will not be long before the import of this acquisition will be realized by the American public." See also letter to Jack B. Yeats, June 23, 1913, Box 1 Folder 73—"The exhibition is a great success in every way. We are all pretty much tired out from the huge work involved, but are all happy to think that it was made possible in America."

[310] Letter to Hans Goltz, April 7, 1913, Box 1, Folder 69, Armory Show Records, AAA.

[311] Untitled clipping, *Globe*, October 25, 1913, D.P. Brinley Papers, Box 12, Folder 23, AAA.

[312] Untitled clipping, *Evening Mail*, October 25, 1913, Brinley Papers, Box 12, Folder 23, AAA.

[313] See Laurette E. McCarthy, "Modernists on Tour: A New Look at a Historic Show," *Archives of American Art Journal* 17 (1997), 2-16. Howard Coluzzi's work was also included. See also Christine I. Oaklander, "Arthur B. Davies, William Fraetas, and 'Color Law,'" *American Art* 18 (Summer 2004): 20-23.

[314] "Art Notes," *The Evening Post,* February 7, 1914, Box 13, Folder 156, Elmer Livingston MacRae Papers, Greenwich Historical Society Archives.

[315] James B. Townsend, "Faddists' at Montross Gallery," *American Art News* (February 7, 1914), clipping in Box 13, Folder 156, MacRae Papers (as in n.51). Henry McBride, " Giving Cube Art a Chance," *New York Sun* January 29, 1914—Montross's comment about the "natural sequel" was penned by Gregg. See McCarthy, "Modernists on Tour.." (as in n. 313), 6-7.

[316] "Artists Divided About Another Cubist Show...Await Return of Walt Kuhn," *New York Press* undated clipping, included with undated letter, September/October 1913, Box 3, Folder 48, Kuhn Papers, AAA.

[317] Quoted in Bennard B. Perlman, *The Lives, Loves, and Art of Arthur B. Davies* (Albany: State University of New York Press, 1998), 222.

[318] Kuhn's letter to Vera Kuhn, [February 1914], Box 3, Folder 49, Kuhn Papers, AAA.

[319] "Art Society Scandal," *American Art News* XII (May 30, 1914): 2. See also "Armory Show Receipts, *American Art News* XII (May 16, 1914): 1 and Brown, *The Story of the Armory Show* (as in n. 31), 228-33, Henri, Luks, Sloan, Bellows, du Bois, Lie, Dabo, Myers, and Fry resigned.

[320] "Secession Fails to Worry Artists," *New York Tribune* May 30, 1914, 9.

[321] Originally published in the May 30 *Tribune* and reprinted in "Art Society Muddle," *American Art News* XII (June 13, 1914), 1.

[322] Brown, *The Story of the Armory Show* (as in n. 31), 233.

[323] "The 'Very Latest' at Montross Gallery," *American Art News* and "Art Notes," *Evening Post,* both March 27,

1915, clippings in Box 13, Folder 154, MacRae Papers, Greenwich Historical Society Archives. Other exhibitors included Sheeler, Schamberg, Charles and Maurice Prendergast, Mowbray Clarke, Glackens, Brinley, and Taylor. On Man Ray, see Francis M. Naumann, *Conversion to Modernism The Early Work of Man Ray* (Montclair Art Museum and Rutgers University Press, 2003), 44.

324 "In Explanation," preface to the catalogue for *The Forum Exhibition of Modern American Painters* (New York: Anderson Galleries, 1916), 5. For a recent discussion of the Forum Exhibition, see Vure, "Independent American Artists"(as in n. 6), 181-188.

325 Ibid, 5 and W.H. De B. Nelson, "Foreword," 34.

326 Ibid, see Henri's "Foreword," 30-32. See also Thomas Hart Benton, *An American in Art* (Lawrence: The University Press of Kansas, 1969), 41. Benton discussed Kuhn's feelings about his exclusion: *Kuhn, as one of the chief organizers of the 1913 Armory Exhibition…, strongly resented the fact that he had not been included in the 1916 Forum [show].…He considered himself…more responsible than Alfred Stieglitz or [critic] Willard Wright [on the selection committee] for the introduction of the modern idioms to America and felt that he should not only have exhibited with the Forum group but should have been included in the selection committee.…*

327 Ibid, 5.

328 Willard Huntington Wright, "The Forum Exhibition," *The Forum* 55 (April 1916): 457, as quoted and discussed in Christopher Knight, *"The 1916 Forum Exhibition and the concept of an American Modernism*, M.A. thesis (State University of New York at Binghamton, 1976), 17. See also Anne Lumsden Harrell, *America's Coming of Age: "The Forum Exhibition of Modern American Painters" and American Cultural Nationalism* (Tallahasee: The Florida State University School of Visual Arts, 1985), 1-10, 64, 66, 105, 108.

329 Kuhn, *The Story of the Armory Show* (as in n. 32), 4-5. For a more detailed discussion, see Gail Stavitsky's forthcoming essay, "Walt Kuhn: Armory Showman," for the New-York Historical Society's *The Armory Show at 100* (as in n.92).

330 Ibid, 24. See also a clipping collected by Kuhn, "Color Combinations of the Futurists Cubist Influence in Fashions,"*The Evening Mail,* March 13, 1913, Scrapbooks: Press II, part I, 1913, Box 2, Folder 34, Armory Show Records, AAA.

331 Pach, *Queer Thing, Painting* (as in n. 74), 201.

332 Ibid, 201,217.

333 Walter Pach, *Modern Art in America* (New York: C.W. Kraushaar Art Galleries, 1928), 17. See also Suzanne LaFollette, *Art in America* (New York and London: Harper & Brothers Publishers, 1929), 313-5, 328.

334 Myers, *An Artist in Manhattan* (as in n. 1), 35.

335 Myers, draft for *An Artist in Manhattan*, Jerome Myers Papers, AAA, reel n68-7, frame 240. See also 214-233, 454, 458, 463, 466, 475 (notes on his submission, *The End of the Walk* (cat 28, p. 89).

336 Ibid, 36.

337 Ibid.

338 Jerome Mellquist, "The Armory Show 30 Years Later," *Magazine of Art* 36 (December 1943): 300. See also Jerome Mellquist, *the Emergence of an American Art* (Port Washington, N.Y.: Kennikat Press, 1942), 213-228.

339 Lloyd Goodrich, *Pioneers of Modern Art in America* (New York: Whitney Museum of American Art, 1946), 13.

340 Ibid.

341 Chloe Hamilton, *The Armory Show: Its History and Significance* (Masters thesis, Oberlin College, 1950), 50.

342 Ibid, 51.

343 Ibid, 45.

344 John I.H. Baur, *Revolution and Tradition in Modern American Art* (Cambridge: Harvard University Press, 1951), 5.

345 Rudi Blesh, *Modern Art USA* (New York: Knopf, 1956), 48.

346 Ibid.

347 Milton W. Brown, *American Painting from the Armory Show to the Depression* (Princeton: Princeton University Press, 1955), 65. For another contemporaneous account, see Margaret Breuning, "A Critic's Notebook: II," *Arts Digest* 29 (May 1, 1955): 4,32.

348 Meyer Schapiro, "Rebellion in Art," (reprinted from *America in Crisis*, 1952) in *The Armory Show International Exhibition of Modern Art 1913* III (New York: Arno Press, 1972), 225, 234.

349 Frank Anderson Trapp, *The 1913 Armory Show in Retrospect* (Amherst: Mead Arts Building, Amherst College, 1958), n.p. [5].

350 Ibid, [8].

351 Ibid.

352 Frank Anderson Trapp, "The 1913 Armory Show in Retrospect," *College Art Journal* 17 (Spring 1958): 295.

353 Aline B. Saarinen, *The Proud Possessors* (New York: Random House, 1958), 214.

354 Emily Genauer, "Armory Show in Retrospect," *Herald Tribune Book Review* (March 2, 1958), 13, Box 17, Folder 189, Holley/MacRae Family Papers, Greenwich Historical Society.

355 Edward H. Dwight, preface to *1913 Armory Show 50th Anniversary Exhibition 1963* (Utica: Munson Williams Proctor Institute and New York: Armory of the Sixty-ninth Regiment, 1963), 5.

356 Brown, essay in *1913 Armory Show 50th Anniversary Exhibition* (as in n. 354), 33.

357 Ibid, 36.

358 Ibid.

359 Ibid, 38.

360 Ibid, 95.

361 Ibid.

362 Transcript of John D. Morse's interview with William Zorach, April 2,1959, p. 17, AAA.

363 Ibid. See also p. 16, referring to Kuhn as a "cross between a tremendous politician and a promoter and a clown" who "was sent over to Europe and saw these wild things, and he thought that would be a marvelous piece of exhibitionism that would jolt the American public."

364 Frank Getlein, "Art: The Armory Disarmed," *The New Republic* 148 (May 4, 1963): 35. Getlein cited Prendergast as the American who "strikes the eye at the Armory now in basically the way Matisse does." He also asserted, however, that the "Armory Anniversary has seen once more the expression of amazement that men who painted like Davies and Kuhn could nevertheless appreciate Matisse and Picasso…Perhaps the nicest thing about the anniversary is that the last few years have seen American acceptance accorded Kuhn…and others of their tradition as it has so long been given the Europeans they introduced us to." (36)

365 Sidney Tillum, "Dissent on the Armory Show," *Arts* 37 (May-June 1963), 96.

366 Ibid. See also Bennard B. Perlman, "A Great Art Event," *American Artist* 27 (February 1963): 64—"…the native productions were largely overlooked, seeming old-hat by comparison."

367 Frank Anderson Trapp, "The Armory Show: A Review," *Art Journal* 23 (Autumn 1963): 4-5.

368 Harold Rosenberg, " "The Armory Show: Revolution Reenacted," *The New Yorker* (April 6, 1963): 102.

369 Lloyd Goodrich, *The Decade of the Armory Show* (New York: Whitney Museum of American Art, 1963), 30.

370 Lloyd Goodrich, "The Decade of the Armory Show," *Art in America* Number One (1963): 61.

371 Leslie Judd Ahlander, "Famed Armory Show Reopens," *The Washington Post*, February 24, 1963, clipping in Box 2, Margaret Carleton Papers, AAA.

372 "The Glorious Affair," *Time* 81 (April 5, 1963), 67.

373 Goodrich, *The Decade of the Armory Show* (as in n. 368), 32.

374 Irma Jaffe, review of Milton W. Brown's *The Story of the Armory Show* in *The Art Bulletin* 46 (September 1964): 420.

375 Ibid, 421—"In France, as in the United States, only a few periodicals dared to defend the new art."

376 Barbara Rose, *American Art Since 1900* (New York and Washington: Frederick A. Praeger, Publishers, 1968), 77.

377 Judith Zilczer, "The World's New Art Center': Modern Art Exhibitions in New York City, 1913-1918," *Archives of American Art Journal* 14 (1973): 2. See also Zilczer's "The Armory Show and American avant-garde", 126.

378 Charles Eldredge, "The Arrival of European Modernism," *Art in America* 61 (July-August 1973): 35. See also Roberta Tarbell, "The Impact of the Armory Show on American Sculpture," *Archives of American Art Journal* 18 (1978): 10 and Judith Zilczer, "The Armory Show and the American Avant-Garde: A Reevaulation," *Arts Magazine* 53 (September 1978): 127. See also Carol Nathanson, "The American Reaction to London's First Grafton Show," (as in n. 67) and her dissertation *The American Response, in 1900-1913, to the French Modern Art Movements After Impressionism* (Johns Hopkins University, 1973), 1 and passim.

379 Zilczer, *The Aesthetic Struggle in America, 1913-1918…* (as in n. 227), 10 and Appendix A, 240-44.

380 Mecklenberg, *American Aesthetic Theory* (as in n. 223), 7-8, Nathanson, *The American Response* (as in n. 377), 237-255, and Peter Morrin et al, *The Advent of Modernism Post-Impressionism and North American Art, 1900-1918* (Atlanta: High Museum of Art, 1986), 26-28.

381 Judith Zilczer, "The Dissemination of Post-Impressionism in North America, 1905-1918," in *The Advent of Modernism* (as in n. 378), 28.

382 Ibid, 31.

383 Zilczer, "'The World's New Art Center,'…" (as in n.377), 2. However, Zilczer in "The Armory Show…" (as in n. 378), 129, maintained the usual tone of criticism, dismissing the American section as "tame by comparison."

384 Erika Doss, *Twentieth Century American Art* (Oxford: Oxford University Press, 2002), 53,56.

385 Ibid, 61.

386 Paul Richard, "Legendary Armory Show," *The Washington Post* February 14, 1988, G5.See also David M. Maxfield, "Show of Shows," *Houston Chronicle,* March 13, 1988, Section Texas Magazine, 10.

387 Garnett McCoy, "Editorial Note," *Archives of American Art Journal* 27 (1997): 2.

388 Brown, "Walt Kuhn's Armory Show," (as in n. 90), 3-4. Taking the opportunity to examine "the new and unsuspected trove" of Kuhn's personal letters, Brown summarized their contents and quoted some verbatim in chronological order, focusing on Kuhn's letters with Vera from December 1911-April 1913. Brown did not discuss other letters in the Kuhn papers, mistakenly observing that "they add relatively little to what we already know about the Armory Show."

389 Brown, *The Story of the Armory Show* (as in n. 31), 10.

390 Ibid, 154.

391 See for example, Bruce Altshuler, *The Avant-Garde in Exhibition New Art in the 20th Century* (New York: Harry N. Abrams, Inc., 1994), 60-77, Altshuler's *Salon to Biennial-Exhibitions That Made History* (London: Phaidon Press Limited, 2008), 153, and Moira McLoughlin, "Negotiating the Critical Discourse: The Armory Show Revisited," in Larry Gross, ed., *On the Margins of Art Worlds* (Boulder: Westview Press, 1995), 17-35. For an overview of the accounts that hew to the standard litany, see Laurette E. McCarthy, "The 'Truths' about the Armory Show: Walter Pach's Side of the Story," *Archives of American Art Journal* 44 (2004): 10, n.1.

392 Christine Oaklander, "Clara Davidge's Madison Art Gallery: Sowing The Seed for the Armory Show" (as in n. 27) and her dissertation *Clara Davidge and Henry Fitch Taylor: Pioneering Promoters and Creators of American Modernist Art* (University of Delaware, 1999)., 98, 118, 135-140, 143-5. See also Susan Larkin, *On*

Home Ground: Elmer Livingston MacRae (as in n. 25), 37-39.

393 See Martin Green, *New York 1913: The Armory Show and the Paterson Strike Pageant* (New York: Charles Scribner's Sons, 1988); Alan Antliff, *The Culture of Revolt* (as in n. 9), Evelyn Carol Hankins, *Homes for the Modern* (as in n.160), Joanne Mancini, "One Term is as Fatuous as Another": Responses to the Armory Show Reconsidered," *American Quarterly* 51 (December 1999): 833-870, John S. Barrett, *Imagining* (Ph.D. diss., Ann Arbor: The University of Michigan, 2005), 13-23,95-105, Daniel H. Borus, *Twentieth Century Multiplicity American Thought and Culture* (Lanham, Maryland: Rowman & Littlefield Publishers, Inc., 2009), 112-126 and Heather Campbell Coyle, *Laughing Matters: Art Caricature in America, 1878-1918*(Ph.D. diss., University of Delaware, 2011), 236-241.

394 Mancini, "One Term is as Fatuous as Another…(as in n. 393), 833.

395 Ibid, 837.

396 Ibid, 842, 867n32,n33.

397 Ibid, 844. See also Mancini's *Pre-Modernism Art-World Change and American Culture from the Civil War to the Armory Show* (Princeton and Oxford: Princeton University Press, 2005),133-157, which is essentially a reprint of the article).

398 Charlotte Laubard,"The 1913 Armory Show, Stakes, Strategies, and Reception of a Media Event, in Eric de Chassy, ed., *American Art 1908-1947 from Winslow Homer to Jackson Pollock* (Paris: Réunion des Musées Nationaux, 2001), 68.

399 See Berman, "'As National as the National Biscuit Company': The Academy, the Critics, and the Armory Show," (as in n. 5), 139-40. See also Avis Berman, *Rebels on Eighth Street Juliana Force and The Whitney Museum of American Art* (New York: MacMillan Publishing Company, 1990),5, 99-105, 375.

400 Laura E. Braden, "From the Armory to academia: Careers and reputations of early modern artists in the United States," *Poetics* 37 (2009): 442.

401 Edward H. Dwight, "The Armory Show—New York 1913," *Canadian Art* XX (March/April 1963): 119.

402 Ibid.

403 John Molleson, "Art, Artful Words at Armory Show," *New York Herald Tribune*, April 25, 1963, 8.

AMERICAN ARTISTS IN THE ARMORY SHOW
by Laurette E. McCarthy

MERICAN ART COMPOSED THE MAJORITY OF WORK in the 1913 Armory Show and while the contemporary press gave it a great deal of coverage and appreciation (see Stavitsky's essay), much of the subsequent literature on this groundbreaking exhibition has overwhelmingly focused on the vanguard Europeans, much to the detriment of the remarkable contributions made by American artists. This neglect of the Americans stems in large part, I would argue, from the existing primary narrative of the Armory Show, an account that previous research began to dispel and which more current scholarship will further alter.[1] The largest legend of the Armory Show is that the ultra-modern European art that was in the exhibition—works by Henri Matisse, Marcel Duchamp, and Constantin Brancusi—was not only thrust upon an unsuspecting and bewildered public but also foisted on a largely uninformed American art world that was woefully behind the times in its knowledge, understanding, and adaptation of modern art. However, in the years preceding the Armory Show, the latest developments of the Parisian art world were reported in the American popular press and in specialized art periodicals on a regular basis, particularly in New York; therefore anyone who read these publications would have at least been aware of these activities.

Many of the avant-garde European paintings and sculptures in the Armory Show had been exhibited before coming to the United States and, beginning as early as the 1905 Salon d'Automne in Paris, in which the Fauves debuted, these works were discussed by American critics.[2] In addition, black-and-white reproductions of their paintings were reproduced in American papers along with long descriptive passages, often tirades, against this kind of art.[3] While we may not know exactly who subscribed to the *New York Times*, *New York Sun*, or the *New-York Tribune* during this period, it would be safe to say that the dailies of that day were the equivalent of the televisions, Internet, cell phones, and other electronic media of today— most people at least had access to them. Though nothing can prepare one for the experience of seeing paintings and sculptures by Matisse, Duchamp, or Brancusi and other European modernists for the first time, and en masse as in the Armory Show, to argue that American audiences, especially artists, were completely unaware of these artists and their work would be to imply that nobody read the newspapers or periodicals, which does not seem plausible.

It has also been clearly established by many art historians that modern art made it to the shores of the United States before the Armory Show, not only in the works of Europeans but also in the paintings of Americans.[4] Much scholarship in the area of American modernism has concentrated on artists such as Alfred Maurer, John Marin, Marsden Hartley, Max Weber, Abraham Walkowitz, and Arthur Dove, who were vigorously promoted by Alfred Stieglitz at his Little Galleries of the Photo-Secession, affectionately known as "291" after its Fifth Avenue address. Yet there were numerous American artists, many in the Armory Show, who were also keenly aware of European modernism and adapted its technique to their art. As Abraham A. Davidson concluded in a 1993 essay, "a great deal was going on even before the Armory Show" and "for all its impact, the Armory Show was but one event in a decade of great venturesomeness and accomplishment in American modernist experimentation."[5]

In large part the misconceptions and misunderstandings about the Armory Show stem from Milton W. Brown's book *The Story of the Armory Show*.[6] First issued in 1963 in conjunction with the Armory Show's 50th anniversary, this publication, which has no footnotes, has been used as the main source of information regarding this event. Reissued in 1988 without the inclusion of new scholarship from the intervening 25 years, and without revisiting the original primary source material, the book continues to hold the seminal place in the literature on the Armory Show, even though some material therein is inaccurate and incomplete. The book is also biased toward Walt Kuhn's version of the event, with the very title taken from Kuhn's 1938 booklet *The Story of the Armory Show*. The current exhibition, *The New Spirit: American Art in the Armory Show, 1913* aims to dispel some of the myths surrounding the original event by re-examining the existing narrative in light of recent scholarship and exciting new findings. In addition, *The New Spirit* is the first exhibition to focus on the American art in the show and while familiar modernists such as Oscar Bluemner, Marsden Hartley, John Marin, and Maurice B. Prendergast are present, other vanguard painters who were prominent in their day but are lesser-known today are also showcased. In addition, women artists and sculptors, as well as some of today's well-known American painters such as Stuart Davis, William Glackens, Edward Hopper, and John Sloan are also represented, serving to highlight the diversity and depth of American art in the Armory Show and restore it to its proper place as an essential and significant part of this important exhibition.

In the decade preceding the Armory Show, clubs, societies, and organizations of American artists were sprouting up like weeds; the Association of American Painters and Sculptors (AAPS), the group that organized the exhibition, was, in many ways, merely one more group looking for a way to be heard and seen amid the cacophonous and competitive art scene of New York City. While the aims of the AAPS were undoubtedly very complicated, one of their stated goals was to strike a blow at the exclusivity of the National Academy of Design (NAD) by creating a permanent annual international exhibition in which all artists, but most especially those Americans rejected by the NAD, had the opportunity to show their works free of the jury and prize system of the academies. However, as Brown noted, seven of the 25 artists of the AAPS were also members of the NAD.[7] In addition, of the almost 200 Americans included in the Armory Show, 75 of them—over 37 percent—had had some work accepted in the NAD annual exhibitions in the years leading up to the Armory Show. In addition, an examination of the NAD records shows that over a dozen pieces displayed at the Armory had, in fact, been shown at the NAD, including: William Glackens's *Bathing Hour* (*The Bathing Hour, Chester, Nova Scotia*, 1910, The Barnes Foundation, Philadelphia, PA), Robert I. Aitken's *Dregs of Love*, *Tired Mercury*, and *George Bellows*, Olaf Bjorkman's *A Vala: Prophetess—Norse Myth*, Nelson Bickford's *Pelican* and *Strutting Turkey*, Edith Burroughs, *Portrait of John Bigelow*, (ca. 1910, Museum of Art, Rhode Island School of Design, Providence), James E. Fraser's *Grief*, Grace Mott Johnson's *Greyhound Pup #2* (cat. 20, p. 24), and Nessa Cohen's *Sunrise*. Also, the NAD accepted two works shown at the Armory—Abastenia St. Leger Eberle's *Girl Seated, Girl Standing, and Sea Treasures (from the Wading series)* (cat. 14, p. 30) and Edward Rook's *Grey Sea, Monhegan*—into their 1913 annual exhibition, which opened after the Armory Show closed in New York.[8]

Another stated goal of the AAPS was to afford exhibition space to the "younger" artists.[9] Who exactly did the AAPS mean by "younger" artists? Of the living Americans invited to participate in the Armory Show, approximately 136 of them were over the age of 30 and about 70 of those were over 40, not exactly youngsters by that day's standard. Also, several of those whose works are mentioned above as having been shown at the NAD were part of the younger generation. Perhaps "younger" was not a chronological term but more of an ideological one, meaning those artists who were more current in their style of painting. Or, maybe "younger" was merely a euphemism for "modern" or for those who were not academicians and therefore not part of what was considered the "old guard." While the AAPS was using publicity to arouse interest in their cause and may have initially intended to have showcased mainly works by "younger" artists, things changed and nothing was definitive as the organization and its plans continued to evolve from its inception to the opening night of the Armory Show, and beyond. The sparring with the NAD has been somewhat exaggerated and has become part of the show's legend, which needs to be modified.

Large-scale international exhibitions of works by living artists were not uncommon in the late 19th and early 20th centuries and many American artists participated in these types of shows. The annual salon of the Société des Artistes des Indépendants in Paris, which had begun in 1884, was still going strong in 1911 when the AAPS was formed, as was the more progressive Salon d'Automne, which debuted in 1903; Americans showed in many of these annuals. In 1908, *London Sunday Times* art critic Frank Rutter founded the Allied Artists Association Limited with the support of the more modernist painters such as Walter Sickert, Walter Bayes, and Wilson Steer. Their main goal was to organize nonjuried exhibitions of international, mainly progressive art, and their first show was held at the Royal Albert Hall in the summer of 1908. From then until 1912, Armory Show artists including Americans Leon Dabo and Alfred Maurer, and Europeans such as Wassily Kandinsky, exhibited there.[10] Americans also participated in the Venice Biennales and in the "Austellung Amerikanischer Kunst" that debuted in Berlin in January 1910 and traveled to Munich.[11] Many of the painters and sculptors in the Armory were selected for inclusion in the "Fine Arts Exposition at Buenos Aires and Santiago," also in 1910.[12] At the International Art Exhibition held in Rome in the summer of 1911, AAPS members George Bellows, D. Putnam Brinley, Arthur B. Davies, William Glackens, Robert Henri, Ernest Lawson, Jonas Lie, George Luks, Jerome Myers, Maurice B. Prendergast, John Sloan, Henry Fitch Taylor, Allen Tucker, J. Alden Weir, and Mahonri Young exhibited their works, as did modernists such as John Marin and Edward Steichen, and Armory Show sculptors Chester Beach, Solon Borglum, Edith Burroughs, and Abastenia St. Leger Eberle.[13]

Many of the artists belonging to, or associated with, the AAPS were also invited to exhibit at large-scale shows held at museums, art associations, and academies across the United States and therefore partook of the established, traditional system of display and patronage. Most had exhibited at the major annuals of the NAD, the Pennsylvania Academy of the Fine Arts (PAFA), the Art Institute of Chicago (AIC), the Boston Art Club, the Carnegie Institute, and dozens of other art institutions like the Buffalo Fine Arts Academy, Albright Art Gallery (now the Albright-Knox Art Gallery), the John Herron Art Institute in Indianapolis (now the IMA), the Worcester Art Museum in Massachusetts, and the Carolina Art Association in Charleston, to name a few. As Cincinnati Museum Association director John H. Gest noted, that in looking over the AAPS membership he found "that ten or eleven of them have already contributed to our annual exhibitions which open in May of each year."[14] Fernando A. Carter, director of the Syracuse Museum of Fine Arts, made a similar observation, "We have had several exhibitions wherein five of your number have done us the honor of exhibiting some of their very beautiful and charming canvases. In our last summer's Show [1911] we had Mr. Henri, Mr. Bellows and Arthur B. Davies. We closed an exhibition of Jonas Lie's last month. The group went from here to Washington D.C."[15] At the PAFA's 1911 Water Color annual, modernist John Marin exhibited "fifteen of his recent works," which constituted "the Academy's earliest display of a body of work by the younger generation of graduates whose sojourns in Paris had encouraged avant-garde approaches to art making."[16] Clearly there were several opportunities for artists associated with the AAPS, including the "younger" ones, to show their work within the traditional, mainstream exhibition circuits in the United States, and one can conjecture from this evidence that the tide seemed to be turning in the years before the Armory Show.

As Roberta K. Tarbell and Ilene Susan Fort recently observed, "In many ways, the history of the international avant-garde movements is also the history of independent exhibitions, as artists whose works and aesthetic philosophies were unacceptable (or incomprehensible) to juries of established organizations created their own associations for exhibitions."[17] Quite a few independent exhibitions were organized in the United States, mainly in New York, prior to the Armory Show. Many scholars have pointed to the *Exhibition of Independent Artists* held in Manhattan in April 1910 as a forerunner to the Armory Show and most of the Americans in the Armory Show participated in this exhibition.[18] With its "no jury, no prizes" policy and over 400 works, it was certainly aligned with the aims of the AAPS. In March of the following year, a smaller display, *An Independent Exhibition of the Paintings and Drawings of Twelve Men*, was held at the Society of Beaux Arts Architects Gallery, organized by Rockwell Kent.[19] Kent, Davies, Luks and modernists such as Marin, Marsden Hartley, Maurer, and Maurice B. Prendergast exhibited. The Art Association of Columbus, Ohio, "invited the New York 'Independents' to show their works there," thus spreading the cause beyond Manhattan. Columbus's outrage over some of the paintings of nudes in this show and the subsequent controversy surrounding them, however, was a stiff reminder of the limits of some American audiences' tolerances and a mild precursor to the much larger furor that would erupt when a very different nude arrived at the 69th Regiment Armory two years later.[20]

A few scholars have noted the role played by the National Arts Club (NAC) in New York in the promotion of works by the younger artists and/or those with more modernist leanings.[21] As early as 1904 the club hosted an exhibition that featured six of "The Eight."[22] In addition, the January 1908 *Special Exhibition of Contemporary Art*, apparently organized by Henri, should also be viewed as a forerunner not only to "The Eight" at Macbeth Gallery the following month, but also to the Armory Show, though on a much smaller scale.[23] This show included work by five of the eight—Henri, Luks, Glackens, Sloan, and Lawson. Others who participated in both this display and the Armory Show were older painters such as Mary Cassatt, Dabo, Childe Hassam, James Abbot McNeil Whistler, and John Twachtman as well as "younger" artists like Homer Boss, Gustave Cimiotti, Eugene Higgins, Steichen, and Van Dearing Perrine. Sculptors in both shows included Solon Borglum, Albert Humphreys, Louis Potter, Eberle, Arthur Putnam, and Beach. There were also etchings and drawings by Sloan and Cassatt. As one critic noted, "The exhibition, in its story of modern tendencies in the development of art interest in New York is most important" and indeed it was.[24] During the 1900s and 1910s, the NAC held annual summer exhibitions of works by former students of the Art Students League, in which Armory artists Bellows, Brinley, Arthur Crisp, Andrew Dasburg, Philip Leslie Hale, Charles Hopkinson, Eberle, and Elmer MacRae participated.[25] In addition, in January 1911, the club began hosting yearly shows of works by "Life Members," the first of which included works by Bellows, Boss, Brinley, Bolton Brown, and Henri, all of whom participated in the Armory.[26]

Most important for the modernist cause, however, was the February 1910 *Exhibition of American Landscape Painting* at the NAC, a show that, as far as I have been able to determine, has not been extensively discussed.[27] Opening three weeks before Stieglitz's famed *Younger*

American Painters show and two months prior to the acclaimed *Exhibition of Independent Artists*, this was an extremely important event. Art critic J. Nielson Laurvik served as chairman and invited approximately 50 painters to submit two of their "most representative landscapes" and furthermore requested them to "send only your best work."[28] The exhibition of about 100 paintings promised to be "the most representative of its kind ever held in America" and was to "give a survey of the achievements in this field of art more completely than it has hitherto been possible to furnish."[29] Traditional, established landscapists like Hassam, George Inness, Homer Martin, and Twachtman were represented, as were Dabo, Henri and Lawson. Remarkably, however, several of "the younger men and those who are just coming to the attention of the public after many years of waiting," such as Bellows, Brinley, Cimiotti, and Kent, were included, as were the "followers of the presumably crazy French painter Matisse, including Marsden Hartley, Glackens, Maurer, Prendergast, and Steichen."[30] This exhibition further shows the NAC's support of modernist art prior to the Armory Show.

Another part of the narrative regarding the Armory Show is that the AAPS was formed because the market for American art, in New York especially, was extremely limited and that the "younger," i.e., more progressive, modern artists had few if any commercial places to show and sell their work, yet research has proven this argument to be inaccurate. Artists were quite sophisticated and savvy in their efforts to get their art in front of potential buyers and there were several layers within the art market of the time—both in the United States and Europe—including galleries, auction houses, museums and art institutions, societies, associations, clubs, artists' studios and studio buildings, and department stores such as Marshall Field and Company in Chicago and Gimbel Brothers in New York.[31] If there was money to be made everyone, including the artists, was going to find a way to do so and to take advantage of the growing interest in American art. While there was not nearly the number of commercial galleries for American art in the early 20th century as there are now, there were quite a few. Some research has suggested that many of these dealers would not represent the more modernist artists but several did, though they might have done so begrudgingly.[32]

Many scholars have discussed Macbeth Gallery's hosting of the famed exhibition of "The Eight" in 1908, yet the dealer supported other contemporary American artists as well during the years prior to the Armory Show.[33] For example, in January 1909, Macbeth mounted an exhibition of *Forty Selected Paintings by Living American Artists*, which included works by Armory Show artists Elmer MacRae, Jerome Myers, and Charles Sheeler.[34] Later that year, the dealer showed a group of 13 Boston artists whose ranks included several who would participate in the Armory Show: Charles Hopkinson, Hermann Dudley Murphy, Charles H. Pepper, and Prendergast.[35] In addition, between 1908 and 1913, Macbeth had annual exhibitions of small bronzes, one of the few dealers to do so during this period.[36] While William Macbeth may not have been as daring in his choice of artists to represent as was Alfred Stieglitz, he did give some of the more progressive artists the opportunity to show their works.

The first dealer to fervently champion the younger generation of American modernists was Alfred Stieglitz; the March-April 1909 Marin and Maurer show at 291 was the earliest exhibition in New York of American modernism.[37] On the heels of the 1910 Matisse show was the *Younger American Painters* exhibition, solidifying the connection between Matisse and the American artists in this show: Brinley, Arthur B. Carles, Arthur Dove, Laurence Fellows, Hartley, Marin, Maurer, Steichen, and Weber.[38] Stieglitz continued to promote these modernists for the next several years. One reviewer's comments regarding a February 1912 show of works by Marsden Hartley referred to "the productions of the followers and imitators of the so-called 'Post-Impressionists,' 'Cubists,' and 'Futurists,' of France," clearly indicating the press's awareness of these art movements and the American artists' relation to them. Furthermore, the writer observed, "The exhibition is not a novelty after those of Weber, Carles, Sterne and others," showing that these artists were also already associated with the advanced art of Europe well before the Armory Show, and had indeed had some opportunity to show their work in New York.[39]

Other supporters of the modern faction of American artists were Bauer-Folsom Galleries (later Folsom Galleries) and the Daniel Gallery. Folsom held group and solo exhibitions devoted to a wide spectrum of American art and many of those who participated in the Armory Show had shown there.[40] In 1908, for example, Gustave Cimiotti had a solo exhibition at Folsom, which included a painting titled *The Hillside*, perhaps the same work as, or one similar to, his Armory Show entry *Hillside* (cat. 7, p. 125).[41] The gallery also hosted two exhibitions of The Pastellists in 1911. Spearheaded by MacRae, the group was composed of both older and younger artists including many Armory Show exhibitors—Marion H. Beckett, Dabo, Jerome Myers, Glackens, Bellows, Edward Adam Kramer, Lie, and Lawson.[42] Other artists influenced by European modernism who showed at Folsom during these years were Alice Schille and Henry G. Keller.[43] Folsom mounted an exhibition of a "group of six painters of New York life," which included works by Luks, Sloan, Bellows, Guy Pène du Bois, Glackens, and Myers.[44] In addition, Maurer's January 1913 "Post-Impressionism" exhibition at Folsom included paintings that went "farther than anything New York has yet seen in its line with the exception of Max Weber's show last year."[45] The Daniel Studio Gallery officially opened its "temporary" doors in March 1912 with the express purpose of exhibiting "pictures by the younger" artists.[46] Its first group exhibition included works by Lawson, Luks, Halpert, Max Kuehne, Kathleen McEnery, and Denys Wortman. Several of these artists were included in the Armory Show, yet none were all that young.[47] This gallery continued to promote vanguard American art until it closed in 1932.[48]

The Madison Art Gallery and the Berlin Photographic Company, both housed at 305 Madison Avenue, also supported the modernist cause. Christine I. Oaklander has shown how essential the Madison Art Gallery was for the formation of the AAPS and, subsequently, the mounting of the Armory Show.[49] A November 1911 show at Madison included works by AAPS founding members Karl A. Anderson, Bellows, Brinley, Glackens, Kuhn, Lawson, MacRae, Myers, Tucker, and Taylor.[50] Kuhn, Lawson, MacRae, and Glackens all had solo shows at the gallery prior to the Armory Show.[51] Martin Birnbaum "was appointed manager" of the American branch of the Berlin Photographic Company in July 1910 and soon thereafter began holding exhibitions of modern art.[52] A review of the January 1912 Maurice Sterne exhibition noted, "Of his paintings only a few are shown. They betray, if not the influence of Cézanne, then certainly acquaintance with the sources from which he drew, and sympathy with his archaic style."[53] The next month there was a showing of paintings by Hamilton Easter Field, with the reviewer observing that the gallery's "management is constantly in search of that which is 'different'."[54] Berlin Photographic Company was also a noted bookseller, specializing in art books and magazines. It was here that Davies bought the foreign, mainly French, periodicals and catalogues that he had Walter Pach translate beginning around 1909. In addition, Davies obtained a copy of the *Sonderbund* catalogue from Birnbaum, who had seen the exhibition in July 1912 and who wrote enthusiastically about it to American lawyer and art collector John Quinn, thus setting the wheels in motion that would lead to the Armory Show as we know it, changing the course of modern art in America.[55]

Although only a few other galleries in New York occasionally held shows of the younger and more modern artists, they are noteworthy. In February 1906, "a new gallery, well named the Modern Gallery, which is to display and exploit the works of a group of young artists, most of whom have not found favor for their canvases or sculptures at the hand of the juries of the routine exhibitions" opened its doors. Among those whose works were presented in the inaugural exhibition were Gutzon Borglum, Dabo, Glackens, Henri, Luks, and Shinn. [56] While most of the exhibitions held at the gallery prior to the Armory Show did not include many of the progressive, modern Americans, the aims of the establishment were decidedly in favor of encouraging "promising" young artists. The Julius C. Haas Gallery held an exhibition of pictures by members of the Painters' Club in December 1908 that included some work by Armory Show artists Gus Mager and Walkowitz.[57] The dealer hosted an exhibition of paintings and drawings by Weber in early 1909 and later that year, and again in 1911, showcased the highly individual and expressionist paintings of Edward Middleton Manigault. [58] The New Gallery also held shows of the younger artists during these years including a 1908 exhibition of works by Lie.[59] Steichen had a display of canvases and photographs at Montross Gallery in January 1910, though the dealer still specialized in more traditional art.[60] On February 17, 1912, exactly one year before the opening of the Armory Show, "Max Weber 'The Futurist'," was the headline that greeted readers of the *American Art News*, regarding his exhibition at the seemingly short-lived Murray Hill Gallery.[61] This was followed by a show of "Another Emotionalist," Samuel Halpert in March 1912.[62] Louis Katz's gallery represented a broad spectrum of American art and mounted a few shows of more progressive artists like Jerome Blum's November 1911 display.[63]

The Carroll Art Galleries announced "their opening for the exhibition of artists' work and sale of paintings, bronzes and other art objects" in the November 9, 1912, issue of *American Art News*.[64] From the first exhibition of paintings by Emeline Abbey Dunn, the noted American art collector Mrs. Edward H. Harriman purchased two watercolors, a very auspicious beginning.[65] The second exhibition at Carroll was quite diverse, consisting of "paintings, sketches, hand-made jewelry, and bronzes" by, among others, Jonas Lie, Eberle, and McEnery.[66] After the Armory Show, the Carroll Galleries, backed by Quinn and aided by Walter Pach, became one of the most significant representatives of American and European modernism. By representing the "younger," more progressive and modern artists, these galleries aligned themselves with those few that were willing to display some of the most experimental American art.

While there were certainly a very limited number of commercial galleries that would exhibit Americans with modernist leanings, there were other venues where they displayed their art. Though studio buildings seemed to have had their heyday in the 19th century, many still existed in the early 20th century including the renowned Tenth Studio Building, and artists often held exhibitions in these spaces. Other prominent studio buildings were Sherwood Studio, Studio Building, Lester Building, Van Dyke Building, and Holbein Studio Building. Among those built beginning around 1906 were the Central Park Studio Building (1906), Colonial Studio Building (1907), Co-Operative Studio Building (1907), Gainsborough Studio Building (1908), Atelier Building (1911) and the Chesterwood Studio Building, founded by sculptor Daniel Chester French around 1912.[67] Several societies and other organizations also had galleries in which artists showed as well. For example, the New York Co-operative Society sponsored Davidson's first solo exhibition at the galleries of The Knickerbocker Trust Building in January 1910.[68] The "Madison House, Down Town Ethical Society" held a show that included works by Davidson, Halpert, Luks, Myers, Weber, and Walkowitz in February 1912, and at the end of that year the German Society for Culture had an "exhibition of paintings" with works by Armory Show participants Dabo, Myers, and Kramer.[69] Further research into this area will undoubtedly uncover other sites that were available for artists to exhibit and which fall outside the mainstream academic, art institutional, and commercial arenas.

The venues for American sculptors to exhibit and sell their works in the years before the Armory Show were much more limited. Like painters, sculptors exhibited at the major institutions including the NAD, as we have seen, the PAFA, AIC, and the Carnegie Institute. The National Sculpture Society, a group to which several Armory Show sculptors belonged, also organized exhibitions in New York as well as traveling shows that were seen in Buffalo, Pittsburgh, Chicago, St. Louis, and elsewhere across the country.[70] Their first show outside Manhattan was held in April 1908 at the Fifth Regiment Armory in Baltimore. "Practically every sculptor on this continent . . . over one hundred in number" was represented by approximately 400 works in bronze, marble, and reliefs.[71] The National Arts Club held its "first annual sculpture exhibition," which included work by Solon Borglum, Eberle, and Yandell, in 1912.[72] Among the dealers, Macbeth Gallery, as noted previously, had group and solo shows during these years that included Armory artists Beach, Fraser, Eberle, Arthur Putnam Young, Myra Musselman-Carr, and Louis Potter.[73] Montross Galleries also hosted some shows of small sculptures with Fraser, Bessie Potter Vonnoh, Robert I. Aiken, Karl Bitter, Solon Borglum, Burroughs, and Sherry C. Fry represented.[74] The most consistent supporters of American sculptors during this period were the Theodore B. Starr Gallery and Gorham Company.

In the years before the Armory Show, galleries, associations, and clubs in other locales also encouraged younger artists and those with more modernist and independent spirits. For example, Prendergast, "a disciple of the school of Matisse," showed at the "rooms of the Franklin Union" in Boston in 1910.[75] In a May 1911 exhibition at the Peabody Gallery in Baltimore organized by the Charcoal Club and the Peabody Institute "a smaller number of the eccentric and 'post' something-or-other things than might have been expected" were on display including at least one painting by Laurence Fellows, "decidedly à la Matisse," which caused "quite as much of a shock to prim and conservative Baltimore as could have been expected."[76] The Greenwich Society of Artists was incorporated in February 1912, with AAPS founder Elmer MacRae as one of its Council members.[77] In Cleveland, the "Secessionist," headed by William Sommer, had organized the progressive art group the Kokoon Club in 1911, and these artists and others such as Henry G. Keller and William Zorach exhibited their works with the club and at the Taylor Art Gallery.[78]

Clubs also played an extremely active and vital part in the American art market in Manhattan in the early 20th century. As mentioned, the NAC certainly promoted the work of some of the younger and more modernist painters. Old-guard clubs like the Century remained supportive of the traditional, conservative, and academic painters, as did the Union League; however, under the guidance of Harry W. Watrous, the Union League hosted an exhibition in April 1911 in which the "Insurgents" were shown. Although a very small exhibition of only 24 paintings, it included pictures by all of "The Eight," as well as canvases by Kent, Bellows, Kuhn, James and May Wilson Preston, and "the curious, weird and crude productions of Max Weber."[79] The City Club also supported some of the younger generations with Luks, Anderson, Henri, Davies, Pepper, and Perrine displaying works there in November 1912.[80]

Another club that promoted more progressive artists was the Women's Cosmopolitan Club of New York, which hosted several exhibitions of diverse artists before the Armory

Show.[81] Incorporated in March 1911, members of this club included art patrons Abby Aldrich Rockefeller and Lillie Bliss as well as artist Adele Herter.[82] In the fall of 1911, a loan show of works by English Post-Impressionist, Matisse follower, and Armory Show exhibitor Phelan Gibb was held at the club.[83] This was followed by a display of "thirty-seven canvases" by Davies "loaned by members of the club."[84] Early the next year, several of Sterne's drawings that had been on display at the Berlin Photographic Company were brought to the Cosmopolitan.[85] Soon thereafter, there was a showing of paintings by Prendergast, "beautiful combinations of color, but incomprehensible as to form."[86] William E. Schumacher, a lesser-known modernist who also sent works to the Armory Show, had his first solo exhibition in America at the Cosmopolitan in January 1913, where his "high-keyed, decorative paintings" showed the artist to be "the strongest and best 'illustrator' of the pointillist method."[87] Clearly some members of the Cosmopolitan Club were interested in modern art.

The New York club that seems to have had an impact on the formation of the AAPS, and therefore, the beginnings of the Armory Show, was the MacDowell Club. In May 1911, plans were announced for "An Art Exhibition Without A Jury System of Awards; The MacDowell Club Has a Plan of Self-Organized Groups of Artists to Give Decisions."[88] John W. Alexander, also president of the NAD, was named head of the organization and Bellows and Henri were also deeply involved. The idea was "to give fifteen art exhibitions during the coming season, for which there will be no prizes and no juries." The notice of the first show also said, "Groups of not less than eight nor more than twelve artists shall pass judgment on all pictures submitted for exhibition."[89] This plan to allow "self-formed groups where artists who combine are judges of each other" was flawed, and after several exhibitions many artists began to feel that the club was simply becoming a venue for Henri and his students. [90] In addition, a very public dispute erupted between the MacDowell and artists who wanted the club to bring exhibitions of modern European art, such as the recent show of the Société Nouvelle of Paris at the Buffalo Fine Arts Academy, to its galleries.[91] Given the substance and tenor of this disagreement, it seems plausible to suggest that an additional motivating factor for the founding of the AAPS was that several American artists had become disenchanted with the motives and operation of the MacDowell Club. As Philadelphia modernist Morton L. Schamberg wrote to Pach in August 1912, "The MacDowell Club sounded fairly good at first" but it was clearly not giving the artists what they wanted.[92] Nonetheless, many of those Americans included in the Armory Show exhibited at the MacDowell Club during 1911, 1912, and early 1913.

In early January 1912, the fledging group of artists who had organized themselves as the AAPS in December 1911 with the intentions of mounting annual exhibitions of "the works of progressive and live painters, both American and foreign; favoring such work usually neglected by current shows and especially interesting and instructive to the public" sent a press release announcing a new show.[93] Later that month, Kuhn, as Secretary of the group, sent a mass mailing to museums, arts organizations, and commercial enterprises soliciting space for an exhibition that would only include works by American artists who formed the membership of this new society.[94] By February 20, however, circumstances had altered dramatically as the AAPS's interest shifted to more international art like the Société Nouvelle of Paris exhibition held at the Albright.[95] Since the first show hosted by the AAPS was quickly morphing into an international exhibition, the American art to be included therein therefore had to be rethought.

Precisely how the works by the American artists in the Armory Show were selected is not fully understood and materials that would clarify this process are missing; however, some-

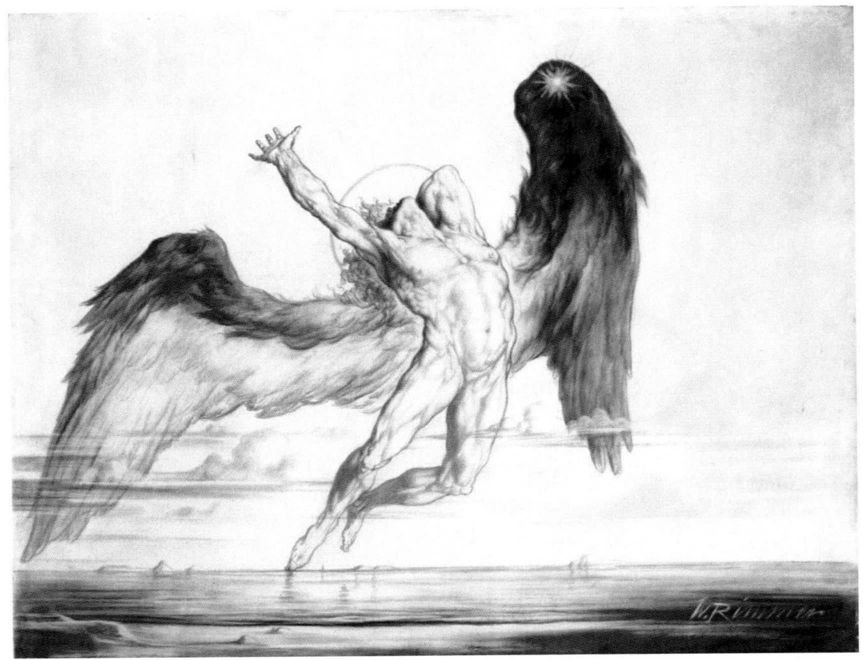

Fig. 13
William Rimmer, *Evening
(The Fall of Day)*, 1869–
70, crayon, oil and
graphite on canvas,
Museum of Fine Arts,
Boston Everett Fund and
William Sturgis Bigelow
Collection, Mrs. J. M.
Forbes and E. W. Hooper,
81.110

time in the spring/summer/ fall of 1912, at least two circulars were sent (cat. 48), inviting artists to participate in a forthcoming exhibition. The AAPS did not restrict the media, style, or subject and furthermore stated, "The Association particularly desires to encourage all art work that is produced for the pleasure that the producer finds in carrying it out. In this way the Association feels that it may encourage non-professionals, as well as professional artists to exhibit the result of any self-expression in any medium that may come most naturally to the individual."[96] The founding members of the AAPS invited other artists to join them and they, in turn, could nominate, select, or solicit colleagues and friends to submit works for the exhibition.

The American artists who participated in the Armory Show were all interconnected, usually in more than one way. Most of the painters were students of William Merritt Chase and/or Robert Henri and often were pupils of the Art Students League as well. Many had also traveled to Europe with the Chase and Henri summer programs and had also studied in Paris. Several of the sculptors were taught by Augustus St. Gaudens and Kenyon Cox and they too had furthered their training in Europe, mainly Paris. In both the United States and Europe these artists formed close-knit groups, often sketching, painting, and exhibiting together and sharing their ideas and passion for art. Many were members of the same clubs and associations like the Country Sketch Club, the Silvermine Group in Connecticut, Woodstock Arts Association, and the Greenwich Society of Artists, to name but a very few. The bonds they shared helped sustain them during difficult times and helped propel their movement toward freedom of expression in all arts.

Most of the Americans in the exhibition lived and worked in the New York City area yet there were a few other geographic "contingents" represented. The Philadelphians included modernists Patrick Henry Bruce, Carles (*The Church*, cat. 6, p. 124), Schamberg, and Sheeler; some non-modernists were also invited. The Boston group was spearheaded by AAPS member Prendergast who invited fellow living artists such as E. Ambrose Webster, Charles Hovey Pepper, Carl Gordon Cutler, Dodge MacKnight, Hale, and Edith L. King to participate.[97] Davies noted that it was "upon the suggestion of Mr. Maurice B. Prendergast" that the drawings of 19th century Boston artist William Rimmer be included; the Museum of Fine Arts, Boston lent *Evening (The Fall of Day)* (Fig. 13) and Caroline H. Rimmer lent three of her father's drawings through the museum.[98] Prendergast probably also suggested the inclusion of the works by another deceased Bostonian, J. Frank Currier, whose daughter lent an oil painting.[99] It is highly likely that Prendergast enlisted Boston gallery Doll & Richards to serve as the packer and shipper for many of the works sent to and from Boston.[100] Progressive Cleveland painter and teacher Henry G. Keller was invited by Kuhn. In

December 1912, Kuhn responded to a letter from Keller saying, "You ask if you will have any chance with the jury—why man you are invited and can send anything you please—If as you say, you are being influenced by Cézanne—all the more reason why your stuff should please the committee—You will hear from them as to details—only back up my judgment by sending the most serious and noncommercial things you may have."[101]

Clearly by the end of 1912, Kuhn, Davies, and perhaps other members of the AAPS wanted to include as much American art influenced by vanguard French painters such as Paul Cézanne as possible. This goal was reinforced by an addendum to the initial invitation, sent by the Domestic Exhibition Committee on January 4, 1913, to those artists who were already "invited exhibitors," which read, "In the forthcoming International Exhibition of Modern Art, the dominant feature of the foreign exhibit is not so much its novelty as its distinct individuality of expression and forceful manifestation of the creative power. For this reason it is held to be the more desirable that our home exhibit be equally conspicuous in like feature. The Domestic Exhibition Committee is therefore addressing this note to such artists upon its list of invited exhibitors as it deems most essential to have represented, with the request that the prospective exhibitor expose works in which the personal note is distinctly sounded."[102] (cat. 49) Probably crafted by Davies and Kuhn after their return from Europe, this note was most likely sent to the American artists who, having lived, studied, and worked in France, were more acutely aware of the modernist art of Europe and whose work had been influenced by it.

The Domestic Exhibition Committee was put in charge of all work by American artists and was, theoretically, tasked with selecting additional works other than those already submitted by members of the society or invited by them. This committee, which passed upon the pictures and sculptures submitted, and the identity of whose members was "kept secret" until a few days before the opening, was really "composed of Arthur B. Davies and William Glackens" only.[103] The AAPS was inundated with letters from American artists who wished to have their works included in the exhibition, and some sense of order had to be established out of the growing chaos. On January 16, 1913, the Domestic Art Committee sent an announcement stating "In response to your request the Committee on Domestic painting suggests that you send for its inspection several examples of your work, the character of which is adapted to the Exhibition." Artists were to have their works to the Artists' Packing & Shipping Co. for review between January 20 and 26.[104] Among the hundreds of paintings sent, the committee narrowed the selection considerably. By February 6, 1913, a mere 10 days before the press preview for the Armory Show, Kuhn wrote that the domestic committee was no longer considering application and that the list was finally, officially closed.[105]

Most scholars acknowledge that the 1912 "Sonderbund" exhibition in Cologne was the primary model for the European section of the Armory Show, yet its impact on the American part has only briefly been touched upon. This exhibition included 19th century European art that was meant to explain the natural chronological progression from Realism through Impressionism, Post-Impressionism, and the Fauves, culminating in the most contemporary work by the Cubists. The composition of the European portion of the Armory Show echoed this plan, though with predominantly French art ranging in date from drawings by Jean Auguste Dominique Ingres to Cubist works by Pablo Picasso, Georges Braque, and Puteaux Group artists including Marcel Duchamp, Jacques Villon, Raymond Duchamp-Villon, Francis Picabia, and Albert Gleizes. When we examine the American section we find that it too had a historical component that, as Brown noted, "was intended to parallel that of the European."[106] While vastly smaller than its European counterpart, the American historical part had some examples of the major 19th- and early 20th-century art movements. In what must not have been mere coincidence, one of the oldest works in the American section was also an Ingres, albeit an 1857 copy of that artist's painting *Andromeda* by Whistler. Other 19th-century American works were three drawings and *Evening (Fall of Day)* by Rimmer (fig. 13) and paintings by Albert Pinkham Ryder. These latter were probably meant to be seen as an American equivalent of the Symbolist paintings and prints by French artist Odilon Redon. Tonalism was represented in the American portion by Whistler's painting *Study in Rose and Brown* (1895, Muskegon Museum of Art) and also by Dabo's paintings such as *Evening, North Sierra* (cat. 8, p. 126) and Perrine's *The Ice Floes* (cat. 30, p. 136). Among the American Impressionists included were Cassatt, Hassam, Theodore Robinson, Twachtman, and Weir.

When it comes to the early 20th-century American art in the Armory Show, much has been written about most of the founders of the AAPS and those associated with "The Stieglitz Group," much to the neglect of the rest of the American painters and to the sculptors in the exhibition. In addition, part of the accepted narrative of the Armory Show pits those of the AAPS with more modernist leanings—mainly Kuhn and Davies—against others in this coterie, especially Henri and his followers, who have been viewed as more conservative. Yet as recent scholarship has noted, modernism can be interpreted in many ways, and as Marian Wardle observed, "both avant-garde European art and adventurous modes of realism were labeled modernist in early twentieth-century America."[107] In discussing the modernists in the exhibition, Brown too focused mainly on those affiliated with Stieglitz—Marin, Walkowitz, Maurer, and Hartley—whereas scholarship since the 1963 and 1988 release of Brown's book has shown that numerous American artists were keenly aware of the avant-garde European art movements, especially of Paris.[108] It is time to re-examine this aspect of the Armory Show with a fresh perspective.

The art worlds of New York and Paris in the 1900s and 1910s were inextricably linked, as artists, dealers, collectors, academies, art institutions, and museums formed an intricate and far-reaching web of interconnections and interrelationships that were exceedingly rich, complex, fluid, and sometimes volatile. While there were hundreds of American artists in Paris in the first decades of the 20th century, those with an interest in avant-garde art tended to congregate together, and since much has been written about this phenomenon only a few of the salient details need to be presented here. As many have noted, anyone with an interest in modern Parisian art eventually made their way to the apartments of the Stein families—Leo and Gertrude and Sarah and Michael—expatriate American collectors who held weekly salons at their homes.[109] There is a long list of American artists who are known to have visited the Steins' homes, and who also exhibited in the Armory Show. These include painters Marion H. Beckett, Bruce, Carles, Andrew Dasburg, Manierre Dawson, Katherine Dreier, Glackens, Anne Goldthwaite, Halpert, Hartley, Henri, Lie, Maurer, Kathleen McEnery, Walter Pach, Katharine Nash Rhoades, Morgan Russell, Schamberg, Sheeler, Steichen, Joseph Stella, Marguerite Thompson (Zorach), and Abraham Walkowitz, as well as sculptors Jo Davidson, Grace Mott Johnson, Arthur Lee, and Mahonri Young, to name but a few.[110] Other Armory participants, including Oscar Bluemner, Leon Kroll, and Marin, were living in Europe in the first decade of the 20th century, though they may not have visited the Steins. Many Americans surely would also have seen the paintings of Cézanne, Van Gogh, Gauguin, Matisse and other Fauves, Picasso, and Braque, among others, at dealers like Daniel-Henry Kahnweiler, Eugène Druet, Bernheim Jeune et Cie, Ambroise Vollard, and the Galleries Durand-Ruel. In addition, they probably saw works by the Puteaux Group of Cubists at the Salon d'Automne in which they showed and at the famous 1912 La Section d'Or exhibition. Many American painters were deeply affected by the large retrospective exhibition of the works of Paul Cézanne held at the Salon d'Automne in Paris in October of 1907; the two major exhibitions of Van Gogh's art in Paris in 1908 surely influenced some as well. Numerous scholars have also noted that scores of Americans were influenced by the art of Matisse and that several attended his short-lived school in Paris. Other Americans had traveled to Germany, where the works of the Blue Rider Group and Wassily Kandinsky affected their art.

The American artists living and working in Paris in the decade before the Armory Show exhibited together frequently and availed themselves of every opportunity to show their work at whatever venue would accept it—whether in France, elsewhere in Europe, or back home. The American Art Association of Paris, which "sponsored more frequent and less restrictive exhibitions" than other venues, held regular shows of works by American artists living in the city from the Association's founding in 1890 until it closed in 1909.[111] Brinley, Walkowitz, and Beach were among those who submitted "sketches" to the winter 1907 show there.[112] In January 1908, Brinley and Steichen organized the *Special Invitational Exhibition of American Impressionist and Tonalist Paintings* at the Association, which included their works as well as pictures by Theodore Scott Dabo (Leon's brother), Marin, and Sterne, and sculptures by Davidson and Young.[113] The following month, the association held a "special exhibition," which included modernists Bruce, Brinley, Marin, Maurer, Steichen, Sterne, and Weber.[114] Later that year, it was reported that Maurer and three other artists were arranging solo exhibitions for early 1909 at the Association.[115] Maurer was also one of the "six American artists resident in France" whose works were shown at the Art Institute of Chicago in January 1908, perhaps arranged by the American Art Association of Paris.[116] In February 1908, Steichen and Brinley formed the New Society of American Artists in Paris with Carles, Bruce, Davidson, Marin, Maurer, and Weber among its members. Though this group did not organize many shows in Paris, two years later these and other Americans exhibited in the *Younger American Painters* show at Stieglitz's gallery.[117]

Also in 1908, yet "another new society," the Allied Artists Association Limited, sprung up in London with the idea of "exhibiting works without first submitting them to a jury." Among the "two or three men" who exhibited "weird landscapes" at the first London Salon in the summer of 1908 was Maurer, who showed landscapes in which "the trees are magenta, while the sky is green, the grass blue and the haystacks violet."[118] In addition, in February 1911, notice was made of "the modest beginning of what may come to be an annual distinctive American salon in Paris" where, among others, Steichen, Maurer, and William E. Schumacher took part in a show held at the Galerie de Vambez.[119] Many American artists exhibited in the various salons in Paris, especially the more progressive Salon d'Automne, where Armory Show artists Beach, Brinley, Bruce, Theodore Earl Butler, Carles, Robert Winthrop Chanler, Davidson, Goldthwaite, Bernhard Gutmann, Halpert, Marin, Maurer, Louise Pope, Boardman Robinson, Russell, Schumacher, Marguerite Thompson, Abel Warshawsky, Charles H. White, Young, and Zorach all showed in the years prior to the Armory Show.[120]

Between 1906 and 1912, numerous Americans artists studied, worked, and exhibited in Paris and elsewhere in Europe and experimented with, adopted, and adapted the modernist aesthetic. While some of them remained in Europe, most returned to the United States, mainly to Manhattan and its vicinity, firmly committed to promoting modern art and its proliferation in the United States and to establishing venues, like the Armory Show, to exhibit their own work. The belief that most American artists in the Armory Show were "provincials"

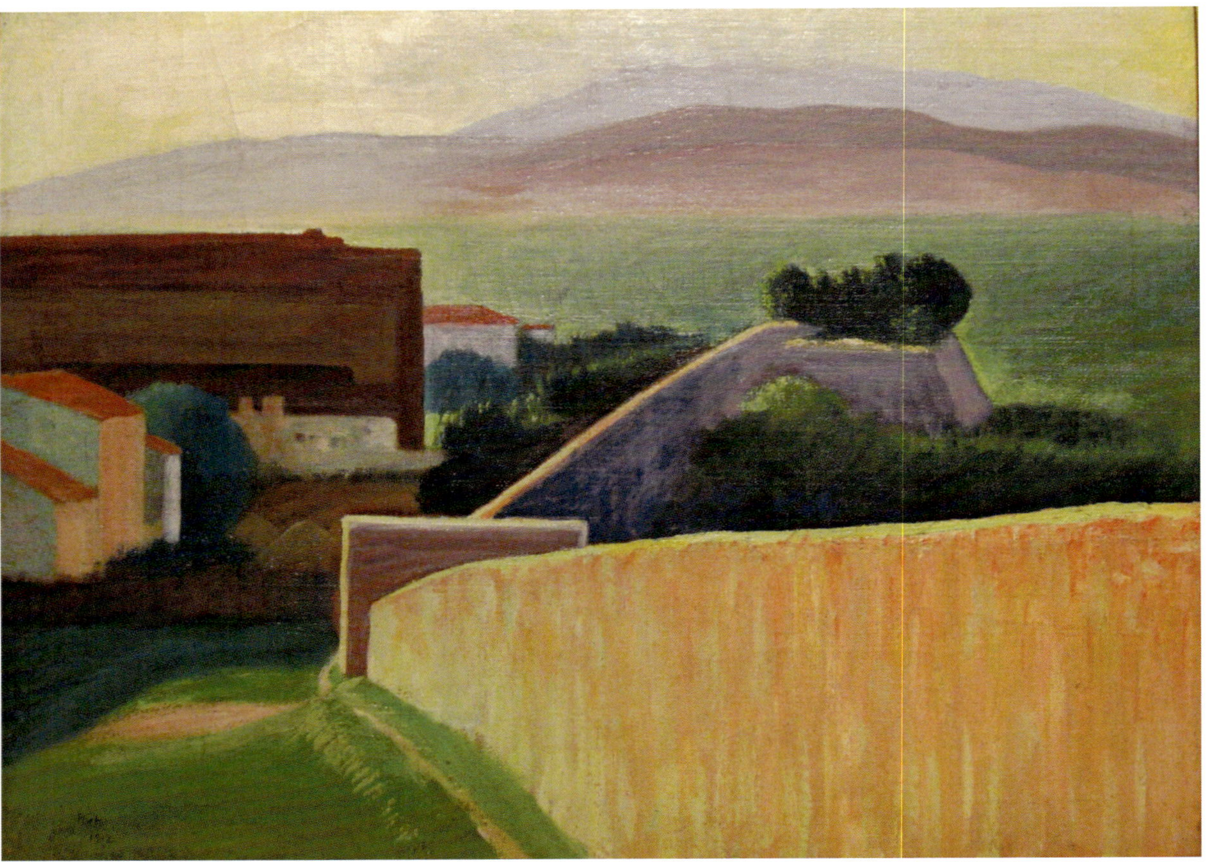

Cat. 29.
Walter Pach, *The Wall of the City*, 1912, oil on canvas, Courtesy of Francis M. Naumann Fine Art, New York

who were woefully behind their European brethren in their experimentations with modernism was promulgated not only by Brown but also, regrettably, by some of the artists themselves.[121] Yet this was not really the case and one of the main goals of *The New Spirit: American Art in the Armory Show, 1913* is to showcase some of the American modernists in the original exhibition who have not been fully recognized in the existing Armory Show literature.

One of the seminal figures in the Armory Show, and in the history of modern art in the United States in general, was painter and critic Walter Pach, who was friends with virtually all of the vanguard artists in the exhibition, American as well as European.[122] Pach's paintings in the show partook of the modernist aesthetic, though he is best known today as the primary curator of the European art who, as he wrote, "put all those canvases into the Armory Show" including Marcel Duchamp's *Nude Descending a Staircase, No. 2* (1912, Philadelphia Museum of Art).[123] Pach first visited Paris in the summer of 1904 and spent a great deal of time with Patrick Henry Bruce. He returned for brief visits in the fall of 1905 and 1906 but lived there from the autumn of 1907 to the summer of 1908 and again from the fall of 1910 until he returned to New York for the opening of the Armory Show. Pach was introduced to Matisse at the Steins' home in Fiesole in the summer of 1907 and the two became close friends, though Pach never formally studied with Matisse at his academy. It was Matisse who suggested that Pach attend the Académie Ranson, where painters Paul Sérusier and Maurice Denis were instructors; Sérusier taught the theory of colors and Denis instructed the students in composition and painting.[124] Pach also learned about color from Auguste Renoir, a painter he greatly admired and whom he knew quite well.[125] As Pach noted in a 1912 article, Renoir recognized that "color has a nature and function apart from the questions of representation."[126] This concept that color could exist as an aesthetic value distinct from its role in the creation of a recognizable object in painting was a primary tenet of avant-garde art theories and a practice endorsed by several of Pach's Parisian contemporaries.[127] Paintings by Matisse, Renoir, Sérusier, and Denis, and the Post-Impressionist works of Cézanne and van Gogh, deeply affected Pach and unquestionably influenced his art during these years.

In the summer of 1912, Pach went to the Tuscan hillside town of Arezzo to study the frescoes of the 15th-century Italian painter Piero Della Francesca and to paint. Several of the works he submitted to the Armory Show were made during this trip, including *The Wall of the City* (cat. 29), a recently rediscovered painting. The somewhat mimetic approach in this painting reveals Pach's admiration for past masters and reflects his belief in their relevance to the modern art of his day. The high-keyed colors, lack of shading, and abstracted composition of *The Wall of the City*, however, are hallmarks of modernism and reminiscent of the Post-Impressionist and Fauve works that Pach had recently been studying in Paris and, more specifically, the paintings of Paul Sérusier.[128] The flat patches of pure and vibrant pigments— pink, purple, white, yellow, and green—are laid onto the canvas and left unblended. Pach combines the intense hues of Post-Impressionism with the structural, geometric forms of Cézanne's paintings to create his powerful vision of the wall hugging the hillside of Arezzo.

In the fall of 1912, after Davies and Kuhn left Paris, Pach was put in charge of all of the art sent from Europe to New York for the Armory Show, including the American works. As Kuhn told Butler, "We would suggest that you select two (2) examples of your most advanced work and ship same to us at our expense. Please present this letter to Mr. Walter Pach, 83 Boulevard Montparnasse, who is our representative and has full authority to act for the Society."[129] Pach also visited the artists in their studios and filled out entry forms for some of them.[130] He noted the dates on the cards for Bruce's four works, simply titled *Nature Morte*, which included *Still Life (with Dish of Fruit)* (cat. 5, p. 26), and it is Pach's handwriting on the card for Davidson's sculpture *La Douleur*.[131] Pach probably saw other Americans like Hartley to offer his assistance with the shipment of their works.

While Pach was in Arezzo in the summer of 1912, he received a note (cat. 83, p. 157) from Schamberg saying that he "got an invitation to exhibit with them [AAPS] the other day" and confessing that he had "done damn little painting."[132] Pach and Schamberg were roommates on the 1903 and 1904 Chase summer programs in Haarlem and London, respectively. They remained close friends and it was through Pach's intercession that Schamberg met Leo Stein in Paris in 1908.[133] On the verso of Schamberg's four-postcard letter are photographs of his paintings, which appear to be similar in subject and style to the one known picture by him in the Armory Show, *Study of a Girl (Fanette Reider)* (ca. 1912, Williams College Museum of Art). These images reveal the same forthright presentation of the figure in shallow space outlined in bold lines. When submitting his entries for the exhibition, Schamberg also included a copy of his January 19, 1913, *Philadelphia Inquirer* article, "Post-Impressionism Exhibit Awaited," thus showing his support and promotion of the Armory Show in his hometown.[134]

One of Sheeler's earliest exposures to the modern art of Cézanne was probably through Pach, his friend and fellow Chase student, who published the first substantial essay on the artist in 1908, "Cézanne—An Introduction."[135] Sheeler's firsthand experience with the paintings of Cézanne, Matisse, and Picasso, however, was in Paris in 1909, when he and Schamberg visited the apartment of Michael and Sarah Stein and met with Leo Stein.[136] When Sheeler returned to Pennsylvania after two months in the French capital, he began assimilating the profoundly new concepts of painting embodied in the art he had seen. Sheeler received the invitation to participate in the Armory Show from Kuhn, writing him on February 10, 1913, "I received the cards for my pictures, which you kindly invited, and the pictures are leaving here to-day" but it was

Davies, apparently, "who chose six paintings for the exhibition" including *Chrysanthemums* (cat.32, p. 25), painted around 1912.[137] The strong, striking, and expressive colors and the concern for structural form in this painting reveal the influence of European modernism.

It was assuredly Pach's dear friend and AAPS member Prendergast who invited Webster to participate in the Armory Show. Webster "was a member of the progressive circle of Boston artists centered around Charles Hovey Pepper," a fellow Armory Show participant and "an ardent champion of the work of Maurice Prendergast and an early patron of Marsden Hartley."[138] (see cat. 68, p. 154) In January 1913, Webster exhibited at the Brooks Reid Gallery in Boston with Pepper, Prendergast and Carl G. Cutler—all of whom sent works to the Armory Show. One of Webster's entries, *Old Hut, Jamaica* (cat. 38, p. 138), shows his use of bold juxtapositions of high-keyed colors with "patterns of sunlight and shadow" that unify the decorative surface patterning in the painting.[139] These techniques, along with his use of broad, flat areas of paint and loose brushwork, are related more to the Post-Impressionist paintings of Gauguin and van Gogh rather than to the canvases of the Impressionists with whom he has sometimes been compared.

When the Armory Show traveled to the Art Institute of Chicago, Pach went with it, and he was instructed by Davies to contact Manierre Dawson, a Chicago painter, civil engineer, and architectural draftsman whom Davies had met in New York in 1910.[140] Dawson recorded his first meeting with Pach in his journal, "The man with the moustache and tremulous hands who seemed in constant attendance saw me as the most lingering of spectators. Engaging me in conversation, I found him most interesting and informative. His name is Walter Pach."[141] During a visit to Dawson's home, Pach selected the painting that the artist "had just varnished," titled it *Wharf under Mountain* (cat. 12, p. 129), and surreptitiously hung it in the American section of the exhibition.[142] Though unrecorded, this was the only abstract painting by an American artist in the Armory Show.

Jonas Lie, a Norwegian by birth, came to the United States in 1893 and had formal lessons in art at the Workingman's School of the Ethical Culture Society, where he may possibly have met Pach, who was also a pupil there at that time. Lie may also have studied at the NAD and the Art Students League. In 1901, he began exhibiting at the NAD and with the Country Sketch Club of New York. Started in 1897 by Perrine and other NAD students to encourage outdoor painting, this club ran until 1912. Fellow members included Glackens, Maurer, and Sterne, among others, and they painted in the Ridgefield, New Jersey, area, the "Barbizon of the Palisades" as it was termed.[143] In his early works, many inspired by his sketching trips to the Palisades, Lie "was attracted ... to the popular Tonalist aesthetic."[144] After trips to Paris in 1906, during which he was influenced by the Impressionists, and 1909, where he visited Leo and Gertrude Stein's home, met Matisse, and frequented the commercial galleries where he saw paintings by Paul Gauguin, his approach changed. [145] In November 1910, Lie had a solo show at the Madison Art Gallery and had two one-person exhibitions at Folsom Galleries in 1911 and 1912, thus placing him within the context of the more progressive art circles in New York; he was also a founding member of the AAPS.[146] While Lie remained realistic in his style and "an ardent advocate of academic standards," his mature works displayed "vigorous brushwork, intense and interpretive coloration, strong chromatic contrasts, and an overwhelming concern for light" that aligned them with some of the modernists' aesthetic.[147] This approach can be seen in paintings like his Armory Show entry, *The Black Teapot* (cat. 21, p. 133), with its vibrant color contrasts and sparking light. Lie had exhibited this painting in his one-person show at the Corcoran Gallery of Art Washington, D.C., in January 1912, and later that year in the Carnegie Institute's annual exhibition, where it won an award.[148]

Another core member of the AAPS was Daniel Putnam Brinley, a pupil at the Art Students League, who gradually became involved with the modernist movement in Paris between 1905 and 1908. Like many of his fellow expatriates, he joined the American Art Association of Paris, "which sponsored more frequent and less restrictive exhibitions" than other venues. He participated in many of these shows and became chairman of the house committee there in 1907.[149] Brinley and his wife became good friends with Steichen as well as Patrick Henry Bruce and his wife.[150] It seems plausible to suggest that Brinley would have been aware of the newest developments in the Parisian art scene, was most likely a guest of the Steins at some point, and probably knew Pach. Since we know that he participated in the Salon d'Automne, he could not have missed the French artists like Matisse and other Fauves who showed there as well. Upon his return to New York in July 1908, Brinley continued to champion the modernist cause and to exhibit with fellow "secessionists," as they were sometimes called. In 1910 alone, he exhibited at the NAC's *Exhibition of American Landscape Painting*, the *Younger American Painters* show at "291," the *Exhibition of Independent Artists*, and had his first solo show at the Madison Art Gallery, another hotbed of modernist ideology.[151]

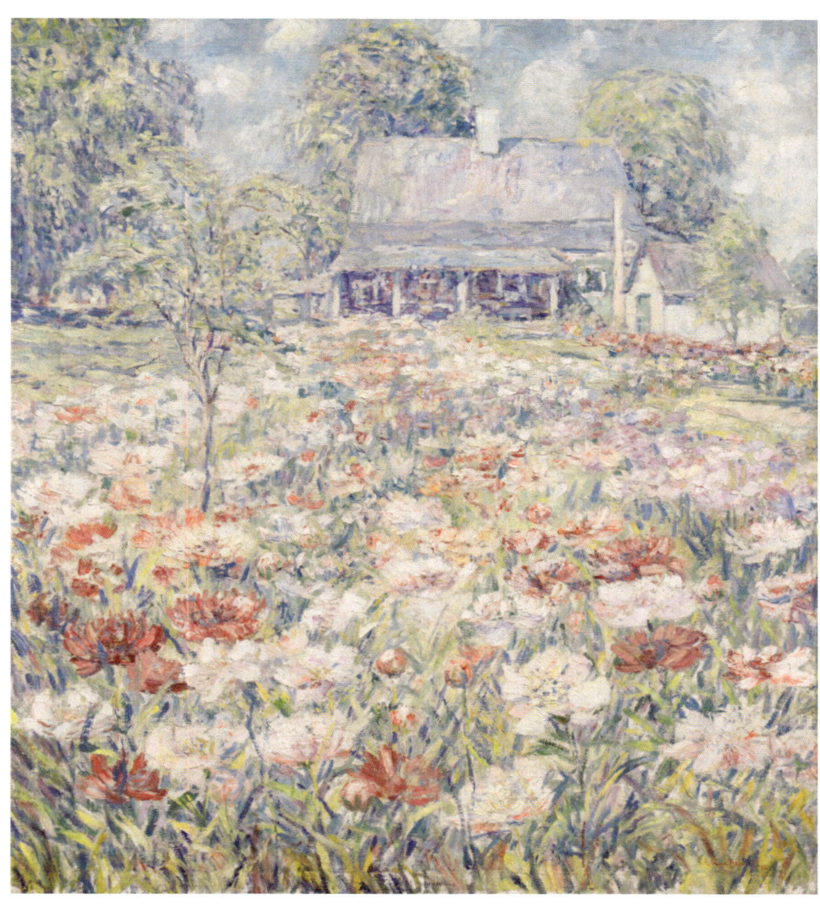

Cat. 4.
Daniel Putnam Brinley, *The Peony Garden*, ca. 1912, oil on canvas, Virginia Museum of Fine Arts, Richmond, Adolph D. and Wilkins C. Williams Fund 78.149

Brinley was also elected a member of the MacDowell Club in 1910 and 1911. He contributed three paintings to the Armory Show including *The Peony Garden* (cat. 4). The subject matter of this work is similar to that of some American and French Impressionists, but the vivid colors, lack of atmospheric effect, and thick, almost sculptural, brushwork show an affinity with the Post-Impressionist paintings of Vincent van Gogh.

Allen Tucker, referred to as the American van Gogh, was another original member of the AAPS. Though a practicing architect for many years, Tucker also took classes at the Art Students League under John Twachtman; at the school's summer classes in Cos Cob, Connecticut, he met Ernest Lawson. During summer trips to Europe between 1889 and 1891, he also became close friends with Henri.[152] Like most artists of his time, Tucker exhibited at the PAFA and the NAD, but as early as 1908 he became involved with the more progressive group of painters that included Henri, Bellows, Sloan, and Lawson. He participated in the *Exhibition of Independent Artists* and undertook the monumental task of putting together the Armory Show exhibition catalogues for the AAPS. From Twachtman, Tucker learned, "I didn't have to be like or unlike anyone else, that it was my job, that the world was mine and that there

83

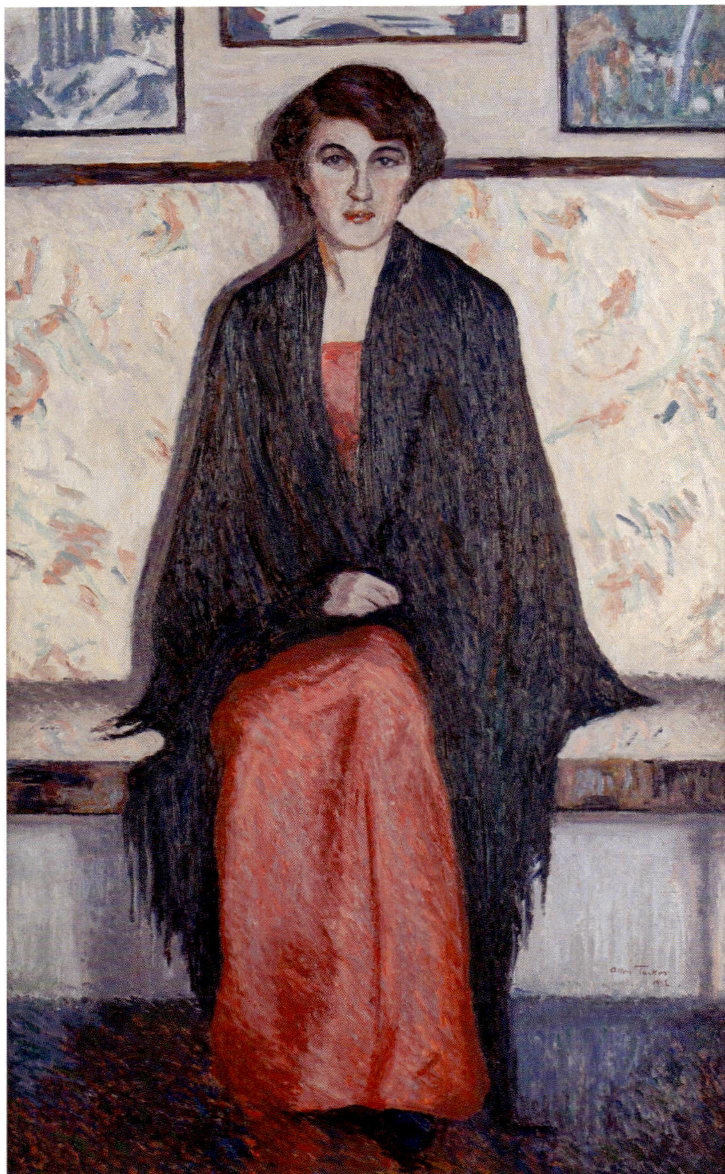

Cat. 36.
Allen Tucker, *Study in Rose and Black*, 1912, oil on canvas, from the Collection of Staten Island Museum

was nothing between me and the wonder of it all but that rectangle of white canvas."[153] This freedom of expression and openness to experimentation became the root of Tucker's art as his early Impressionist and Tonalist paintings gave way to the influence of the expressive potential of Post-Impressionism, especially the canvases of Vincent van Gogh.[154] In December 1912, Tucker held a three day exhibition of his "Rocky Mountain Pictures" at his studio, which attracted a considerable crowd.[155] Among the paintings shown was *Mount Aberdeen—Gray Day*, suggesting that his Armory Show work with a similar title may also have been done during this western trip. One of his other Armory entries was *Study in Rose and Black* (cat. 36), which is decidedly different from Robert Henri's very similar subject *The Spanish Gypsy* (cat. 17, p. 131). While both are boldly forthright portraits of young women, Tucker's is more of a study in colors with more emphasis on the well-designed composition of decorative patterns. As art critic Forbes Watson observed, "Even in his portraits, the 'sitter' is rarely as absorbing to him as the design," and indeed Tucker's book on the subject, *Design and the Idea*, reveals these concepts as the foundation of his art. [156]

The "decorative quality" of Edward Middleton Manigault's art, as well as its similarities to Davies's figurative paintings like *Sea Drift* (cat. 10, p. 127) and the visionary aspects of Albert Pinkham Ryder's canvases, may have been one of the reasons that his works *Adagio* (cat. 23, p. 29) and *The Clown* (1912, Columbus Museum of Art, Ohio) were selected, likely by Davies, for the show.[157] As Manigault scholar Beth A. Venn noted, Manigault's association with the *Exhibition of Independent Artists*, as well as his exhibitions at Haas Gallery, probably also precipitated his invitation. In the summer of 1912, Manigault traveled to France and England, visiting the major museums and finding inspiration in the "art of the more distant past." [158] These paintings by Manigault, as well as the numerous other Post-Impressionist, Fauvist, and Expressionist works by Americans in the Armory Show, could be construed as the American equivalent of that "distinct individuality of expression and forceful manifestation of the creative power" that Davies, Kuhn, and others in the AAPS were looking for and that they felt was present in the European art assembled for the show.

One aspect of the American art in the Armory Show that was decidedly different from the European section was the larger number of women artists; they composed over 20 percent of the

American exhibitors and were represented by paintings, sculptures, drawings, and illustrations, as well as painted china and embroidery; the AAPS had specifically requested that invited artists be on the lookout for "someone who is not a professional artist and yet produces original designs in needlework of art value."[159] Of the female artists in the Armory Show, several had studied with Robert Henri including some whose works are featured in *The New Spirit*: Barkley, *Jerome Avenue Bridge (Landscape over the City)* (cat. 1, p. 121), McEnery, *Going to the Bath* (cat. 25), p. 135), Ethel Myers, *The Gambler: Joe Johnson* (cat. 27, p. 39), and Hilda Ward, *The Kennels* (cat. 37).[160] It is not surprising, therefore, that many women artists in the Armory also showed at the 1910 *Exhibition of Independent Artists* that Henri helped organize. As Marian Wardle observed, "Henri's women students contributed significantly to the structure of American modernism. They produced a large body of work, exhibited widely, won major art awards, belonged to and administered art organizations, and taught art classes across America."[161]

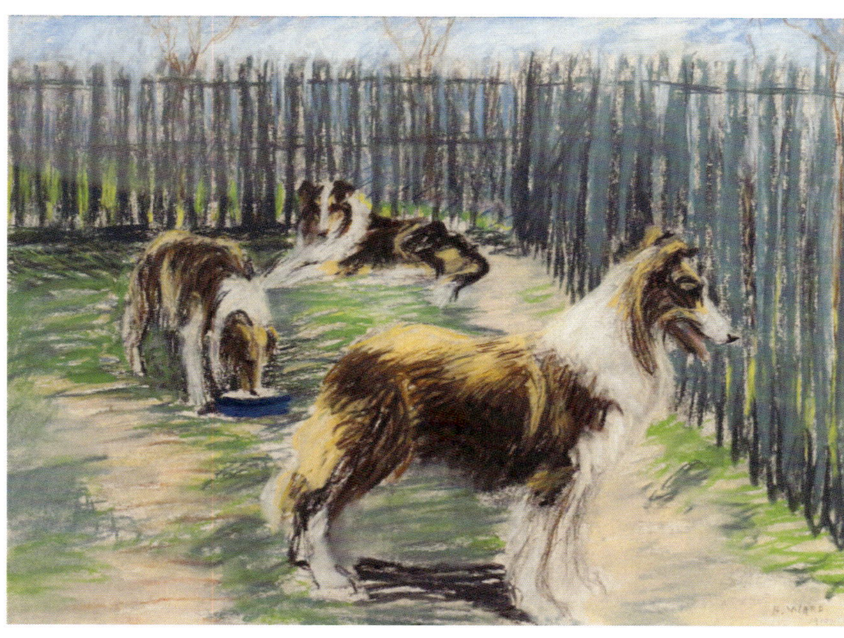

Cat. 37.
Hilda Ward, *The Kennels*, 1910, pastel on paper. Collection of Francis M. Naumann and Marie T. Keller, Yorktown Heights, NY

In the early years of the 20th century it was more difficult for women artists to find venues to show and sell their art because many organizations were male-dominated and did not allow females to exhibit. Nevertheless, women joined as many societies, associations, and clubs as they could, including the American Water Color Society, New York Water Color Club, Mural Painters, American Society of Miniature Painters, Society of Illustrators, National Association of Portrait Painters, and the National Sculpture Society. Women formed their own groups as well, which were designed to promote their art in shows in New York, Paris, and elsewhere.[162] In Manhattan, the National Association of Women Artists, originally called the Woman's Art Club, was founded in 1889 and still holds yearly exhibitions.[163] Early annuals were held at commercial galleries in New York such as Bauer-Folsom and Knoedler's, as well as at the National Arts Club. Armory Show participants Burroughs, Eberle, Goldthwaite, Johnson, Josephine Paddock, and May Wilson Preston became members.[164] In 1896, the Catharine Lorillard Wolfe Art Club was established "to provide aid, counsel and exhibition opportunities to young women artists in New York City" and regular shows of paintings, arts and crafts, and photographs by women artists, both students and professional, began that year and continue to this day.[165] The American Girls' Club of Paris held annual exhibitions starting in 1893, and in 1895 the American Woman's Art Association of Paris was formed to organize yearly shows.[166] In 1911, the Society of Women Painters was formed with the purpose of circulating "exhibitions of women's art outside of New York City."[167] Women artists were also included in the shows of the MacDowell Club and at several commercial galleries as well. In addition, they participated in the large-scale shows at the NAD, PAFA, AIC, and elsewhere across the United States.

Hundreds of American women artists, like their male counterparts, also studied and exhibited in Paris, and some visited the Steins' households and became part of the American modernist circle that developed in the French capital between 1906 and 1912. Perhaps the earliest to develop a knowledge and understanding of European modernism before the Armory Show was Anne Goldthwaite, who arrived in Paris in 1906 and, like many American women artists, resided at the American Girls' Club.[168] Goldthwaite served as president of the American Woman's Art Association of Paris, which, as mentioned above, held yearly exhibitions. The 1910 show included works by a few Armory Show artists including Goldthwaite, Grace Mott Johnson, Kathleen McEnery, and Marguerite Thompson (Zorach).[169]

McEnery studied with the Henri class in Spain during the summer of 1906, where Pach served as agent for the class, and in 1908. Soon after the last course, she moved to Paris, rented a studio, and experienced "a prolific period of work" during her two-year stay from 1908 to 1910.[170] McEnery surely came under the influence of European modernism during this period as is evident in her Armory Show entry, *Going to the Bath* (cat. 25, p. 135). This vision of two large, full-length female nudes placed in a shallow space, with one boldly confronting the viewer, must have been seen as quite daring for the time. The strong lines, flattened forms, and bold palette are hallmarks of a modernist aesthetic. Armory Show participants Marion H. Beckett and Katharine Nash Rhoades also arrived in Paris in 1908 and visited the Steins' households, becoming involved with the modernists.[171] One of Beckett's Armory Show entries was *Portrait of Mr. Edward J. Steichen,* and it was he who suggested a show of Rhoades's work to Stieglitz as early as 1912; Beckett and Rhoades showed at 291 in 1915.[172] Around this same time, Thompson (Zorach) arrived in Paris and worked with Scottish artist John Duncan Fergusson at the Ecole de La Palette, one of the schools where Post-Impressionism was taught. An introduction from an aunt brought her to the Steins' homes.[173] Katherine Dreier, who attended the Brooklyn School of Art and was a pupil of Walter Shirlaw at the Pratt Institute, also studied in Europe and was a guest of the Steins in Paris. She had her first solo show in 1911 at the Doré Galleries in London. While her Armory Show entry, *The Blue Bowl* (cat. 13, p. 18), is not a modernist painting, Dreier was well aware of vanguard European art movements; she lent Vincent van Gogh's painting *Mademoiselle Ravoux* (1890, Cleveland Museum of Art), which she had purchased from the *Sonderbund Exhibition*, to the Armory Show.[174]

Women accounted for a significant portion of the American sculpture at the Armory Show, and although the American work was not as radical as the pieces by Europeans such as Raymond Duchamp-Villon and Constantin Brancusi, except perhaps for Andrew Dasburg's *Lucifer*, it was not all academic or traditional.[175] There was also a variety of subjects and a diversity of media including bronze, marble, terra cotta, plaster, painted plaster, carved plaster, and medals. American work, like European, was dominated by the figure with portraits and nudes prevailing. Allegorical and mythological themes—Norse, Greek, and Japanese among them—and American Indian subjects were popular as were sculptures of animals. Drawings and medals by some of these sculptors were also included in the exhibition. Finally, as with the paintings and prints, some sculptures were not catalogued and some were listed as catalogued but not received, meaning there were probably other three-dimensional objects in the Armory Show.

Most of the American sculptors, like the painters, had studied at the academies in the United States and many had also trained and exhibited in Paris including George Gray Barnard, Chester Beach, Burroughs, Musselman-Carr, Davidson, Cecil de Blaquere Howard, Johnson, Bessie Potter Vonnoh, and Enid Yandell. While many of the sculptors in the show relied heavily on the Beaux-Arts academic tradition, several had come under the influence of the more expressive and experimental sculpture of French artists Auguste Rodin, Aristide Maillol, and Antoine Emile Bourdelle. Art historians Ilene Susan Fort and Roberta K. Tarbell have noted, "The works by Americans [in the Armory Show] were closer in style to those of Rodin than those of the fifteen European sculptors...who demonstrated more modern aesthetic convictions."[176] Barnard, Beach, Davidson, Arthur Putman, Vonnoh, and Yandell all had personal encounters with Rodin. [177] Others, such as Robert I. Aiken of San Francisco, learned of Rodin's art through fellow sculptors, while still more read about Rodin's art in the press or saw it in various exhibitions in the United States prior to the Armory Show.[178] As Fort observed, "Rodin and his art signaled the introduction of a modernist aesthetic to American sculpture."[179] She furthermore observed, "Modernity ... for Americans ... meant an openness toward subject matter, style, cultural ideals, and personal beliefs and attitudes."[180] In the American sculpture in the Armory Show, and in those in *The New Spirit*, we see these concepts realized.

Chester Beach, like many American sculptors in the early 20th century, was a member of the National Sculpture Society and the NAD, and also studied in France, where he belonged to and exhibited at the American Art Association of Paris. Fellow American sculptor Paul W. Bartlett furnished him with a letter of introduction to Rodin.[181] Beach was represented in the Armory Show by several works, including the marble sculpture, *Unveiling of Dawn* (cat. 2). The voluptuous female form in this piece awakens from her sleep enveloped in an aura of sensuality and subtle eroticism. The manner in which the woman and man emerge from the unfinished portion of the marble is reminiscent of the nudes of Michelangelo. Beach used undulating and flowing forms to portray the figures, revealing the influence of Rodin's "irregular surface modulations." Unlike Rodin, however, who "conceived his sculptures by building up malleable clay and had artisan-carvers transfer them to marble," Beach became noted for his direct carving technique, his "masterful workmanship" and his "clear and individual expression."[182] In the early 1900s, Beach's skillful interpretation of "Rodin's poetic mode" earned him recognition as a "leader of the 'new movement' of modernists."[183] Beach showed *Unveiling of Dawn* (cat. 2, p. 122) just before the Armory Show, at the Pratt Institute in Brooklyn in January 1913, and also exhibited two other Armory Show entries, *The Big Wave* and *Mermaid*, at his solo show at Macbeth Gallery in December 1912.[184]

Another American sculptor who was influenced by the powerful forms of Rodin's art was Jo Davidson, who was part of the modernist circles in Paris before the Armory Show. At the 1908 Salon des Artistes Indépendants, Davidson saw artists "painting and sculpting as they like, expressing themselves." It was, for him, an "open door to freedom."[185] He firmly believed that "plastic art is a form of expression by which emotions can be made visible" and he captured the essence of his figures through forceful and direct modeling of the clay. While best known today for his portraits of famous men and women, most of Davidson's Armory Show works were depictions of ordinary individuals, mainly women. Unlike much of the other sculpture in the exhibition, many of Davidson's pieces were bronze, such as *Seated Female (Study in Repose)* (cat. 9, p. 24). In this work, the artist contrasted the smooth and subtle surface of the dark bronze figure against the rough-hewn texture and bright tone of the stone base. Davidson exhibited a version of *Seated Female (Study in Repose)* and a series of *Studies in Action* (also in the Armory Show) in his January 1913 solo exhibition at the gallery Henry Reinhardt & Sons in New York.[186] He had also sent plasters of two of his other Armory Show sculptures, *Yoshinosan* (statuette) and *Yoshinosan* (bust), to the 1912 Salon d'Automne in Paris.[187]

One of the female sculptors in the Armory Show, Grace Mott Johnson, married fellow artist Andrew Dasburg, and in 1909 the couple sailed for Paris and "became part of the

American modernist coterie in Paris that included Arthur Lee, Russell, and Davidson."[188] Johnson studied sculpture with Hermon A. MacNeill, James Earle Frazier, and Gutzon Borglum at the Art Students League. She made a specialty of animal sculpture, mostly small-scale three-dimensional works. Four of her pieces were in the Armory Show, including a version of *Greyhound Pup #2* (cat. 20, p. 24). Like Davidson, whom she certainly knew, Johnson also exhibited a relief panel in the Armory Show, *Chimpanzees*, which bears a resemblance to Davidson's decorative panel of stylized nude figures in the exhibition and, to a lesser extent, French artist Aristide Maillol's bas-relief of a nude female. Though relatively traditional, Johnson's sculptures in the round, like *Greyhound Pup #2*, have simplified forms and her bas-reliefs show minimal and mainly surface incisions, techniques that differ from the more academic methods of strictly realistic representation.

The American sculpture that caused the most controversy at the Armory Show, *The White Slave* (fig. 14), was by a woman artist, Abastenia St. Leger Eberle.[189] A pupil of Barnard (also in the exhibition) at the Art Students League in New York, Eberle had gained fame in the years before the famed exhibition with her small bronze sculptures of "poor immigrants on New York's Lower East Side," which she exhibited at the NAD, PAFA, and elsewhere. Many art historians have noted that her sculpture was viewed as the "counterpart of the paintings of the Ashcan school."[190] "This shift to genre realism was actually the first challenge to the hegemony of Beaux-Arts sculpture in the early twentieth century" scholar Daniel Robbins observed, and Eberle was among the most prominent sculptors in this vein.[191] *Girl Seated, Girl Standing, and Sea Treasures (from the Wading series)* (cat. 14, p. 30), which depicts three young girls on the sandy shores of a beach, is typical of her popular sculptures of scenes of everyday life. It was one of her other contributions, however, that sparked outrage.[192] *The White Slave*'s forthright, uncompromising, and biting depiction of a scruffily clothed man selling a nude young girl into prostitution was too real and politically charged for many Americans.[193] As art historian and curator Susan P. Casteras noted, the work "managed to encompass several of the day's critical issues—the white slavery scandal, socialist ideology, women's rights, nudity in art, and modern art."[194]

Another female sculptor married to a fellow Armory Show artist was Ethel Myers, wife of Jerome. Ethel studied art with Chase, Henri, and Kenneth Hayes Miller and was a painter before she turned to sculpture, in which she specialized in subjects similar to the "Ashcan school tradition" of which her husband was also a part.[195] She began modeling clay and wax figures around 1905 and used expressive and exaggerated forms to portray the foibles of the human character, often defining her subjects by their clothing. In all of her statuettes, Myers presented "particular types … with consummate skill and rare human sympathy." One critic ranked her "as a sculptor with the power of presenting through her work a knowledge of life and understanding of human psychology as rare as it is interesting."[196] Most of her sculptures were of women, *The Gambler, Joe Johnson* (cat. 27, p. 39), an image of a famous African American gambler from North Carolina being an exception.[197] While many of Myers's sculptures were cast in bronze others, including this one, were tinted with brown, green, or blue tones to resemble more durable

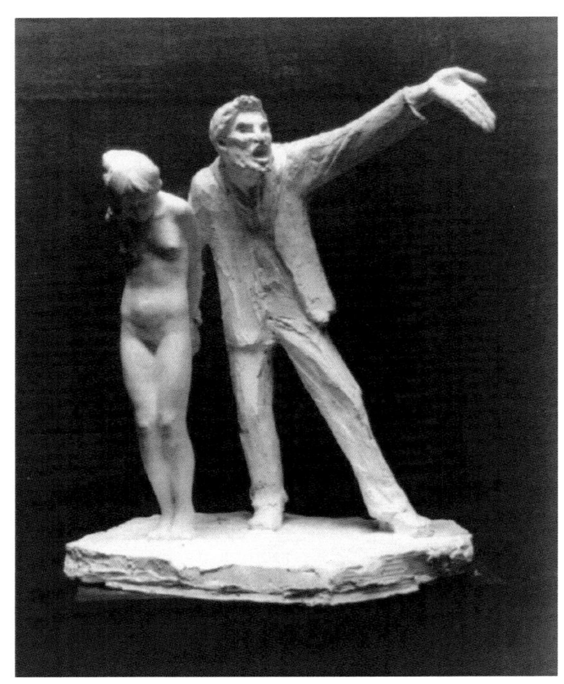

Fig. 14
Abastenia St. Leger
Eberle, *The White Slave,*
n.d., plaster, location
unknown

substances like bronze or other metals.[198] All of Myers's works in the Armory Show were exhibited early in 1913; as she recalled later in life, "At the Folsom Gallery I had an exhibition of my statuettes with Alfie Maurer and it was there that Arthur B. Davies selected 9 of my figures for the Armory Show." [199]

Although there was some discussion among the executive committee of the AAPS about only selecting works for the Armory Show that had not been exhibited before, Myers's statement reveals that not only was

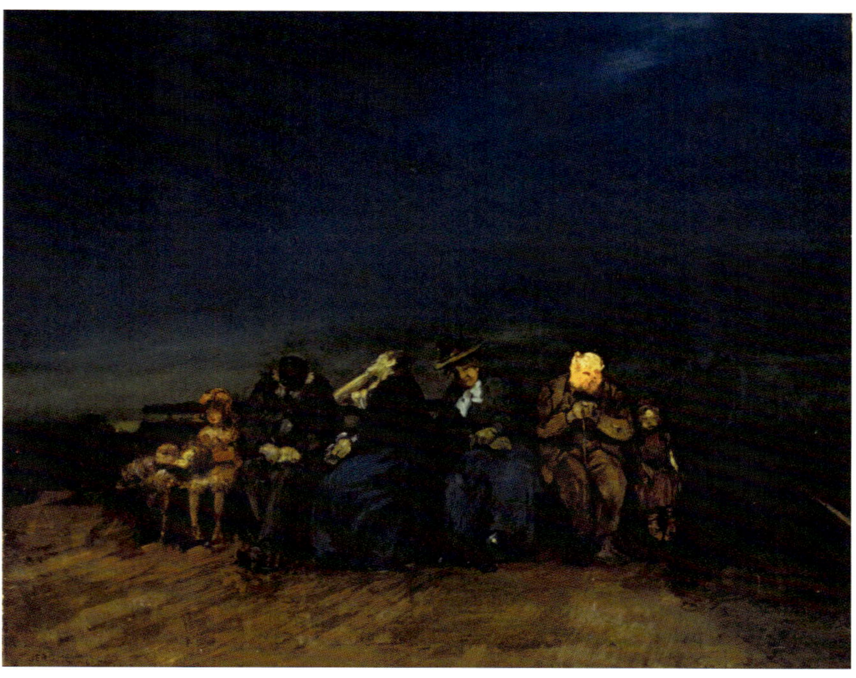

Cat. 28.
Jerome Myers, *End of the Walk*, 1907, oil on canvas, Greenville County Museum of Art, Museum Purchase with funds donated by The Museum Association Inc and Mrs. S. M. Beattie; Mrs. Robert S. Conahay III; Paul Doll; Ronald Green Jr.; Mr. and Mrs. Maxine Hermanos; Sigmund Rothschild

Davies choosing American art for the show mere weeks before it opened, but also that some of the work in the exhibition had indeed been shown previously, and most of it was not created specifically for the show.[200] Other evidence further supports this idea. Kuhn wrote cartoonist and illustrator Arthur Young, "Don't think you have got to make something special for this occasion."[201] A few days later Kuhn further explained, "I think you rather misunderstand the exact purpose of the show. It will not be necessary for you to make any special drawings. What we want is a representation by you irrespective of whether the thing has been seen before."[202]

Over a dozen works had been shown at the NAD, as noted previously, and numerous other American paintings and sculptures were exhibited in the United States in the years preceding the Armory Show; a few are cited here.[203] Myers's, *End of the Walk* (cat. 28) was in his solo show at Macbeth Gallery in 1908 and Bellows's *Docks in Winter* (1911, Private Collection) was in the first MacDowell Club show in November 1911.[204] J. Alden Weir's *Coronation Week, Madrid* and MacRae's *New York Yacht Club Fleet at Newport* and *Feeding Ducks* (1912, The Historical Society of the Town of Greenwich, Connecticut) were shown at the First Annual Exhibition of the Greenwich Society of Artists in the fall of 1912.[205] MacRae's *Fairy Stories (Fairy Tales)* (cat. 22, p. 90), is similar in style to his works shown at Greenwich. In January 1913, Leon Kroll's *Terminal Yards* (fig. 6, p. 31) and Henry J. Glintenkamp's *The Village Cemetery* were both in the eighth MacDowell Club exhibition, and Alfred Maurer showed *Old Faience* at the Folsom Galleries. [206] While the Armory Show catalogues and Brown's books list the works of Marin and Walkowitz as "lent by the artist," they were done so through the aegis of Stieglitz, who had shown these works in recent exhibitions of these artists' works at "291," including Marin's *St. Paul's Lower Manhattan (Broadway, St. Paul's Church)* (cat. 24 p. 134).[207]

Several American works in the Armory Show had been exhibited in Paris as well. For example, Charles H. White showed an edition of his print *The Condemned Tenement* at the Salon d'Automne in 1909, and the following year William E. Schumacher exhibited *Dans la jupe bleu (In Her Blue Skirt)* there.[208] As Andrew Martinez observed, the 1912 Salon d'Automne "featured works by many of the European and American modernists, including some that the two Americans [Davies and Kuhn] were trying to secure for the International Exhibition."[209] Other Americans represented in this show were Bruce, Butler, Carles, Goldthwaite, Maurer, and Pope, so it is quite possible that some works by them went from Paris to the Armory. All of this documentation challenges the AAPS's initial statements that one of the main reasons that they organized themselves and the Armory Show was because the "younger" American artists had few or no places to exhibit their art. It also shows that much of the American art in the exhibition was selected at the last minute, thus giving a much better picture of the chaotic conditions surrounding the final days before the opening of the International Exhibition of Modern Art.

It is impossible to account for all of the art in the Armory Show as titles have been changed, dozens of pieces were added to the show without documentation, and last minute changes were accepted; yet

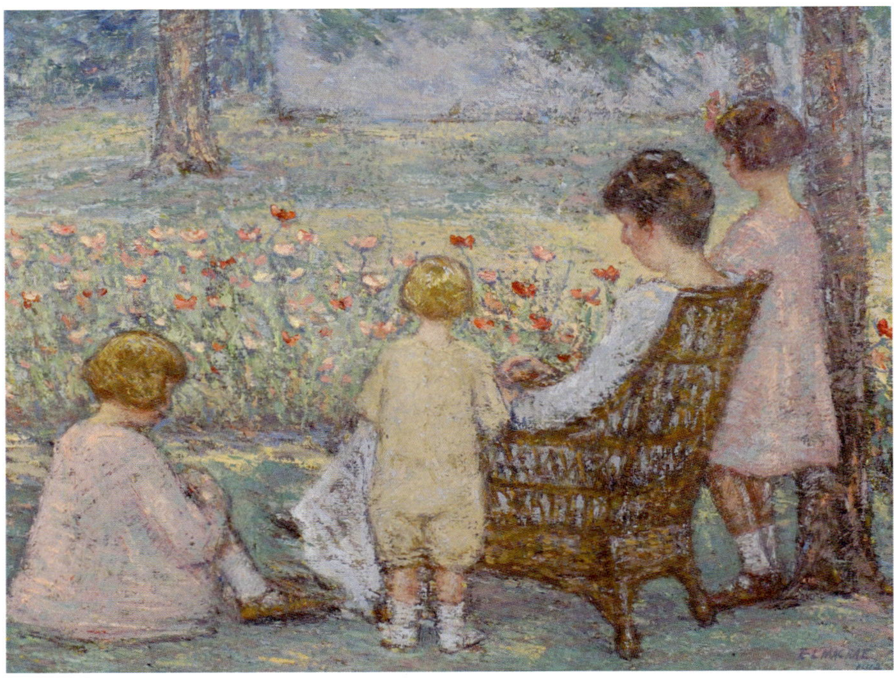

Cat. 22.
Elmer MacRae, *Fairy Stories (Fairy Tales)*, 1912, oil on canvas, Parrish Art Museum, Southampton, NY,
Gift of the Littlejohn Foundation, Littlejohn Collection, 1966.1.10

tremendous strides have been made to document, locate, and/or identify many of them, and more progress has occurred during the course of researching *The New Spirit*. We found from correspondence between Doll & Richards and the AAPS that two drawings by J. Frank Currier were sent to New York; however, no lender was noted.[210] MacRae asked Kuhn to "Send telegram to Budworth information regarding your picture called Study for Buffalo Albright," though this work has not yet been uncovered.[211] Davidson lent a bust titled *Portrait of Doris Keane*, which had also been in his January 1913 show at the Henry Reinhardt Gallery, yet its whereabouts remain a mystery.[212] Pach noted that there was a "small picture without number" titled *Boy and Goat* by Karl Anderson in the show; also not yet found.[213] In a letter to Kuhn, Art Young gave the title of a fourth drawing of his in the show, *The Freedom of the Press*, and Charles Hovey Pepper mentions his work, *Saffron Kimono*, also not listed in the catalogues, in a note to Kuhn.[214] The rediscovery of some photographic images have led to the identification of some unlocated works. For example, an article about the Armory Show written by the AAPS's publicity man Frederick James Gregg illustrates an Arthur B. Davies painting titled *Fording the Stream*, which seems to be another uncatalogued work.[215] A 1913 article by James William Pattison, cited by Brown, reproduces two paintings that, as far as I have been able to determine, are undocumented: Ernest Lawson's *Weeds and Willow Trees* and one of William Nicholson Taylor's decorative screens with the title *Nude Women in a Meadow*.[216] A closer inspection of the AIC installation photographs of the American section reveals Davies's *Hill Wind*, Hassam's *Naples,* Prendergast's *Crépuscule,* Kenneth Frazier's *The Winter Garden*, May Wilson Preston's *Girl with Print*, and Sheeler's *The Waterfall*. Perhaps more works will be recognized through further examination of these images. Finally, since the 50th anniversary of the Armory Show in 1963, paintings, sculptures, and works on paper by American artists have been located, including several in this exhibition such as Pach's *The Wall of the City* (cat. 29, p. 80)and Henri's drawing #838 (cat. 18, p. 42).[217]

On the occasion of the 100th anniversary of the Armory Show, *The New Spirit: American Art in the Armory Show, 1913* seeks to re-examine and re-evaluate many of the accepted ideas about the show in light of new scholarship and recent rediscoveries, to dispel some of the legends surrounding it, and to develop a fuller and richer understanding of this complex, fluid, and important event in the history of American and modern art. Among the main assumptions about the Armory Show are that the AAPS mounted the exhibition as a direct attack on the National Academy of Design, that they did so because "younger" American artists had been rejected by the NAD, and that the show was necessary because these artists had few places to exhibit their work. The evidence, however, does not fully support this argument. A more logical explanation for the group's formation and the subsequent show was a desire to host large-scale international shows in New York like those of Paris, London, Venice, and Rome, thereby placing the United States and its artists on a more equal footing with the Europeans on the world stage.

Another element of some Armory Show narratives is that European modernism was completely unknown to the vast majority of American artists and to the population in general; but this too has been disproven. An additional myth is that most of the American art in the Armory Show was traditional and provincial. Yet works inspired by the modern art of Paul Cézanne, Vincent van Gogh, Paul Gauguin, Henri Matisse, and other advanced French art of the late 19th and early 20th centuries were a significant part of the American section of the Armory Show and, contrary to Brown's observations, held up quite well beside their European counterparts in the press of the time (see Stavitsky's essay). These Post-Impressionist, Fauvist, Expressionist, and abstract works by Americans were vibrant contributions to the Armory Show, but they have been overshadowed by the spectacle created by the more radical European works not only in the original exhibition and the press of that time but also in the subsequent Armory Show literature. As noted scholar Judith Zilczer observed, "Ironically, the international scope of the Armory Show resulted in a partial eclipse of the American Post-Impressionists. Although American entries were as numerous as those of the European Post-Impressionists, public attention focused on the Europeans, particularly the French."[218] While there is a great deal of scholarship on American modernism and on many individual artists involved with the modernist aesthetic, many of the painters in the current exhibition have been somewhat neglected, are relatively unrecognized outside a small coterie of enthusiasts, and remain outside the mainstream of American modernism. This exhibition places emphasis on these lesser-known and underappreciated vanguard American painters, as well as on women artists and sculptors. The works in this exhibition represent a tiny microcosm of the larger world of early 20th-century American art and a small cross-section of the Americans who participated in the International Exhibition of Modern Art. *The New Spirit: American Art in the Armory Show, 1913* strives to offer new perspectives on the Armory Show and the American art therein, laying the groundwork for further investigations into this rich, exciting, and dynamic field of study.

FOOTNOTES

1 Doreen Bolger, "Hamilton Easter Field and the Rise of Modern Art in America" (unpublished Master's thesis, University of Delaware, 1973), Charles C. Eldredge, "The Arrival of European Modernism," *Art in America* 61 (July-August 1973): 34-41, Carol Arnold Nathanson, "The American Response, in 1900-1913, to the French Modern Art Movements after Impressionism" (unpublished Ph.D. diss., the John Hopkins University, 1973), Judith C. Zilczer, "The World's New Art Center: Modern Art Exhibitions in New York City 1913-1918," *Archives of American Art Journal* 14 (1974): 2-7 and "The Aesthetic Struggle in America, 1913-1918: Art and Theory in the Stieglitz Circle, "(unpublished Ph.D. diss., University of Delaware, 1975), William Innes Homer, *The Avant-Garde Painting & Sculpture in America, 1910-25* (Wilmington, DE: Delaware Art Museum, 1975), Ann Uhry Abrams, "Catalyst for a Change: American Art and Revolution, 1906-1915," (unpublished Ph.D. diss., Emory University, 1975), Howard Anthony Risatti, "American Critical reaction to European Modernism, 1908-1917," (unpublished Ph.D. diss., University of Illinois at Urbana-Champaign, 1978), Judith Zilczer, "The Armory Show and the American Avant-Garde: A Re-evaluation," *Arts* 53 (September 1978): 126-30, J. Meredith Neil, "The Impact of the Armory Show," *The South Atlantic Quarterly* 79 (Autumn 1980): 375-385, Abraham A. Davidson, *Early American Modernist Painting, 1910-35* (De Capro, 1981 and 1994), Carol A. Nathanson, "The American Reaction to London's First Grafton Show," *Archives of American Art Journal* 25(1985): 3-10, Peter Morrin and Judith Zilczer, *The Advent of Modernism: Post-Impressionism and North American Art, 1900-1918,* (Atlanta, GA: High Museum of Art, 1986), and William H. Gerdts, "The American Fauves: 1907-1918," in *The Color of Modernism: The American Fauves* (NY: Hollis Taggart Galleries, 1997).

2 "Various Art Matters," *New York Times*, April 22, 1905, "Salon Given Over To Freak Paintings," *New York Times*, October 11, 1908, 3, "News and Notes of the Art World," *New York Times*, October 24, 1909, "Echoes From France," *Art and Progress* 1 (January 1910): 74, "'Futurists' Desire To Destroy Venice," *New York Times*, July 24, 1910, "Futurists Condemn Nudity in Painting," *New York Times*, August 20, 1911, "'Futurism' Ad Nauseam," *New York Times*, September 3, 1911, "Freaks of the Futurists," *New York Times*, February 25, 1912, C3, "Independent Salon Opens," *American Art News* 10 (March 23, 1912): 5, Felix Grendon, "What is Post-Impressionism?" *New York Times*, May 12, 1912, BR294, Eric Tayne, "The Art Trend in France," *New York Times*, July 21, 1912, "Art Notes From London," *New York Times*, November 3, 1912, Warren Barton Blake, "Crazy-Quilt Art," *The Independent* (December 19, 1912), 1419.

3 "Post-Impressionist 'Art'," *New York Times*, November 27, 1910 (Vincent van Gogh's *Girl with Sunflower* reproduced), "The 'Cubists' Dominate Paris' Fall Salon," *New York Times*, October 8, 1911. Among the works illustrated was Henri Matisse's *Le Madras rouge* which would cause a sensation at the Armory Show. In addition Auguste Chabaud's *La Place aux Affiches* and paintings by Jean Metzinger and André Derain were reproduced. "Is Post Impressionism a New Disease or a New Religion?" *Current Literature* 52 (May 1912): 584-88. Works by Gauguin, Van Gogh, and Matisse illustrated. "Art At Home and Abroad: Some Typical Pictures by Van Gogh, the Post Impressionist, Whose Works Will Be Seen Here This Season," *New York Times*, September 15, 1912, several works illustrated. James Huneker, "Decade of The New Art Movement Shows Big Changes," *New York Times*, November 10, 1912, SM12. Auguste Chabaud's Armory Show entry *The Flock After the Rain* and Matisse's *The Dance*, 1910, illustrated.

4 See note 1.

5 Abraham A. Davidson, "The Armory Show and Early Modernism in America," in *American Art in the 20th Century: Painting and Sculpture, 1913-1993,* edited by Christos M. Joachimides and Norman Rosenthal, Co-ordinating editor, David Anfan (Prestel, 1993), 41 and 46.

6 Milton W. Brown, *The Story of the Armory Show* (NY: The Joseph H. Hirshhorn Foundation, 1963 and Abbeville Press Publishers and The Joseph H. Hirshhorn Foundation, 1988).

7 Brown, *The Story of the Armory Show*, 1988, 51.

8 Peter H. Falk, *Annual Exhibition Record of the National Academy of Design, 1901-1950* (Madison, CT: Sound View Press, 1990).

9 J. Alden Weir to Henry Fitch Taylor, January 3, 1912, Association of American Painters and Sculptors (AAPS) Records: Membership, 1911-1912, Box 3, Folder 3, #39. Walt Kuhn, Kuhn Family Papers and Armory Show Records, 1859-1978, Bulk 1900-1949, Archives of American Art, Smithsonian Institution, Washington, D.C. (hereinafter Armory Show Records, AAA). The Archives of American Art will hereafter be abbreviated AAA.

10 "History of Art: Dictionary of Art and Artists, http://www.all-art.org/artists-a-allied_artists.html, accessed, August 6, 2012. Dabo personally brought five of his "Hudson riverscapes" to the premier exhibition in 1908. See, "London Letter," *American Art News* 6 (July 11, 1908): 2.

11 Bennard B. Perlman, *The Lives, Loves and Art of Arthur B. Davies* (Albany, NY: SUNY, 1999), 182 and 183.

12 "News and Notes of the Art World," *New York Times*, April 25, 1910. Among those selected were: Beach, Bellows, Borglum, Burroughs, Davies, Leger, Glackens, Philip L. Hale, Hassam, Lawson, Vonnoh, Weir, and Young.

13 "The Roman Art Exhibit," *American Art News* 9 (June 17, 1911): 2. Other artists in both shows include Childe Hassam, Robert I Aitken, James Fraser, and Bessie Potter Vonnoh.

14 John H. Gest to Walt Kuhn, February 2, 1912, Association of American Painters and Sculptors (AAPS) Records: Exhibition Venues, 1912, Box 3, Folder, 2, #12, Armory Show Records, AAA.

15 Fernando A. Carter to Walt Kuhn, January 30, 1912, Association of American Painters and Sculptors (AAPS) Records: Exhibition Venues, 1912, Box 3, Folder, 2, #5, Armory Show Records, AAA.

16 Sylvia Yount, "Rocking the Cradle of Liberty: Philadelphia's Adventures in Modernism," in *To Be Modern: American Encounters with Cézanne and Company* (PA: Museum of American Art of the Pennsylvania Academy of the Fine Arts Distributed by University of Pennsylvania Press, 1996), 11.

17 Roberta K. Tarbell and Ilene Susan Fort, "America Sculpture and Rodin," in *Rodin and America: Influence and Adaptation, 1876-1936* (Milan, Italy: Silvana Editoriale, 2011), 17.

18 "The Independent Artists," *American Art News*, 8 (April 9, 1910): 2. Elizabeth Milroy, "The Legacy of The Eight: Independent Exhibitions and the 'National Salon'," in *Painters of a New Century: The Eight & American Art* (Milwaukee, WI: The Milwaukee Art Museum, 1991) 87-90, Brown, *The Story of the Armory Show*, 1988, 48, 51, 61, and 88, Perlman, *The Lives, Loves and Art of Arthur B. Davies*, 181-86.

19 Perlmann, *The Lives, Loves, and Art of Arthur B. Davies*, 190-92.

20 "Nudes Shock Columbus (o.)," *American Art News* 9 (February 25, 1911): 2. See also Perlmann, *The Lives, Loves and Art of Arthur B. Davies*, 190-91.

21 Jay Boechner, *An American Lens: Scenes from Alfred Stieglitz's New York Secession* (London, England and Cambridge, MA: The MIT Press, 2005), 37. Perlmann *The Lives, Loves, and Art of Arthur B. Davies*, 140-41.

22 Perlman, *The Lives, Loves and Art of Arthur B. Davies*, 140.

23 Boechner, *An American Lens: Scenes from Alfred Stieglitz's New York Secession*, 37.

24 "Exhibitions Now On," *American Art News* 6 (January 11, 1908): 6.

25 "Exhibitions Now On," *American Art News* 7 (May 15, 1909): 6 and "Exhibitions Now On: Old Students at Art Club," *American Art News* 31 (May 14, 1910): 6.

26 "Artists at Arts Club," *American Art News* 9 (January 14, 1911): 6.

27 The exhibition was held February 2-23, 1910. See J. Nilsen Lauvrik to D. Putnam Brinley, January 10, 1910, D. Putnam Brinley Papers, Organization Files, National Arts Club, Box 11 folder 4, AAA.

28 Ibid.

29 James B. Townsend, "American Landscapes at Art Club," *American Art News* 8 (January 29, 1910): 6.

30 Townsend, "American Landscapes at Art Club," *American Art News* 8 (January 29, 1910): 6 and "Landscapes at Arts Club," 8 (February 12, 1910); 6.

31 "Gimbel Brothers Announce Their First Exhibition of Paintings by American Artists," *American Art News* 10 (April 13, 1912): 2.

32 Julie Mellby, "A Record of Charles Daniel and the Daniel Gallery," (unpublished thesis, Hunter College, 1993), 6. According to Mellby, galleries other than Stieglitz's "refused to exhibit modern American art. A few like Haas Gallery would grudgingly rent artists space. Abraham Walkowitz had to clear out the garbage before hanging his first solo exhibition in Haas' backroom….. Almost no one was willing to take a chance on financing the young, modern American artist." She also noted, "Other dealers had been coerced into showing modern paintings, like William Macbeth, who required a guarantee of five hundred dollars for the exhibition of The Eight."

33 See especially, Gwendolyn Owens, "Art and Commerce: William Macbeth, The Eight and the Popularization of American Art," in *Painters of a New Century: The Eight & American Art* (as in. n. 18), 61-69.

34 See, *Forty Selected Paintings by Living American Artists on Exhibition*, January 7-21, 1909, Macbeth Gallery, Miscellaneous Exhibition Catalogues, Series 5, Art Exhibition Catalogues: M-O, Box 3, Reel 4859, AAA.

35 "Boston Artists at Macbeth's," *American Art News* 7 (April 24, 1909): 6.

36 Louise R. Noun, *Abastenia St. Leger Eberle, Sculptor (1878-1942)* (Des Moines, IA: Des Moines Art Center, 1980), 10-11.

37 "Marin's and Maurer's Works," *American Art News* 7 (April 10, 1909): 6

38 "Followers of Matisse,"*American Art News* 23 (March 19, 1910): 6.

39 "Hartley at Photo-Secession," *American Art News* 10 (February 17, 1912): 2.

40 "Exhibitions Now On," *American Art News* 6 (November 30, 1907): 6. This was an announcement of the opening of the gallery and its inaugural exhibition.

41 "Cimiotti at Bauer-Folsom's," *American Art News* 7 (December 5, 1908): 6.

42 "First Exhibition of 'The Pastellists' Suggests the Revival of a Charming Form of 18th Century Art," *New York Times*, January 15, 1911 and "News and Notes of the Art World: The Pastellists," *New York Times*, December 17, 1911. Powell Gallery hosted an exhibition of the Pastellists in February 1912 which included works by Bellows, Dabo, Samuel Halpert, Edward E. Kramer, George Luks, Elmer MacRae, Walt Kuhn, Jerome Myers, Allen Tucker, and Arthur B. Davies. "News and Notes," *New York Times*, February 11, 1912. See also, *The Sun*, February 25, 1912, 10.

43 "Russell and Schille at Folsom's," *American Art News* 10 (March 9, 1912): 2, "Dabo at Folsom's," *American Art News* 10 (March 30, 1912): 2.

44 "Paintings of City Life," *American Art News* 11 (October 19, 1912): 2.

45 "'Post-Impressionism' at Folsom's," *American Art News* 11 (January 18, 1913): 2.

46 "Around the Galleries," *American Art News* 23 (March 16, 1912): 8. A year earlier, Daniel had "rented an office at 2 West 47th Street, where the artists could come to see him and show him their work." Mellby, "A Record of Charles Daniel and the Daniel Gallery," 5.

47 "Around the Galleries," *American Art News* 10 (March 16, 1912): 8.

48 Julie Mellby, *Charles Daniel and the Daniel Gallery, 1913-1932* (NY: Zabriskie Gallery, 1993), 7.

49 Christine I. Oaklander, "Clara Davidge's Madison Art Gallery: Sowing the Seed for The Armory Show," *Archives of American Art Journal* 36 (1996): 20-37 and *Clara Davidge and Henry Fitch Taylor: Pioneering Promoters and Creators of American Modernist Art* (Ph.D. diss., University of Delaware, 1999).,98,118,135-140, 143-5.

50 "Madison Gallery Display," *American Art News* 10 (November 11, 1911): 2.

51 "News and Notes of the Art World," *New York Times*, March 6, 1910 (review of MacRae show), "Kuhn at Madison," *American Art News* 10 (December 2, 1911): 2 and "News and Notes of the Art World: A Painter of the Sea," *New York Times* December 19, 1911, "Landscapes by Lawson," *American Art News* 10 (January 6, 1912): 2, "Pictures by MacRae," *American Art News* 10 (March 2, 1912): 2, and "Glackens' Recent Work," *American Art News* 10 (March 16, 1912): 2.

52 "With the Dealers," *American Art News* 8 (July 16, 1910): 3.

53 "News and Notes of the Art World: An Artist of Fifteenth Century Inspiration," *New York Times*, January 28, 1912. According to one newspaper report, more than twenty-five of the drawings "found new owners, among the buyers being painters as wells as collectors and amateurs." See *New-York Tribune*, February 18, 1912.

54 "Weber & Field on Madison Ave.," *American Art News* 10 (February 24, 1912): 2. Also that spring the gallery hosted a large exhibition of works by Mahonri Young, who would later participate in the Armory Show. See, "Works by Mahonri Young," *American Art News* 10 (April 20, 1912): 2.

55 Perlman, *The Lives, Loves, and Art of Arthur B. Davies*, 212.

56 "A New Gallery," *American Art News* 4 (March 3, 1906): 2.

57 "Exhibitions Now On," *American Art News* 7 (December 5, 1908): 6.

58 "Weber at Haas Gallery," *American Art News* 7 (May 1, 1909): 6 and Beth A. Venn, *Middleton Manigault: Visionary Modernist* (NY: Hollis Taggart Galleries for an exhibition organized by the Columbus Museum of Art, 2002), 20-21. See also, "Pictures by Manigault," *American Art News* 9 (April 1, 1911): 2.

59 "Exhibitions Now On," *American Art News* 6 (January 4, 1908): 6.

60 "Steichen at Montross's," *American Art News* 8 (January 22, 1910): 6.

61 "Max Weber, 'The Futurist'," *American Art News* 10 (February 17, 1912): 2.

62 "Another Emotionalist 'Erupts,'" *American Art News* 10 (March 9, 1912): 2.

63 "Obituaries: Louis Katz," *American Art News* 11 (January 11, 1913): 7.

64 "The Carroll Art Galleries" *American Art News* 11 (November 9, 1912): 7.

65 "Watercolors at Carroll Gallery," *American Art News* 11 (December 7, 1912): 4.

66 "Art at Carroll Gallery," *American Art News* 11 (December 21, 1912): 2.

67 For the Chesterwood Studio see "With the Artists," *American Art News* 9 (December 7, 1912): 3. In spring 1907, Robert Vonnoh, Irving R. Wiles, and Childe Hassam, among others, bought four lots on West 57th Street "to erect thereon a co-operative studio building to cost $800,000, and to be called the Renaissance." See, *American Art News* 5 (May 11, 1907): 1. In January 1909 "A New Studio Building" was announced, the "Manhattan" on West 70th Street, "the largest in the city . . .with ten rooms and a studio." See, *American Art News* 7 (January 30, 1909): 8.

68 "News and Notes of the Art World," *New York Times*, January 23, 1910 and "Calendar of Exhibitions," *New-York Tribune*, January 23, 1910, 3.

69 *The Sun*, February 25, 1912, 10 and "Exhibitions Now On," *American Art News* 11 (December 14, 1912): 2.

70 Noun, *Abastenia St. Leger Eberle, Sculptor (1878-1942)*, 12.

71 "Coming Sculpture Exhibit," *American Art News* 6 (March 7, 1908): 3.

72 "Sculpture Show at Arts Club," *American Art News* 10 (May 11, 1912): 2.

73 "Bronzes at Macbeth's," *American Art News* 10 (December 9, 1911): 2 and "Beach's Sculptures at Macbeth's," *American Art News* 11 (December 7, 1912); 4. See also, Guy Pène Du Bois, *The Art of Chester Beach* (NY: The Macbeth Gallery, 1912) in the Chester Beach Artist's Vertical File, National Portrait Gallery/Smithsonian American Art Museum, Washington, D.C.

74 "Small Sculptures at Montross's," *American Art News* 10 (March 2, 1912): 2.

75 "Boston," *American Art News* 8 (February 26, 1910): 2.

76 "Baltimore (MD)," *American Art News* 9 (May 6, 1911): 5.

77 "Artists Organize," *The Greenwich News*, February 16, 1912, Greenwich Art Society Records, 1912-1987, unmicrofilmed, AAA. See also, "Greenwich, Conn.," *American Art News* 10 (March 2, 1912): 9.

78 "Cleveland," *American Art News* 10 (March 2, 1912): 9 and "William Zorach," in *The Figure in American Sculpture: A Question of Modernity* (Los Angeles County Museum of Art in association with University of Washington Press, 1995), 235.

79 "Art at Union League" *American Art News* 9 (April 15, 1911): 5 and "Exhibitions Now On: Insurgents Capture League," *American Art News* 9 (April 22, 1911): 6. See also, Perlman, *The Lives, Loves, and Art of Arthur B. Davies*, 195-97.

80 "Pictures at City Club," *American Art News* 11 (November 2, 1912): 2.

81 "New Club For New York Women," *New York Times*, March 22, 1911. According to this notice, "Albany, March 21.—The Woman's Cosmopolitan Club of New York was incorporated to-day to maintain a club for women engaged in the liberal arts or professions. The Directors include Mary Bosworth of New York, Josephine Hendrick of Simsbury, Conn; Mary A. Hewitt of Bingwood, N.J.; Ethel S. Hoyt of Darien, Conn., and Edith Macy of Scarsborough-on-Hudson."

82 "Women's Cosmopolitan Club," *The Sun*, March 19, 1911, 9.

83 "Gibbs at Cosmopolitan Club," *American Art News* 10 (November 11, 1911): 2.

84 "Davies at Cosmopolitan," *American Art News* 10 (December 23, 1911): 2.

85 "Art at Cosmopolitan," *American Art News* 10 (March 16, 1912): 2.

86 "Prendergast at Cosmopolitan," *American Art News* 10 (April 13, 1912): 2.

87 "Paintings by W. E. Schumacher," *American Art News* 11 (January 25, 1913): 8.

88 "An Art Exhibition Without A Jury System of Awards; The MacDowell Club Has a Plan of Self-Organized Groups of Artists to Give Decisions," *New York Times*, May 14, 1911.

89 "MacDowell Club Displays," *American Art News* 32 (June 17, 1911):

90 "An Art Exhibition Without A Jury System of Awards," *New York Times*, May 14, 1911.

91 "Club Loses Opportunity," *American Art News*, 10 (December 23, 1911): 4, G.P. Goodwin, "Correspondence: A Good Suggestion," *American Art News* 10 (December 30, 1911): 4, "Alexander's Criticisms," *American Art News* 10 (January 6, 1912): 4. The dispute was also recorded in newspapers such as the *Evening Sun* and the *Evening Post*, December 30, 1911.

92 Morton L. Schamberg to Walter Pach, August 23, 1912, Walter Pach Papers, AAA, Gift of Francis M. Naumann, unprocessed and unmicrofilmed.

93 December 11, 1911 notes of the Association of American Painters and Sculptors, Association of American Painters and Sculptors (AAPS) Records: Minutes, 1911-1914, Box 3, Folder 5, #2, AAA.

94 See letters to and from Walt Kuhn and AAPS to various museums and art institutions, in Association of American Painters and Sculptors (AAPS) Records: Exhibition Venues, 1912, Box 3, Folder, 2, #4-32, Armory Show Records, AAA.

95 This change was noted by Cornelia B. Sage, director of the Buffalo Fine Arts Academy, in her response to Kuhn's inquiry regarding "the expense of a foreign exhibition, transportation, insurance, brokerage, etc." See Cornelia B. Sage to Walt Kuhn, March 16, 1912, Association of American Painters and Sculptors (AAPS) Records: Exhibition Venues, 1912, Box 3, Folder, 2, #25, Armory Show Records, AAA. The new plan was reiterated in a letter Kuhn sent to the John Herron Art Institute, dated March 5, 1912, wherein he stated, "At a recent meeting of the Society, extensive changes were made in the program for the ensuing year. All action pertaining to the giving of Exhibitions outside of New York has been postponed until after our first comprehensive show in this city." See Walt Kuhn to Milton Matter, Acting Director, The John Herron Art Institute, March 5, 1912, Association of American Painters and Sculptors (AAPS) Records: Exhibition Venues, 1912, Box 3, Folder, 2, #16, Armory Show Records, AAA.

96 The Association of American Painters and Sculptors, New York, First International Exhibition," Circular invitation, Artists and Lenders Correspondence: Domestic, A-D, 1912-1913, Box 1, Folder 9, #4, Armory Show Records, AAA.

97 Maurice B. Prendergast to Walt Kuhn, March 17, 1913, Artists and Lenders Correspondence: Domestic, K-R, 1912-1913, Box 1, Folder 13, #20, Armory Show Records, AAA.

98 Arthur B. Davies to Mr. Fairbanks, Museum of Fine Arts, Boston, February 5, 1913, Archives, Museum of Fine Arts, Registrar Records, Loans by Museum. I wish to thank Karen E. Quinn, Kristin and Roger Servison Curator of Paintings Art of the Americas, Patrick Murphy, and the Archivist at the MFA, Boston for locating these materials and confirming this loan. See also, Arthur B. Davies to Miss Caroline H. Rimmer, June 20, 1913, Insurers, Packers and Shippers Correspondence: Doll and Richards Inc., 1913, Box 1, Folder 34, #6. According to these letters, the AAPS returned the three drawings by Rimmer lent by his daughter via Doll & Richards. In addition, although signed Walt Kuhn this letter is clearly Walter Pach's handwriting; therefore, Walter Pach to Messrs. Doll & Richards, June 18, 1913, Insurers, Packers and Shippers Correspondence: Doll and Richards Inc., 1913, Box 1, Folder 34, # 5, Armory Show Records, AAA.

99 Arthur B. Davies to Miss Currier, March 13, 1913, Artists and Lenders Correspondence: Domestic, A-D, 1912-1913, Box 1, Folder 9, #29, Armory Show Records, AAA.

100 Doll & Richards to Arthur B. Davies, March 24, 1913, Armory Show Records, Insurers, Packers and Shippers Correspondence: Doll and Richards Inc., 1913, Box 1, Folder 34, #3, Armory Show Records, AAA.

101 Walt Kuhn to Henry G. Keller, December 20, 1912, Artists and Lenders Correspondence: Domestic, Keller, Henry G., 1912-1913, Box 1, Folder, 12, #1, Armory Show Records, AAA.

102 Note to invited artists from the Domestic Exhibition Committee, January 4, 1913, Artists and Lenders Correspondence: Domestic, A-D, 1912-1913, Box 1, Folder 9, #6, Armory Show Records, AAA.

103 "Coming Painters and Sculptor's Show," *American Art News* 11 (February 15, 1913): 2.

104 "Important Notice" by AAPS, January 16, 1913, Domestic Art Committee Records: Record Book, 1913, Box 1, Folder 75, #2, Armory Show Records, AAA.

105 Walt Kuhn to F. William Brown, February 6, 1913, Artists and Lenders Correspondence: Domestic, A-D, 1912-1913, Box 1, Folder 9, #22, Armory Show Records, AAA.

106 Brown, *The Story of the Armory Show*, 1988, 98.

107 Marian Wardle, "Thoroughly Modern: The 'New Woman' Art Students of Robert Henri," in *American Women Modernists: The Legacy of Robert Henri, 1910-1945*, edited by Marian Wardle (New Brunswick, New Jersey and London: Brigham Young University Museum of Art in association with Rutgers University Press, 2005): 1.

108 Brown, *The Story of the Armory Show*, 1988, 88-89.

109 For more on the Stein families see James R. Mellow, *A Charmed Circle: Gertrude Stein and Company* (Boston: Houghton Mifflin Company, 1974) and *The Steins Collect: Matisse, Picasso, and the Parisian Avant-garde*, edited by Janet Bishop, Cécile Debray, and Rebecca Rabinow (New Haven and London: San Francisco Museum of Modern Art in association with Yale University Press, 2011).

110 See, Emily Braun, "Saturday Evenings at the Steins'," in *The Steins Collect: Matisse, Picasso, and the Parisian Avant-garde*, 49-67. See also, H. Nicols B. Clark, "Katharine Nash Rhodes (1885-1965)" and Michele De Angelus, "Katherine S. Dreier (1877-1952)," in William Innes Homer, *Avant-Garde Painting & Sculpture in America, 1910-25* (Wilmington, DE: Delaware Art Museum, 1975), 118. See also, Eleanor Tufts, *American Women Artists, 1830-1930* (Washington, D.C.: National Museum of Women in the Arts, 1987): No. 55. According to the UVA website on the Armory Show, "in the summer of 1912, Robert Henri took several of

his summer school 'students to visit Gertrude Stein in Paris." See, "The Part Played by Women: The Gender of Modernism at the Armory Show," http://xroads.virginia.edu/~museum/armory/gender.html, Accessed August 8, 2012.

[111] Margaret Burke Clunie, "D. P.B.," in *Daniel Putnam Brinley: The Impressionist Years* (Bowdoin College Museum of Art, 1978): unpaginated. See also, *American Art News* 5 (August 17, 1907): 2 and 8 (October 16, 1909): 5.

[112] "Exhibitions—Past and to Come," *Brush and Pencil* 19 (January 1907): 5.

[113] Clunie, "D.P.B.," unpaginated.

[114] "Paris Letter," *American Art News* 6 (February 8, 1908): 5.

[115] "Paris Letter," *American Art News* 7 (December 26, 1908): 5.

[116] "Chicago," *American Art News* 6 (January 18, 1908): 6.

[117] Barbara Ann Boese Wolanin, *The Orchestration of Color: The Paintings of Arthur B. Carles* (NY: Hollis Taggart Galleries, 2000), 35.

[118] "The London Salon: An Experiment in the Way of an Art Show Without the Aid of a Jury," *The Sun*, August 2, 1908, 3.

[119] "Paris Letter," *American Art News* 9 (February 25, 1911): 5.

[120] Pierre Sanchez, *Dictionnaire du Salon d'Automne: Repertoire des Exposants et Listes Des Oeuvres Presentees, 1903-1945*, preface d"Olivier Meslay (Dijon, France: L'Echelle de Jacobs, 2006).

[121] Jerome Myers, *Artist in Manhattan* (New York: American Artists Group, Inc., 1940), Guy Pène du Bois, *Artists Say the Silliest Things* (New York: American Artists Group, Inc., 1940). Art historian Jerome Mellquist also viewed the situation this way, Jerome Mellquist, *The Emergence of an American Art* (New York: Charles Scribner's Sons, 1942).

[122] For more on Pach see Laurette E. McCarthy, *Walter Pach (1883-1958): The Armory Show and the Untold Story of Modern Art in America* (University Park, PA: Penn State Press, 2011).

[123] Walter Pach to Mrs., Pollak, College Art Association, December 11, 1931, Eddy Collection File Folder, Archives, Art Institute of Chicago.

[124] Walter Pach to Paul J. Sachs, October 26, 1939, Paul J. Sachs Papers, Harvard University Archives, Harvard Archives HUG 4764.12 [Miscellaneous Correspondence.] Also quoted in Bennard B. Perlman, *American Artists, Authors, and Collectors*, 347.

[125] Pach had also met and interviewed Renoir on his previous stay in Paris, on June 2, 1908. See Walter Pach Papers, AAA, Reel 4220, fr. 566, June 2, 1908, 43, rue Caulaincourt, chez Renoir, notes from interview. See also Pach to Klauber, June 20, 1908, Alice Klauber Papers, AAA, Reel 583, fr. 572. For the 1911 interview, see Pach's notes and a copy of a letter from Auguste Renoir to Walter Pach, Pach Papers, AAA, Reel 4217, frs. 19-20.

[126] Walter Pach, "Pierre Auguste Renoir," *Scribner's Magazine* 51 (May 1912): 607.

[127] Denis, too, proclaimed this idea of painting in his oft-quoted phrase: "It is well to remember that a picture—before being a battle horse, a nude woman, or some anecdote—is essentially a plane surface covered with colors assembled in a certain order." Maurice Denis, "Definition of Neotraditionism," quoted in *Theories of Modern Art: A Source Book by Artists and Critics*, edited by Herschel B. Chipp (Berkeley and Los Angeles: University of California Press, 1968), 94.

[128] I wish to thank Löic Malle for pointing out this resemblance to me.

[129] Walt Kuhn to Theodore E. Butler, December 21, 1912, Artists and Lenders Correspondence: Europe, Butler, Theodore E., 1912-1913, Box 1, Folder 19, #2, Armory Show Records, AAA.

[130] Cecil Howard to Walter Pach, undated, Artists and Lenders Correspondence: Europe, General, H-N, 1912-1913, Box 1, Folder 25, #4, Armory Show Records, AAA. Howard notes, "Very sorry not to have been in when you called."

[131] Pach recorded the date of 1910 for Bruce's entries 1, 3, and 4 and 1911 for number 2. See European Entry Cards, French, circa 1912, Box 1, Folder 77, #9 and 10, Armory Show Records, AAA. For *La Douleur* See European Entry Cards, French, circa 1912, Box 1, Folder 77, #15, Armory Show Records, AAA.

[132] Morton L. Schamberg to Walter Pach, August 23, 1912, Pach Papers, AAA, Naumann donation. Schamberg seems to have received the invite from Kuhn. See Morton L. Schamberg to Walt Kuhn, January 24, 1913, Artists and Lenders Correspondence: Domestic, S-Y, 1912-1913, Box 1, Folder 16, #1, Armory Show Records, AAA. Schamberg wrote, "In the fall [of 1912] I received a list to be filled out and returned by January first, which I did. But since then I have had no information. Should I have received entry blanks or are they still to come, or has my invitation been reconsidered. I see by your circular that the entry blanks need not be in until February 5th but my reason for writing you for information is that should I be sending any pictures it would be necessary it would be necessary to order frames made in time."

[133] William C. Agee, "Morton Livingston Schamberg," in *The Advent of Modernism*, 157. Pach wrote one of the first essay's on Schamberg after his untimely death in 1918. See Walter Pach, "The Schamberg Exhibition," *The Dial* 66 (17 May 1919): 505-506.

[134] Morton Livingston Schamberg, "Post-Impressionism Exhibit Awaited," *Philadelphia Inquirer*, January 19, 1913, 3, cited in William C. Agee, "Morton Livingston Schamberg," in *The Advent of Modernism*, 157.

[135] Walter Pach, "Cézanne—An Introduction," *Scribner's Magazine* 44 (December 1908): 765-768.

[136] Rick Stewart, "Charles Sheeler," in *The Advent of Modernism*, 161.

[137] Charles Sheeler to Walt Kuhn, February 10, 1913, Artists and Lenders Correspondence: Domestic, S-Y, 1912-1913, Box 1, Folder 16, #6, Armory Show Records, AAA.

[138] Joseph Coburn Smith, *Charles Hovey Pepper* (Portland, ME: The Southworth-Anthoensen Press, 1945), 39-

40 and 46, quoted in Peter Morrin, "E. Ambrose Webster" in *The Advent of Modernism*, 179.

[139] Morrin, "E. Ambrose Webster," *The Advent of Modernism*, 179.

[140] Randy J. Ploog, "The First American Abstractionist: Manierre Dawson and His Sources," in *Manierre Dawson: American Pioneer of Abstract* Art (NY: Hollis Taggart Galleries, 1999), 69.

[141] Appendix 1 *Transcription of Manierre Dawson's Journal, 1908-40*, March 25, 1913, in *Manierre Dawson: American Pioneer of Abstract* Art, essays by Dr. Henry Adams and Dr. Randy Ploog (NY: Hollis Taggart Galleries, 1999), 172.

[142] Dawson's Journal, March 27, 1913, 172.

[143] William H. Gerdts, *Jonas Lie (1880-1940)* (NY: Spanierman Gallery, LLC, 2006), 8 and 19-20.

[144] Gerdts, *Jonas Lie*, 8.

[145] Gerdts, *Jonas Lie*, 22.

[146] Gerdts, *Jonas Lie*, 10.

[147] Gerdts, *Jonas Lie*, 9-10

[148] *Exhibition of Oil Paintings by Jonas Lie*, The Corcoran Gallery of Art, Washington, D.C., January 5-17, 1912, no. 9, Artist's File, National Portrait Gallery/Smithsonian American Art Museum Library, Washington, D.C. Peter H. Falk, *Record of the Carnegie Institute's International Exhibitions 1896-1996* (Madison, CT: Sound View Press, 1998). *Sixteenth Annual Exhibition*, Carnegie Institute, April 25-June 30, 1912.

[149] Clunie, "D.P.B.," unpaginated.

[150] Clunie, "D.P.B.," unpaginated.

[151] Clunie, "D.B.P.," unpaginated.

[152] Lisa Peters, *Allen Tucker: The Force of Emotion—A Post-Impressionist Rediscovered* (NY: Spanierman Gallery, LLC, 2010): 3.

[153] Peters, *Allen Tucker: The Force of Emotion*, 3.

[154] Forbes Watson, "Allen Tucker: A Painter with a Fresh Vision," *International Studio* 52 (March 1914): xix-xi, quoted in Peters, 5. See also James W. Lane, "Vincent in America: Allen Tucker, Whitney memorial to a U.S. Post-Impressionist," *Art News* 38 (December 16, 1939): 13.

[155] "Exhibitions Now On," *American Art News* 11 (December 14, 1912): 2.

[156] Forbes Watson, "Allen Tucker" in *Allen Tucker Memorial Exhibition* (NY: Whitney Museum of American Art, 1940): unpaginated.

[157] "Pictures by Manigault," *American Art News* 9 (April 1, 1911): 2. See Venn, *Middleton Manigault: Visionary Modernist*, 26.

[158] Venn, *Middleton Manigault: Visionary Modernist*, 25.

[159] "The Association of American Painters and Sculptors, New York, First International Exhibition," Circular invitation, Artists and Lenders Correspondence: Domestic, A-D, 1912-1913, Box 1, Folder 9, #4, Armory Show Records, AAA.

[160] Stephanie Andrews McNairy, "Artists' Biographies," in *American Women Modernists*, 234. Others included: Marion H. Beckett, Bessie Brewer, Kate Thompson Cory, Florence Dreyfous, Edith Haworth, Marjorie Organ (Mrs. Robert Henri), Margaret Wendell Huntington, Amy Londoner, Helen J. Niles, Josephine Paddock, Louise Pope, Katharine Nash Rhoades, and Mary Rogers. Little is known about Florence Barkley or Hilda Ward. Ward, apparently, stopped painting altogether in 1918. See, "Hilda Ward," in Reviews and Previews, *Art News* 56 (September 1957): 12.

[161] Wardle, "Thoroughly Modern: The 'New Woman' Art Students of Robert Henri," 4.

[162] Ronald G. Pisano, *One Hundred Years: A Centennial Celebration of the National Association of Women Artists* (Roslyn Harbor, NY: Nassau County Museum of Fine Art, 1988), 11.

[163] National Association of Women Artists, http://thenawa.org, accessed August 6, 2012.

[164] Pisano, *One Hundred Years*, 10.

[165] "Wolfe Art Club Show," *American Art News* 18 (February 10, 1912): 2.

[166] Mariea Caudill Dennison, "The America Girls' Club in Paris: the Propriety and Imprudence of Art Students, 1890-1914," *Woman's Art Journal* 26 (Spring/Summer 2005): 35.

[167] Pisano, *One Hundred Years*, 11.

[168] Dennison, "The America Girls' Club in Paris," 34 and Patricia E. Phagan, "Anne Goldthwaite," in *the Advent of Modernism*, 91.

[169] Dennison, "The American Girls' Club in Paris," 34 and 37 note 44.

[170] Eleanor Tufts, *American Women Artists, 1830-1930* (Washington, D.C.: National Museum of Women in the Arts, 1987): No. 55.

[171] H. Nichols B. Clark, "Katharine Nash Rhoades," in William Innes Homer, *Avant-Garde Painting & Sculpture in America, 1910-25* (Wilmington, DE: Delaware Art Museum, 1975), 118.

[172] Brown, *The Story of the Armory Show*, 1988, 246 and Clark, "Katharine Nash Rhoades," 118.

[173] William H. Gerdts, "The American Fauves: 1907-1918," in *The Color of Modernism: The American Fauves* (NY: Hollis Taggart Galleries, 1997), 31.

[174] Tufts, *American Women Artists, 1830-1930*, no. 26 and John Angeline, "Chronicles of Modernism: Dreier the painter," *Art in America* 94 (June/July 2006): 102.

[175] For the first detailed study of American sculpture at the Armory Show see Roberta K. Tarbell, "The Impact of the Armory Show on American Sculpture," *Archives of American Art Journal* 18 (1978): 2-11. In a letter to Grace Mott Johnson, his wife, Dasburg explained, "'From morn till noon from noon till dewy eve he fell.' And my Lucifer looks it. I did not start out to model a bad angel nor a convict, but the title will give those who don't know what it is about something to ease their minds with. They will think it is the key to all that

is strange in my angles face." Andrew Dasburg to Grace Mott Johnson, October 14, 1912, Andrew Dasburg and Grace Mott Johnson Papers, AAA. The work was "Carved from a block of plaster in sculptor Arthur Lee's studio in New York." See Tarbell, "The Impact of the Armory Show on American Sculpture," 11, note 15. *Lucifer* was quite expressionist, its sharp planes and emphasis on structure creating exaggerated forms, much like Pablo Picasso's *Head of a Woman* in the Armory Show.

176 Roberta K. Tarbell and Ilene Susan Fort, "Armory Show of 1913," in *Rodin and America*, 129.

177 Ilene Susan Fort, "The Cult of Rodin and the Birth of Modernism in America," in *The Figure in American Sculpture: A Question of Modernity* (Los Angeles County Museum of Art in association with University of Washington Press, 1995). In same volume see, "George Grey Barnard," 176, "Chester Beach," 178, "Jo Davidson, " 188, "Arthur Putnam," 219, "Bessie Potter Vonnoh, " 228 and "Enid Yandell," 234.

178 Fort, "The Cult of Rodin," 30.

179 Fort, "The Cult of Rodin," 23.

180 Fort, "Introduction," in *The Figure in American Sculpture*, 20.

181 Fort, "Cult of Rodin," 29.

182 Tarbell and Fort, "Armory Show of 1913," in *Rodin and America*, 133. See also, Lorado Taft, quoted in Tarbell and Fort, "Armory Show of 1913," in *Rodin and America*, 133.

183 Fort, "Cult of Rodin," 46 and Mary L. Alexander, "Sculpture to Be Shown Here," in unidentified Cincinnati newspaper clipping, 1910, in Chester Beach Scrapbook, private collection and Chester Beach papers, 1846-1999, bulk circa 1900-1999, AAA, Reel N727, fr. 293, quoted in Fort, "Cult of Rodin," 46.

184 Chester Beach papers, 1846-1999, bulk circa 1900-1999, AAA. See also "Beach's Sculptures at Macbeth's," *American Art News* 11 (December 7, 1912); 4 and Guy Pène Du Bois, *The Art of Chester Beach* (NY: The Macbeth Gallery, 1912) in the Chester Beach Artist's Vertical File, National Portrait Gallery/Smithsonian American Art Museum, Washington, D.C.

185 Quoted in, Tarbell and Fort, "Armory Show of 1913," in *Rodin and America*, 131.

186 "Sculptures and Drawings by Jo Davidson," *American Art News* 11 (January 25, 1913): 8. See also "Sculptures and Drawings by Jo Davidson," *New York Times*, February 2, 1913.

187 Sanchez, *Dictionnaire du Salon d'Automne*, vol. I, A-E, 389.

188 Charlotte Streifer Rubinstein, *American Women Sculptors: A History of Women Working in Three Dimensions* (Boston, MA: G.K. Hall & Co., 1990), 238.

189 I have recently identified this photograph of *The White Slave* as one of the presumed long-lost, original images taken by Hagelstein Brothers, the official photographers for the Armory Show. This photograph is in the collection of the Prints and Photographs Division, Library of Congress, Washington, D.C.

190 "Abastenia St. Leger Eberle," in *The Figure in American Sculpture*, 192.

191 Daniel Robbins, "Statues to Sculpture: 1890-1930," in *200 Years of American Sculpture* (NY: Whitney Museum of American Art, 1976), quoted in Fort, *The Figure in American Sculpture*, 11.

192 Susan P. Casteras "Abastenia St. Leger Eberle's *White Slave*," *Woman's Art Journal* 7 (Spring-Summer 1986): 32-36.

193 Rubinstein, *American Women Sculptors*, 211.

194 Casteras, "Abastenia St. Leger Eberle's *White Slave*," 35.

195 "Ethel Myers," in *The Figure in American Sculpture*, 214.

196 "Notes of General Interest: At the Folsom Galleries," *The Craftsman* (March 1, 1913): 23.

197 We wish to thank Barry and Helene Downes for providing this information.

198 Rubinstein, *American Women Sculptors* 219. See also, Paula Ann Snorf, "The Sculpture of Ethel Myers," 12-13, typed manuscript, dated May 22, 1967, Ethel Myers Papers, 1913-1960, AAA, Reel N68-6, frame number undecipherable.

199 Ethel Myers, "Leaves from the Diary of Ethel Myers, no dates, 23 pp." Ethel Myer Papers, 1913-1960, AAA, Reel N68-6, frame 42.

200 Minutes of Executive Committee, December 20, 1912, MacRae Diary, AAA. See chronology.

201 Walt Kuhn to Arthur Young, February 7, 1913, Artists and Lenders Correspondence: Domestic, S-Y, 1912-1913, Box 1, Folder 16, #17, Armory Show Records, AAA.

202 Kuhn to Young, February 10, 1913, Artists and Lenders Correspondence: Domestic, S-Y, 1912-1913, Box 1, Folder 16, #18, Armory Show Records, AAA.

203 This is an incomplete list, but other works shown before the Armory include: Robert I. Aitken's small bronze *The Tired Mercury*, which had actually been "partially sold" when The Gorham Company lent it to the Armory Show. See W. Frank Pudy, The Gorham Company, to the AAPS, March 17, 1913, Artists and Lenders Correspondence: Domestic, E-J, 1912-1913, Box 1 Folder 10, #18, Armory Show Records, AAA. In addition, *The Dregs of Love* was shown at the NAD and PAFA in 1907, *Tired Mercury* NAD 1908, *George Bellows* NAD 1910-W, *A creature of God Until now Unknown*, NAD-W 1910. James E. Fraser's *Grief*, NAD 1910-W, Montross Gallery in 1912; Bolton Coit Brown's *Green Fire*, Louis Katz Galleries in the spring of 1912, see, "Bolton Brown at Katz's," *American Art News* 10 (March 30, 1912): 2; Homer Boss's *Young Woman in Blue and Gold*, PAFA 1910 and "Circuit Exhibition of Contemporary Art of the National Arts Club," February 11- March 10, 1911, no. 8; Edith Burroughs's *Portrait of John Bigelow*, PAFA 1911; G. Ruger Donoho, *A Garden*, Carnegie Institute 1911 and PAFA 1912, a prize winner; Childe Hassam's *The Spanish Stairs*, AIC 1897 and *The Spanish Steps* PAFA, 1898 ; Edward Rook, *Grey Sea, Monhegan* AIC 1911 and PAFA 1912; Victor Salvatore, *Portrait of Susanna Richardson*, AIC and PAFA 1911; J. Alden Weir, *Willimantic Factory Village*, Carnegie 1911 and *The Orchid*, PAFA 1900; Mahonri Young, *Carrying Coal*, PAFA 1911; Nessa Cohen, *Sunrise*, NAD 1912 -W and AIC 1912; Grace Mott Johnson, *Greyhound Pup 1 and 2*, NAD and AIC 1912; Charles Hovey Pepper, *Irene*, AIC

1912; Charles H. Davis, *L'Allegro*, Carnegie Institute 1912; Van Dearing Perrine, *Ice Floes*, Carnegie Institute 1907, *The Ice Flows*, Carnegie Institute 1912; Nicholas Bickford, *Pelican* and *Strutting Turkey*, NAD 1905.

[204] *Paintings by Jerome Myers*, January 6-18, 1908, Macbeth Gallery, Miscellaneous Art Exhibition Catalog Collection, 1813-1953, Series 5: Art Exhibition Catalogs: M-O, Box 3, Reel 4859. "MacDowell Display," *American Art News* 10 (November 4, 1911): 2.

[205] First Annual Exhibition, Greenwich Society of Artists, Bruce Art Museum, September 28-October 26, 1912, Greenwich Art Society Records, AAA, unmicrofilmed.

[206] "Eight Group at MacDowell," *American Art News* 11 (January 11, 1913): 2. See also, Walt Kuhn to Hy J. Glintenkamp, c/o MacDowell Club, January 17, 1913, Artists and Lenders Correspondence: Domestic, E-J, 1912-1913, Box 1 Folder 10, #16, Armory Show Records, AAA and "'Post-Impressionism' at Folsom's," *American Art News* 11 (January 18, 1913): 2.

[207] Alfred Stieglitz to Walt Kuhn, February 4 and 26, 1913, Artists and Lenders Correspondence,: Domestic, Stieglitz, Alfred, 1912-1913, Box 1, Folder 14, #1, 2, 5 and 6, Armory Show Records, AAA. "Marin Show at Photo-Secession Gallery," *American Art News* 11 (January 25, 1913): 8. The notice states, "in the 15 water-colors 5 are different aspects of the Woolworth Building." *Broadway, St. Paul's Church (St. Paul's Lower Manhattan)* was also shown.

[208] Sanchez, *Dictionnaire du Salon d'Automne*, vol. III, 1397 and 1240, respectively.

[209] Andrew Martinez, "A Mixed Reception for Modernism: The 1913 Armory Show at The Art Institute of Chicago," *Museum Studies, The Art Institute of Chicago* 19 (1993): 37.

[210] See note 100 and Arthur B. Davies to Messrs. Doll & Richards, March 22, 1913, Insurers, Packers and Shippers Correspondence: Doll and Richards, Inc., 1913, Box 1, Folder 34, # 2, Armory Show Records, AAA.

[211] Elmer MacRae to Walt Kuhn, Hotel Touraine, Boston, Mass, April 28, 1913, Artists and Lenders Correspondence: Domestic, K-R, 1912-1913, Box 1, Folder 13, #1, Armory Show Records, AAA.

[212] "Sculptures and Drawings by Jo Davidson," *American Art News* 11 (January 25, 1913): 8.

[213] Notes by Pach on letter from Dave H. Morris to Walt Kuhn, March 5, 1913, Sales Correspondence: General, L-P, 1913, Box 1, Folder 71, #13, Armory Show Records, AAA.

[214] Art Young to Walt Kuhn, February 25, 1913, Sales Correspondence: General, Q-Z, 1913, Box 1, Folder 73, #31, Armory Show Records, AAA and Charles Hovey Pepper to Walt Kuhn, undated, Artists and Lenders Correspondence: Domestic, K-R, 1912-1913, Box 1, Folder 13, #16, Armory Show Records, AAA. Pepper writes "Glad to have it [his watercolor *Sunny Windows*] in Chicago," so the letter must be dated toward the middle of March 1913.

[215] I would like to thank Gail Stavitsky, who rediscovered this article, for sharing this information with me.

[216] James William Pattison, "Art in an Unknown Tongue," *Fine Arts Journal* 28 (May 1913): 297 and 306. Also reproduced on page 305 is Childe Hassam's *Nude Woman with Mirror*, a photograph of which is in the Peter Juley Collection of the AAA.

[217] Casteras, "Abastenia St. Leger Eberle's *White Slave*," 33. We would like to thank Heather Smith Coyle, curator at the Delaware Art Museum, for sharing her rediscovery of Robert Henri's drawing #838 in their archives.

[218] Judith Zilczer, "The Dissemination of Post-Impressionism in North America: 1905-1918," in *The Advent of Modernism*, 31.

COLLECTORS OF AMERICAN ART FROM THE ARMORY SHOW

by Laurette E. McCarthy

ACCOUNTS OF EXACTLY HOW MANY WORKS OF ART SOLD during the entire run of the Armory Show and just afterwards differ; however, over 250 paintings, prints, and sculptures were sold and at least 50 of those sales, or close to one-fifth, were works by American artists.[1] Almost all of these transactions took place in New York as little American art traveled to the Art Institute of Chicago and no American works were sent to the Copley Society in Boston. The number of sales of American art in just over three weeks should be viewed as a great success for the Americans, yet the majority of the scholarship has, unfortunately, concentrated on the European art and its purchasers, including major collectors such as John Quinn, Arthur Jerome Eddy, Lillie Bliss, Walter C. Arensberg, Albert E. Gallatin, and Agnes Ernst Meyer.[2] Little research has focused on the American art bought by Quinn, Eddy, and Meyer and even less attention has been paid to the seemingly unfamiliar women who purchased American art, such as Mrs. James Sibley Watson, Mrs. Marshall Orme Wilson, and Mary Livingston Willard. These and other female buyers, however, were scions of some of the oldest, wealthiest, and most powerful families in the United States. Several of those who bought American art were involved with the law and politics, many had business interests in railroads, steel, and other industries, and a few were artists themselves. Some had already begun collecting American art prior to the Armory Show and quite a few were personal friends of some of the American painters and sculptors. Like the American artists in the Armory Show, the patrons of American art were also very closely interconnected through professional, political, economic, and social spheres, and several were related through familial ties.

Among the collectors of the American art at the Armory Show who were attorneys or had relatives in the legal profession were Quinn, Eddy, Dave H. Morris, Amos Pinchot, Edward Wales Root (son of Elihu Root), Walter Clyde Jones, Charles F. Williams, and Mrs. Samuel Untermyer.[3] Many of these individuals were undoubtedly familiar with one another socially as well. A great deal has been written about John Quinn who, as good friends with Arthur B. Davies and Walt Kuhn and as legal counsel for the AAPS, was intimately involved with the exhibition and its successful outcome.[4] Although the vast majority of works bought by Quinn were European and while these acquisitions established him as a prominent collector of European modernism, he also purchased American art from the Armory, including two paintings by Kuhn, *Morning* (see cat. 72, p. 35) and *Girl with Red Cap*.[5] He also acquired two watercolors by Edith Dimock but noted "I am not especially crazy about the two Dimock things. I think I can get some more amusing ones of her's at some other time."[6] There is conflicting information about exactly which paintings by Dimock were purchased by Quinn and these and other contradictions about works in the Armory Show have caused much confusion in the scholarship on this topic.[7]

Another New York lawyer who knew artists involved with the exhibition was Amos Richards Eno Pinchot. A founder of the Civil Liberties Union and a staunch supporter of labor, Pinchot was deeply involved with government and politics, like many attorneys of his time. He briefly worked in Washington, D.C., in 1905 as a lobbyist for Theodore Roosevelt and later became part of Roosevelt's inner circle during the latter's 1912 campaign. Pinchot's father and siblings were leaders in the conservation movement in the United States and probably knew fellow Armory Show patron George Dupont Pratt. Like most men of his economic class and social status, Pinchot was engaged in numerous cultural, social, and philanthropic activities. A music enthusiast, he served as a trustee of the New York Philharmonic and was a member of the University and Players Clubs as well as the Racquet and Tennis Club in Manhattan.[8] In 1911, Pinchot helped fund and support the radical journal *The Masses* and became friends with the artists who worked on this periodical, including Armory Show participants John Sloan, Art Young, and Boardman Robinson.[9] Though well known as a collector of paintings and fine furniture, Pinchot asked the AAPS, "Will you be kind enough not to publish my name in connection with this sale?" when he purchased Robert Henri's painting *The Red Top* at the exhibition in New York.[10] Obviously, he did not wish to draw any attention to his acquisition.

Dave H. Morris, a wealthy New York lawyer who had business affiliations with railroads, hotels, and thoroughbred racehorses, was also the husband of Alice Vanderbilt Shepard, granddaughter of William Henry Vanderbilt.[11] The Morris family, which hailed from the south, owned Morris Park Racetrack in the Bronx, a horse and automobile racecourse, and Dave's father was a founder of the New York Jockey Club. At his wife's urgings and through her family's connections, Morris became involved in politics and was appointed ambassador to Belgium by Franklin D. Roosevelt in the 1930s.[12] Morris wrote a letter to the AAPS on March 5, saying that a "client" of his wanted the prices of all the paintings by Edward Adam Kramer and Karl Anderson.[13] Ten days later he bought two works by Kramer, *Meditation* and *Rock Encompassed*.[14] These paintings would probably have graced the walls of one of the Morris's many homes such as the mansion at 19 East 70th Street in New York, which was built in 1909 and served as the home of Knoedler Gallery for many years, or their summer place in Bar Harbor, Maine, the favored retreat of many of the Vanderbilt clan.[15]

The two Chicago attorneys who bought American works at the Armory Show, Arthur Jerome Eddy and Walter Clyde Jones, probably knew one another. After Quinn and Bliss, Eddy made the most acquisitions from the exhibition, purchasing the majority of pieces from the New York venue. While most of the paintings and prints that he bought were by Europeans, he also acquired four paintings by American artists: Leon Kroll's *Terminal Yards* (fig. 6, p. 31), E. Middleton Manigault's *The Clown* (1912, Columbus Museum of Art, OH), and two of William N. Taylor's decorative panels referred to as *Spring*, one of which is illustrated in a 1913 periodical with the title *Nude Women in a Meadow*.[16] Eddy was emphatic that the American paintings he purchased be sent to the Art Institute of Chicago venue of the exhibition. He wrote Davies, "I have told Mr. French of the Art Institute that all the pictures I purchased would come on to Chicago, and that includes the painting by Kroll; two by Taylor and one by Manigault, all Americans. I particularly desire that these pictures be exhibited with the foreign pictures I purchased, because taken all together they illustrate my attitude in art, which is exceedingly catholic. While if the foreign pictures alone were exhibited, it would naturally give rise to the inference that I had lost interest in the strong and virile American pictures…. It is needless to say that I also have in mind the fact that the exhibition of those American pictures will be of benefit to the artists who painted them."[17] These four works did indeed go to Chicago and were displayed in the American section of the exhibition (fig. 11, p. 41). Eddy began collecting American art around the time of the 1893 World's Columbian Exposition in Chicago and soon thereafter acquired works by James Abbott

McNeill Whistler, Winslow Homer, and Gifford Beal, among others. After the Armory Show, Eddy embarked on a collecting frenzy, buying more European modernists, especially German and Russian expressionists like Wassily Kandinsky, but also paintings by American artists such as Kroll, Rockwell Kent, Charles Demuth, Man Ray, Manierre Dawson, Preston Dickinson, and Albert Bloch.[18]

A graduate of the Chicago College of Law and well-known senior member of the firm of Jones, Addington, Ames & Seibold, Walter Clyde Jones also served as state senator from the fifth district of Illinois from 1906 to 1914 and was nominated as the Progressive Republican candidate for governor of Illinois in 1911. Jones was a leader in the movement for civil service, election, and legislative procedure reform as well as the author "of the ten hour day law for women."[19] He was also a close friend and ally of liberal Wisconsin Senator Robert La Follette. [20] Since Jones's law firm had offices in Manhattan, it is likely that he, along with Eddy, knew some of the New York lawyers, especially Morris and Pinchot, who were also involved in politics.[21] At the Chicago venue of the Armory Show, Jones acquired Kate Thompson Cory's painting *Arizona Desert*.[22] Cory was from a politically active Waukegan, Illinois, family that had personal ties to Abraham Lincoln and whose home was a stop on the Underground Railroad. In addition, Cory's father, James, was a prominent newspaper editor of the *Waukegan Gazette*. Jones might have been familiar with the Cory family because of their political activities.[23]

Edward Wales Root was a major American modernist collector with ties to the law and politics. He was the youngest son of Elihu Root, renowned attorney and Secretary of State under Theodore Roosevelt, and was surely acquainted with the aforementioned Manhattan, and possibly Chicago, lawyers. Soon after graduating from Hamilton College in 1905, Edward Root went to work as a reporter for *The New York Evening Sun*, where art critic Frederick James Gregg and journalist Charles Fitzgerald argued "violently about 'art'—and contemporary art at that—as if it were a vital part of life. As if it were something you got mad about like politics and finance and law."[24] Root was fascinated by these heated discussions and quickly became part of the New York circle of artists and writers who frequented Mouquin's restaurant. He also began supporting young artists whose lives, Root found, "were poverty-stricken and wretched." When Gregg mentioned that Ernest Lawson was in need of funds, Root went to Kuhn's studio and bought one of Lawson's small paintings, his first purchase of contemporary American art.[25] To the Armory Show, Root lent drawings by George Luks, *Ten Studies in the Bronx Zoo* (1904, Addison Gallery of American Art, Phillips Academy, Andover, MA). During the first week of the Armory Show, he bought Maurice B. Prendergast's *Landscape with Figures* (fig. 15, 1913, Munson-Williams-Proctor Institute, Utica, NY).[26] "I was excited by the fauve Matisses and by Duchamp but I felt it was my business to buy the Prendergast," he once told biographer Aline B. Saarinen.[27] His acquisition of Prendergast's painting might also have been influenced by a more personal reason as both Root and the artist were deaf. Regardless of the motive, the feeling that it was his "business" to purchase American art such as *Landscape with Figures* compelled and propelled Root to amass one of the most significant collections of modern American art in the country. In 1953, a portion of Root's remarkable collection was shown at the Metropolitan Museum of Art. Four years later, he bequeathed 277 works by 80 American artists that ranged in date from 1902 to 1953 to the Munson-Williams-Proctor-Institute (MWPI). In 1961-2 an exhibition of the *Edward Wales Root Bequest* was held at the MWPI and the following year the museum hosted the 50th anniversary exhibition of the famed 1913 Armory Show.

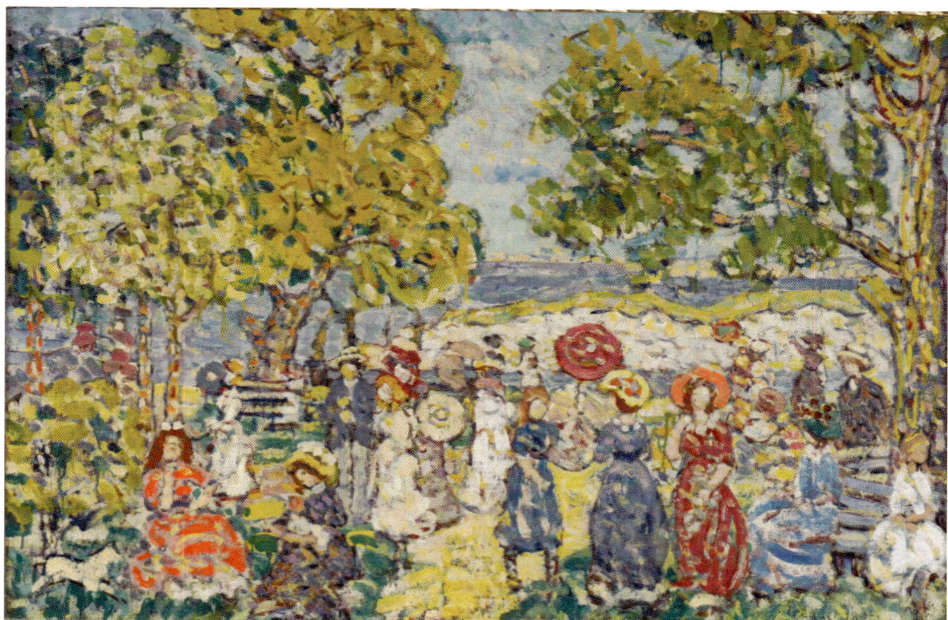

Fig. 15
Maurice Prendergast,
Landscape with Figures, ca.
1912, oil on canvas,
Munson-Williams-
Proctor Arts Institute,
Museum of Art, Utica, NY,
57.212

Another newspaperman who was friends with several of the American artists involved with the Armory Show and who bought a painting from the exhibition was Charles M. Lincoln. "A descendant of Governor Bradford of Plymouth Colony," Lincoln "was a member of the Sons of the American Revolution and the Society of Mayflower Descendants."[28] He began his newspaper career as a cub reporter for *The New Haven Palladium* then took a job with *The Philadelphia Press* in 1891 and subsequently met John Sloan, George Luks, Williams Glackens, and Everett Shinn, who were illustrators for the paper. At the young age of 28, Lincoln was appointed managing editor of the paper and eventually became the managing editor of *The New York Herald* and *The New York World*. From 1926 until his retirement in 1943, Lincoln served as the foreign editor of *The New York Times*.[29] It is very likely that Lincoln knew Lawson before he bought the artist's painting *Upper Manhattan* (now called *Harlem River, Winter*, 1910, Chrysler Museum, Norfolk, Virginia) (see cat. 73, p. 155) at the Armory Show.[30]

Newspaperwoman Agnes Ernst Meyer, who bought at least one work from the exhibition, was an early and strong supporter of American modernism.[31] In April 1908, she became acquainted with Alfred Stieglitz and Edward Steichen when she interviewed the former as part of her job as a reporter for the *New York Sun*, and her interest in modern and American art was ignited. That summer she traveled to Europe to study at the Sorbonne, renewed her friendship with Steichen, and was introduced to the Stein families at their evening salons. During this time she undoubtedly came to know other American artists living in Paris who were part of this circle and who would participate in the Armory Show, such as Alfred Maurer, John Marin, and Arthur B. Carles. Shortly after she returned to New York, she married Eugene Meyer, Jr., owner of *The Washington Post*, and the two devoted much time, money, and energy to supporting the avant-garde art movement in New York. She was among the earliest patrons of Steichen, Marin, and Max Weber and collected European modernism as well—including works by Cézanne and Rodin. Most of her early acquisitions were made at or through Stieglitz and 291. On the last day of the Armory Show in New York, Meyer sent a telegram to Pach, buying a watercolor of a western landscape by Francis McComas.[32] After the exhibition closed, she acquired several of Marin's Woolworth series watercolors that had been in the artist's February 1911 solo show at 291 and also in the Armory Show. She also purchased *In the Tyrol* and *Lake and Mountain, Tyrol* when they were returned to Stieglitz after the exhibition.[33] Subsequently, Meyer donated these works to the National Gallery of Art in Washington, D.C.

Several of the women who bought works from the Armory Show were wives and daughters of the some of the oldest, wealthiest, and most powerful families in the United States, and while much has been written about the role of women in the patronage of art at the turn of the century in the United States, little has been written about some of these women.[34] Mrs. James Sibley Watson, née Emily Sibley, of Rochester, New York, was the daughter of Hiram Sibley, founder of Western Union Telegraph Company and an art collector and philanthropist. Her first husband, Isaac S. Averell, was related to the Averells of Ogdensburg, New York, most of whom were bankers and railroad men. When this marriage ended in divorce, Emily wed James Sibley Watson, who was the son of Don Alonzo Watson, a former business partner of her father.[35] Emily and James Sibley Watson, Sr., were among Rochester's social elite and "were said to have one of the finest private collections of art in the country."[36] She founded the Memorial Art Gallery in Rochester, New York, in memory of her late son James George Averell, nephew of Mrs. Edward H. Harriman (née Mary Williamson Averell). Among the initial donations to the museum were works by contemporary American artists including Willard Metcalf and Jonas Lie.[37] These paintings were part of the institution's inaugural exhibition, held in October 1913, and helped form the basis of the museum's outstanding collection of American Art.[38] Several months before the Memorial Art Gallery opened, Kramer's pastel *The Evangelist* was sold to Mrs. Watson, though it is unclear whether she bought the work in person at the Armory Show, or acquired the work through the agency of George Hurdle, president of the Rochester Art Club and first director of the Memorial Art Gallery.[39]

Related by marriage to Mrs. Watson was Mrs. Charles Cary Rumsey, née Mary Harriman, daughter of railroad magnate Edward E. Harriman and Mary Williamson Averell. Rumsey's mother was an avid collector of traditional American art with Arden, the family home in Ramapo Hills near Tuxedo, New York, full of paintings, sculptures, textiles, and furnishings, including bronze andirons, wooden gargoyles, and marble reliefs by Charles Cary Rumsey.[40] Following in her mother's footsteps, Mary Rumsey also collected American art but she preferred more contemporary works. From the Armory Show she bought Howard Coluzzi's *Mahabarata*, another uncatalogued work.[41] An admirer of Davies, Rumsey had five of his paintings in her collection which, by 1917, also included works by Armory Show artists James E. Fraser, Manigault, John Marin, Victor Salvatore, Whistler, Charles H. White, Eugene Higgins, Jerome Myers, and Robert Chanler. She also collected paintings by Demuth and Thomas Dewing and sculptural pieces by Hunt Diederich.[42] Along with other family members, she helped establish the Colony Club in New York in 1907. Among the first year's membership were fellow Armory Show collectors: Mrs. Marshall Orme Wilson, Mary Livingston Willard, and Annie B. Jennings, as well as the wives of Amos Pinchot and Dave H. Morris.[43] The first social club exclusively for women in Manhattan, it still exists today.[44] The Colony Club held several exhibitions of American art in the years prior to the Armory Show and Rumsey and other collectors were probably involved with these displays.

While the Harrimans were certainly among America's wealthiest families in the late 19th and early 20th centuries, the Astors were at the apex of the social and financial elite, and one member of this prestigious family, Mrs. Marshall Orme Wilson, née Caroline "Carrie" Astor, youngest daughter of Mr. and Mrs. William Astor, purchased a painting at the Armory Show. Carrie's husband was the eldest son of Richard T. Wilson, head of a Wall Street banking firm who began accumulating his fortune during the Civil War, working with the Commissariat Department of the Southern Confederacy. The elder Wilson's business skills enabled him to become "English agent of the entire Southern cotton crop," and he parlayed this opportunity into growing his wealth through the cotton industry and Southern railways after the Civil War.[45] In 1884, after he graduated from Columbia University, Marshall Orme Wilson married

Carrie Astor in a lavish wedding that garnered considerable national press.[46] A few years later, his youngest sister, Grace, married Cornelius Vanderbilt III, thus firmly intertwining two of the most powerful families in the United States.[47] Carrie Wilson bought Morton L. Schamberg's painting *Landscape* at the Armory Show.[48] It is possible that the landscape she purchased was similar in style to one reproduced on the verso of a postcard that Schamberg sent to Walter Pach in August 1912 (cat. 83, p. 157).

A blue-blooded Daughter of the American Revolution (DAR), Mary Livingston Willard was another member of America's upper class who bought American art at the Armory Show.[49] She was the great-granddaughter of Revolutionary war surgeon Elias Willard and in 1894, at the age of 21, she inherited substantial wealth from a cousin related to the Vanderbilt family, and thereby became financially independent.[50] Like many of her social standing, Willard lived in various houses in Manhattan, had summer homes in Maine and elsewhere, and traveled regularly to Europe—all of these activities being reported in the society columns of the *New York Times*. Willard had a keen interest in art and may have attended the Art Students League of New York. She had a collection of American and European art that included paintings and prints by Claude Monet, Mary Cassatt, and Odilon Redon.[51] She bought three American works at the Armory Show: J. Alden Twachtman's *Coronation Week, Madrid*, Morgan Russell's *Capucines*, and Robert Henri's drawing #839, *Nude (Drawing)*.[52]

Another purchaser at the exhibition, Mrs. Barend van Gerbig, née Edith Olcott, who hailed from one of the first families of Connecticut, was also a member of the DAR. Her relative, Thomas Olcott, emigrated from England in 1630 and was one of the original settlers of the city of Hartford and the colony of Connecticut.[53] Frederic P. Olcott, her father, was a prominent New York banker and politician. As President of the Central Trust Company of New York, Mr. Olcott helped reorganize many of the country's railroads and probably knew the Averells, Harrimans, and Morrises.[54] In 1900, Edith married musician and Amsterdam native Barend van Gerbig.[55] The couple had homes in New York and New Canaan, Connecticut, and they were generous supporters of educational, charitable, and political organizations.[56] One of Mrs. van Gerbig's primary passions was collecting glass, and she left her 3,000-object collection to the Wadsworth Athenaeum in Hartford, Connecticut, in 1957.[57] From the Armory Show, she purchased Arthur Freund's painting *The Pig* (Property of Ginger H. and H. Richard Dietrich III).[58]

Mrs. Nicholas M. Pond, née Nanine Woodward Lawrence, served as regent of the Freelove Baldwin Stow Chapter of the DAR and was an officer of the Milford Historical Society in Connecticut.[59] A descendant of Revolutionary soldier Charles Pond, Nanine married a distant relative, Nicholas Misplee Pond of Milford, who was president of the Baldwin Mat Manufacturing Company.[60] The Ponds resided in both Manhattan, where Mr. Pond was a member of the New York Athletic Club and the West Side Club, and in Milford.[61] Mentioned in the society pages alongside the Astors, Vanderbilts, and Wilsons, Mrs. Pond was involved with several schools and hospitals devoted to physically challenged children.[62] She purchased Van Dearing Perrine's painting *When the Wind Blows* at the Armory Show, but other information about her interest in art is unknown.[63]

Arguably the most famous of the Connecticut women to buy an American painting from the exhibition was Annie Burr Jennings, daughter of Oliver Burr Jennings, who made his fortune through the Standard Oil Company. She was an art lover, philanthropist, social activist, and the "First Lady" of Fairfield, Connecticut, where she lived from 1909 to her death in 1939 at her palatial home, Sunnieholme, on the Long Island Sound.[64] A graduate of the prestigious Miss Porter's School in Farmington, Connecticut, Jennings was a member of the Connecticut Society of Colonial Dames and a vice-regent for the state of Connecticut for the Mount Vernon Ladies' Association. She was "widely known for her philanthropies and for her keen interest in public affairs" and was heavily involved in politics and social reform activities.[65] She also had an art collection, mainly 19th-century works, and added to it with her purchase of Elmer MacRae's painting *New York Yacht Club Fleet at Newport* at the Armory Show.[66]

A fellow Standard Oil heir was George Dupont Pratt whose father, Charles, was an officer and director of the company and a founder of the Pratt Institute in Brooklyn. The young Pratt's business activities included work for the Long Island Rail Road, the Chelsea Fiber Mills, and the financial firm of Charles Pratt & Company. A patron of the arts, founder of the Society of Medalists, and a major collector, Pratt donated numerous works to the Metropolitan Museum of Art, where he served as a trustee for many years.[67] The natural world and its wonders, however, were his true passions. He was an avid conservationist and deeply involved with the Boy Scouts of America, serving as treasurer from the organization's inception in 1910 until 1934. He was appointed conservation commissioner of the state of New York from 1915 to 1921, president of the American Forestry Association from 1924 to 1934, and was a trustee of the American Museum of Natural History.[68] It is highly likely that he was acquainted with Amos Pinchot's family, who were also very active in the conservation movement in the United States. At the Armory Show, Pratt purchased Theodore Robinson's painting *Two in a Boat* (1891, The Phillip Collection, Washington, D.C.), the subject of which, two figures in a canoe, surely would have appealed to this outdoorsman.[69]

Another American painting with a boating theme that sold at the show was Edward Hopper's *Sailing* (cat. 19, p. 132), his first sale, to Thomas F. Vietor.[70] The son of George F. Vietor, founder of the wholesale dry goods and textile firm Frederick Vietor and Achelis, Thomas worked for the family business and was also involved in banking.[71] He married Elizabeth Bacon Allen, daughter of Oliver Allen, a prominent manufacturer from the Rochester and Buffalo, New York, areas.[72] Unlike other wealthy Americans, who summered in Newport, Rhode Island, or on Long Island, the Vietor and Achelis families had seasonal "cottages" on the New Jersey Shore and were founders of the Rumson Country Club in 1908.[73] Thomas Vietor's interest in art may have been influenced by the Achelises', who were avid collectors. The Fritz Achelis Memorial Collection of Old Master prints at Yale University was begun in 1925 and formally established this institution's Print Room.[74] The younger Vietor's taste, however, was for more contemporary art, and in addition to his purchase of the Hopper painting he bought John Mowbray-Clarke's plaster *The Bloomers*, one of only three American sculptures sold at the exhibition.[75]

A few of the collectors at the Armory Show had connections with the textile industry, including Vietor, Wilson, and Pratt, and also James Temple Gwathmey.[76] Gwathmey hailed from a prominent clan "of old Virginia stock, the first American members of the family coming to Virginia from Wales in Colonial times."[77] Their vast wealth stemmed from the southern cotton business. His father was a well-known broker on Wall Street and Gwathmey & Company were members of the New York Cotton Exchange, where James served on the Board of Governors and as president.[78] In 1906, Gwathmey headed a syndicate that assumed controlling interest in the Mutual Alliance Company after William Rockefeller, Cornelius Vanderbilt, and other members of the Board of Directors retired; clearly these men were all business associates.[79] James and Archibald, his brother, also owned steeplechase and thoroughbred horses and both collected American art; Archibald once owned George Luks's famous painting *The Spielers*.[80] After making inquiries on the prices of several American paintings at the Armory Show, James T. Gwathmey bought Jonas Lie's painting *Hill Top*.[81]

Some of the purchasers of American art from the exhibition were artists themselves including Alfred Stieglitz, Edith Dimock (Mrs. William Glackens), George Warrington Curtis, and George E. Marcus. Stieglitz was the first to buy an American work, purchasing Arthur B. Davies's pastel drawing *Reclining Woman* (1913, The Metropolitan Museum of Art) a few days after the show opened.[82] Mrs. Glackens bought a drawing by Walt Kuhn.[83] George Warrington Curtis, who bought Eugene Higgins's painting *Weary* (Greenville County Museum of Art, South Carolina), was a marine painter and sculptor who may have known Stieglitz and Marsden Hartley before the show. [84] Around 1912, New York art dealer Charles Daniel hired poet Alanson Hartpence as an assistant to manage the Daniel Gallery. At the time, Hartpence was a salesman, along with writer Alfred Kreymbourg, at Aeolian Hall, where they demonstrated the pianola and the orchestrelle instruments. Hartpence left the music business to write poetry and "took a room at a boarding house in 14th Street where Marsden Hartley also happened to be living" and through Hartley, Hartpence met Stieglitz.[85] Since George W. Curtis was a director of the Aeolian Company, a manufacturer of organs, pianolas, and other musical instruments that was affiliated with Aeolian Hall, it seems plausible to suggest he may have been acquainted with Hartpence and, hence, Hartley and Stieglitz. A graduate of Columbia University, Curtis became a member of the Racquet and Tennis Club and the National Golf Links.[86] Like others of his social and financial status, Curtis had a grand estate in Southampton on Long Island, where he and his wife entertained regularly during the summer months, hosting balls, masques, and concerts, as well as foreign royalty and other dignitaries.[87]

Artist and master jeweler George Elder Marcus may well have designed some of the fabulous jewels worn by the Vanderbilts, Astors, and Harrimans. In 1892, Marcus helped found the renowned house of Marcus & Company Jewellers with his father and brother. Marcus studied at the Polytechnic Institute of Brooklyn and in Lausanne, Switzerland, and Heidelberg, Germany.[88] After their father's death in 1899, the Marcus brothers moved their business to 544 Fifth Avenue and "opened a Department for Silversmithing" alongside their exquisite jewelry business. George E. Marcus's designs were exhibited at the *First Exhibition of the Arts and Crafts* at Copley Hall in Boston in 1897 and he thereafter catapulted to fame as a jewelry designer.[89] At the Armory Show, Marcus bought "eight little pictures by E. Dimock" for his wife.[90] Pach, who was in charge of sales at the exhibition, subsequently wrote Marcus about these watercolors, saying he had an interested buyer for at least one work, *Mother and Daughter*. Marcus refused to sell, telling Pach that "The value and charm of each of the pictures is enhanced by the presence of the others. To eliminate one would impoverish the lot."[91] While Brown stated that Quinn purchased this work, it seems that the set of eight watercolors remained with Marcus, yet another unsolved mystery.[92]

While most of the American works were sold to New Yorkers, a few were bought by Chicago natives including George French Porter, son of Chicago railroad, shipping, lumber, and steel magnate Henry H. Porter.[93] The younger Porter served as the director of the Chicago Transfer and Clearing Company, secretary and treasurer of The Nevada Land Company, and president of the Wisconsin and Michigan Construction and Manufacturing Company. He also helped organize the vast freight transfer yards at Clearing on Chicago's south side.[94] Keenly interested in art, music, and literature, Porter was heavily involved with the Art Institute of Chicago and went to New York with Arthur T. Aldis to see the Armory Show firsthand.[95] "It is entirely due to the efforts of Arthur Aldis and George Porter that the exhibit of modern impressionists, post impressionists, and futurists" was brought to the AIC, one newspaper reported.[96] Porter furthermore suggested, "the inclusion among the pictures which come out to Chicago"—Childe Hassam's *Naples* and J. Frank Currier's *Forest Interior*—with the idea that "there would be a possibility in each case of the Friends of American Art liking and purchasing these pictures for their collection."[97] On March 1, 1913, Pach wrote Prendergast, "Will you please let me know at once whether the 'Currier' painting is for sale... I have reason to believe that the Chicago Institute will purchase it if the price is not too high," clearly a reference to this possible sale.[98] A collector of both American and European art, Porter was a founding member of the AIC's Friends of American Art and served as a vice-president from 1913-14. This society was organized in 1910 "to promote the development of American Art by the purchase of works by American artists to be presented to the Art Institute of Chicago, and by any other appropriate means."[99] It is probable that Porter had a hand in the purchase of Mary Foote's *Portrait (Old Lady)* for the AIC's collection, which was acquired through the Friends of American Art after the Armory Show left Chicago.[100] For his personal collection, Porter negotiated directly with Pach about the purchase of one of Robert Chanler's screens from the exhibition.[101] Porter also lent his Arthur B. Davies painting *Golden Sea Garden* (ca. 1912, Art Institute of Chicago) to the AIC venue.[102] The other Chicago buyer of an American work was Dr. Daniel D. Vandegrift, who bought Chester Beach's sculpture, *The Big Wave*.[103] He donated this piece to the AIC in 1922 but it has since been deaccessioned. Though little is known about him, Vandegrift obviously had an abiding interest in art and artists, for he established the Daniel D. Vandegrift Scholarship Fund at the School of the Art Institute of Chicago.

Among the other American works sold at the Armory Show were "four small panels" by D. Putnam Brinley, and a painting and a print by Walter Pach. Much has been written about San Francisco art dealer Frederick C. Torrey's acquisition of the most scandalous work in the Armory Show, Marcel Duchamp's painting *Nude Descending a Staircase, No. 2*.[104] (see cat. 79, p. 156) Since Pach was surely responsible for this sale, he probably also handled the purchase of the Brinley oils by the collector. These were apparently unsigned as Torrey wrote the AAPS, "It is understood that Mr. Brinley is to sign these panels and send them to me without frames at the close of the exhibition."[105] Henry Clay Frick's purchase of Pach's painting *Flowers* was probably made as a personal favor to Pach since Frick's primary area of collecting was not contemporary American art.[106] The other work by Pach that sold was a small etching, *Renoir's "Liseuse,"* to New York lawyer and businessman Richard Sheldrick.[107]

As the person in charge of the sales staff, Walter Pach was responsible for overseeing all the sales, American as well as European, at all three venues of the Armory Show. While Elmer MacRae kept records of sales as his duties as treasurer of the AAPS, Pach kept two small, private record books in which he recorded the daily sales activities at the exhibition (cats. 54, 55, pp. 151-2). These crucial materials have not been seen since 1963, when Pach's widow lent them to the 50th anniversary exhibition at the MWPI, and they are among the most significant recent rediscoveries related to the famed 1913 Armory Show. These notebooks contain a gold-mine of information that somewhat contradicts some of MacRae's and Brown's accounts, although Brown clearly had access to them as he referenced them in his writings on the show.[108] According to Pach's records, for example, the first purchases were made February 18, 1913, the day after the show opened, by Lillie Bliss and John Quinn; Brown states the first purchase was made by Daniel H. Morgan on February 19, 1913.[109] In addition to these record books, Pach kept detailed notes of sales in his annotated copy of the exhibition catalogue, which Brown mistakenly refers to as the "Kuhn catalogue" in the catalogue raisonné section of his book *The Story of the Armory Show*. In his 1991 essay "The Armory Show and Its Aftermath," Brown observed, "Curiously, the prices for American works were much higher than those for Europeans," perhaps one reason why more foreign works sold.[110] In addition, correspondence shows that, for the most part, purchasers paid the asking price. As an artist first and foremost, Pach surely would have had his colleagues' best interest in mind when negotiating the sale of their works and would have tried to get the highest price possible. While major collectors like Quinn and Eddy certainly would have bought on their own, Pach helped cultivate a taste for modern art among other collectors and personally brokered the sale of numerous American paintings, sculptures, prints, and drawings. As art historian Laura Coyle has noted, "The Armory Show was a financial success in part because [Walter] Pach not only knew the work inside and out and fervently promoted it, but also because he seems to have had a knack for matching buyers with works appropriate for their collections."[111]

The collectors of American art at the Armory Show were intricately intertwined with one another not only through family ties, wealth, and class but also through professional, political, and social affiliations. While the names may sound unfamiliar at first, a closer investigation reveals that many buyers were related to the Astors, Vanderbilts, Averells, and Harrimans— American royalty. Railroads, steel, textiles, and other industries as well as law and politics were common threads that bound these individuals to one another, and many of them, especially the women, probably knew one another quite well. Most of the collectors were also deeply involved with social causes and philanthropy. Many of the men belonged to the same organizations like the New York Athletic Club, University Club, and the Union League Club, to name a few. Several also shared a passion for thoroughbred racehorses and automobiles and belonged to various related organizations like the Automobile Club of America. Several of the women were members of the DAR as well as clubs like the Colony and Cosmopolitan in Manhattan. All of these collectors clearly had a keen interest in art; however, while their grandparents and parents might have collected Old Masters, the Barbizon School, and perhaps French Impressionists, these patrons chose to buy contemporary American art. Their presence at, and purchases from, the exhibition not only signaled a shift in taste and in collecting but also served to legitimize the American art in the exhibition, as well as the Armory Show itself, in the eyes and minds of an entirely new generation of Americans.

FOOTNOTES

1 One week after the exhibition opened, the *New York Sun* announced, "Walter Pach of the committee in charge" of sales stated that "fifty-one of the exhibits have been sold." See "They're Buying the New Art: Fifty-one Sales Reported in First Week of International Show," *New York Sun*, February 26, 1913. On March 6, the same paper reported, "125 Art Works Sold: Armory Show Breaks All Records With 10 Days Yet to Hear From," *New York Sun*, March 6, 1913. From Chicago, Pach wrote to Michael Stein, "Total number of sales in N.Y.—237." Walter Pach to Michael Stein, March 30, 1913, Gertrude Stein and Alice B. Toklas Papers YCAL MSS 76, Series II, Gertrude Stein Correspondence, 1893-1946, box 11, folder 2529, Beinecke Rare Book and Manuscript Library, Yale University, New Haven, CT. Also quoted in, Perlman, *American Artists, Authors, and Collectors*, 384.

2 For more information on these collectors see: Judith Zilczer, *"The Noble Buyer": John Quinn, Patron of the Avant-Garde* (Washington, D.C.: The Hirshhorn Museum and Sculpture Garden, Smithsonian Institution Press, 1978), Benjamin Laurance Reid, *The Man from New York: John Quinn and His Friends* (New York: Oxford University Press, 1968), Paul Kruty, "Arthur Jerome Eddy and His Collection: Prelude and Postscript to the Armory Show," *Arts Magazine* 61 (February 1987): 40-47, Rona Roob, "Patrons: A Noble Legacy," *Art in America* 9 (November 2003): 73-83, Francis M. Naumann, "Walter Conrad Arensberg: Poet, Patron, and Participant in the New York Avant-Garde, 1915-20," *Philadelphia Museum of Art Bulletin* 76 (1980): 2-32, and Douglas K.S. Hyland, "Agnes Ernst Meyer, Patron of American Modernism," *The American Art Journal* 12 (Winter 1980): 64-81. Albert E. Gallatin made a minor acquisition from the Armory Show, a "Red Chalk" drawing by Boardman Robinson. See Walter Pach's Red Record Book of Sales, "Mar. 11th, Sold to A. E. Gallatin 14 E. 65th St Boardman Robinson's Red Chalk Drwg. 25.00," Walter Pach Papers, Archives of American Art, Smithsonian Institution, Washington, D.C., unprocessed and unmicrofilmed, donated by Francis M. Naumann, 2011 (hereinafter Pach's Red Record Book of Sales).

3 Little is known about Charles F. Williams of the law firm Conway, Williams & Kelly. He purchased Edward A. Kramer's painting *Dawnlit*, now in the collection of the Munson-Williams-Proctor Institute. When Williams sent his payment he asked "At the close of the Exhibition, kindly send this to me in care of my picture framer, L. A. Dubernet, 24 East 8th Street, City" indicating that he likely owned other works of art. See Charles F. Williams to the Treasurer, AAPS, February 25, 1913, MacRae Papers, AAA, Reel 4131, fr. 1031. See also Pach's Red Record Book of Sales, "Feb. 24, Sold to Mr. Chas F. Williams 300 Lexington Ave Kramer No 881 'Dawnlit' 700." Born Minnie Carl in St. Louis, Missouri, Mrs. Untermyer and her husband, noted lawyer Samuel Untermyer, were great patrons of art, music, and literature and supported numerous philanthropies and charities. See "Death of Mrs. Untermeyer," *The Jewish Exponent*, August 22, 1924, 7 and "Mrs. Samuel Untermyer Dies," *The Sun*, August 17, 1924, 12. According to Pach's Red Record Book of Sales, "Mar. 10th, Sold to Mrs. Samuel Untermeyer #887 Kramer 'Pastel' 100." However, on February 26th Pach recorded that #887 *The Evangelist* was sold to Mrs. James S. Watson which, in fact, recent research has concluded was accurate. Kramer's *The Evangelist* was part of a loan exhibition of works from private collections held at the Memorial Art Gallery, Rochester in October 1915, undoubtedly lent by Mrs. James Sibley Watson. Email from Marjorie Searl, Chief Curator to the author, September 20, 2013. I wish to thank Dr. Searl for her assistance with this research. Therefore, the pastel sold to Mrs. Untermyer was not #887 but another one of his pastels.

4 See Reid, *The Man from New York: John Quinn and His Friends* and Zilczer, *"The Noble Buyer": John Quinn, Patron of the Avant-Garde*.

5 According to Pach's Red Record Book of Sales, he "Sold to B&B Kuhn 2 paintings total 950" on February 19; whereas Brown has Quinn buying the works on February 26, 1913. See, Milton W. Brown, *The Story of the Armory Show* (NY: Abbeville Press and The Joseph Hirshhorn Foundation, 1988), 283.

6 John Quinn to Walt Kuhn, June 2, 1913, MacRae Papers, AAA, Reel 4131.

7 George E. Marcus had, in fact, purchased all eight of Dimock's watercolors on February 22, 1913. Pach's Red Record Books of Sales, "Feb 22, Sold to G.E. Marcus 544 Fifth Ave. E. Dimock whole group 280." Marcus wrote Pach on February 28, 1913, "It would give me pleasure to gratify the lady who expressed a wish for it [*Mother & Daughter*] but unfortunately there is a lady to be considered on my side. I have given the little group of pictures to my wife and I cannot ask her to part with even one of them." See George E. Marcus to Walter Pach, February 28, 1913, Armory Show Papers, AAA, reel D-72, frame 1317. In his March 17, 1913, letter to the AAPS Marcus asks, "Will you kindly deliver to the bearer the eight little pictures by E. Dimock, which were sold to me at the exhibition." On March 13, Pach noted in his Red Record Book of Sales, "Sold to Mrs. Quinn 2 watercolors by E. Dimock 70.00." According to Brown's book, Quinn bought Dimock's *Sweat Shop Girls in the Country* and *Mother and Daughter* on March 13, 1913, but this is not accurate. According to the AAPS records, the total paid to Dimock was $315.00, which was $350.00 less the 10% commission the AAPS received. Therefore, ten works by Dimock were sold at $35.00 each—eight went to Marcus and two to Quinn.

8 "Amos Richards Eno Pinchot," in *The National Cyclopaedia of American Biography*, (New York: James T. White & Co., 1941), 379-80.

9 "Amos Pinchot," Spartacus Educational, http://www.spartacus.schoolnet.co.uk/USApinchotA.htm. Accessed February 16, 2011.

10 Amos Pinchot to Treasurer, AAPS, February 24, 1913, MacRae Papers, AAA, Reel 4131, fr. 1006. Pach's Red Record Book of Sales, "Feb. 23, Sold to Mr Pinchot Henri 'Red Top' 900." An additional note on this entry reads "Brinley Pd.", perhaps indicating that artist D. Putnam Brinley made the purchase for Pinchot.

[11] "A Society Surprise: An Unexpected Wedding in New York," *San Francisco Chronicle*, June 20, 1895, 1.

[12] "Vanderbilt Heiress in Politics: Mrs. David Hennen Morris Helps Her Husband Get a Nomination," *Boston Daily Globe*, October 3, 1900, 6 and "What is Doing in Society," *New York Times*, July 27, 1900, 7.

[13] Dave H. Morris to Secretary, March 5, 1913, Armory Show Records, AAA, Reel D-72, fr. 1324.

[14] Pach's Red Record Book of Sales, "Mar 15, Sold to Dave H. Morris 19 E. 70th St. No 883 No 884 Kramer 625."

[15] "Dave Hennen Morris Residence," on "The New York Chapter of the American Guild of Organists," http://www.nycago.org/Organs/NYC/html/ResMorrisDH.html, accessed, August 28, 2012 and Brad Emerson, "Vanderbilts Under the Pines," *The New York Social Diary*, http://www.newyorksocialdiary.com/node/1905363, accessed, October 19, 2012.

[16] According to Pach's Red Record Book of Sales, he noted on March 2nd, "Sold to Mr. Eddy No 85 Kroll" with no price listed. According to Brown, this transaction was not run through the AAPS. See Brown, *The Story of the Armory Show*, 1988, 283. Also see Pach's Red Record Book of Sales, "March 3rd, Sold to Mr. A. J. Eddy Nos 83A and 83B W.N. Taylor 600 No 47 Manigault The Clown 300." For the illustration of the Taylor painting, see James William Pattison, "Art in an Unknown Tongue," *Fine Arts Journal* 28 (May 1913): 306.

[17] Arthur J. Eddy to Arthur B. Davies, March 15, 1913, Armory Show Records, D72, fr. 1523. While Eddy was enthusiastic about these American paintings, Kruty notes in his essay that "In May [1913] he altered his will to establish a prize for American artists at the Art Institute," the clause in his will that allowed for these prizes "only went into effect if there were no descendants," and hence "No Eddy Prize was ever established." See Kruty, "Arthur Jerome Eddy," 44 and 47, n. 41.

[18] See Kruty, "Arthur Jerome Eddy," 45 and 47, ns. 65-71.

[19] "Walter C. Jones, Lawyer, Reformer, Legislature, Dies," *Chicago Daily Tribune*, June 29, 1928, quoted in "Walter Clyde Jones (1870-1928)-Find a Grave Memorial," http:/www.findagrave.com/cgi-bin/fg.cgi?page=gr&Grid=61667603, accessed September 15, 2012.

[20] "Asks Election Reform Law," *Chicago Daily Tribune*, October 9, 1910, 4, "Jones Confers with Merriam," *Chicago Daily Tribune*, May 1, 1911, 13, "W. Clyde Jones Heads 'Merriam' Ticket in State," *Chicago Daily Tribune*, July 21, 1911, 1, "W. Clyde Jones Open Campaign For Governorship," *St. Louis Post-Dispatch*, July 30, 1911, A4, and "Launch New Club To Aid Lorimer," *Chicago Daily Tribune*, August 25, 1911, 4.

[21] *The Book of Chicagoans: A Biographical Dictionary of Leading Living Men and Women of The City of Chicago*, edited by Albert Nelson Marquis (Chicago: A.N. Marquis & Company, 1917), 370.

[22] Walter Pach's Brown Record Book of Sales, "Mar. 24, "Sold to Mr. W. Clyde Jones 5541 Woodlawn Ave office 105 W. Monroe St Kate Cory 'Arizona Desert' 150," Walter Pach Papers, Archives of American Art, Smithsonian Institution, Washington, D.C., unprocessed and unmicrofilmed, donated by Francis M. Naumann, 2011 (hereinafter Pach's Brown Record Book of Sales).

[23] Lucas Bucholtz "Kate Cory," *Waukegan Historical Society* (July 2006), http://www.waukeganhistorical.org/people-journal/kate-cory.html, accessed September 8, 2012.

[24] Aline B. Saarinen, "Prologue," in *Edward Wales Root Bequest* (Utica, NY: Munson-Williams-Proctor Institute, 1962), unpaginated.

[25] Saarinen, "Prologue," in *Edward Wales Root Bequest*, unpaginated.

[26] Pach's Red Record Book of Sales, "Feb 22, Sold to Mr. E.W. Root 998 Fifth Ave Prendergast #895 'Lands.w.Fig.' 800." The address listed was the elder Root's address. Since Edward W. Root did not marry until 1917, it is likely that he lived with his parents.

[27] Quoted in Saarinen, "Prologue," in *Edward Wales Root Bequest*, unpaginated.

[28] "C.M. Lincoln Dies; Retired Editor, 84," *New York Times*, December 23, 1950, 15.

[29] Ibid.

[30] Pach's Red Record Book of Sales, "Feb. 26 Sold to C.M. Lincoln, N.Y. World Lawson 'Upper Manhattan' 660."

[31] For more information on Agnes Ernst Meyer see Hyland, "Agnes Ernst Meyer, Patron of American Modernism."

[32] See Mrs. Eugene Meyer to Walter Pach, March 15, 1913, MacRae Papers, AAA, Reel 4131, fr. 1002. Pach's Red Record Book of Sales, "Mar 15, Sold to Mrs. Eugene Meyer 135 Central Park West McComas 'Landscape California' 200." She may also have acquired a work by Arthur Freund as a note dated March 20, 1913, reads, "Recd from Amer Assn P&S for Mrs. E. Meyer 135 Central Park West 1 Drawing Arthur Freund," MacRae Papers, AAA.

[33] Hyland, "Agnes Ernst Meyer, Patron of American Modernism," 70.

[34] Among recent books on this topic is *Power Underestimated: American Women Art Collectors*, edited by Inge Reist and Rosella Mamoli Zorzi (Venice: Marsilio, 2011), Dianne Sachko Macleod, *Enchanted Lives, Enchanted Objects: American Women Collectors and the Making of Culture, 1800-1940* (Berkeley, Los Angeles, and London: University of California Press, 2008), *Before Peggy Guggenheim: American Women Art Collectors*, edited by Rosella Mamoli Zorzi (Venice: Marsilio, 2001), Kathleen D. McCarthy, *Women's Culture: American Philanthropy and Art, 1830-1930* (Chicago and London: University of Chicago Press, 1991), and Avis Berman, *Rebels on Eighth Street: Juliana Force and the Whitney Museum of American Art* (New York: Atheneum, 1990)..

[35] "Emily Sibley Watson, Founder of the Memorial Art Gallery," http://mag.rochester.edu/centennial/emily-sibley-watson/ and "James Sibley Watson" http://en.wikipedia.org/wiki/James_Sibley_Watson.

[36] Marie Via, "William Ordway Partridge *Memory*," in *Seeing America: Painting and Sculpture from the Collection of the Memorial Art Gallery of the University of Rochester*, 1 (Rochester, NY: Memorial Art Gallery, 2006), 81.

[37] I wish to thank Jessica Marten, Curator of Art at the Memorial Art Gallery for providing me information about Mrs. James Watson Sibley and the museum's collection.

38 Michael Kammen, "Introduction," in *Seeing America: Painting and Sculpture from the Collection of the Memorial Art Gallery of the University of Rochester* (Rochester, NY: Memorial Art Gallery, 2006), 14.

39 Pach's Red Record Book of Sales reads, "Feb. 26, Sold to Mrs. James E. (or S.) Watson 11 Prince St, Rochester N.Y. Kramer 887—The Evangelist 100." There is some confusion about this sale. According to a letter sent to the AAPS which was written by George Hurdle on his personal stationery, Mrs. Watson sent "a cheque for one hundred dollars in payment for that small pastel by Edward Adam Kramer (not in the catalogue) but hanging near 887 & which she was told has for title 'April?'." See George Hurdle to AAPS, February 27, 1913, MacRae Papers, AAA, Reel 4131, fr. 1026. However as stated in note 3, *The Evangelist* was sold to Mrs. Watson. I wish to thank Dr. Searl for providing me with the identity of the author of this letter.

40 Guy Pène du Bois, "Mistresses of Famous American Collections: The Collection of Mrs. E. H. Harriman," *Arts & Decoration* 7 (September 1917): 291-96.

41 Pach's Red Record Book of Sales, "Mar. 1, "Sold to Mrs. Rumsey Coluzzi Mahabarata 200.00." In his annotated catalogue Pach crossed out Coluzzi's entry #93 drawing and wrote "Maharabarata 300 sold."

42 Guy Pène du Bois, "Mistresses of Famous American Collections: The Collection of Mrs. Charles Cary Rumsey," *Arts & Decoration* 7 (September 1917): 556-62.

43 The Colony Club's Full List of members in Its First Year," on "The History Box: The Most Unique Site Regarding History," http://www.thehistorybox.com/ny_city/society/printerfriendly/nycity_society_colony_club_article00206.htm, accessed September 5, 2012.

44 Surprisingly, the Colony Club does not have a website. See, "Colony Club, Woman's Latest Effort to Imitate Mere Man, Opens Its Handsome Madison Avenue House," *The Evening World*, March 11, 1907, 3, "and "Colony Club" http://en.wikipedia.org/wiki/Colony_Club, accessed September 24, 2012.

45 "Wilson Death Puts Many in Mourning," *New York Times*, November 27, 1910, 13.

46 "New York: The Wedding of Miss Carrie Astor and Mr. Orme Wilson Today," *Chicago Daily Tribune*, November 18, 1884, 2, "Wedded Wealth, New York Society in an Unparalleled Flutter, The Marriage of William Astor's Youngest Daughter to a Broker's Son, More Than a Quarter of a Million Dollars' Worth of Presents," *Boston Daily Globe*, November 19, 1884, 5, and "A Georgia Cracker's Nuptials: Miss Carrie Astor Wedded to a Hall County Boy," *The Atlanta Constitution*, November 19, 1884, 1.

47 "Wilson Death Puts Many in Mourning," *New York Times*, November 27, 1910, 13.

48 Pach's Red Record Book of Sales, "Feb. 28, Sold to Mrs. Orme Wilson 3 E. 64th St. no 22 Schamberg 'Landscape' 100."

49 *National Society of the Daughters of the American Revolution*, www.dar.org.

50 "Mme. Surberbeille's Wills: One of Them Divides More Than a Million Between Husband, Daughter, and Cousin," *New York Times*, January 18, 1894, 9.

51 "Wills Art to Museum: Miss Willard's Paintings Go to Metropolitan—Estate $750, 000," *New York Times*, January 29, 1926, 18. Willard bought Odilon Redon's oil painting *The Red Boat* from the Armory Show.

52 Pach's Red Record Book of Sales, "Mar 15, Sold to Miss M. L. Willard 13 E 77 No 778 Alden Twachtman 100 No 839 Henri Drwg 25 No 254 Russel's Capucines 60." Brown mistakenly lists #838 as the Henri drawing sold to Willard, see Brown, *The Story of the Armory Show*, 1988, 275. The 50th anniversary exhibition catalogue states that either #838 *Nude (Drawing)*, sanguine or 839 was purchased by Willard. See, *1913 Armory Show 50th Anniversary Exhibition 1963* (Utica, NY: Munson-Williams-Proctor Institute, 1963), 192. However, Heather Smith Coyle, curator at the Delaware Art Museum, discovered Henri's #838 in their archives (cat. 18). Therefore, the work sold to Willard is, in fact, #839 as Pach recorded and is the work recorded in the Munson catalogue as #838 *Nude (Drawing)*, sanguine.

53 "Hudson-Mohawk Genealogical and Family Memoirs: Olcott," http://www.schenecdatyhistory.org/families/hmgfm/olcott.html. Accessed September 6, 2012.

54 "Frederic P. Olcott" Schenectady Digital History Archive: Hudson-Mohawk Genealogical and Family Memoirs: Olcott," http://www.schenectadyhistory.org/familes/hmgfm/olcott.html, accessed September 9, 2012.

55 "Marriage announcement," *New-York Tribune*, May 27, 1900, 11.

56 "East Side Residence Sold After Forty Years," *New York Times*, September 9, 1941, 40, "Town Receives Gift of Schoolhouse Site," *The Christian Science Monitor*, November 19, 1925 and "For Fighting Prohibition," *Boston Daily Globe*, July 6, 1926.

57 Ethel Beckwith, "The Last Word: Glass Collectors," *Sunday Herald*, September 1, 1957, 51.

58 Pach's Red Record Book of Sales, "Mar. 7, Sold to Mrs. Barend van Gerbig 129 E. 61st Freund's 'Pig' 150.00."

59 "Aviator Escapes When Plane Nose Dives into Sound," *The Hartford Courant*, October 9, 1926, 1 and "Milford Historical Society," *The Hartford Courant*, May 20, 1930, 2.

60 www.dar.org.

61 "Nicholas M. Pond Dies of A Stroke," *New York Times*, April 16, 1931, 23.

62 "Society at Home and Abroad," *New York Times*, February 27, 1910, X1, "Christmas Sale for Darrach House," *New York Times*, November 25, 1914, "Officers Chosen For Children's Institutions," *New York Times*, May 10, 1925, X9, "Campaign For St. Vincent's: Card party To Aid Crippled Children," *New York Times*, December 6, 1925, X16. "Obituary 1," *New York Times*, February 3, 1950, 23, and "New London Hospital to Observe Half-Century of Service Sunday," *The Hartford Courant*, April 7, 1962, 11D.

63 Pach's Red Record Book of Sales, "Mar. 6, Sold to Mrs. N.M. Pond 53 West 75th St. Perrine 'When the Wind Blows' 650."

64 "Annie B. Jennings, Oil Heiress, Dies in Fairfield, 83," *The Hartford Courant*, July 28, 1939, 4.

[65] "Personal Mention," *The Hartford Courant*, December 4, 1915, 9 and "Annie B. Jennings," *The Hartford Courant*, July 29, 1939, 6.

[66] Edward Alden Jewell, "Museum Arranges Walter Gay Show," *New York Times*, April 9, 1938, 18 and "Second Annual Winter Exhibition at Mount Vernon," *The Washington Post*, January 28, 1940, F6. Pach's Red Record Book of Sales, "Mar. 12, Sold to Miss A.B. Jennings 48 Park Ave MacRae's 'Yacht Club at Newport' 800." The painting was exhibited at the first exhibition of the Greenwich Society of Artists in 1912 with this title. Little is known about another women buyer at the Armory Show, Mrs. V.P. Snyder, who purchased a still life painting by Paul Rohland. Her husband was Deputy Controller of the Currency and "appointed Examiner of the National Banks at the cities of New-York, Brooklyn, and Jersey City" in 1887. "New Year's At Washington," *New York Times*, January 1, 1887, 5. Once in New York, she became involved in the social world surrounding the Vanderbilts, Goulds, and other wealthy families. "The Social World," *New York Times* April 11, 1894, 8, "Topics in New York," *The Sun*, December 27, 1897, 8, "Cost of a Thirst," *Chicago Daily Tribune*, December 26, 1897, 1, "Regatta Interests Lake George Colony," *New York Times*, August 2, 1934, 21, and "Large Card party Draws Colonists," *New York Times*, August 2, 1935, 21.

[67] "Loans from the Collection of George D. Pratt," *Metropolitan Museum of Art Bulletin* 35 (December 1940), 237.

[68] "George Dupont Pratt," *National Cyclopaedia of American Biography*, Vol. 29 (New York: James T. White & Co., 1941), 143.

[69] Pach's Red Record Book of Sales, "Feb. 26, Sold to Geo D. Pratt, 245 Clinton Ave Brooklyn No. 731 T. Robinson 350." The list price of the work was $500.

[70] Pach's Red Record Book of Sales, "Mar 14, Sold to Mr. Vietor Hopper's 'Sailing' 250."

[71] "Social Notes," *New York Times*, November 15, 1913, 11.

[72] I would like to thank Dr. Searl for providing information on the Allen family.

[73] "Borough of Rumson—History—Sheep's Run," http://www.rumsonnj.gov/history_sheeps_run.php, accessed February 16, 2011.

[74] "'Art for Yale' charts growth of gallery's collections," *Yale Bulletin & Calendar* 29 (April 20, 2001), http://www.yale.edu/opa/arc-ybc/v29.n27/story2.html, accessed October 19, 2012.

[75] Pach's Red Record Book of Sales, "Mar. 12, Sold to Mr. Thos F. Vietor 38 E. 25th St Mr. Clark's sculpture 'Bloomers' 200."

[76] Little is known about Tilda Colsman who purchased Arthur Lee's bronze sculpture *Aphrodite*. See Pach's Red Record Book of Sales, "Feb. 27, Miss Colsman Langenberg, Rheinland Haus Tanne not to be sent before beg May c/o Mrs. Schniewind 8 East 79th St Arthur Lee's 'Aphrodite' 500." The receipt for this work was on letterhead from the Susquehanna Silk Mills Company, so Colsman must have been connected with this business somehow.

[77] "Fall in Horse Race Kills J. T. Gwathmey," *New York Times*, October 16, 1932, 1. This was James T. Gwathmey's son.

[78] "A.B. Gwathmey, Jr. Is Sued By Wife," *New York Times*, December 3, 1919, 15 and "J. Temple Gwathmey," *New York Times*, June 13, 1924, 19, obituary notice.

[79] "Cotton Men in Trust Co.," *New York Times*, January 18, 1906, 10.

[80] "Gwathmey Buys Steeplechasers," *The Washington Post*, April 10, 1903, 9 and "James Huneker, "The Seven Arts," *Puck*, May, 23, 1914, 16.

[81] Pach's Red Record Book of Sales, "Feb 22, Sold to Mr. Gwathmey Lie 'Hilltop' #877 800" and Bolette Sunturn to Walter Pach, February 25, 1913, Armory Show Papers, AAA, Reel D-72, fr. 1291. According to Carol Lowery in her "Chronology" on Jonas Lie, "One of his figural works, a depiction of Norwegian peasants dancing, is sold from the [Armory Show] exhibition." See Carol Lowery, "Chronology," in *Jonas Lie (1880-1940)* (NY: Spanierman Gallery LLC, 2006), 112. Pach's Red Record Book of Sales, "Feb. 21, Mr. Gwathmey offers on Lie & Bellows." Gwathmey also offered $500 for George Bellow's painting *Docks in Winter*, the list price was $800. See Pach's Red Record Book of Sales, "Feb. 28, Mr. Jas. Temple Gwathmey 11 East 55th St leaves offer of 500 on Bellows 'Docks'."

[82] Pach's Red Record Book of Sales, "Feb. 20, Mr. Davies Drawing 65.00."

[83] Pach's Red Record Book of Sales, "Mar 15, Sold to Mrs. William Glackens 29 Washington Sq Drawing by Walt Kuhn 50."

[84] Pach's Red Record Book of Sales, "Mar. 1, Sold to Geo. W. Curtis, Southampton L.I. Higgins No 17 'Weary' 200."

[85] Julie Mellby, Julie Mellby, "A Record of Charles Daniel and the Daniel Gallery," (unpublished thesis, Hunter College, 1993), 7.

[86] "George W. Curtis Dead," *New York Times*, September 12, 1927, 23.

[87] "Society," *The Washington Post*, September 3, 1912.

[88] "Blue Dinosaur Press: Peter Marcus (1889-1934)," http://www.bluedinasaupress.com/profiles_marcus.php, accessed July 3, 2012.

[89] "Marcus & Co., Jewelry Artists—Artists Biographies, Macklowe Gallery," http://www.macklowegallery.com/education.asp/art+nouveau/Artist+Biographies/antiques/Jewelry+Artists/education/Marcus+%26amp%3B+Co./id/166, accessed July 3, 2012.

[90] George E. Marcus to AAPS, March 17, 1913, Armory Show Records, AAA, Sales Correspondence: General L-P, 1913.

[91] Marcus to Pach, February 28, 1913, Armory Show Records, AAA, Reel D-72, fr. 1317.

[92] See note 7 above.

[93] Paul Gilbert and Charles Lee Bryson, "H.H. Porter," in *Chicago and Its Makers: A Narrative of Events from the Day of the First White Man to the Inception of the Second World's Fair* (Chicago, IL: Felix Mendelsohn, Publisher, 1929), 804.

[94] *Clark J. Herringshaw's City Blue Book of Current Biography: Chicago Men of 1913*, edited by Mae Felts Herringshaw (Chicago, IL: American Publishers' Association, 1913), 272.

[95] Andrew Martinez, "A Mixed Reception for Modernism: The 1913 Armory Show at the Art Institute of Chicago," *The Art Institute of Chicago Museum Studies* 19 (1993): 39 and Brown, *The Story of the Armory Show*, 1988, 191.

[96] Untitled newspaper clipping from *Chicago Daily Tribune*, March 16, 1913, Art Institute of Chicago Scrapbook, v. 29-37, March 5, 1912-August 4, 1918, Microfilm 1969 25 reel 5, Ryerson Library, AIC.

[97] Arthur T. Aldis to Arthur B. Davies, March 17, 1913, Armory Show AIC Correspondence, March 17-June 27, 1913 folder, Archives, Art Institute of Chicago. I wish to thank Bart Ryckbosch and Deborah Webb of the Archives for their assistance in providing me these materials. See also Brown, *The Story of the Armory Show*, 1988, 194.

[98] Walter Pach to Maurice B. Prendergast, March 1, 1913, Armory Show Records, AAA, Reel, D-72 fr. 1339.

[99] *Bulletin of the Art Institute of Chicago* 4 (July 1910), 1.

[100] Martinez, "A Mixed Reception for Modernism," 105, note 86 and Brown, *The Story of the Armory Show*, 1988, 267. See also Assistant Secretary Art Institute of Chicago to Walt Kuhn, May 28, 1913, Sales Correspondence: Tuttle, William F. (Friends of American Art, Art Institute of Chicago), 1913, Box 1, folder 72, Armory Show Records, AAA.

[101] There is some confusion about which screen Porter purchased. Porter wrote Pach that he was interested in #1024, which was *Screen. Swan*. See George F. Porter to Walter Pach, March 15, 1913, Armory Show Records, AAA, Reel D-72, fr. 1331. Pach's Brown Record Book of Sales shows that he "Sold to George F. Porter Chanler's Screen "Swans" 1500." Chanler wrote to the AAPS that he received funds "from the sale of my blue screen in Chicago." See Robert Chanler to AAPS, June 9, 1913, MacRae Papers, AAA, Reel 4131, fr.900. However, Brown records that Chanler's *Screen, In Red*" #1031, sold for $1,500. See Brown, *The Story of the Armory Show*, 1988, 255.

[102] Brown, *The Story of the Armory Show*, 1988, 260.

[103] Telegram Pach to Davies and Kuhn, April 14, 1913, Armory Show Records, AAA, Reel D-72, fr. 1263. See also Kuhn to Pach, April 15, 1913, Armory Show Records, AAA, Reel D-72, fr. 1264. Pach's Brown Record Book of Sales, "April 15, Sold to Dr. D.D. Vandergrift 4436 Drexel Bd Beach's 'Big Wave' 500."

[104] See especially Francis M. Naumann, "Frederick C. Torrey and Duchamp's *Nude Descending a Staircase*," in *West Coast Duchamp*, ed. by Bonnie Clearwater (Miami Beach: Grassfield Press, 1991).

[105] Frederic C. Torrey to AAPS, March 6, 1913, MacRae Papers, AAA, Reel 4131. For this sale see Pach's Red Record Book of Sales, "Feb 22, Sold to Frederic C. Torrey 550 Sutter St. San Fran Brinley 843-846 inc 115." The works were listed as oils and titled simply "Color Note." The list price was $40 each or $160 for all four.

[106] Pach's Red Record Book of Sales, "Mar. 5, Sold to H. C. Frick (Knoedler) Pach No 263 'Flowers' 87.50."

[107] Pach's Red Record Book of Sales, "Mar 13, Sold to Mr. Sheldrick 16th St. & Bway. Metropolis Bldg Pach's Etching 'Liseuse' 10." Little is known about Richard Sheldrick. He served as secretary to the Chemical Manufacturing Company, Franklin H. Kalbfleisch Company. "Meetings and Elections," *New York Times*, December 31, 1907, 9. See also, "Society News and Gossip," *New York Times*, March 26, 1905, 33 and "Society at Home and Abroad," *New York Times*, November 28, 1909, X2.

[108] Brown, *The Story of the Armory Show*, 1988, 241 and 242.

[109] Brown, *The Story of the Armory Show*, 1988, 120.

[110] Milton W. Brown, "The Armory Show and Its Aftermath," in *1915, The Cultural Moment: The New Politics, the New Woman, the New Psychology, the New Art & the New Theatre in America*, edited by Adele Heller and Lois Rudnick, (New Brunswick, NJ: Rutgers University Press, 1991), 172.

THE ARMORY SHOW:
THE STORY OF ITS PRIMARY SOURCES

By Charles H. Duncan

AT THE CENTURY MARK, the International Exhibition of Modern Art is recognized as the single most important event in the history of American art. Its organizing body, the Association of American Painters and Sculptors (AAPS), existed only from 1911 to 1914, yet its sole achievement—the Armory Show — was unquestionably a formidable catalyst for the assimilation of modernism into American visual culture. In 1938, 25 years after the exhibition, AAPS Secretary Walt Kuhn published his pamphlet-length *The Story of the Armory Show*, and Walter Pach, one of the exhibition's principal organizers, recalled events in the autobiographical *Queer Thing, Painting*. In 1963, art historian Milton W. Brown's book-length chronicle, also titled *The Story of the Armory Show*, provided a more complete picture of the historic events of 1913. This important study was among the first to benefit from primary records of the AAPS, which only emerged many years after the original event, and today it stands as the most widely referenced work on the International Exhibition of Modern Art.[1]

The story of the Armory Show's primary sources begins at the nexus of three events in the 1950s: the discovery of the Elmer Livingston MacRae papers; the founding of the Archives of American Art (AAA); and a plan to recreate the Armory Show as a 50th anniversary commemorative exhibition. Prior to the late 1950s, the quest to locate original records of the AAPS was met with frustration. In the 1930s, while researching his book *American Painting from the Armory Show to the Depression*, Milton W. Brown queried Walt Kuhn about the whereabouts of the Association's records, only to be informed that none existed.[2] In 1951, two years after Kuhn's death, Elmer MacRae similarly denied knowledge of any extant AAPS records.[3] A letter dated February 16, 1951, to Virginia Vanderbilt Teague, wife of sculptor R. Lewis Teague, confirms that MacRae either placed little value on his own records as Treasurer or had long forgotten about them: "Walt Kuhn, Secretary, had everything—correspondence, knowledge of the organization's formation and growth, those who were sponsors, the aims and aspirations of the Society—well, just about everything you want. Most lamentable, Walt Kuhn is dead. I don't know what was done with all this."[4]

In 1958, the MacRae records were discovered at the Holley House in Connecticut, the gathering place from the early 1890s until the 1920s for the group of artists and writers who formed the Cos Cob Art Colony. MacRae lived at the house from the time of his marriage to Constant Holley in 1900 until his death in 1953. In 1957, the Historical Society of the Town of Greenwich purchased the Holley House from MacRae's widow, and while converting it into a museum stumbled upon the AAPS records, which had been packed in "an old orange crate, stored in the barn behind the house, and then completely forgotten."[5] In 1959, portions of the MacRae papers were exhibited as part of a retrospective at the Milch Gallery, and in 1961 the collection was acquired by the Joseph H. Hirshhorn Foundation, which commissioned Milton W. Brown to publish the papers as a memorial volume on the Armory Show.

Concurrent to the discovery of the MacRae papers, Joseph S. Trovato, assistant to the director of the Munson-Williams-Proctor Institute in Utica, New York, was organizing a large-scale commemorative exhibition on the Armory Show scheduled to open five decades to the day after the original exhibition. One of the first contacted by Trovato was Brenda Kuhn, who confirmed that papers of her father, Walt Kuhn, remained intact. As she recalled later, "In 1952, Mother and I stood in Walt Kuhn's New York studio, collecting his Armory Show papers into a couple of old straw suitcases.… The Papers were sent to our house in Maine, from there, in summer of 1961, they went to our New York Storage warehouse."[6]

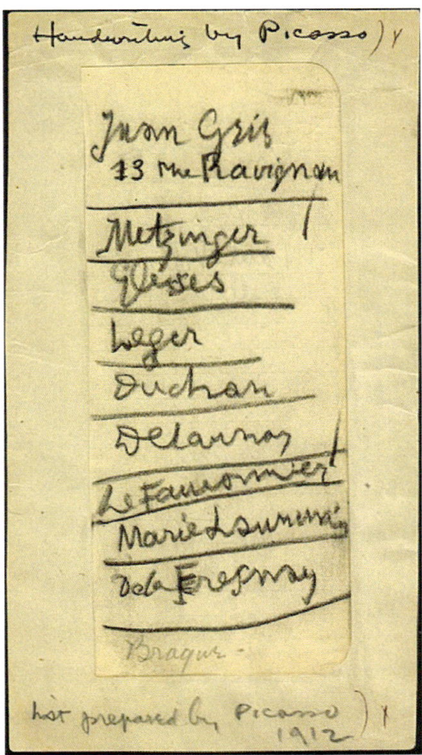

Fig. 16
List of European artists to be included in the Armory Show, 1912, compiled by Pablo Picasso, Walt Kuhn, Kuhn family papers, and Armory Show records, 1858–1978 (bulk 1900–1949), Archives of American Art, Smithsonian Institution

Trovato's entreaties spurred Brenda Kuhn to turn over a substantial portion of her father's papers to the Archives of American Art in 1962, affording access for the first time to one of the most important troves of the Association's official correspondence and records of transactions.[7] Additional donations would include over 800 personal letters from Kuhn to his wife Vera from 1909 to 1948, as well as photographs and ephemera. For the Archives, founded in 1954 as a microfilm repository of papers housed in other institutions and expanded in the late 1950s to collect and preserve original materials, the Walt Kuhn, Kuhn Family papers, and Armory Show records rapidly became one of its most important and frequently accessed collections.[8]

Together, the Kuhn and MacRae collections contain the majority of known original records of the AAPS and the Armory Show. As secretary of the Association, Kuhn was heavily involved in the conception, organization, and production of the exhibition; his papers document the selection of art work in Europe (Fig. 16) and the United States, as well as the selection of venues, negotiation of contracts, production of the exhibitions, publicity (Fig. 17), promotion, sales, and the wide array of responses to the exhibition in New York, Chicago, and Boston. Kuhn's papers additionally house the lion's share of official AAPS business documents, including the group's constitution, articles of incorporation, drafts of minutes of meetings, and briefs and correspondence relating to lawyer and collector John Quinn's work to lift duties on imported art.

In contrast, the MacRae papers are heavily weighted toward financial records and correspondence, including ledgers with credit and debit payments, information concerning foreign lenders to the exhibition, and records of financial obligations of the Association itself. Particularly illuminating are invoices for works of art, as often they mark the initial bridge between prominent European avant-garde artists and American collectors. Both the Kuhn and MacRae papers contain selections of printed materials and ephemera, including Armory Show catalogues, pamphlets, postcards and scrapbooks. Photographic albums and important loose photographs appear in the Kuhn papers, including images of the Duchamp-Villon brothers, artworks and, until recently, the only identified installation photographs from New York's 69th Regiment Armory.[9]

In 2010, an exciting discovery of original Armory Show records was brought to the attention of the AAA by Adam Bergmann, a playwright in New York City. While cleaning the home of his late father, Bergmann discovered several folders of original, yellowed AAPS documents unknown to contemporary scholarship. Research suggests that Bergmann's father, Rudolph, who lived for many years in Rockland County, New York, may have been friendly with or purchased the home of Virginia Vanderbilt Teague, who lived in Rockland County during in the 1950s. Correspondence in this collection dating from the early 1950s between Teague, MacRae and Vera Kuhn, wife of Walt Kuhn, as well as between Teague and Vera Kuhn in the

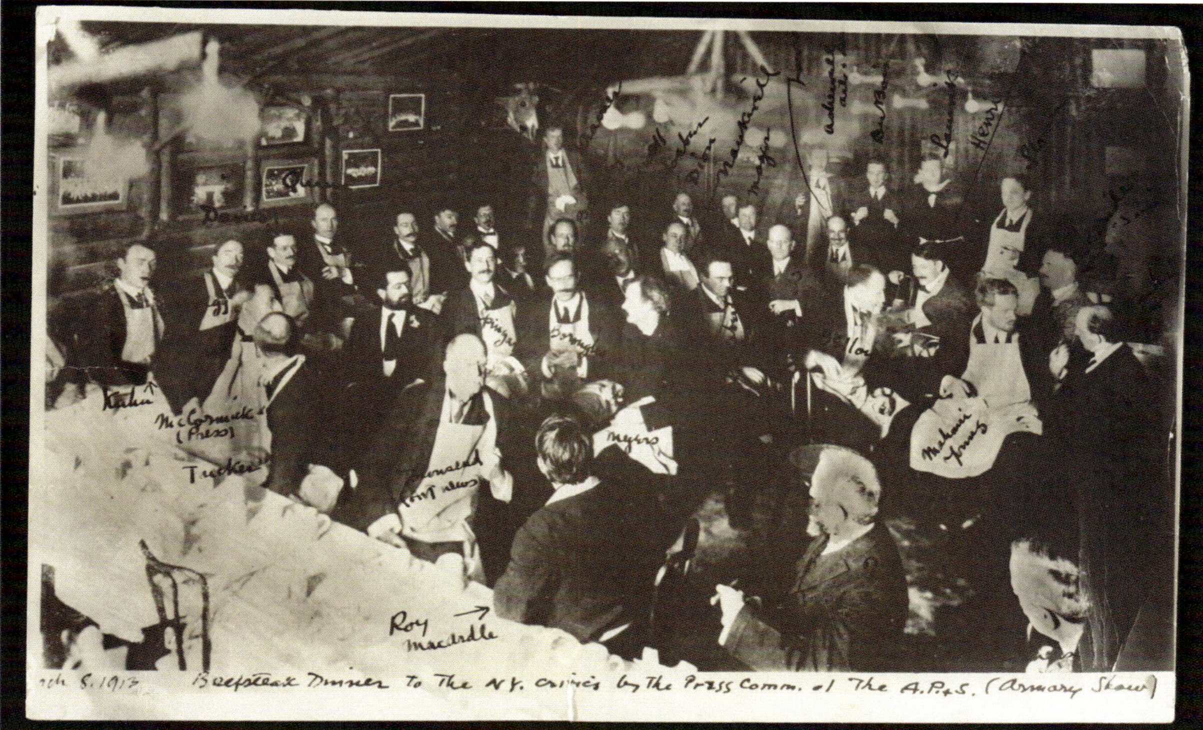

Fig. 17
Beefsteak Dinner to the New York Critics by The Press Committee of the Association of American Painters and Sculptors, March 8. 1913, Walt Kuhn, Kuhn family papers, and Armory Show records, 1858–1978 (bulk 1900–1949), Archives of American Art, Smithsonian Institution

Walt Kuhn papers, reveals that Virginia Teague sought to write a history of the Armory Show, and actively pursued materials to support her study. The AAPS records in the Teague papers may have originated from the estate of Kuhn, although another likely source may be Mary Mowbray-Clarke, a friend of Teague whose husband John had been vice-president of the Association.[10] The Virginia Teague papers relating to the Armory Show correct an important lacuna in details regarding the third and final leg of the exhibition, staged at the Copley Society of Boston from April 28 to May 19, 1913. While the particulars of the Boston exhibition were introduced by Brown in *The Story of the Armory Show* and later considered in detail by Garnett McCoy, the paucity of original AAPS documentation on Boston had remained an issue.[11] The Teague papers largely complete gaps in correspondence between members of the AAPS and leadership of the Copley Society, as well as correspondence and memoranda between members of the AAPS regarding developments in Boston. A large concentration of material concerns the disagreement over sharing financial proceeds as stipulated in the original Boston contract, also included in the Teague collection. Numerous spirited letters between Walt Kuhn, Arthur B. Davies and John Quinn of the AAPS and Holker Abbott, Edward Warren, L. Flanders and the law firm of Brandeis, Dunbar & Nutter on behalf of the Copley Society reveal that the matter was ultimately resolved by Henry Fitch Taylor just prior to arbitration during a personal visit to Boston. A congratulatory letter from Quinn lauds Taylor for his diplomacy and concludes with his assessment of the sensibilities of the Boston constituents: "I have had experience with the 'Puritan Conscience'. It certainly adhereth to the letter but killeth the spirit, strangleth the spirit, and they do it all with such a suave and tender care of words and forms."[12] The Teague papers additionally contain previously unknown minutes of the Association's meetings, including a gathering on November 1, 1915, concerning a final settlement from the New York Customs House and damage claims levied by the French courts; a date later than previously known official AAPS business meetings. (Fig. 18, p. 118)

Artist, critic, lecturer, art adviser and art historian Walter Pach played an integral role in soliciting participation in the exhibition from European avant-garde artists and dealers, and his wide-ranging knowledge of art trends on both sides of the Atlantic guided the conceptual

117

development of the Armory Show. The first distribution of Pach papers was acquired by the Archives of American Art in 1988, purchased by the Brown Foundation, Inc., on behalf of the Archives from the Salander O'Reilly Galleries. In 1990, Pach's son, Raymond, donated eight additional family photographs. The Pach papers are rich in personal and family materials, extensive professional correspondence with noted artists and art world figures, handwritten versions of manuscripts by Pach, as well as drawings, printed material, photographs, a scrapbook and selections from Walter Pach's library. Of particular importance is Pach's correspondence from the years immediately predating the Armory Show with American and European artists including Prendergast, Ryder, Rodin, Matisse and the Duchamp-Villon brothers, as it offers extraordinary insight into the developing affinities between modernist artists on both continents.

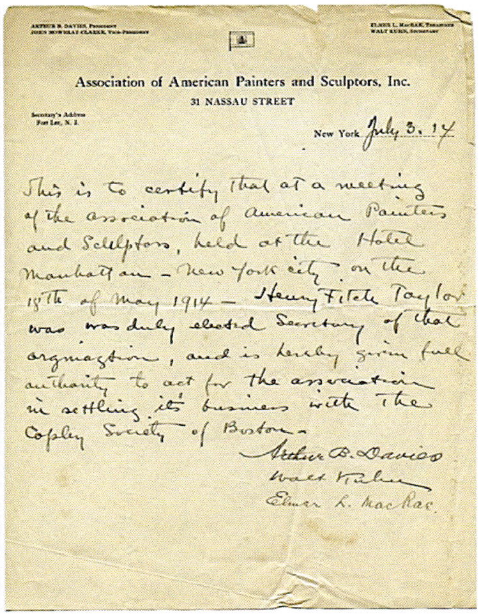

On the eve of the 100th anniversary, an exciting and important addition to the Walter Pach papers was purchased and generously donated to the Archives of American Art by scholar and dealer Francis M. Naumann, who recalled the circumstances of its discovery:

At the recommendation of Laurette E. McCarthy, I went to Athens in mid-August of 2011 to visit a man named Tony, who is the nephew of Nikifora Iliopoulos, Pach's widow. I was mostly interested in the possibility of acquiring paintings by Walter Pach, since I was planning a show at my gallery in the fall.[13] Tony took me by subway to an apartment located in a northern suburb... on the top floor of a four-story cinderblock building with no air conditioning, so you can only imagine how hot it was. I told him that I was also interested in whatever Pach papers might have remained with his aunt, for I knew about ledger books Pach kept during the Armory Show in New York and Chicago that recorded the prices for works of art sold and the names of the collectors who purchased them.[14] Tony showed me a large closet filled with papers, and after about an hour of looking I came across the two ledger books and immediately recognized them as the important historical documents I was seeking.[15]

Among the treasures in this substantial addition to the Walter Pach papers are an unpublished, illustrated book of lectures, titled *Aesthetics*; manuscripts of writings; and two groups of letters and photographs documenting exchanges between Pach and Raymond Duchamp-Villon, who died shortly after World War I, and his brother Jacques Villon. Armory Show materials include the two sales ledgers, a letter composed on four postcards from Morton Schamberg to Pach during the summer of 1912 regarding plans to mount a major exhibition of modern art in New York (both are discussed by Laurette E. McCarthy elsewhere in this volume), postcards of works of art, and copies of booklets Pach wrote especially for the exhibition on Raymond Duchamp-Villon and Odilon Redon. Of special interest is a letter from Theodore Roosevelt dated 1914, one year after Pach resumed residence in the United States, providing Pach *entrée* from the former president and Armory Show critic during Pach's travels in Europe to secure works of art for a forthcoming modernist exhibition at the Carroll Gallery and Montross Gallery in New York.[16] (Fig. 19, p. 119)

The Archives of American Art preserves numerous additional collections of papers from figures who played roles in organizing the original Armory Show, including painters Jerome Myers and Daniel Putnam Brinley, as well as papers of historians who have brought the Armory Show into contemporary focus. Rich resources for Armory Show scholarship can

Fig. 18
Memorandum dated July 3, 1914, certifying Henry Fitch Taylor as Secretary of the Association of American Painters and Sculptors, Virginia Teague papers relating to the Armory Show, 1913–1952 (bulk 1913–1917), Archives of American Art, Smithsonian Institution

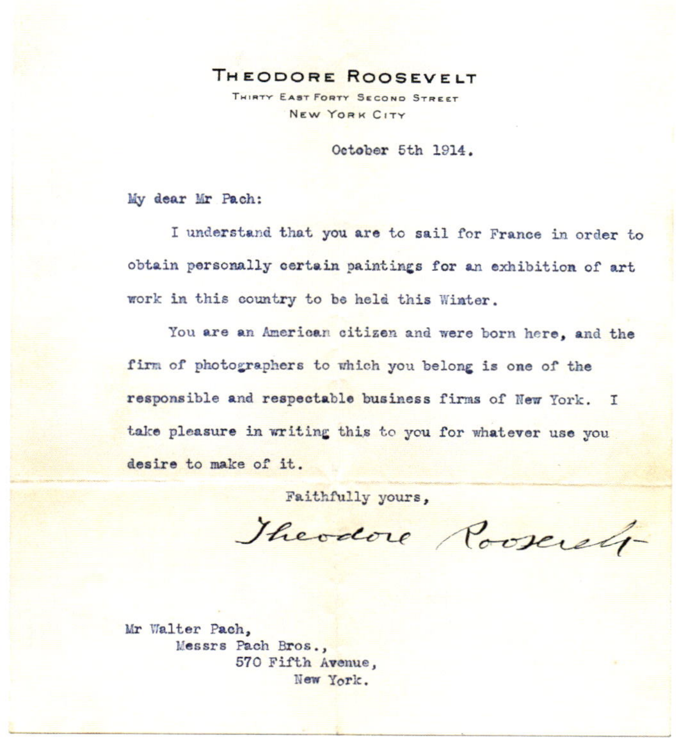

THEODORE ROOSEVELT
THIRTY EAST FORTY SECOND STREET
NEW YORK CITY

October 5th 1914.

My dear Mr Pach:

I understand that you are to sail for France in order to obtain personally certain paintings for an exhibition of art work in this country to be held this Winter.

You are an American citizen and were born here, and the firm of photographers to which you belong is one of the responsible and respectable business firms of New York. I take pleasure in writing this to you for whatever use you desire to make of it.

Faithfully yours,

Theodore Roosevelt

Mr Walter Pach,
Messrs Pach Bros.,
570 Fifth Avenue,
New York.

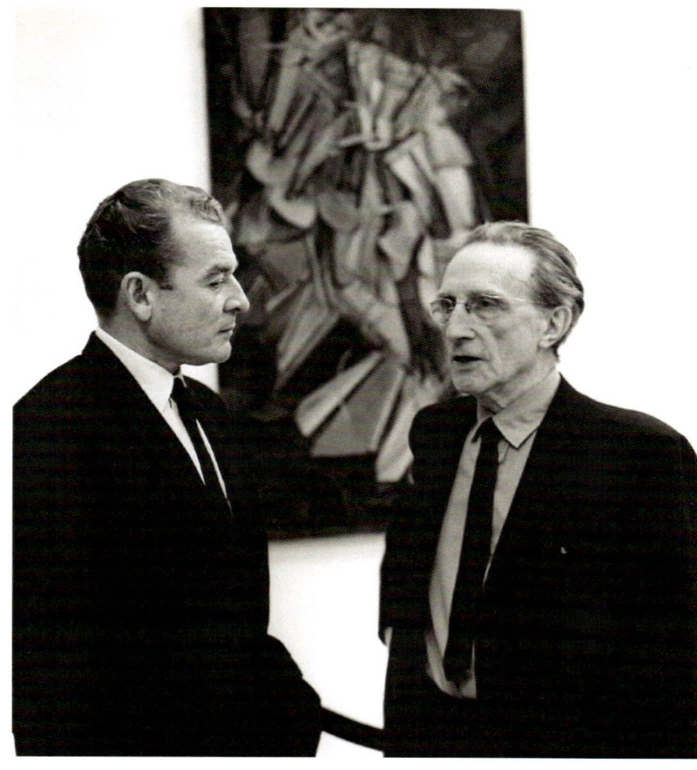

Fig. 19
Letter from Theodore Roosevelt to Walter Pach, October 4, 1914, Walter Pach papers, 1857–1980, Archives of American Art, Smithsonian Institution

Fig. 20
Marcel Duchamp and CBS news anchor Charles Collingwood at the Munson-Williams-Proctor Arts Institue, Utica, New York. Papers relating to the 1913 Armory Show 50th Anniversary Exhibition, circa 1962–1995, Archives of American Art, Smithsonian Institution

also be found in collections documenting the 50th Anniversary of the Armory Show exhibitions staged in Utica and at the original 69th Regiment Armory site. Records donated by the Munson-Williams-Proctor Institute, and personal papers of its organizer, Joseph S. Trovato, contain in-depth research on works exhibited at the original exhibition, practical documentation of the Armory Show's recreation, and recollections solicited for the occasion from Charles Sheeler, Stuart Davis, William Zorach, Alexander Archipenko, and other artists. Records of the New York City event, sponsored by the Henry Street Settlement, originate with its co-chair Margaret Carlton, and include two recently acquired scrapbooks offering letters, clippings, ephemera, and copious photographs of the exhibition and its visitors. Also included in the Carlton papers are commemorative posters featuring *Nude Descending a Staircase, No. 2* designed by Marcel Duchamp for the benefit of the Henry Street Settlement, including an artist's proof inscribed to Margaret Carlton.[17]

Oral history interviews, recorded lectures, and moving image records complete the wide variety of primary Armory Show resources housed at the Smithsonian Institution. Particularly resonant are materials created by Marcel Duchamp, who assumed the role of elder statesman for the exhibition during 50th anniversary commemorations. A lecture by Duchamp, delivered at the Munson-Williams-Proctor Institute on February 17, 1963, summarizes the art historical heritage leading up to the Armory Show, and an interview conducted by Milton W. Brown for the Martha Deane radio program reveals that for Duchamp the celebrity of the *Nude Descending a Staircase, No. 2* "really beat me, in that I disappeared for forty years because people talked about the painting… but they never named me."[18] And finally, moving image interviews conducted at the Munson-Williams-Proctor Institute by Charles Collingwood with Marcel Duchamp and Sir Kenneth Clarke, broadcast on April 5, 1963, as part of the CBS Television program *Eyewitness*, provide firsthand perspectives set within the context of the recreated exhibition itself. (Fig. 20)

FOOTNOTES

[1] For an extensive bibliography on the International Exhibition of Modern Art see Laurette E. McCarthy, "The 'Truths' about the Armory Show: Walter Pach's Side of the Story, *Archives of American Art Journal*, Vol. 44, No. 3/4 (2004), footnote no. 1.

[2] As Brown noted, Walt Kuhn had likely been reluctant to give public access to the records "because there were things among the papers that might reopen the wounds of the old unpleasantness surrounding the dissolution of the Association." Milton W. Brown, *The Story of the Armory Show* (New York: Abbeville Press and the Joseph H. Hirshhorn Foundation, 1988), p. 16

[3] In a letter to Bernard Karpel, librarian of the Museum of Modern Art, November 29, 1951. Brown, p. 16

[4] Virginia Teague papers relating to the Armory Show, 1913-1952 (bulk 1913-1917), Archives of American Art.

[5] Brown, p. 16

[6] Letter from Brenda Kuhn, Cape Neddick, Maine, November 29, 1971 to Roberta Van Horn, Membership Secretary, Archives of American Art, Detroit. Collection file, Walt Kuhn papers, Archives of American Art.

[7] Joseph S. Trovato, "Acknowledgements" in Armory Show 50th Anniversary Exhibition, 1913-1963 (New York and Utica: Henry Street Settlement and the Munson-Williams-Proctor Institute, 1963) p. 8

[8] The Archives of American Art was founded in Detroit, MI by Edgar P. Richardson, Director of the Detroit Institute of Arts, and collector Lawrence A. Fleischman. It became a unit of the Smithsonian Institution in 1970.

[9] See Laurette E. McCarthy, "The Armory Show: New Perspectives and Recent Rediscoveries," *Archives of American Art Journal*, vol. 51, nos. 3-4 (2012).

[10] The Teague papers contain an Exhibition catalogue inscribed "Mowbray-Clarke." At the time of writing this essay, archival materials from the estate of Mary and John Mowbray-Clarke are being processed by the Harry Ransom Center, University of Texas, that may shed additional light on the relationship between Teague and the Mowbray-Clarkes.

[11] Brown pp. 215-222; Garnett McCoy, in "The Post-Impressionist Bomb," *Archives of American Art Journal*, Vol. 20, No. 1 (1980), p. 13, noted "Moreover, the Association's records on Boston are Skimpy."

[12] Letter from John Quinn, July 11, 1914, Virginia Teague papers relating to the Armory Show, 1913-1952 (bulk 1913-1917), Archives of American Art.

[13] *The Paintings of Walter Pach*, Francis Naumann Fine Art, New York, NY: November 11 - December 23, 2011.

[14] The Pach ledgers were made available to Brown and Trovato during preparations for 50th Anniversary exhibitions but not acquired with the first distribution of Pach papers. See Brown, p. 12.

[15] Written statement from Naumann to the author, Sept. 6, 2012

[16] According to Laurette E. McCarthy, "The letter by Theodore Roosevelt was written when Pach was in NY and was intended, I believe, to give Pach safe passage during wartime when he traveled to Paris to continue the work started by the Armory Show, by gathering modern European art for exhibitions at Montross Gallery and Carroll Galleries for the 1914-1915 season and beyond." Correspondence with the author, Sept. 26, 2012.

[17] For more information on the Armory Show poster see Schwarz, Arturo, *The Complete Works of Marcel Duchamp*, Delano Greenridge Editions; 3 Rev Sub edition (April 1997), p. 828.

[18] Transcript of tape recorded interview with Marcel Duchamp originally broadcast on the Martha Deane radio show, 1963. Interviewer Milton W. Brown. p. 5. Archives of American Art.

PLATES

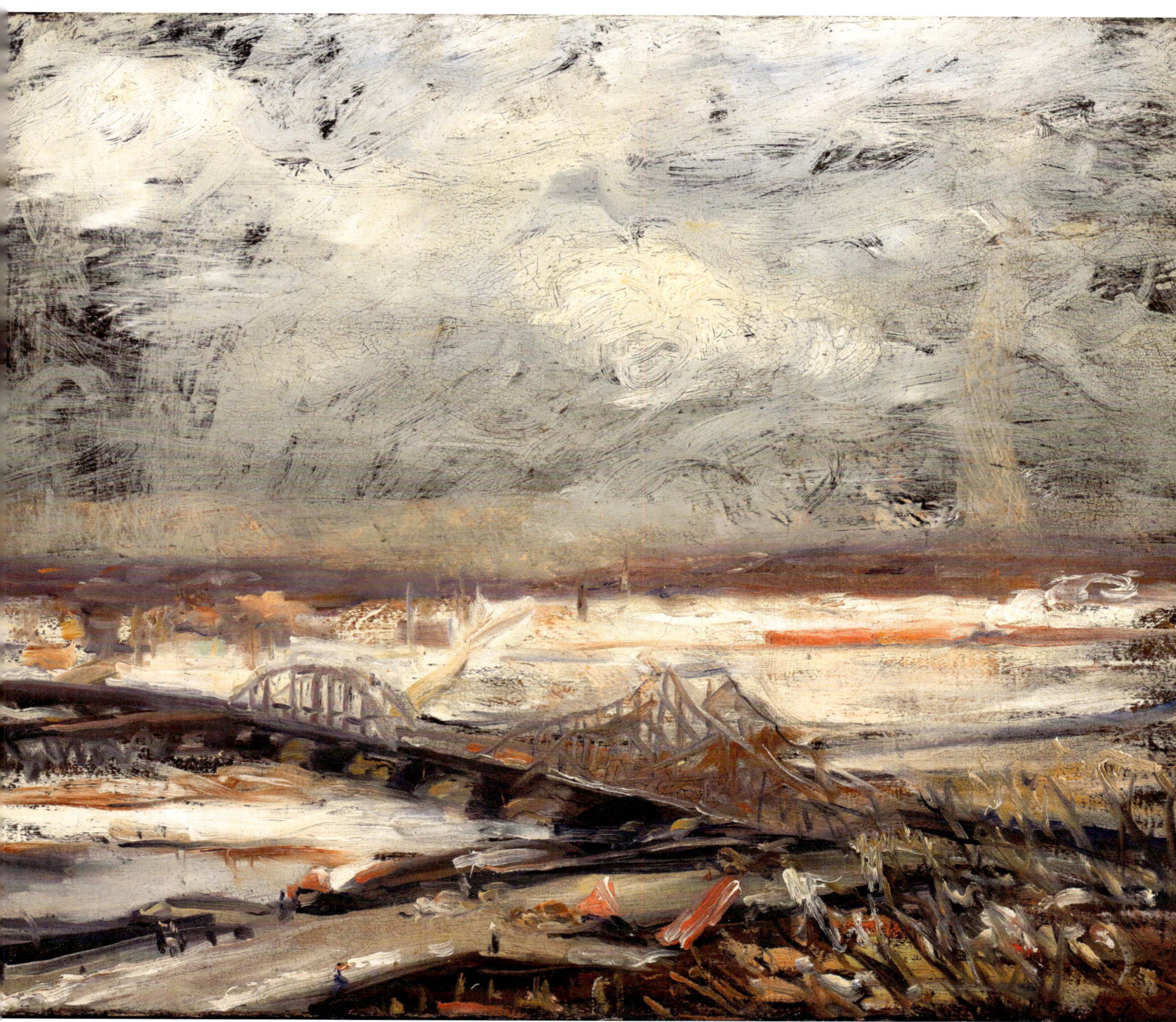

Cat. 1.
Florence Howell Barkley. *Jerome Avenue Bridge (Landscape over the City)*,
1910-11, oil on canvas, Museum of the City of New York, Gift of Miss Florence Howell Barkley, 53.401

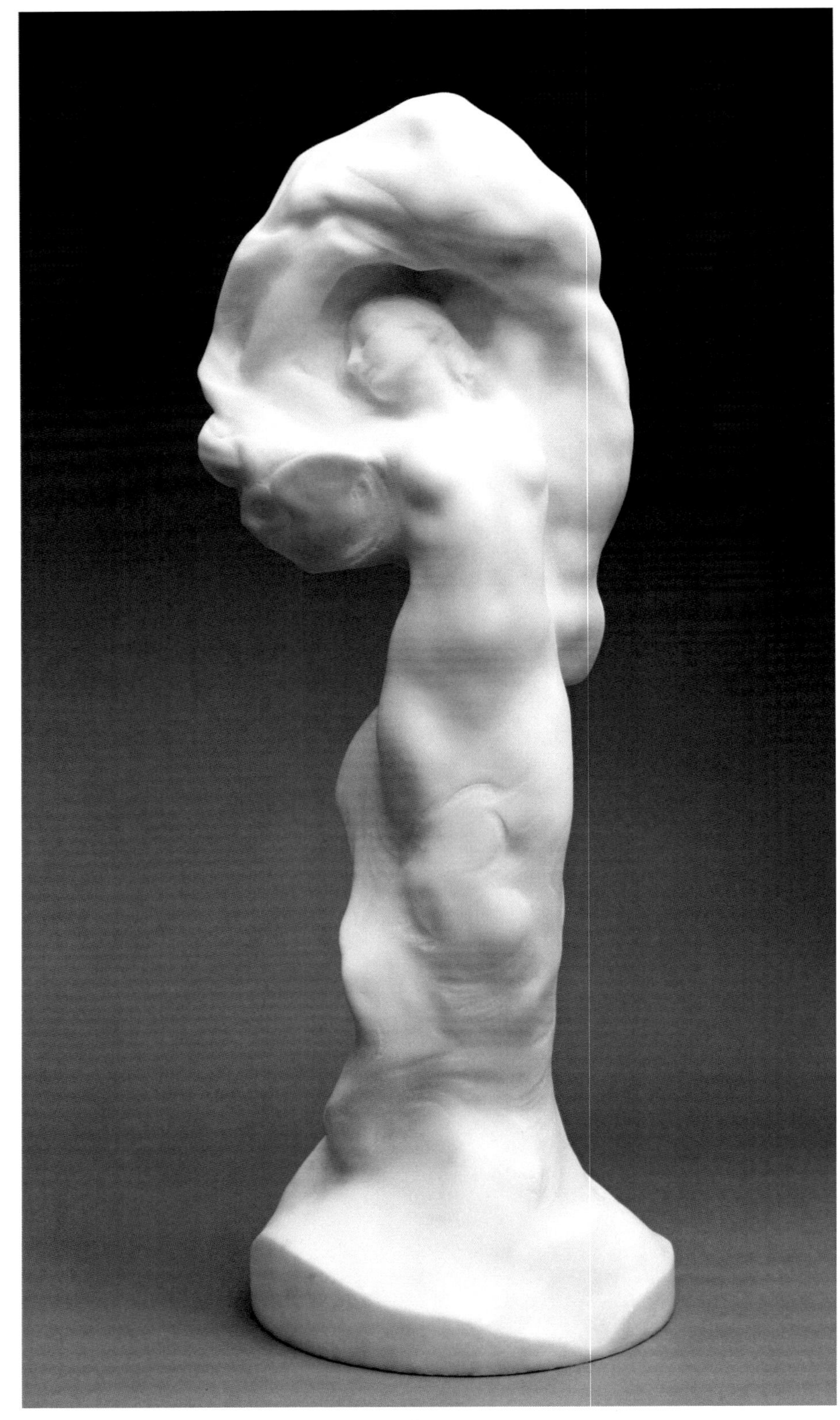

Cat. 2.
Chester Beach, *Unveiling of Dawn*, 1913, marble, The Metropolitan Museum of Art,
Gift of Mr. and Mrs. George W. Davison, 1943 (43.20)

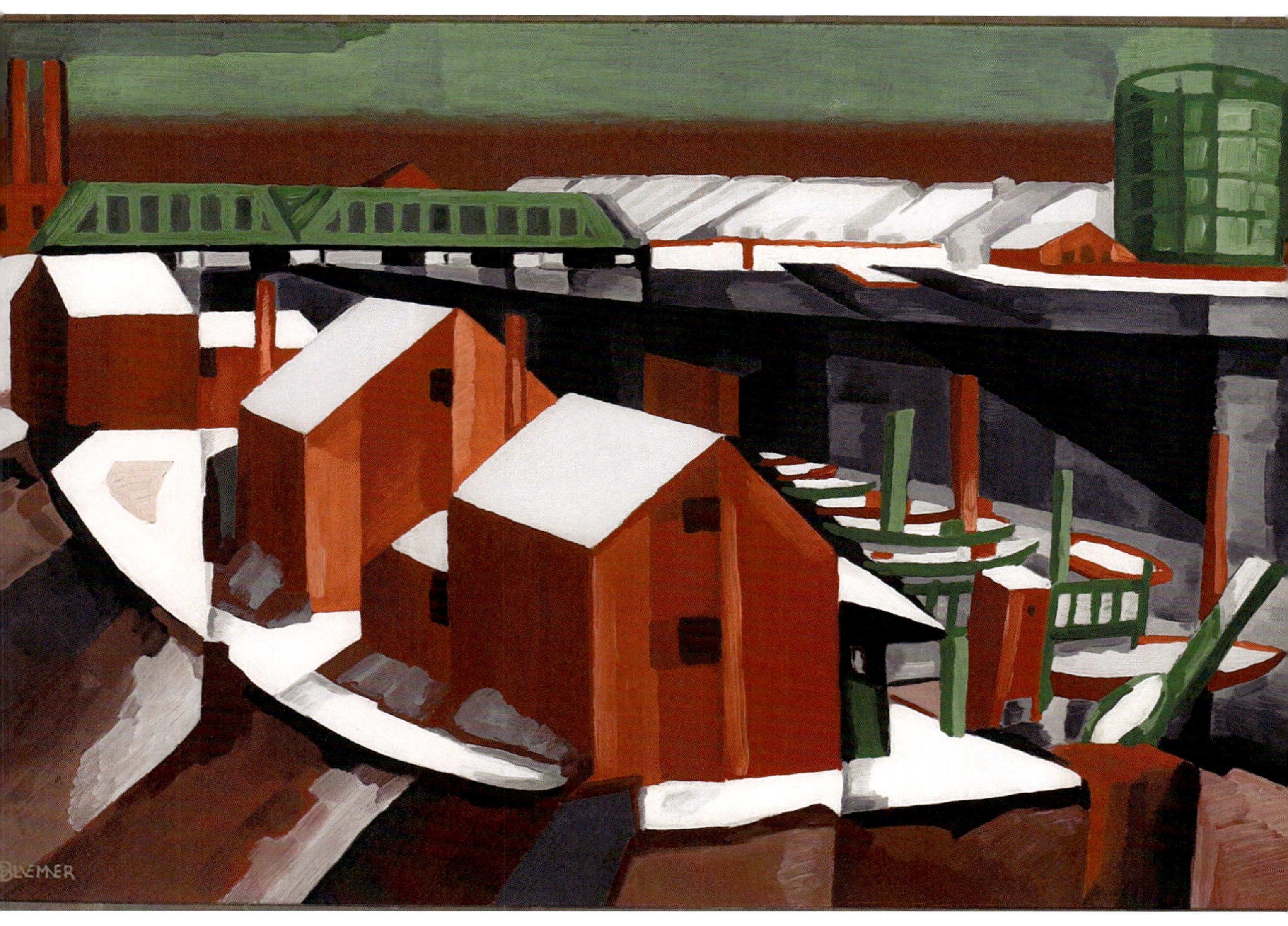

Cat. 3.
Oscar Bluemner, *Hackensack River*, 1911 (repainted 1914 and 1916-17), oil on canvas, Collection of the Naples Museum of Art, Naples, FL. 2000.15.011,
Museum purchase made possible by William J. and Suzanne V. von Liebig

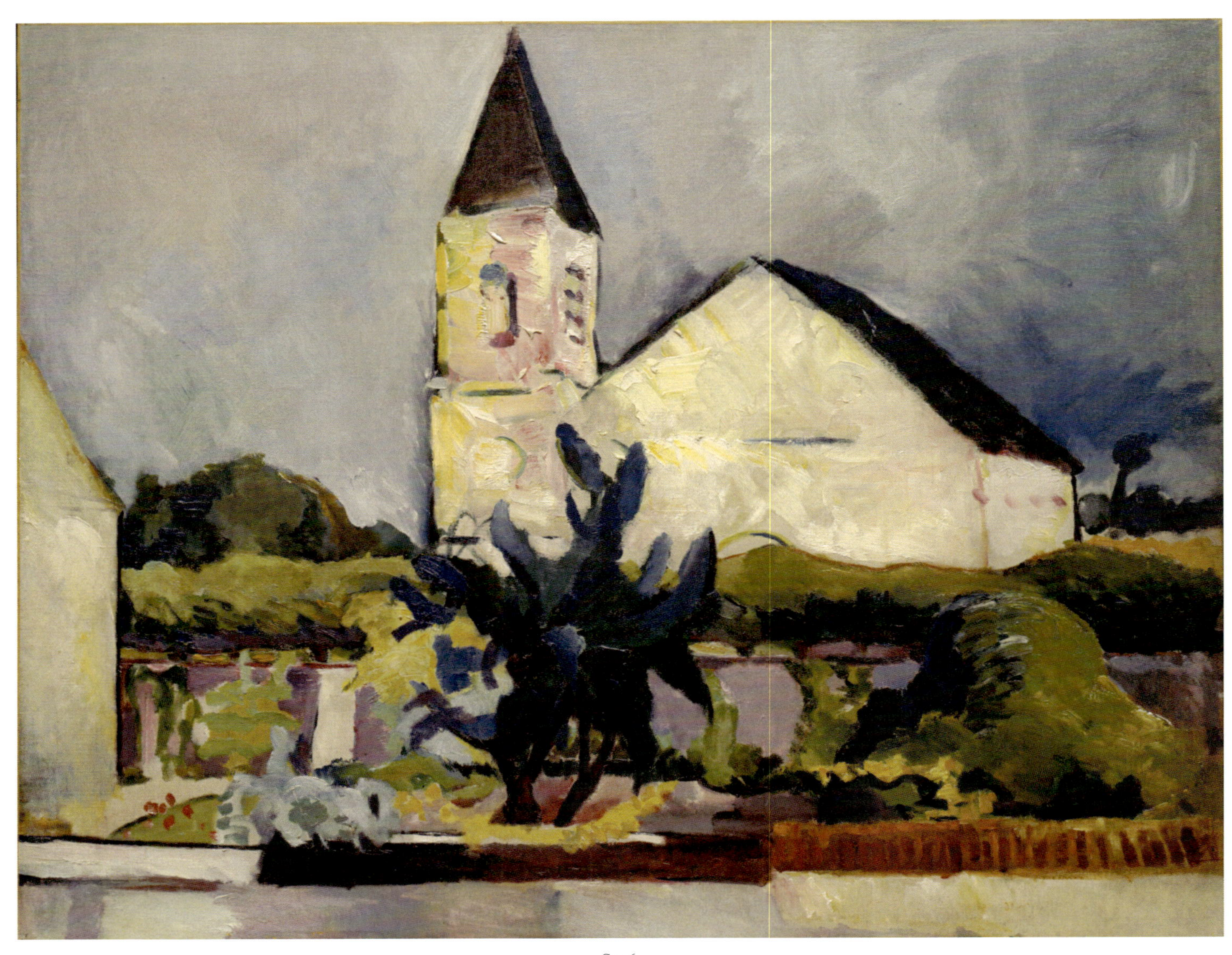

Cat. 6.
Arthur B. Carles, *The Church*, ca. 1910, oil on canvas, The Metropolitan Museum of Art, Arthur Hoppock Hearn Fund, 1962 (62.203)

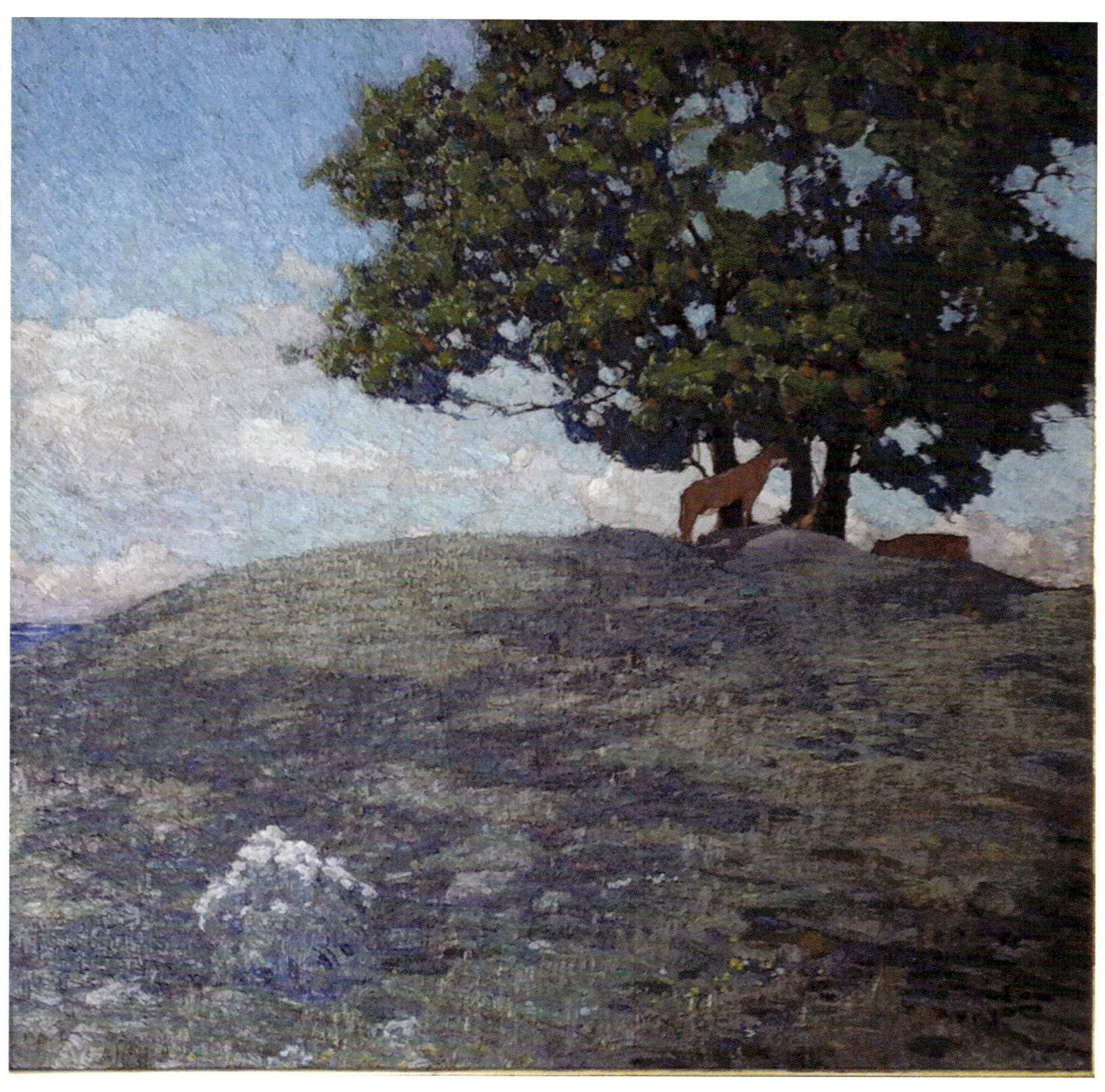

Cat. 7.
Gustave Cimiotti, *Hillside*, 1912, oil on canvas, Collection of Lazar Spasovic

Cat. 8.
Leon Dabo, Evening, North Sierra, 1910, oil on canvas, Collection of Robert di Domizio, courtesy of Stillwell House Fine Art and Antiques

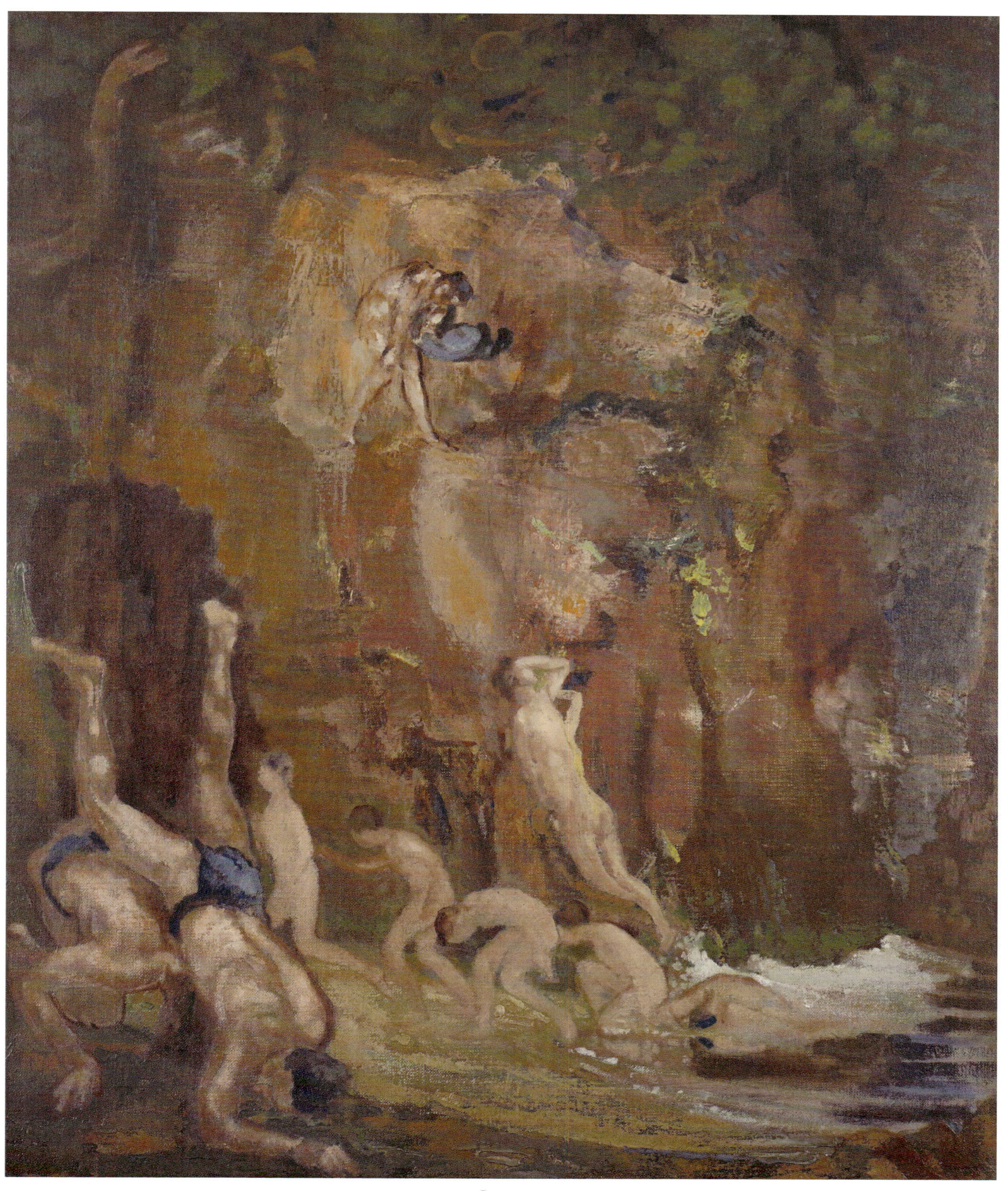

Cat. 10.
Arthur B. Davies, *Sea Drift*, n.d., oil on canvas, Private Collection

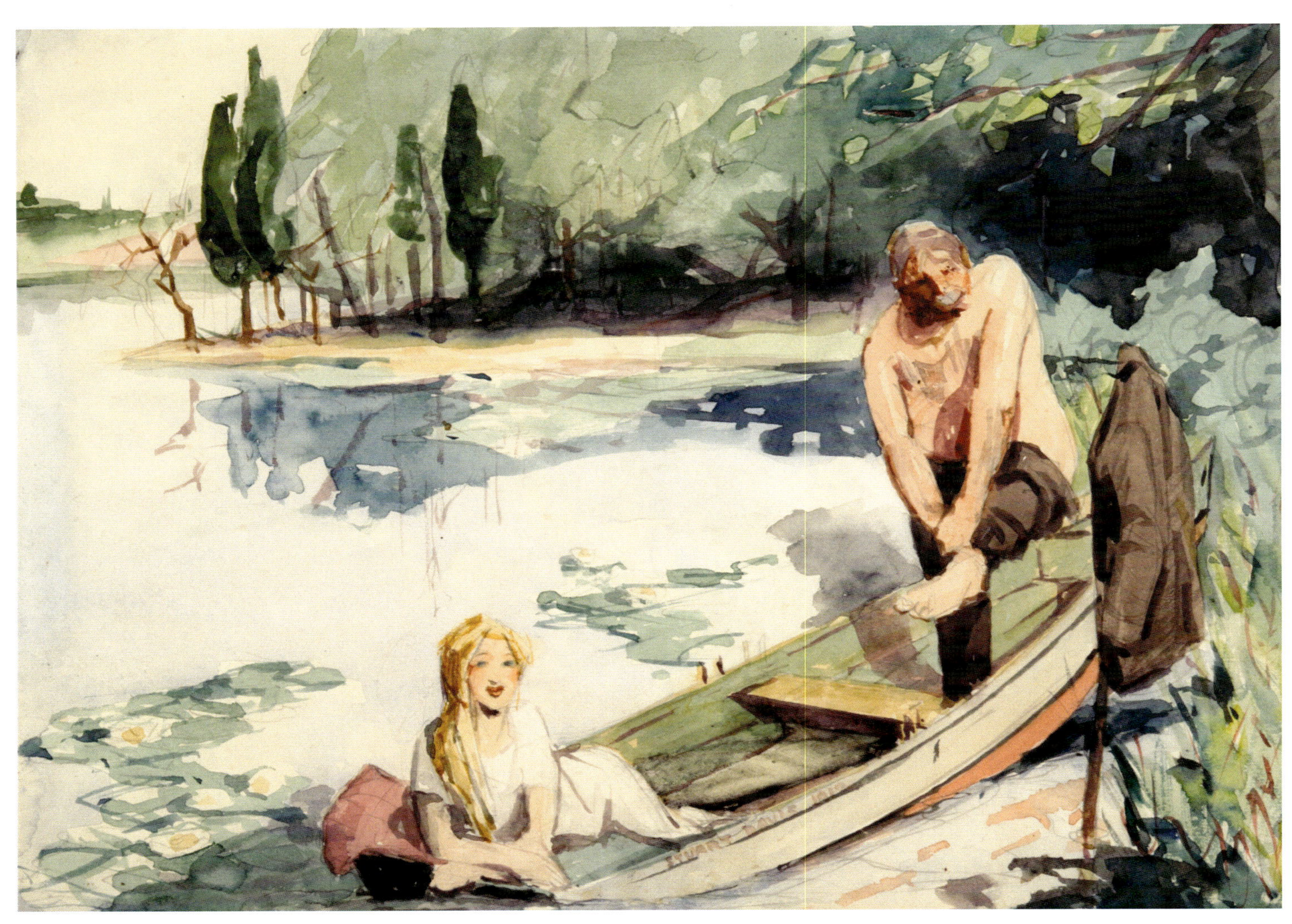

Cat. 11.
Stuart Davis, *Romance/The Doctor*, 1912, watercolor and pencil on paper, Collection of Earl Davis

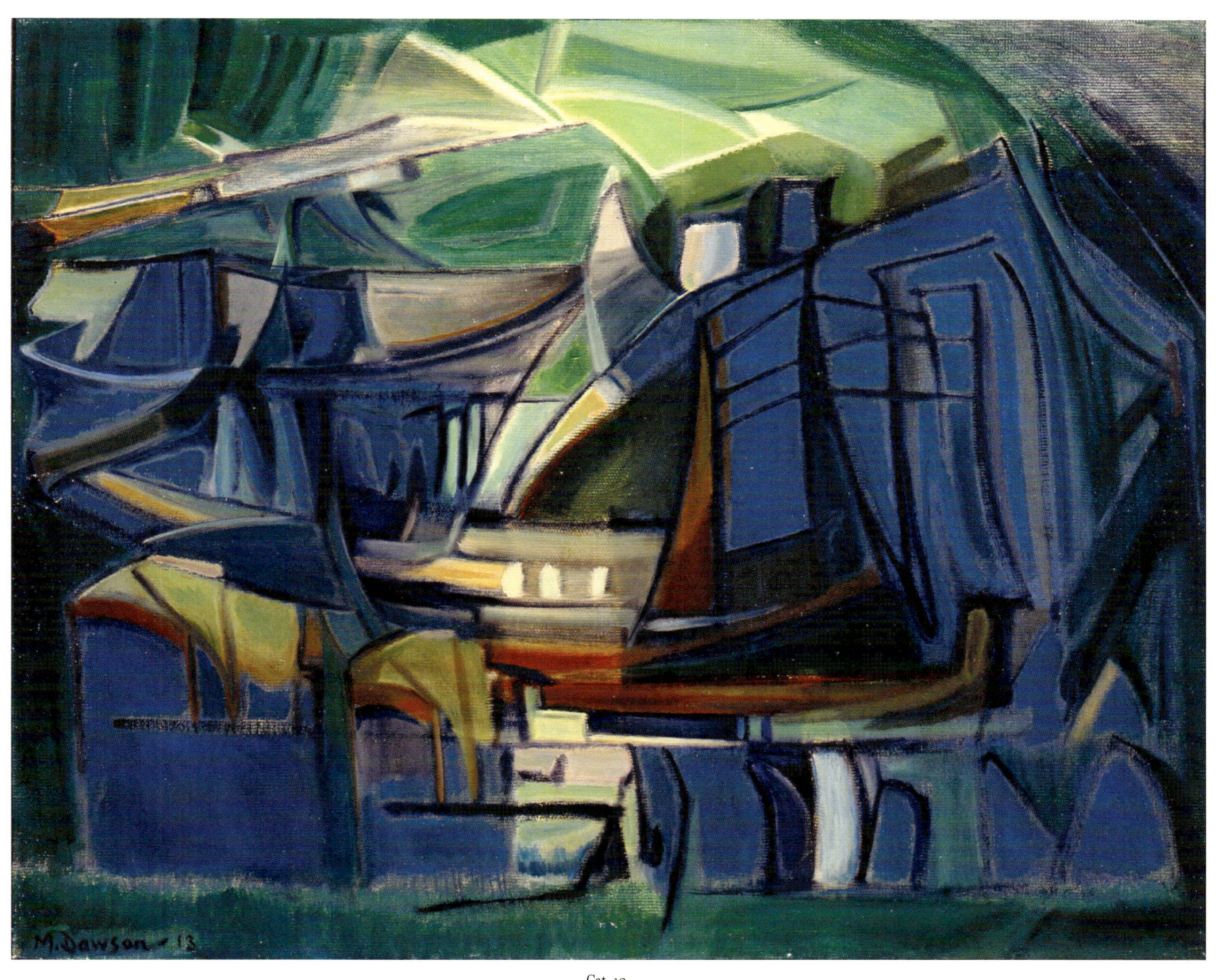

Cat. 12.
Manierre Dawson, *Untitled (Wharf Under Mountain)*, 1913, oil on canvas, Norton Museum of Art, Purchase, the R.H. Norton Trust, 69.5

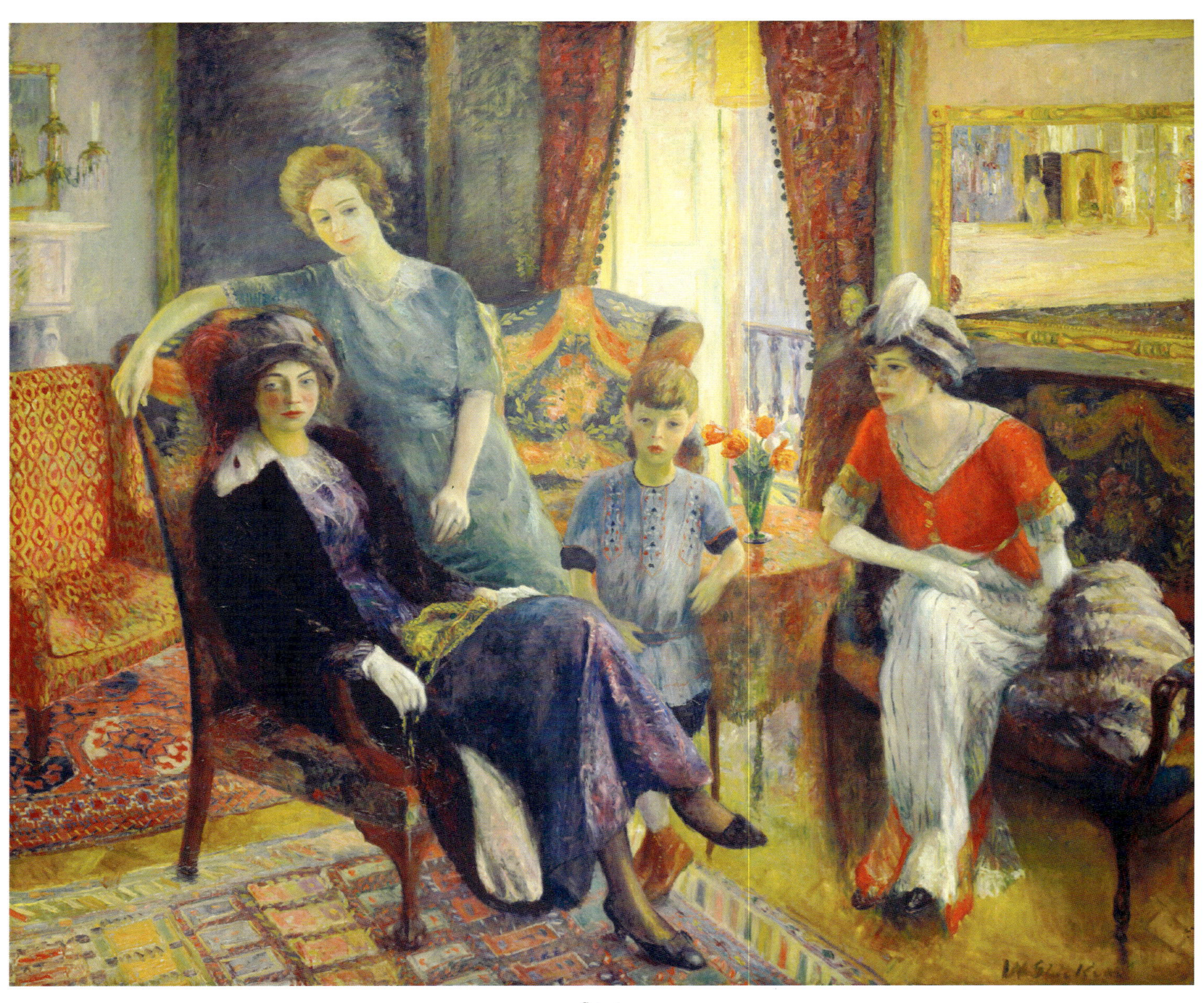

Cat. 15.
William Glackens, *Family Group*, 1910-11, oil on canvas, National Gallery of Art, Washington, Gift of Mr. and Mrs. Ira Glackens 1971.12.1

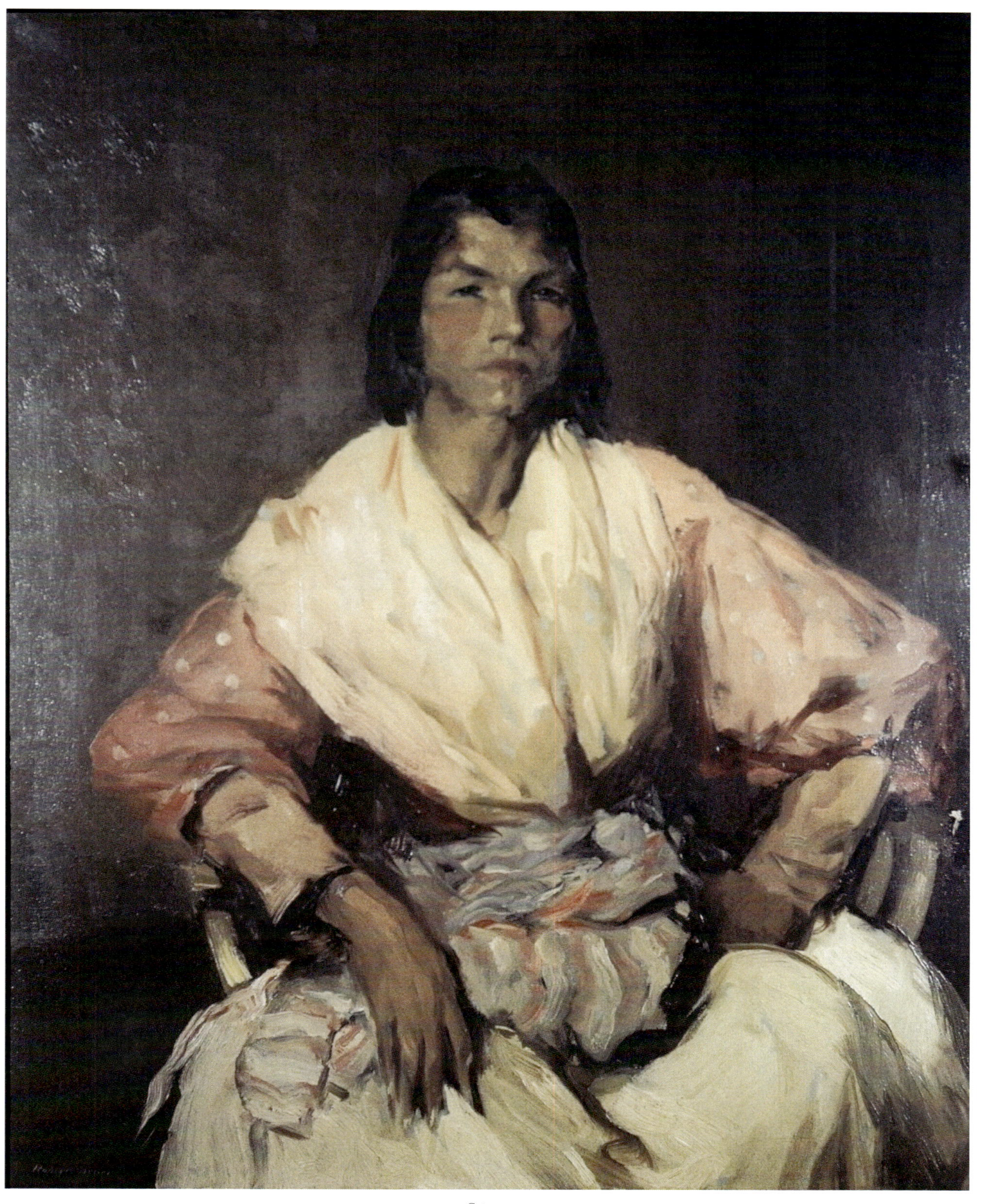

Cat. 17.
Robert Henri, *The Spanish Gypsy*, 1912, oil on canvas, The Metropolitan Museum of Art, Arthur Hoppock Hearn Fund, 1914 (14.80)

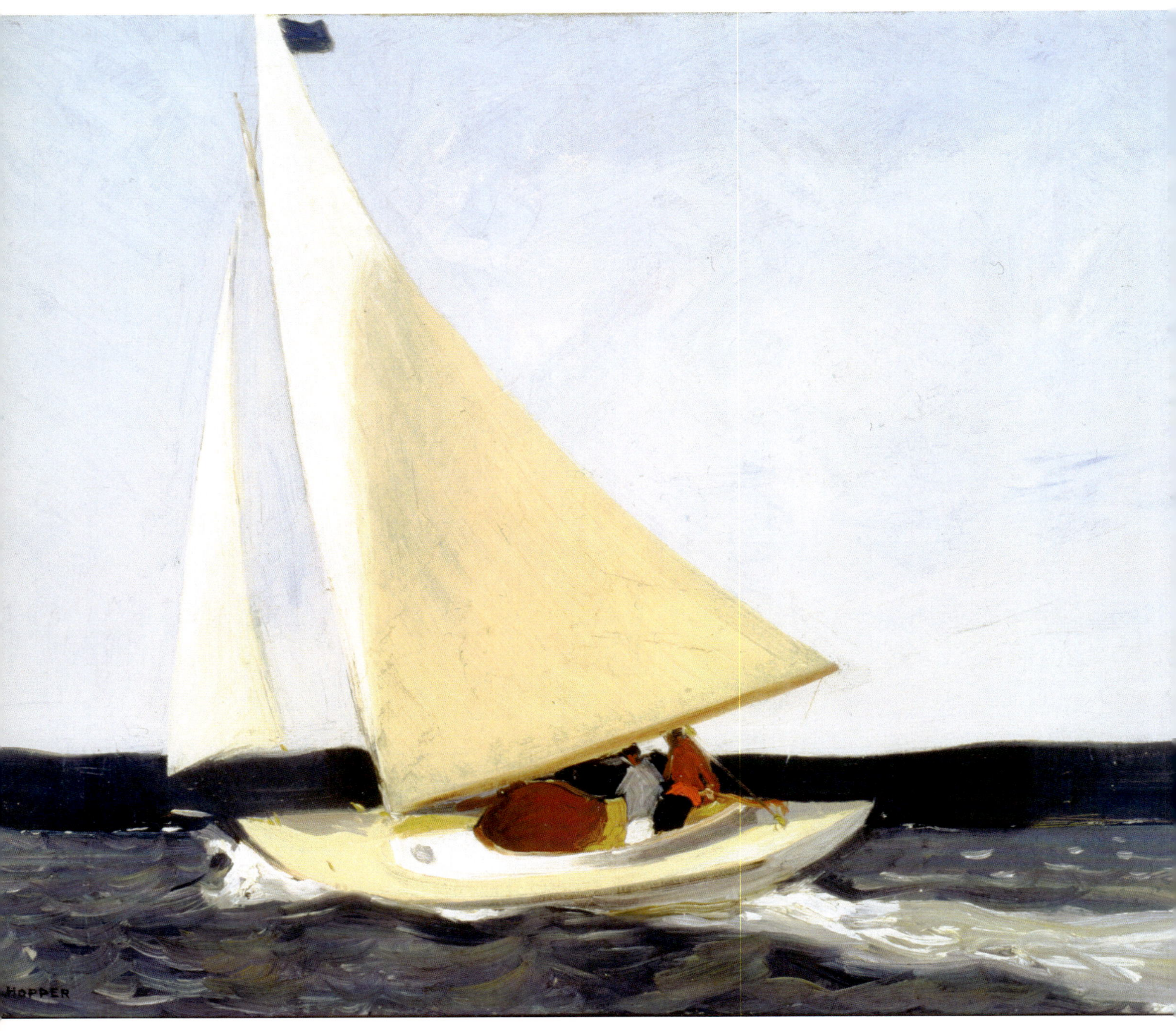

Cat. 19.
Edward Hopper, *Sailing*, 1911, oil on canvas, Carnegie Museum of Art, Pittsburgh; Gift of Mr. and Mrs. James H. Beal in honor of the Sarah Scaife Gallery, 72.43

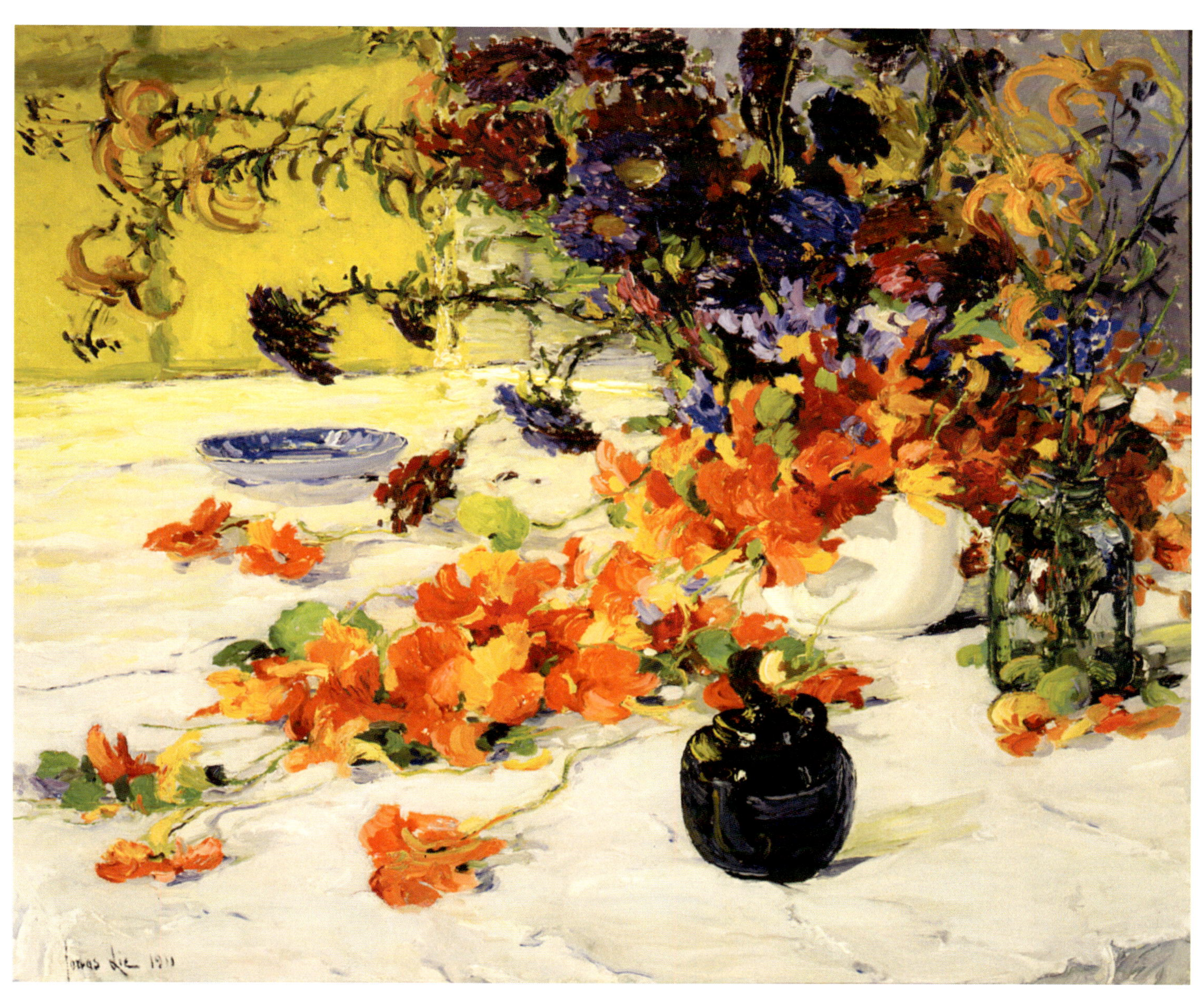

Cat. 21.
Jonas Lie, *The Black Teapot*, 1911, oil on canvas, Collection Everson Museum of Art, Museum Purchase; 13.121

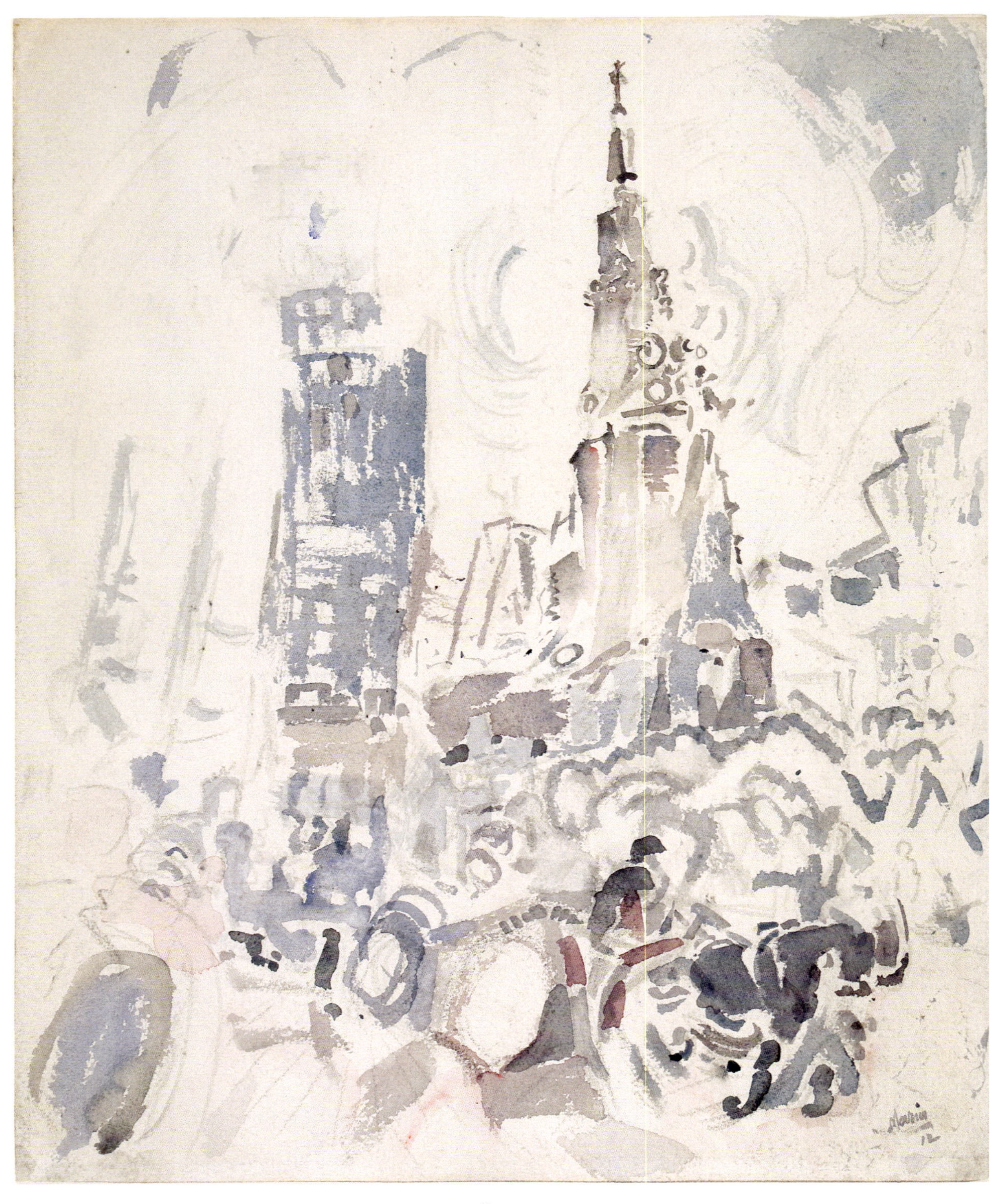

Cat. 24
John Marin, *St. Paul's, Lower Manhattan (Broadway, St. Paul's Church)*, 1912,
watercolor on paper, Delaware Art Museum, Gift of John L. McHugh, 1957

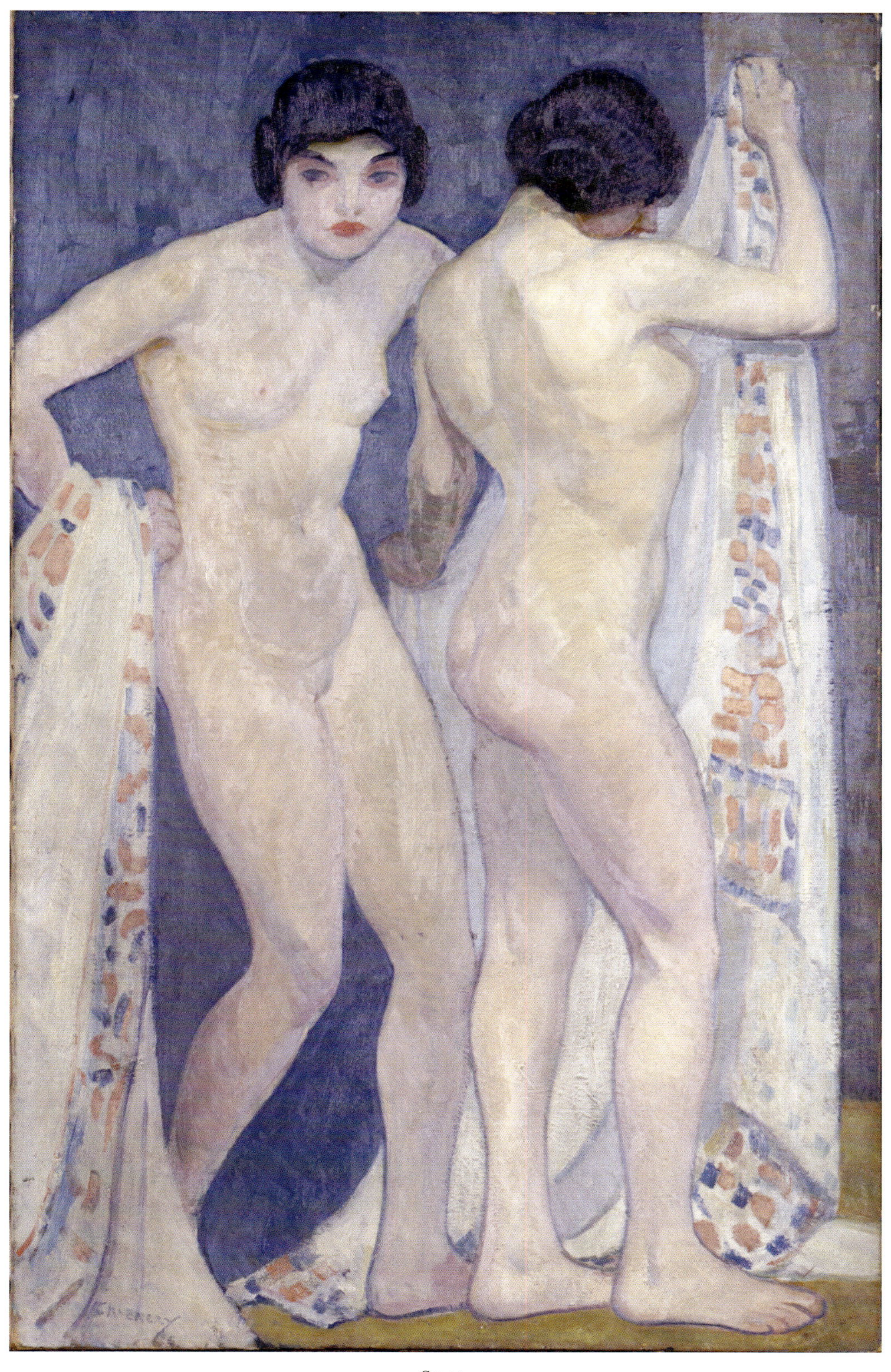

Cat. 25.
Kathleen McEnery (Cunningham), *Going to the Bath*, ca. 1905-1913, oil on canvas, Smithsonian American Art Museum,
Gift of Peter Cunningham and Joan Cunningham Williams

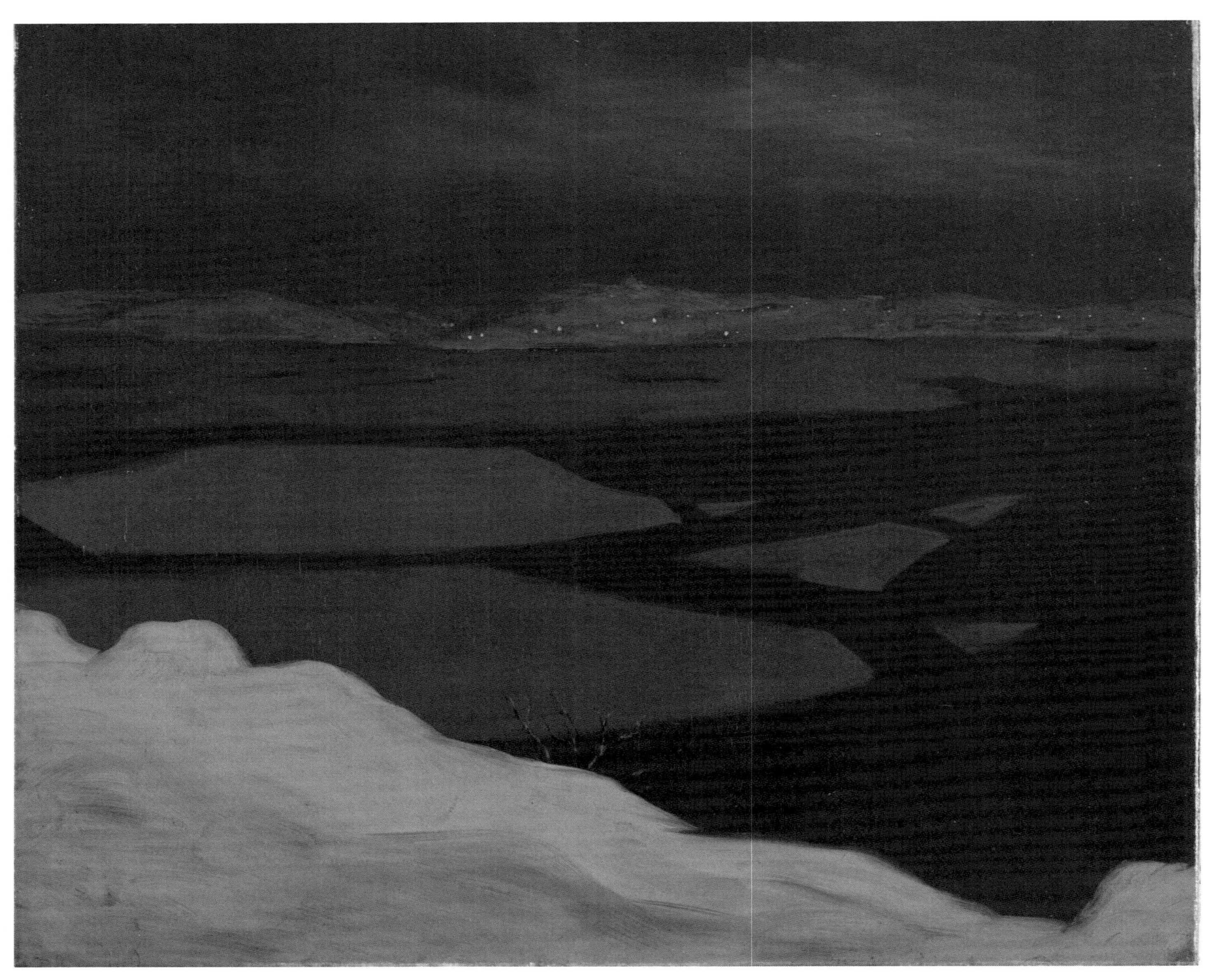

Cat. 30.
Van Dearing Perrine, *The Ice Floes*, ca. 1910, oil on canvas, Whitney Museum of American Art, New York, Purchase ,68.19

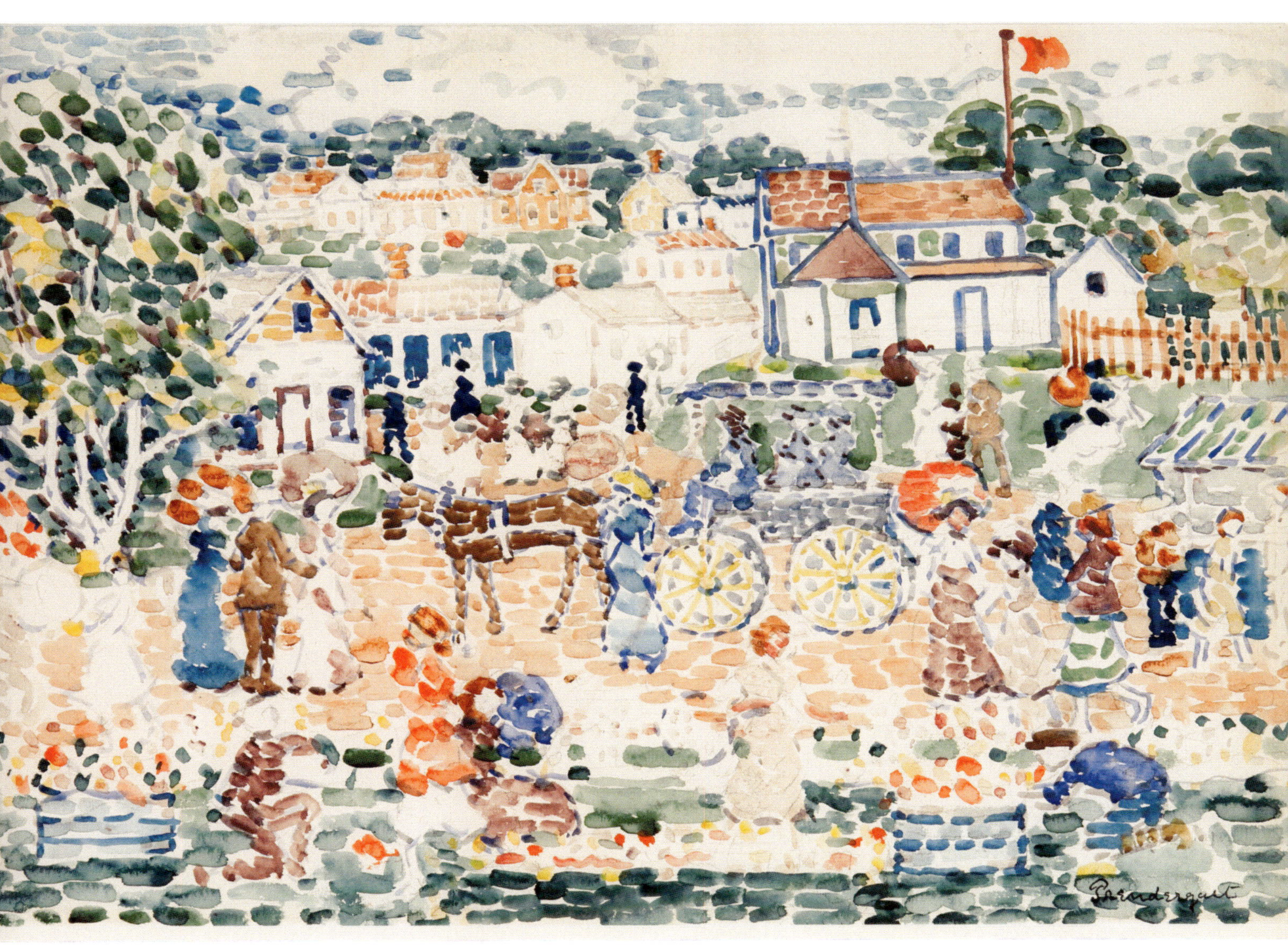

Cat. 31.
Maurice Prendergast, *Study*, ca. 1912-13, watercolor and graphite on paper, Collection of the Museum of Art | Fort Lauderdale, Nova Southeastern University,
Bequest of Ira Glackens

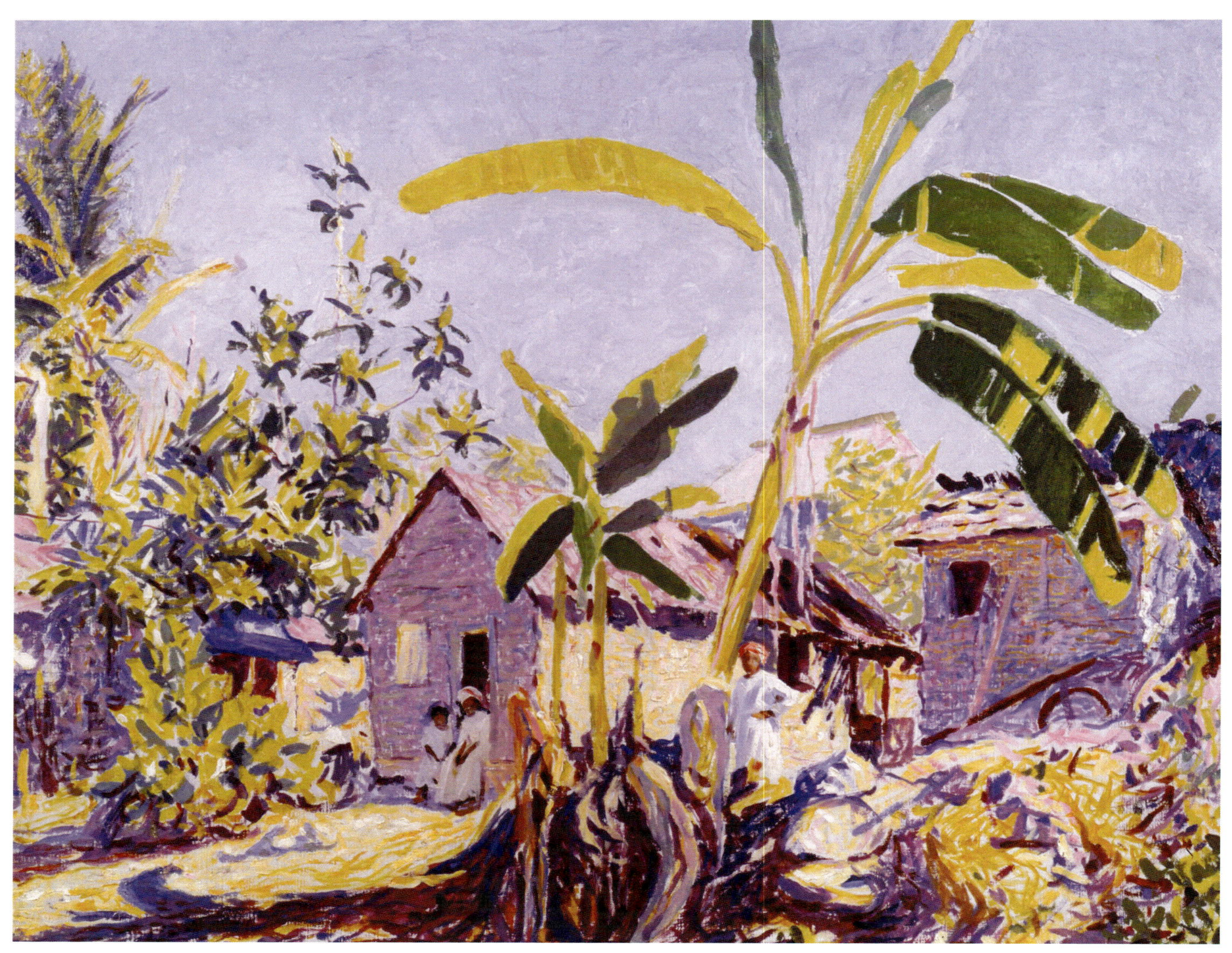

Cat. 38.
E. Ambrose Webster, *Old Hut, Jamaica*, 1912, oil on canvas, Collection of Mr. and Mrs. Hurdle Lea

SELECTED CHRONOLOGY

1904 A **January** loan exhibition is selected by Robert Henri of his work and his colleagues Arthur B. Davies, William Glackens, George Luks, Maurice B. Prendergast, and John Sloan at the National Arts Club in New York. All will later participate in the Armory Show.

1908 A special exhibition of contemporary art is held in **January** at the National Arts Club. Painters represented include Leon Dabo, George Luks, William Glackens, John Sloan, Robert Henri, Mary Cassatt, Eugene Higgins, James McNeill Whistler, John Henry Twachtman, Van Dearing Perrine, Childe Hassam, Gustave Cimiotti, and Homer Boss. Among the sculptors, there are works by Solon Borglum, Albert Humphreys, Louis Potter, Abastenia St. Eberle, Arthur Putnam, and Chester Beach. All will be represented in the Armory Show. Landmark independent exhibition of "The Eight" from February 3-15 at the Macbeth Galleries, New York. Paintings by Arthur B. Davies, Glackens, Henri, Ernest Lawson, Luks, Prendergast, Everett Shinn, and Sloan, all of whom, with the exception of Shinn, will be represented in the Armory Show.

December, Walter Pach's article "Cézanne—An Introduction," appears in *Scribner's Magazine*—first substantial essay on the artist published in the United States. Arthur B. Davies reads it.

1908-09 Weekly receptions/salons in the studio of Robert Henri bring together the New York members of the Eight, Henri's former students Walter Pach, George Bellows, and others, especially future Armory Show co-organizer Walt Kuhn. Likely a frequent topic of their encounters is exhibition opportunities for progressive artists as an alternative to the conservative National Academy of Design shows. September-May, national tour of the Eight's exhibition.

1909 Paintings by Alfred Maurer and watercolors by John Marin, **March 30-April 17**, 1909, "291" Gallery, New York, Alfred's Stieglitz's pioneering gallery on Fifth Avenue. Davies and Pach meet. Davies begins sending Pach foreign periodicals that he buys from Martin Birnbaum at the Berlin Photographic Company and has Pach translate articles on modern European, mainly French, art. Over the next three years, Davies also reads more of Pach's writings, including an unpublished essay on Henri Matisse.

Opening of the Madison Art Gallery on November 20 (closed April 1912), established by Clara Potter Davidge as the first gallery exclusively dedicated to American art, intended to promote the work of new young artists.

1910 A *Contemporary Art Exhibition* is held at the National Arts Club **February 2-23**. It includes work by Hassam, Twachtman, Dabo, Henri, Lawson, Bellows, Cimiotti, D. Putnam Brinley, Marsden Hartley, Glackens, Alfred Maurer, and Prendergast, all to be represented in the Armory Show. *Younger American Painters*, **February 23-March 8**, "291," New York. Includes work by Brinley, Arthur B. Carles, Hartley, John Marin, and Maurer, all of whom will later be represented in the Armory Show.

The Exhibition of Independent Artists, **April 1-27** at 29-31 W. 35 Street, New York. Featuring over 400 examples of paintings, drawings, and sculptures by 103 artists, the first large scale exhibition in this country of contemporary American art brings together the artists who will play a key role in the organization of the Armory Show—Davies, Kuhn, Pach who organized it with Henri and Sloan. The show attracts record-breaking attendance and significant publicity.

Extensive publicity for London's Grafton Gallery exhibition, *Manet and the Post Impressionists*, **November 8, 1910-January 15, 1911**, generates curiosity about Post-Impressionism.

Founding of the MacDowell Club as a setting for small, progressive shows by self-selected artists, many of whom will be represented in the Armory Show.

Formation of the Pastellists Society for the purpose of exhibiting works in pastel. Its members include future co-organizers of the Armory Show, Davies, Kuhn, and Elmer MacRae, as well as Edward A. Kramer, Jerome Myers and Leon Dabo.

1911 *An Independent Exhibition*, **March**, assembled by Rockwell Kent at the Society of Beaux-Arts Architects, combines works by ex-Henri students Homer Boss, Glenn O. Coleman, Guy Pène du Bois, and Julius Golz, with artists in the circle of Alfred Stieglitz— John Marin and Marsden Hartley, as well as Davies, Alfred Maurer, Prendergast, Luks, and Kent. All, with the exception of Kent, are later featured in the Armory Show.

Union League exhibition of "Insurgents" in April features work by Henri, Kuhn, Edith Dimock (Glackens), James Preston, Rockwell Kent, George Bellows, Glackens, Davies, Luks, Shinn, Lawson, and Prendergast, all of whom, except Kent, will show in the Armory Show.

Pastellists' exhibition, **December**, includes works by MacRae, Marion Beckett, Mary Cassatt, Dabo, Davies, Glackens, Henri, Kramer, Lawson, Jonas Lie, Myers, Henry Reuterdahl, John H. Twachtman, and J. Alden Weir, all of whom will be represented in the Armory Show.

Group show, **November**, Madison Art Gallery, New York, with Allen Tucker, Lawson, Glackens, Bellows, D. Putnam Brinley, MacRae, Karl Anderson, Henry Fitch Taylor, Myers, and Kuhn, who will have a one-man show there in December. Director Henry Fitch Taylor and owner Clara Davidge will play important roles in the organization of the Armory Show. Kuhn's exhibition and especially the preceding group exhibition spark the coalition of the future Association of American Painters and Sculptors (AAPS).

December 14, first meeting of the AAPS at the Madison Art Gallery with Kuhn, MacRae, Myers, and Taylor present. The gallery serves as the association's official headquarters until December 1912. The possibilities are discussed of organizing a society to exhibit "progressive and live painters, both American and foreign, favoring such work usually neglected by current shows and especially interesting and instructive to the public."

December 18, Stieglitz's letter to the editor of the *Evening Sun* is published. He proposes that the Metropolitan Museum of Art organize an exhibition of Post-Impressionist painting. A dispute between the MacDowell Club and those progressive artists who want the club to bring exhibitions of modern European art to its galleries, such as the recent show of the Société Nouvelle at the Buffalo Fine Arts Academy, is also aired in newspapers such as the *Evening Sun* and the *Evening Post*, December 30, 1911, as well as *American Art News* on December 23 and 30, 1911, and January 6, 1912.

December 19, first official meeting of the AAPS at the Madison Art Gallery, with 13 artists present— D. Putnam Brinley, Gutzon Borglum, John Mowbray-Clarke, Davies, Leon Dabo, Glackens, Kuhn, Lawson, Lie, Luks, MacRae, Myers, and Taylor (by proxy—Karl Anderson, James Earle Fraser, Allen Tucker, J. Alden Weir). A statement is made by Taylor as host, defining the goal of "an association of live and progressive men and women who shall lead the public taste in art rather than follow it. The National Academy of Design is not expected to lead the public taste. It never did and…never will." The fundamental platform was defined as an organization, called The American Painters and Sculptors, "for the purpose of developing a broad interest in American art activities, by holding [nonjuried] exhibitions of the best contemporary work…representative of American and foreign art." The following officers are elected: J. Alden Weir, President; Gutzon Borglum, vice-president; Walt Kuhn, secretary; and Elmer MacRae, treasurer. Davies, Borglum, and Mowbray-Clarke are elected to the Constitutional Committee to devise the constitution.

1912 **January 2**, AAPS meeting. Discussion of proposed constitution to be further refined and adopted at next meeting. Various artists are proposed for membership, including Bellows, Prendergast, George

Grey Barnard, Kramer, and. Sloan. That evening Kuhn provides a statement from the tentative constitution to newspaper reporters, quoted in the papers the following morning—'The society has been founded for the purpose of developing a broad interest in American art activities, by holding exhibitions of the best contemporary work that can be secured representative of American and foreign art." Various newspaper articles promote the new organization on January 3 as a society that will give the artists who are not members of the Academy and in some cases opposed to its methods a chance to exhibit their work. It is also noted that one of the goals of the AAPS is to erect a building in New York, where exhibitions can be staged, which will not be dominated by any school of art or artists. Gutzon Borglum is cited as the leader of those opposed to the Academy's previous efforts to secure a site in Central Park.

The publicized anti-Academy stance of the AAPS prompts the immediate resignation of Weir from the presidency. He is soon succeeded by Davies. At the **January 9** meeting of the AAPS, Davies is elected to replace Weir, the constitution is adopted/voted upon, and a board of trustees is elected, as well as a committee to speak for the AAPS. Taylor, as chairman, issues a statement of purpose and policy which is reprinted at length in newspapers. The primary goal to hold annual, non-juried exhibitions is reaffirmed, as is the intent to make them "as interesting as they will be representative…of American and European art activities."

January 23, AAPS meeting, Davies officially assumes presidency. Kuhn is elected Secretary and part of eight member board of trustees, also in charge of the Catalogue and General Printing Committee.

January 29, Kuhn writes extensively to potential venues for travel of the show across America, to inquire whether they are willing to hold an exhibition of works by members of the Association.

February 20, Kuhn writes to Cornelia Sage, Director of the Buffalo Fine Arts Academy, Albright Art Gallery, asking about shows of international art like the Société Nouvelle of Paris exhibition that she brought to her institution.

March 5, change in direction for plans of the first show of the AAPS, to feature more loans of foreign art, as reflected in a letter of that date from Kuhn to Milton Matter, Acting Director, The John Herron Institute, Indianapolis.

April-May, search for exhibition space. Suggestion of Borglum to rent an armory since the Baltimore Armory had been large enough to accommodate the 1908 sculpture show. First steps taken on securing a lease for the 69th Regiment Armory between 25th and 26th Streets, the training ground and meeting place of the New York National Guard.

May, Walter Pach, "Le mouvement artistique a l'étranger. Etats-Unis," *L'art et les artistes* 15 (May 1912): 92. Mentions the upcoming exhibition.

June 19, Davies writes Pach: "Hope I may see you in Paris in October."

Summer, Davies and Kuhn are preoccupied with what is initially a rather tame list of foreign exhibitors as announced in the press on June 27, including the turn-of-the century artists Jean-François Raffaelli, a French realist painter, and Edmond Aman-Jean, a Symbolist, neither of whom are ultimately in the show. This list is evidently based on Sage's exhibition of works by members of the Sociéte Nouvelle of Paris, since these artists were all represented in the Albright Art Gallery show. Deepening friendship of Davies and Kuhn results in many conversations about the projected exhibition.

July, Martin Birnbaum, Director of Berlin Photographic Company, sees Cologne Sonderbund exhibition of modern art and writes enthusiastically about it to American lawyer and art collector John Quinn.

July 31, First regular meeting of Board of Directors, Submission of the proposed lease of the 69th Regiment Armory for one month sometime between January 1 and April 1, 1913. The Secretary is authorized to write to lenders.

By **August 23**, Schamberg receives an invitation to exhibit with the AAPS. (cat. 83)

Summer, Davies obtains copy of the Sonderbund catalogue from Birnbaum at Berlin Photographic Company.

September 2, letter from Davies to Kuhn, enclosing the catalogue for the Cologne Sonderbund exhibition and urging Kuhn to go see it before it closed on September 30.—"I wish we could have as good a show as the Cologne Sonderbund…" Received September 4, 1912, while Kuhn was vacationing in Nova Scotia.

September, Walter Pach, "Le mouvement artistique a l'étranger. Etats-Unis," *L'art et les artistes* 15 (September 1912): 281-282. Mentions the upcoming exhibition and the possibility of Davies's trip to Paris.

September 30-October 2, Kuhn sees the Sonderbund exhibition in Cologne, Germany. In almost daily touch with Davies who appears to provide directions for his European tour, possibly influenced by correspondence with Pach.

October, Davies writes to Pach: "The reason for writing now is with reference to Walt Kuhn and the coming exhibition at the 69th Inf [antry Regiment] Armory in Lexington Ave. Kuhn sailed for Hamburg to see the Sonderbund at Cologne & to enlist for our show such artists as may promise of the newest tendencies—good work of an International character anywhere—The hanging space will be very large and lots of new men we hope to bring to the front. . . . To those of us and men like yourself the possibilities loom tremendous yet so many can only see another opportunity of showing their work—we look for the higher organic life in the intuitive future. I believe that you can do much for Kuhn in every way. . . So I am asking a favor of you again for which I hope I may reciprocate happily some time."

October, Davies writes to Kuhn suggesting he "go back to The Hague stopping in Brussels where there is a big movement and lots of interesting things. Pach can inform you of much of the work done there."

October 5-7 Kuhn visits The Hague and sees the work of Odilon Redon at Artz & de Bois, starting negotiations to bring a large group of his work to America.

October 7 Kuhn in Amsterdam, may see the first Moderne Kunst Kring exhibition at the Stedelijk Museum (opened October 6) with works by Picasso and Braque 1908-9.

October 8-15 Kuhn in Berlin, evidently went to Düsseldorf on the way.

October 15-25 Kuhn in Munich, meets Hans Goltz, sees works by Braque, Cézanne, Delaunay, Derain, Gauguin, Kirchner, Kandinsky, Matisse, Picasso, Van Gogh, Vlaminck in the Neue Kunst show.

October 25- November 5 Kuhn in Paris. Views the Salon d'Automne on October 27, which is influential for the Armory Show. Sees works by Archipenko, Bonnard, Courbet, Degas, Duchamp, Duchamp-Villon, Gauguin, Segonzac, Gleizes, Matisse, Picabia, Toulouse-Lautrec, Vuillard as well as the American artists Bruce, Carles, Whistler, and Maurer.

October 28-31 Kuhn's visits to local artists and dealers, mostly guided by Pach, also Jo Davidson, visited Maurer who introduced him to Vollard.

Late October—lease on the Armory is finalized. Kuhn cables Davies for assistance.

November 6-12 Pach takes Davies and Kuhn around Paris and shows them the best and most advanced art, including examples in the Stein collections, such as Matisse's *Blue Nude (Souvenir of Biskra)* (1907, Baltimore Museum of Art) and *Red Madras Headdress (Le Madras rouge)*, (1907, Barnes Foundation, see cat. 74, p. 15)—one of the most controversial works in the Armory Show. They also visit Redon, the Duchamp-Villons, Brancusi, and Marsden Hartley. It is likely that the work of other American artists living in Paris is solicited at this time, such as Davidson and Maurer, as well as Patrick Henry Bruce, and Morgan Russell. The assistance of key dealers is also secured, including Vollard, Bernheim-Jeune, Daniel-Henry Kahnweiler, and especially the Galerie Emile Druet, from which the largest loan of post-impressionist and modern works will come. There is also an important meeting on November 7 of Kuhn and Davies with Arthur T. Aldis, governing member of the Art Institute of Chicago, who promises them that this museum will take the show after it closes in New York.

Davies and Kuhn leave Paris and Pach becomes the European agent for the Armory Show. The final selection of virtually all of the art sent from Paris to New York is left to Pach, making him the primary curator of most of the 19th-century and contemporary European art in the Armory Show.

November 12-21 To London where Davies and Kuhn see the second Grafton Gallery show of Post Impressionism, which will be a fruitful source of loans, especially of Matisse's work. They leave London on November 21, having arranged for about 430 examples of European art.

November 21-30 On the *S.S. Celtic* back to the United States, Davies and Kuhn plan publicity and publications. Kuhn translates the text for Gauguin's *Noa Noa*, which will be published as a pamphlet for the Armory Show, and a series of Van Gogh's letters, which he dictates to Davies, that are not published, with the exception of one that will be published as an essay by Van Gogh entitled "The Spirit of Modern Art" in the special issue of *Arts and Decoration* (March 1913).

December 12 Memo from the Sub-Committee of the Council of the AAPS reporting that it has secured works by European artists "of the new movement in art," ranging from Ingres, to Cézanne, Gauguin, Van Gogh, Redon, Matisse, Picasso, and others, for the forthcoming exhibition in February 1913. Further examples will be added; the list of works by Americans "is in progress and the result will be announced later."

December circular signed by Davies and Mowbray-Clarke inviting American artists by January 1 "to send a list of works which you would wish to exhibit," marked in order of preference. Only two works are guaranteed to be hung. Goal to "encourage non-professional as well as professional artists to exhibit the result of any self-expression in any medium…"

December 13: Moved into offices rented across the street from the Armory and a stable nearby for the storage of European works.

Mid-December Kuhn launches a publicity campaign of sending out buttons and posters, including to Prendergast in Boston, Schamberg in Philadelphia, and Henry G. Keller in Cleveland. Adoption of the Revolutionary War pine tree emblem. Plans being made for an inexpensive catalogue and a de Luxe illustrated catalogue (never realized). Pach in Europe handling details of packing, shipping, and insurance.

December 20, Executive Committee meeting, AAPS vote on price of admission as 25 cents; $5 for season ticket. Chooses Monday February 17 for the official opening. According to MacRae's diary, they have a discussion pertaining to "Restriction about pictures being publically exh[ibited] before in New York—laid over." This would not be enforced. Formation of General Executive Committee, and committees for Foreign Exhibits, Domestic Exhibits, Reception and Publicity, Catalogue and General Printing. Glackens appointed Chairman of the Domestic Exhibits committee. Members: Borglum, Brinley, Clarke, Nankivell, Prendergast, Taylor, Tucker, Fry.

Late December -early January 1913 The names of many of the European artists are released to the Press (including Cassatt). List of works by Americans in progress, to be announced later. Advance publicity states that there will be 27 temporary rooms on the drill floor of the Armory with 2,000 works of American and foreign artists. Receipt of letters of inquiry from artists interested in having their work selected for the show. Outreach and invitations to American artists.

1913 **January 6** AAPS meeting—construction bid is accepted with David Morison, carpenter and builder.

January 13 Executive meeting, proposal by Borglum to add a Sculpture Committee to address the question of sculpture space for the show. Upon Borglum's motion it is decided to add three members to this committee.

January 18, Board of Directors meeting, acceptance of Davies's floor plans for the Armory Show, as per motion by Kuhn. Changes must be subject to the approval of the Board of Directors. Full approval of the Sculpture Committee as it stands is voted upon, without adding new members, to the dissatisfaction of Borglum who is absent. Authorization of Quinn "to urge on behalf of this Association the removal of the present duty on foreign contemporary art." Quinn's argument that if American art "is strong enough to compete on its own ground with contemporary foreign art, then…it needs no protection."

January 18 — publicity for Alfred Maurer's show at Folsom Galleries provides advance press for Post-Impressionism and the Armory Show.

January 22 Motion that "the policy as expressed by Mr. Davies in the selection of painting and sculpture be approved by the members," carried. Also approved is the "improved plan of arrangement as submitted on this date, as well as Mr. Davies's policy regarding the distribution of works be approved."

January 20-26 Domestic Art Committee to receive art work at the Artists' Packing & Shipping Co., 130 W. 54 Street. Entry blanks (no longer extant) due February 5.

February 1 Borglum writes a long resignation letter to the AAPS, protesting the "unauthorized gathering" on the part of Davies and Mowbray-Clarke of sculpture "unknown to the committee as a whole."

February 2 Publicity in *The New York Times* stating that some 1,500 works by American artists will be on view. The committee on domestic art "is now so far along with its work as to be able to report the following as among those Americans who will be represented."

February 6 Resignation letter of Borglum, published in the *Post*, with a repudiation of "the three or four men that pretend to be the Association." Response released to the press by Davies and Kuhn denying that the constitution has been broken and that the work of the Sculpture Committee has not been completed.

February 7 Members meeting Acceptance of resignation of Borglum, motion that to "qualify for membership of this association it must be shown that a candidate is a practitioner of the art of painting or sculpture or any of the graphic arts." Publicity announcing Borglum's resignation as Vice-President and as a member of the AAPS and Chair of the Sculpture committee because the "selection of exhibits for the forthcoming exhibition has been performed improperly" via favoritism and surreptitious invitations and "that consequently the exhibition will not be representative of America's ability in sculpture." Resignation ultimately has little impact other than more publicity for the show.

February 13-14, Reception of art work and unpacking. Note in MacRae Diary—"start to hang pictures at Armory" Feb. 14 — "Hanging pretty much finished." Pach had returned to NYC for the show and was involved with the installation of the art and most likely had a hand in the design of the European section.

February 13-16 Show is hung, arranged in 18 octagonal rooms lettered from A to R in chronological order from French neo-classicists to Fauves and Cubists, with intermixing of old and new, encouraging the public to apprehend the advanced European art at the end of a continuous historical and stylistic evolution. Varying accounts of how many works in the show, 1,044 listed in catalogue.

February 13 Evening lecture by Mowbray-Clarke on the coming International Exhibition of Modern Art, for the alumnae of the Young Women's Christian Association School of Art, 7 E. 15th Street.

Sunday February 16 Press View, 2-6 pm.

Monday February 17 8-11 pm. formal opening of the International Exhibition of Modern Art. Some invitations are for 3 to 7 p.m. 4,000 invited guests, uniformed attendants. Fanfare of trumpets.

Exhibition open weekdays, 10 to noon, admission $1.00; noon to 10 p.m. 25 cents; Saturdays 10 a.m. to 10 p.m, 25 cents; Sundays 2 p.m. to 10 p.m., 25 cents. Slow attendance until second Saturday, March 1. Students admitted between 5 and 10 p.m. every day except weekends. Guides on hand to direct visitors. Accompanying publications on Redon, Raymond Duchamp-Villon's architectural façade, Gauguin, and Cézanne written and translated by Pach, plus "Extracts from Gauguin's *Noa Noa*" translated by Kuhn sold for 10 cents each. Availability of 57 postcards of works in show for purchase. Photographs of works of art also available for purchase. March issue of *Arts and Decoration*—displayed and sold at special both.

March 4 President Theodore Roosevelt takes a tour of the exhibition, later writing an article for *Outlook* magazine.

March 8, Beefsteak dinner at Healy's, 66th Street and Columbus Avenue, 7:30 p.m. to celebrate the success of the Armory Show. Seven-foot-tall Brinley reportedly dances, sings, and wins a high-kicking contest. Quinn announces that the show had had 50,000 visitors in 19 days and more than 100 works of art had been sold.

March 15 Closing of Armory Show in New York. Record attendance of about 5,500 that day. The artists and others parade with regimental fife and drum, led by Brinley as drum major, through each room, cheering all who are represented in the show. Attendance recorded as 87,620 (MacRae Papers, Roll 4132, frame 69), other sources state almost 100,000.

Mid-late March Exhibition at the New York Public Library of reprints of Cubist and Futurist art shown at the Armory Show.

March 23 Opening of the Academy of Misapplied Art's parody of the Armory Show's "cubist, past-impressionistic, futuristic, neurotic, psychopathic, and paretic schools," comprised of paintings by Bellows and various academic artists such as Kenyon Cox, held in the Lighthouse for the Blind, 111 E. 59th Street, as a benefit for that institution.

March 24-April 16 International Exhibition of Modern Art at the Art Institute of Chicago, over 100,000 attend, It is about half the size of the New York Show; many of the Americans and much of the historical section as well as most of the American sculpture are eliminated. The catalogue goes into a second edition at the end of the first week. So many inquiries about the modern art on view are received that the Committee of the AAPS in Chicago, also discouraged by the lack of thoughtful commentary in the Chicago press, which often alternated between jeering parodies and moralistic condemnations, publishes *For and Against: Views on the International Exhibition Held in New York and Chicago.*

April 28-May 19 Copley Hall, Boston. Press preview on Sunday afternoon April 27. After various proposals for the limited space, no American art is shown. Only 244 works are received; almost none of the early French work was included. 12,676 paid admissions.

June 7 Paterson Strike Pageant held at Madison Square Garden, organized by Sloan, patron Mabel Dodge, journalist John Reed, and leaders of the Industrial Workers of the World, to dramatize the plight of striking textile workers in Paterson, New Jersey.

November 12 Meeting of the AAPS directors. Davies congratulates the society "on having success-fully held in New York City the first real International Exhibition of Modern art." It is also resolved "to recommend that the Association hold no exhibition during this season." The Treasurer plans to submit complete accounts of the financial affairs of the AAPS at the regular Annual meeting of the Association in January 1914. The successful outcome of Quinn's efforts on behalf of duty-free contemporary art is also noted.

December 1913-May 1914 Opening at the Carnegie Institute, a show of modern American art that Davies, Kuhn, and Pach organize as a sequel to the Armory Show, travels to New York, Detroit, Cincinnati, and Baltimore.

1914 **May 18** Meeting of the AAPS, resignations of du Bois, Bellows, Henri, Myers, Fry, Luks, Sloan, Lie, Dabo, due to incomplete financial reports. Effective end of the organization which lasts another two years mostly to clear up administrative details.

The Exhibition of Contemporary Art at the National Arts Club from **February 5 through March 7**, featuring over 200 works by American artists.

1915 Robert Henri organizes a Modern American Art exhibit for the Panama-California Exposition in San Diego, which focuses primarily on the Eight and is overshadowed by the larger Panama-Pacific International Exposition in San Francisco.

1916 Forum Exhibition held at the Anderson Gallery focuses, in reaction to the Armory Show, on American modernism with nearly 200 paintings and drawings by 17 artists.

1917 Formation of the Society of Independent Artists to organize large, annual, non-juried exhibitions.

1918 Founding of the Whitney Studio Club in Greenwich Village.

1920 Founding of the Société Anonyme by Katherine Dreier, Man Ray, and Marcel Duchamp, which sponsors lectures, concerts, publications, and exhibitions of modern art until 1940.

1921 Opening of the Phillips Memorial Art Gallery in Washington D.C, the country's first museum of modern art.

1922 Dr. Albert C. Barnes established the Barnes Foundation for the purpose of "promot[ing] the advancement of education and the appreciation of the fine arts." A 24-room gallery is constructed in Merion, Pennsylvania and dedicated in 1925. Limited access to the collection which includes works by some American artists, especially Glackens, Maurer, and Charles Demuth.

1926 International Exhibition of Modern Art at the Brooklyn Museum.

1927 A.E. Gallatin's Gallery of Living Art opens at New York University as the country's first museum of modern and contemporary art in the center of the art world.

1929 Opening of the Museum of Modern Art, New York.

1931 Founding of the Whitney Museum of American Art, New York.

1935 The Whitney Museum of American Art mounts Abstract Painting in America, the first museum show on this subject.

1938 Kuhn self-published *The Story of the Armory Show* on the occasion of the 25th anniversary. Pach's *Queer Thing, Painting* is published with his recollections of the Armory Show.

1940 Myers's *An Artist in Manhattan* and Du Bois's *Artists Say the Silliest Things* are published, which include their observations on the Armory Show.

1944 *Pictures for Peace: A Retrospective Exhibition Organized from the Armory Show of 1913* is held at the Cincinnati Art Museum from **March 18-April 16**.

1958 45th Anniversary of the Armory Show and the exhibition *The 1913 Armory Show in Retrospect* at the Mead Arts Building, Amherst College, **February 17-March 17**. Discovery of MacRae's papers in the barn of the Holley House in Cos Cob, Connecticut, subsequently acquired by the Joseph H. Hirshhorn Foundation.

1962 Donation of Kuhn's papers and records of the Armory Show by his daughter Brenda Kuhn to the Archives of American Art.

1963 50th Anniversary exhibition at Munson-Williams-Proctor Institute, **February 17 March 31**, and the Henry Street Settlement at the 69th Regiment Armory, **April 6- 28**. Publication of Milton Brown's *The Story of the Armory Show. Decade of the Armory Show* at the Whitney Museum of American Art.

1964 *The Organizers of the Armory Show* is held at Museum of Art, The University of Kansas from **March 1 through April 15**.

1965 Brenda Kuhn donates to the Archives of American Art a new trove of letters by her father to her mother Vera, related to the formation of the AAPS, Kuhn's travels abroad in 1912 to secure work for the show, and also to his travel to Chicago and Boston to manage aspects of it.

1988 75th Anniversary exhibitions at the Hirshhorn and Archives of American Art. Publication of special issue of the Archives of American Art Journal.

1988 Sale of Walter Pach Papers to the Archives of American Art by Pach's widow Nikifora L. Iliopoulos.

1995 & Donation of the Margaret Gillies Carlton papers to the Archives of American Art,
2009 relating to the 1913 Armory Show, 50th Anniversary exhibition sponsored by the Henry Street Settlement, of which Margaret Carlton was co-chair.

2010 Discovery of the Virginia Vanderbilt Teague papers by Adam Baumann, which are donated to the Archives of American Art and fill in gaps in our knowledge of plans for the presentation of the Armory Show at the Copley Society in Boston.

2011 Discovery and donation of more of Walter Pach Papers to the Archives of American Art by Francis M. Naumann.

2013 Centennial celebrations of the Armory Show; exhibitions held at the Montclair Art Museum, the Greenwich Historical Society, and the New-York Historical Society.

EXHIBITION CHECKLIST
WORKS IN THE ARMORY SHOW

1. Florence Howell Barkley (1880-1954)
Jerome Avenue Bridge (Landscape over the City), 1910-11
Oil on canvas
20 x 24 in.
Museum of the City of New York, Gift of Miss Florence
Howell Barkley, 53.401.

2. Chester Beach (1881-1956)
Unveiling of Dawn, 1913
Marble
26 ¼ x 10 x 9 in.
Lent by The Metropolitan Museum of Art, Gift of Mr. and
Mrs. George W. Davison, 1943 (43.20)

3. Oscar Bluemner (1867-1938)
Hackensack River, 1911 (repainted 1914 and 1916-17)
Oil on canvas
20 x 30 ¼ in.
Collection of the Naples Museum of Art, Naples, FL.
2000.15.011.
Museum purchase made possible by William J. and Suzanne
V. von Liebig.

4. Daniel Putnam Brinley (1879-1963)
The Peony Garden, ca. 1912
Oil on canvas
43 ¾ x 38 ¾ in.
Virginia Museum of Fine Arts, Richmond, The Adolph D. and
Wilkins C. Williams Fund 78.149

5. Patrick Henry Bruce (1881-1936)
Still Life (with Dish of Fruit), 1911
Oil on canvas
12 ½ x 16 in.
Greenville County Museum of Art, Museum purchase from
the Arthur and Holly Magill Fund

6. Arthur B. Carles (1882-1952)
The Church, ca. 1910
Oil on canvas
31 x 39 in.
Lent by The Metropolitan Museum of Art, Arthur Hoppock
Hearn Fund, 1962 (62.203)

7. Gustave Cimiotti (1875-1969)
Hillside, 1912
Oil on canvas
25 x 25 x 2 in.
Collection of Lazar Spasovic

8. Leon Dabo (1864-1960)
Evening, North Sierra, 1910
Oil on canvas
36 x 27 in.
Collection of Robert di Domizio, courtesy of Stillwell House
Fine Art and Antiques

9. Jo Davidson (1883-1952)
Seated Female Nude (Study in Repose), 1913
Bronze
13 ½ x 7 ½ x 14 in.
The Angerman Collection

10. Arthur B. Davies (1862-1928)
Sea Drift, n.d.
Oil on canvas
28 x 23 in.
Private Collection

11. Stuart Davis (1892-1964)
*Romance/The Doctor**, 1912
Watercolor and pencil on paper
10 ½ x 14 5/8 in.
Collection of Earl Davis
*Exhibited in the 1913 Armory Show as *The Doctor*

12. Manierre Dawson (1887-1969)
Untitled (Wharf Under Mountain), 1913
Oil on canvas
18 x 22 in.
Norton Museum of Art, Purchase, the R.H. Norton Trust,
69.5

13. Katherine S. Dreier (1877-1952)
The Blue Bowl, 1911
Oil on canvas
31 ½ x 18 in.
Yale University Art Gallery, Gift of Barbara B. and
Theodore Dreier, Jr., in honor of the Katherine S. Dreier
Bequest

14. Abastenia St. Leger Eberle (1878-1942)
Three bronze sculptures from the *Wading Series* exhibited as
a group:
Girl Seated: 8 ¼ x 13 x 7 in.
Girl Standing: 13 ½ x 6 x 7 ½ in.
Sea Treasures: 10 x 13 ¼ x 9 ¾ in.
Modeled 1911; cast 1913 or later
Corcoran Gallery of Art, Washington, DC, Museum
Purchase, Special Authority of the Director, 68.28.5,
68.28.6, 68.28.7

15. William Glackens (1870-1938)
Family Group, 1910-11
Oil on canvas
71 15/16 x 84 in.
National Gallery of Art, Washington,
Gift of Mr. and Mrs. Ira Glackens 1971.12.1

16. Marsden Hartley (1877-1945)
Still Life No. 1, 1912
Oil on canvas
31 ½ x 25 5/8 in.
Columbus Museum of Art, Ohio; Gift of Ferdinand Howald,
1931.184

17. Robert Henri (1865-1929)
The Spanish Gypsy, 1912
Oil on canvas
40 ¾ x 33 in.
Lent by The Metropolitan Museum of Art, Arthur Hoppock
Hearn Fund, 1914 (14.80)

18. Robert Henri (1865-1929)
Where We Dined in the Latin Quarter, Paris, in 1896, 1904
Ink on paper
11 x 8 7/16 in.
Delaware Art Museum, Gift of Helen Farr Sloan, 2011

19. Edward Hopper (1882-1967)
Sailing, 1911
Oil on canvas
24 x 29 in.
Carnegie Museum of Art, Pittsburgh; Gift of Mr. and Mrs. James H. Beal in honor of the Sarah Scaife Gallery, 72.43

20. Grace Mott Johnson (1882-1967)
Greyhound Pup #2, 1911
Bronze
Height: 9 in. Base: 7 x 6 3/4 in.
Collection of Arthur A. Anderson

21. Jonas Lie (1880-1940)
The Black Teapot, 1911
Oil on canvas
35 x 42 in.
Collection Everson Museum of Art, Museum Purchase; 13.121

22. Elmer MacRae (1875-1955)
Fairy Stories (Fairy Tales), 1912
Oil on canvas
28 3/8 x 36 1/8 in.
Parrish Art Museum, Southampton, NY, Gift of the Littlejohn Foundation, Littlejohn Collection, 1966.1.10

23. Edward Middleton Manigault (1887-1922)
Adagio, 1912
Oil on canvas
26 x 33 in.
Lent by the Mint Museum of Art | the Mint Museum of Craft + Design, Charlotte, North Carolina. Museum Purchase with exchange funds from various donors; lead matching funds generously provided by Welborn and Patricia Alexander and Charlie and Beth Murray; and additional matching support from The Dickson Foundation, James and Marguerite Hardy, Ben and Marianne Jenkins in appreciation of James and Marguerite Hardy, and the Curator's Circle for American Art. 2010.66

24. John Marin (1870-1953)
St. Paul's, Lower Manhattan (Broadway, St. Paul's Church), 1912
Watercolor on paper
18 1/4 x 14 3/4 in.
Delaware Art Museum, Gift of John L. McHugh, 1957

25. Kathleen McEnery (Cunningham) (1885-1971)
Going to the Bath, ca. 1905-1913
Oil on canvas
50 1/8 x 31 1/4 in.
Smithsonian American Art Museum,
Gift of Peter Cunningham and Joan Cunningham Williams

26. John Mowbray-Clarke (1869-1953)
The Tree, ca. 1912
Plaster Medallion
5 1/4 x 4 1/4 in. Oval
Harry Ransom Center, The University of Texas at Austin, The Sunwise Turn Bookshop Collection

27. Ethel Myers (1881-1960)
The Gambler, Joe Johnson, 1912
Painted Plaster
Height: 9 in. Base: 4 in. diameter
Collection of Barry and Helene Downes

28. Jerome Myers (1867-1940)
End of the Walk, 1907
Oil on canvas
25 x 30 in.
Greenville County Museum of Art, Museum Purchase with funds donated by The Museum Association Inc and Mrs. S. M. Beattie; Mrs. Robert S. Conahay III; Paul Doll; Ronald Green Jr.; Mr. and Mrs. Maxine Hermanos; Sigmund Rothschild

29. Walter Pach (1883-1958)
The Wall of the City, 1912
18 x 24 in.
Oil on canvas
Courtesy of Francis M. Naumann Fine Art, New York

30. Van Dearing Perrine (1869-1955)
The Ice Floes, ca. 1910
Oil on canvas
35 x 42 in.
Whitney Museum of American Art, New York
Purchase
68.19

31. Maurice Prendergast (1858-1924)
Study, ca. 1912-13
Watercolor and graphite on paper
14 1/2 x 21 in.
Collection of the Museum of Art | Fort Lauderdale, Nova Southeastern University, Bequest of Ira Glackens

32. Charles Sheeler (1883-1965)
Chrysanthemums, 1912
Oil on canvas
24 x 20 in.
Whitney Museum of American Art, New York
Gift of the artist
55.24

33. John Sloan (1871-1951)
Night Windows, 1910
Etching on paper
8 3/4 x 11 in.
Montclair Art Museum, Gift of an anonymous donor, 1982.23

34. John Sloan (1871-1951)
The Picture Buyer, 1911
Etching on paper
8 1/2 x 11 3/8 in.
Montclair Art Museum, Gift of an anonymous donor, 1982.24

35. John Sloan (1871-1951)
Anshutz on Anatomy, 1912
Steel-faced (removed) copper plate etching, ink on paper
7 3/8 x 9 in.
Delaware Art Museum, Gift of Helen Farr Sloan, 1963

36. Allen Tucker (1866-1939)
Study in Rose and Black, 1912
Oil on canvas
50 x 30 in.
From the Collection of Staten Island Museum

37. Hilda Ward (1878-1950)
The Kennels, 1910
Pastel on paper
14 7/8 x 19 7/8 in.
Collection of Francis M. Naumann and Marie T. Keller, Yorktown Heights, NY

38. E. Ambrose Webster (1869-1935)
Old Hut, Jamaica, 1912
Oil on canvas
28 ½ x 34 in.
Collection of Mr. and Mrs. Hurdle Lea

39. Paul Cézanne (1839-1906)
The Bathers, large plate (Les baigneurs, grand planche), 1896-97
Lithograph
16 ¾ x 20 ¼ in.
The Museum of Modern Art, Lillie P. Bliss Collection, 1934
4.1934

40. Henri Matisse (1869-1954)
Nude in a Wood (Nu dans la forêt; Nu assis dans le bois), 1906
Oil on board mounted on panel
16 x 12 ¾ in.
Brooklyn Museum, Gift of George F. Of 52.150

Archival Objects

41. "Information" Button from Armory Show Material. 1913.
Metal, oval
1 3/16 x 1 5/8 in.
Armory Show Material. The Museum of Modern Art
Archives, New York. ARCH 189

42. Armory Show Poster, 1913
20 5/8 x 14 1/8 in.

Elmer McRae Papers,
Collection Archive,
Hirshhorn Museum and Sculpture Garden,
Smithsonian Institution,
Gift of the Joseph H. Hirshhorn Foundation, 1966.

43. John Sloan's admission ticket to the Armory Show,
2 ½ x 5 ½ in., John Sloan Manuscript Collection, Delaware
Art Museum

44. Invitation to the Beefsteak dinner, 3 ½ x 5 ½ in., John Sloan
Manuscript Collection, Delaware Art Museum

45. Backing Board with Armory Show label for Robert Henri's
Drawing (Where We Dined in the Latin Quarter, Paris, in 1896),
1904, 11 ¼ x 9 11/16 in., Delaware Art Museum

46. Mary Mills Lyall (1879-?), author and Earl Harvey Lyall
(1877-1932), illustrator
The Cubies' ABC (New York and London: G.P. Putnam's Sons,
1913)
6 x 8 in.
Francis M. Naumann and Marie T. Keller, Yorktown Heights,
NY

Objects on Loan from the Archives of American Art, Smithsonian Institution

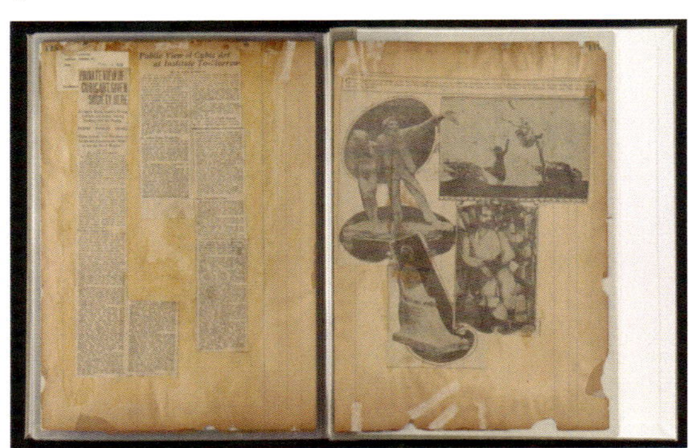

47. Scrapbook of the International Exhibition of Modern Art,
Press II, Part 2, 1913
Walt Kuhn. CONSERVED Scrapbook, 182 p. bound volume
with printed material
18 ½ x 28 x 2 in. opened
Walt Kuhn, Kuhn Family Papers, and Armory Show Records,
1859-1978, bulk 1900-1949, Archives of American Art,
Smithsonian Institution

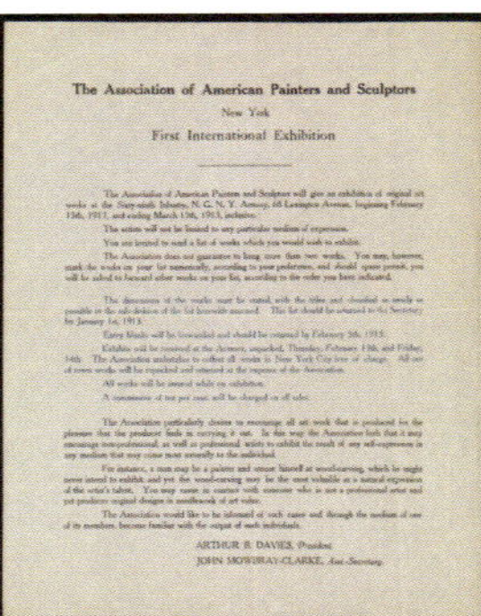

48. The Association of American Painters and Sculptors invitation to participate in the Armory Show, Association of
American Painters and Sculptors (New York, N.Y.)
Typescript flyer, 1p.
1912(?)
11 x 8 ½ in.
Walt Kuhn, Kuhn Family Papers, and Armory Show Records,
1859-1978, bulk 1900-1949, Archives of American Art,
Smithsonian Institution

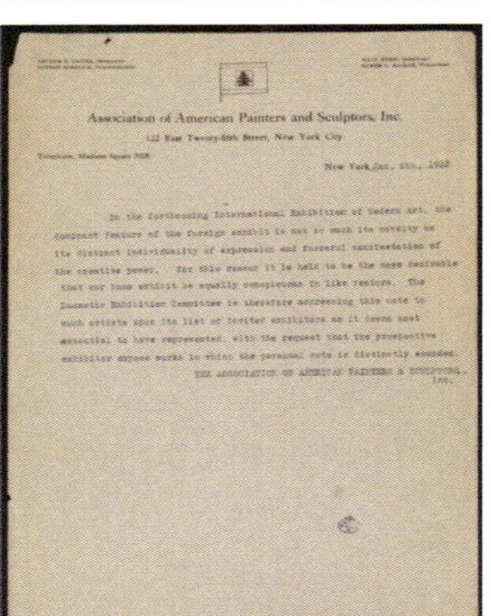

49. The Association of American Painters and Sculptors statement on the Armory Show, 1 p. typescript, January 4, 1913
11 x 8 ½ in.
Walt Kuhn, Kuhn Family Papers, and Armory Show Records,
1859-1978, bulk 1900-1949, Archives of American Art,
Smithsonian Institution

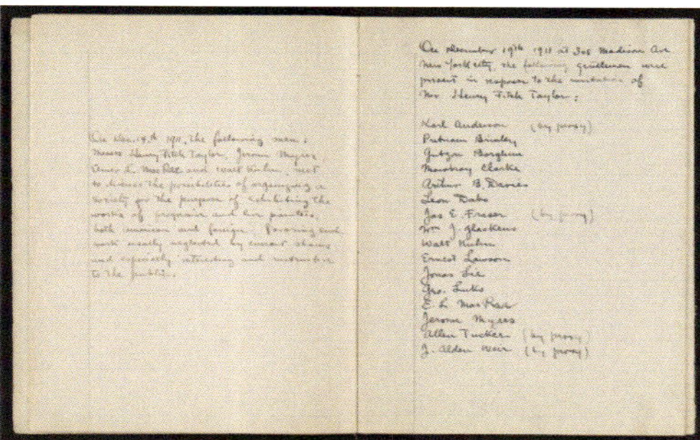

50. Meeting Minutes, Association of American Painters and
    Sculptors (New York, N.Y.)
    December 19, 1911–January 2, 1912
    11 p. notebook
    10 x 14 ½ in.
    Walt Kuhn, Kuhn Family Papers, and Armory Show
    Records, 1859–1978, bulk 1900–1949, Archives of
    American Art, Smithsonian Institution

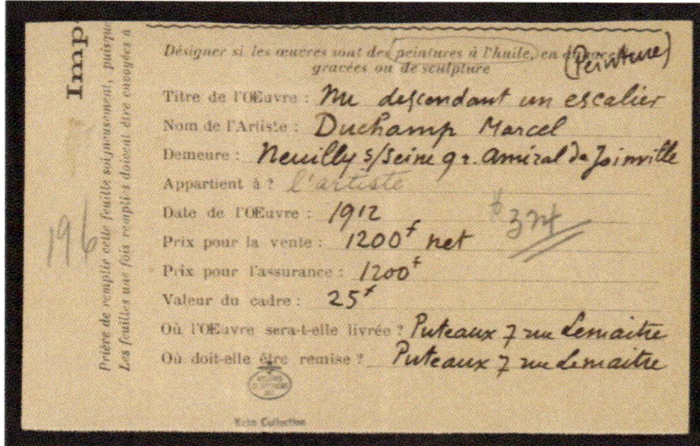

51. Armory Show entry form for Marcel Duchamp's painting
    *Nu Descendant un Escalier (Nude Descending the Staircase,
    No. 2)*, 1912
    1913
    3 1/3 x 5 ¾ in.
    Walt Kuhn, Kuhn Family Papers, and Armory Show
    Records, 1859–1978, bulk 1900–1949, Archives of
    American Art, Smithsonian Institution

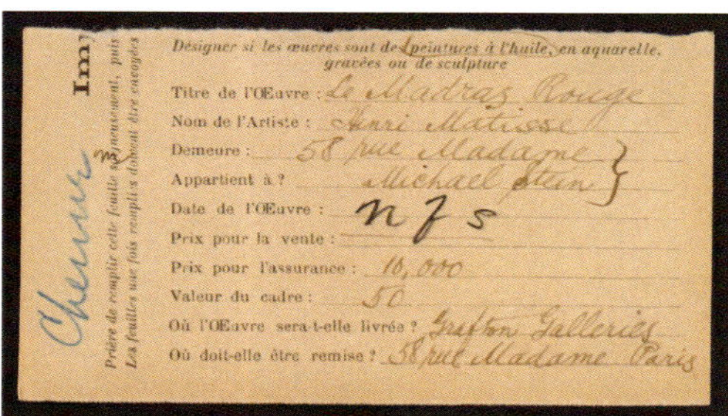

52. Armory Show entry form for Henri Matisse's 1907 painting
    Le Madras Rouge
    1913
    3 1/3 x 5 ¾ in.
    Walt Kuhn, Kuhn Family Papers, and Armory Show
    Records, 1859–1978, bulk 1900–1949, Archives of
    American Art, Smithsonian Institution

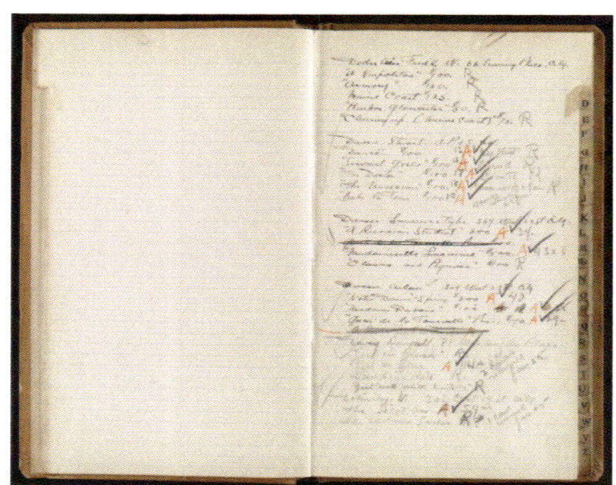

53. Domestic Art Committee Record Book, by the Association
    of American Painters and Sculptors, 25 p., 1913
    12 1/8 x 13 in. (open)
    Walt Kuhn, Kuhn Family Papers, and Armory Show
    Records, 1859–1978, bulk 1900–1949, Archives of
    American Art, Smithsonian Institution

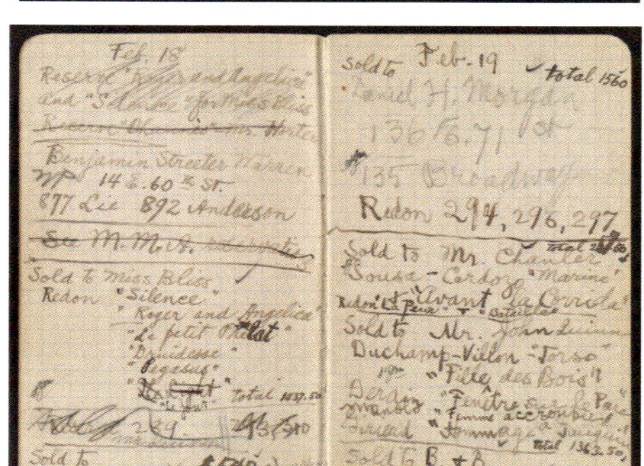

54. Walter Pach's Red Record Book of Sales, New York
    February 18–March 15, 1913
    6 ¾ x 8 in. (open)
    Walter Pach Papers, 1857–1980, Archives of American Art,
    Smithsonian Institution, donated by Francis M. Naumann

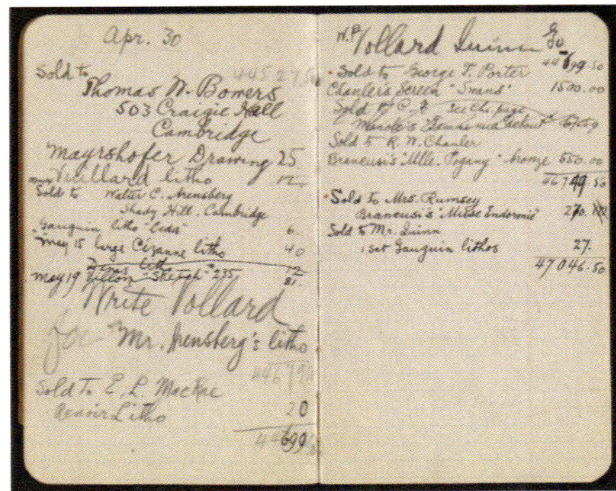

55. Walter Pach's Brown Record Book of Sales, Chicago,
Boston, and beyond
6 ¾ x 8 in. (open)
Walter Pach Papers, 1857–1980, Archives of American Art,
Smithsonian Institution, donated by Francis M. Naumann

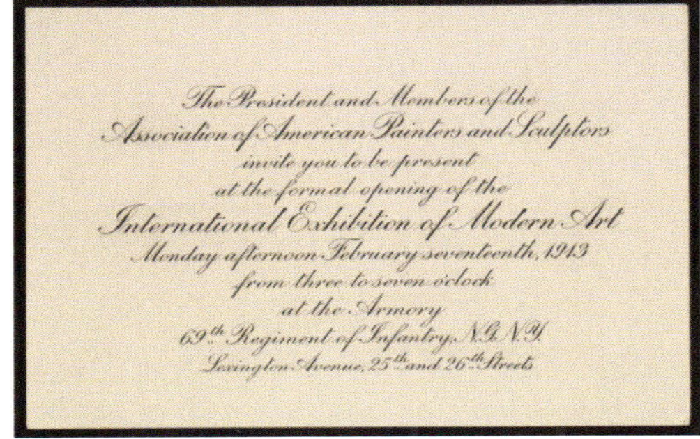

56. Invitation to the opening of the Armory Show, Association
of American Painters and Sculptors (New York, N.Y.), typescript
1913
4 1/3 x 6 ¾ in.
Walt Kuhn, Kuhn Family Papers, and Armory Show
Records, 1859–1978, bulk 1900–1949, Archives of
American Art, Smithsonian Institution

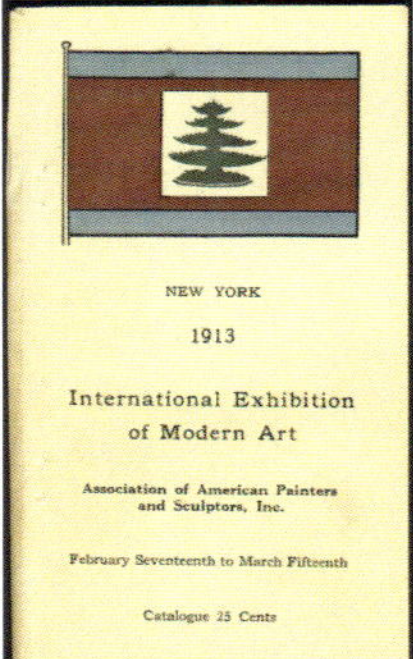

57. *International Exhibition of Modern Art*, Association of
American Painters and Sculptors (New York, N.Y.)
Exhibition Catalog, 112 p. annotated
1913
7 7/8 x 4 in.
Walt Kuhn, Kuhn Family Papers, and Armory Show
Records, 1859–1978, bulk 1900–1949, Archives of
American Art, Smithsonian Institution

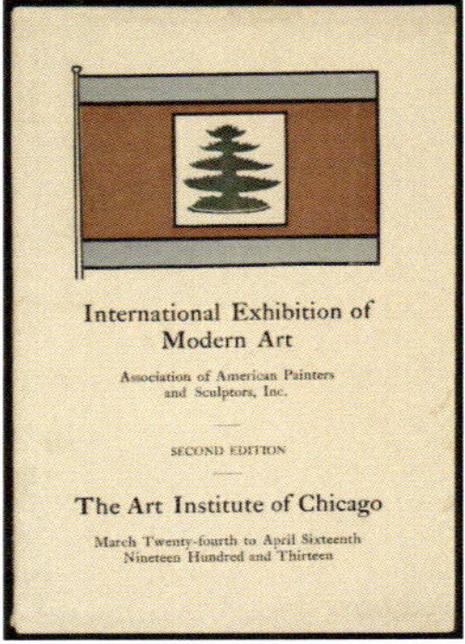

58. *International Exhibition of Modern Art*,
Art Institute of Chicago, Chicago, Ill. Second edition,
Association of American Painters and Sculptors (New York,
N.Y.) Exhibition Catalog, 74 p. annotated
1913
7 7/8 x 4 in.
Walt Kuhn, Kuhn Family Papers, and Armory Show
Records, 1859–1978, bulk 1900–1949, Archives of
American Art, Smithsonian Institution

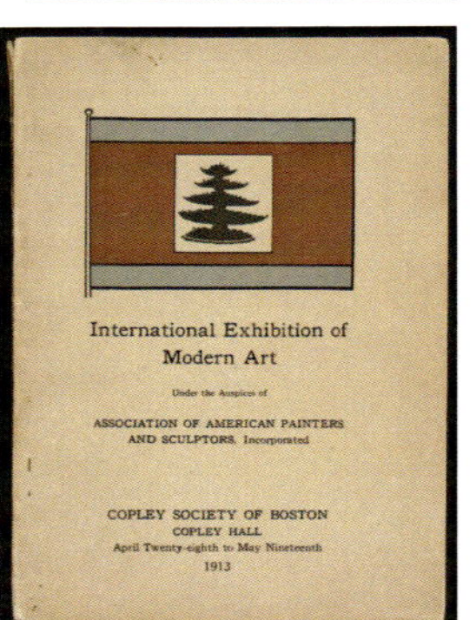

59. *International Exhibition of Modern Art*, Copley Society of
Boston, Copley Hall, Boston, Mass., Association of
American Painters and Sculptors (New York, N.Y.)
Exhibition Catalog, 28 p. annotated
1913
7 7/8 x 4 1/3 in.
Walt Kuhn, Kuhn Family Papers, and Armory Show
Records, 1859–1978, bulk 1900–1949, Archives of
American Art, Smithsonian Institution

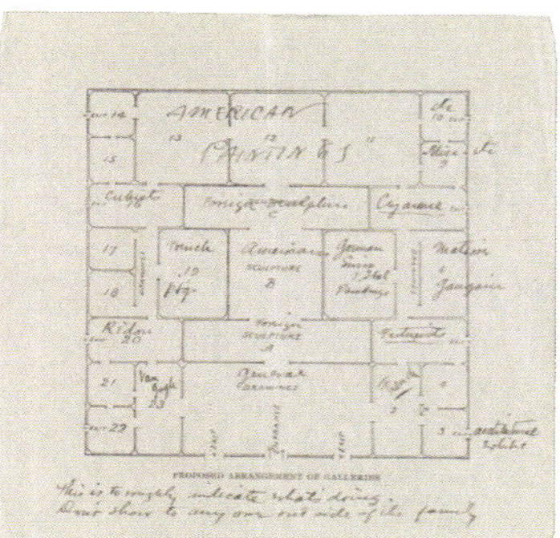

60. Arthur B. Davies letter to Walt Kuhn, 1 p. handwritten
September 2, 1912
10 x 8 in.
Walt Kuhn, Kuhn Family Papers, and Armory Show
Records, 1859–1978, bulk 1900–1949, Archives of
American Art, Smithsonian Institution

61. Arthur B. Davies letter to Walt Kuhn, October 1912: hand-
written, ill. 2 p., letter and floor plan
10 x 8 in.
Floorplan: 7 1/4 x 7 2/3 in.
Walt Kuhn, Kuhn Family Papers, and Armory Show
Records, 1859–1978, bulk 1900–1949, Archives of
American Art, Smithsonian Institution

62. Walt Kuhn letter to Walter Pach, 8 p. handwritten
December 12, 1912
6 3/16 x 7 3/4 in.
Walt Kuhn, Kuhn Family Papers, and Armory Show
Records, 1859–1978, bulk 1900–1949, Archives of
American Art, Smithsonian Institution

63. Walt Kuhn, New York, N.Y. letter to Vera Kuhn, 4 p. hand-
written, illustrated
December 14, 1912
p. 1–2: 10 x 8 in. p. 3–4: 6 1/2 x 10 in.
Walt Kuhn, Kuhn Family Papers and Armory Show
Records, Archives of American Art, Smithsonian
Institution

64. Arthur B. Davies letter to Walter Pach, 2 p. handwritten
October 2, 1912
10 x 8 in.
Walter Pach papers, 1857–1980, Archives of American Art,
Smithsonian Institution

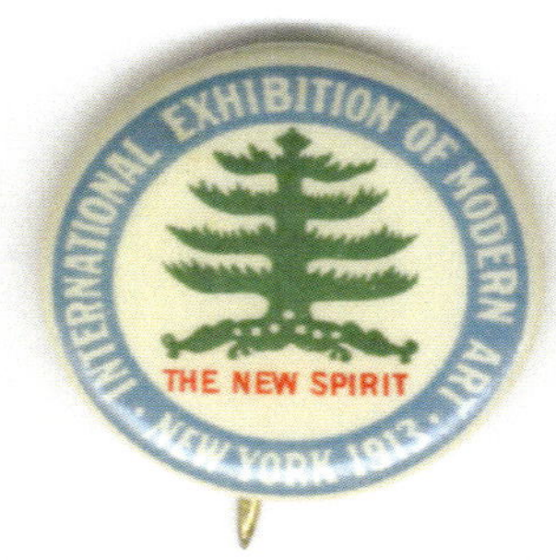

65. *International Exhibition of Modern Art* Button, 1913
1 ¼ x 1 ¼ in.
Walt Kuhn, Kuhn Family Papers, and Armory Show
Records, 1859-1978, bulk 1900-1949, Archives of
American Art, Smithsonian Institution

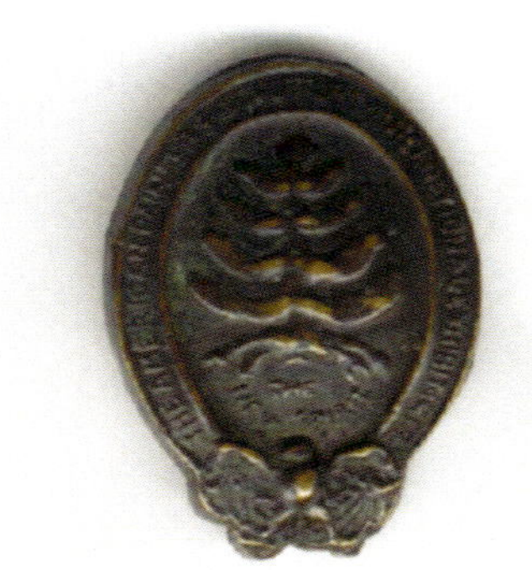

66. *International Exhibition of Modern Art* Lapel Pin, 1913
1 ¼ x 1 ¼ in.
Walt Kuhn, Kuhn Family Papers, and Armory Show
Records, 1859-1978, bulk 1900-1949, Archives of
American Art, Smithsonian Institution

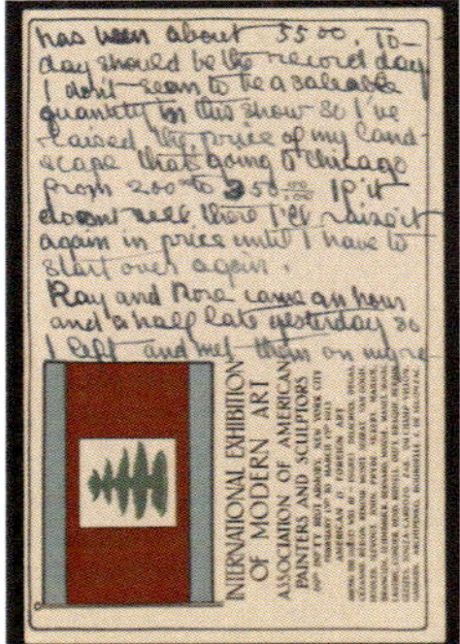

67. Andrew Michael Dasburg postcard to Grace Mott Johnson,
handwritten
March 15, 1913
3 ½ x 5 in.
Andrew Dasburg and Grace Mott Johnson Papers, 1833-
1980, bulk 1900-1980, Archives of American Art,
Smithsonian Institution

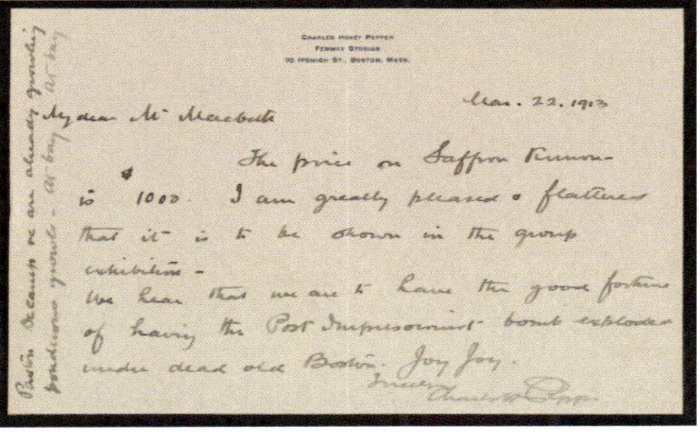

68. Charles Hovey Pepper to Robert W. MacBeth, 1 p. hand-
written
March 22, 1913
4 ¾ x 8 in.
MacBeth Gallery Records, 1838-1968, bulk, 1892-1953,
Archives of American Art, Smithsonian Institution

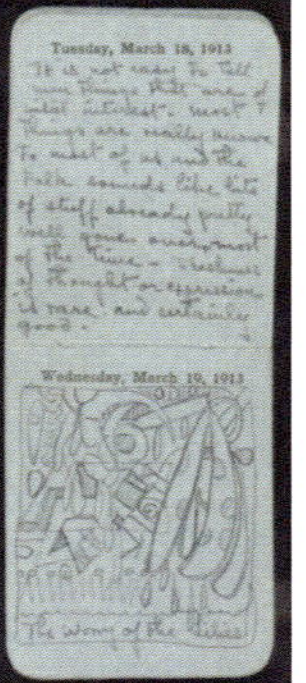

69. F. Luis Mora pocket diary of the artist, 32 p., handwritten,
illustrated
March 1913
5 7/8 x 2 in. (open)
F. Luis Mora papers, 1895-1969, bulk 1895-1922, Archives
of American Art, Smithsonian Institution

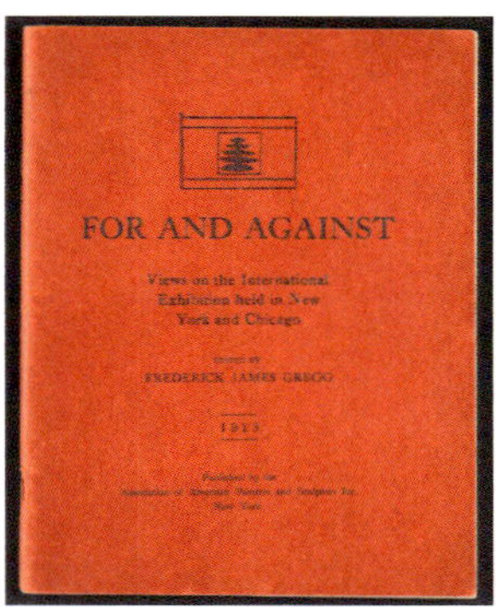

70. *For and Against Views on the International Exhibition held in New York and Chicago*, Association of American Painters and Sculptors (New York, N.Y.) published pamphlet, 64p. Edited by Frederick James Gregg, 1913
6 ½ x 5 1/8 in.
Walt Kuhn, Kuhn Family Papers, and Armory Show Records, 1859-1978, bulk 1900-1949, Archives of American Art, Smithsonian Institution

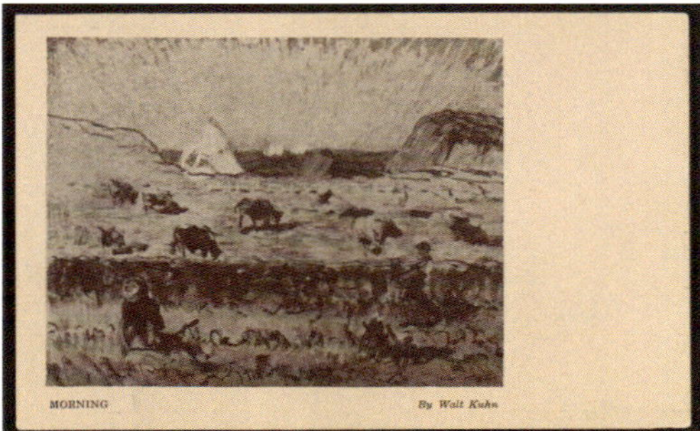

71. "On Sale at the Entrance Booths," announcement card for the Armory Show, Association of American Painters and Sculptors (New York, N.Y.) 1913
3 1/3 x 5 ½ in.
Walt Kuhn, Kuhn Family Papers, and Armory Show Records, 1859-1978, bulk 1900-1949, Archives of American Art, Smithsonian Institution

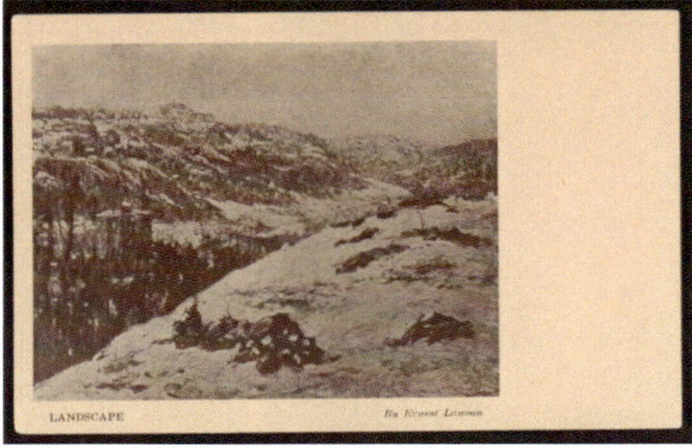

72. *Morning* by Walt Kuhn
International Exhibition of Modern Art postcards, Association of American Painters and Sculptors (New York, N.Y.)
1913
5 ½ x 3 ½ in.
Walt Kuhn, Kuhn Family Papers, and Armory Show Records, 1859-1978, bulk 1900-1949, Archives of American Art, Smithsonian Institution

73. *Landscape* by Ernest Lawson
International Exhibition of Modern Art postcards, Association of American Painters and Sculptors (New York, N.Y.)
1913
5 ½ x 3 ½ in.
Walt Kuhn, Kuhn Family Papers, and Armory Show Records, 1859-1978, bulk 1900-1949, Archives of American Art, Smithsonian Institution

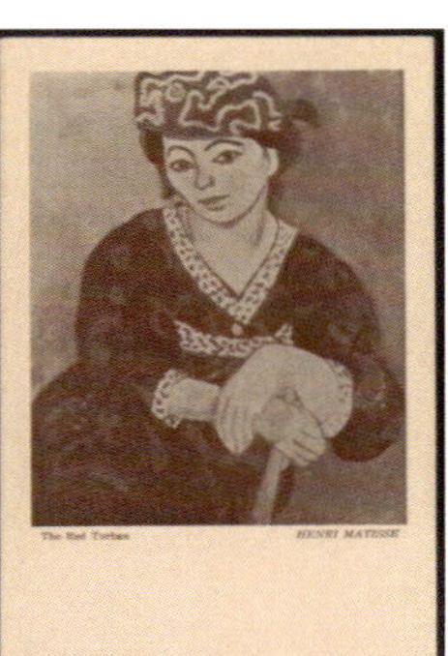

74. *The Red Turban* by Henri Matisse
International Exhibition of Modern Art postcards, Association of American Painters and Sculptors (New York, N.Y.)
1913
5 ½ x 3 ½ in.
Walt Kuhn, Kuhn Family Papers, and Armory Show Records, 1859-1978, bulk 1900-1949, Archives of American Art, Smithsonian Institution

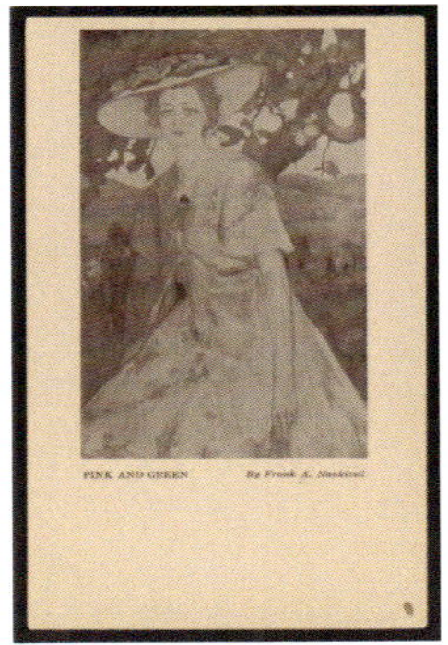

75. *Pink and Green* by Frank A. Nankivell
International Exhibition of Modern Art postcards,
Association of American Painters and Sculptors (New York,
N.Y.)
1913
5 ½ x 3 ½ in.
Walt Kuhn, Kuhn Family Papers, and Armory Show
Records, 1859–1978, bulk 1900–1949, Archives of
American Art, Smithsonian Institution

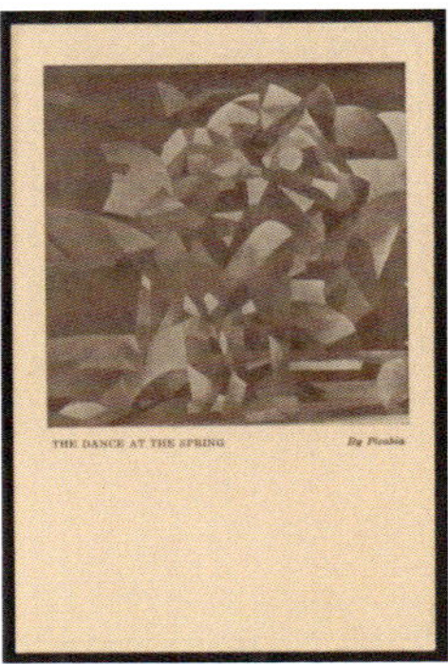

76. *The Dance at the Spring* by Picabia
International Exhibition of Modern Art postcards,
Association of American Painters and Sculptors (New York,
N.Y.)
1913
5 ½ x 3 ½ in.
Walt Kuhn, Kuhn Family Papers, and Armory Show
Records, 1859–1978, bulk 1900–1949, Archives of
American Art, Smithsonian Institution

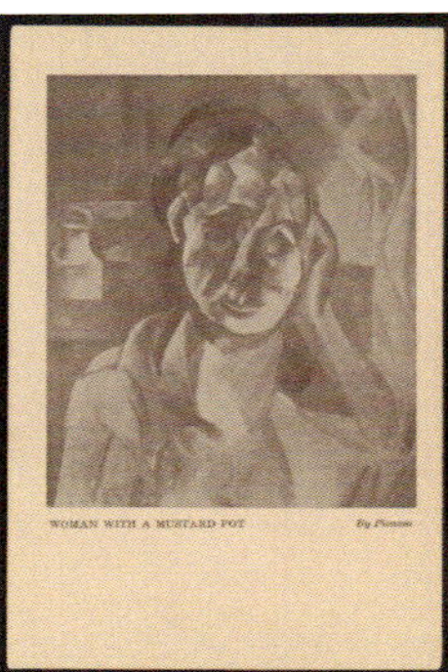

77. *Woman with a Mustard Pot* by Pablo Picasso
International Exhibition of Modern Art postcards,
Association of American Painters and Sculptors (New York,
N.Y.)
1913
5 ½ x 3 ½ in.
Walt Kuhn, Kuhn Family Papers, and Armory Show
Records, 1859–1978, bulk 1900–1949, Archives of
American Art, Smithsonian Institution

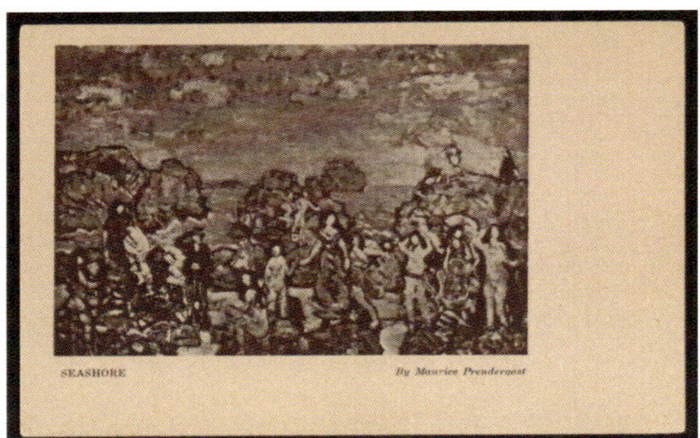

78. *Seashore* by Maurice Prendergast
International Exhibition of Modern Art postcards,
Association of American Painters and Sculptors (New York,
N.Y.)
1913
5 ½ x 3 ½ in.
Walt Kuhn, Kuhn Family Papers, and Armory Show
Records, 1859–1978, bulk 1900–1949, Archives of
American Art, Smithsonian Institution

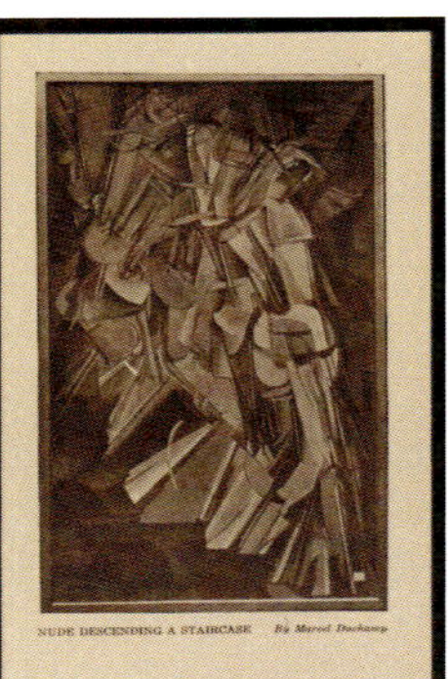

79. *Nude Descending a Staircase* by Marcel Duchamp
International Exhibition of Modern Art postcards,
Association of American Painters and Sculptors (New York,
N.Y.)
1913
5 ½ x 3 ½ in.
Walt Kuhn, Kuhn Family Papers, and Armory Show
Records, 1859–1978, bulk 1900–1949, Archives of
American Art, Smithsonian Institution

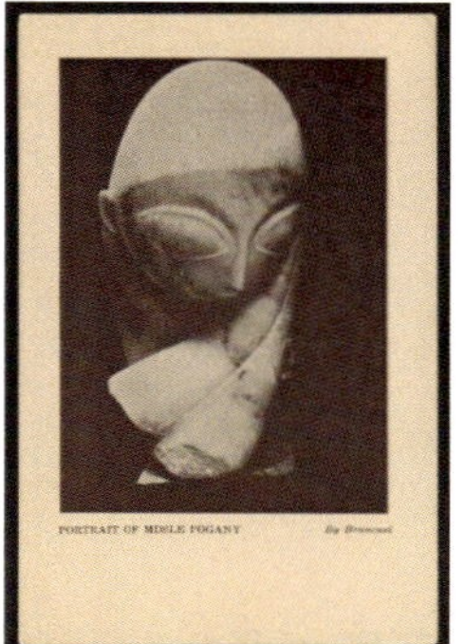

80. *Portrait of Mlle. Pogany* by Brancusi
International Exhibition of Modern Art postcards,
Association of American Painters and Sculptors (New York,
N.Y.)
1913
5 ½ x 3 ½ in.
Walt Kuhn, Kuhn Family Papers, and Armory Show
Records, 1859-1978, bulk 1900-1949, Archives of
American Art, Smithsonian Institution

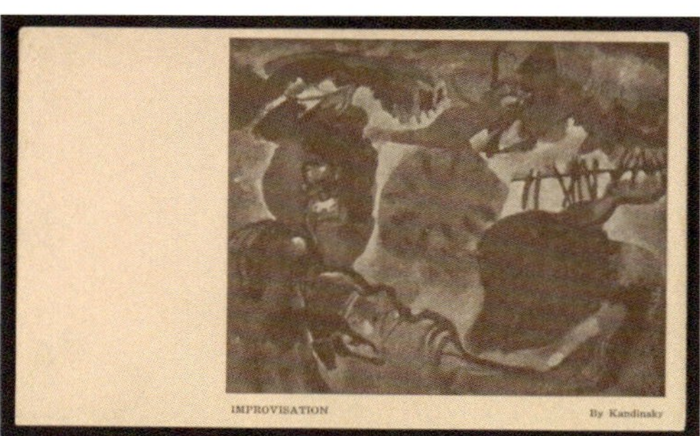

81. *Improvisation* by Kandinsky
International Exhibition of Modern Art postcards,
Association of American Painters and Sculptors (New York,
N.Y.)
1913
5 ½ x 3 ½ in.
Walt Kuhn, Kuhn Family Papers, and Armory Show
Records, 1859-1978, bulk 1900-1949, Archives of
American Art, Smithsonian Institution

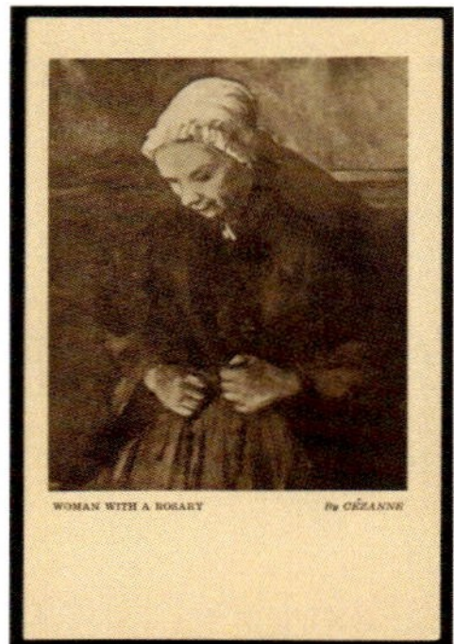

82. *Woman with a Rosary* by Cézanne
International Exhibition of Modern Art postcards,
Association of American Painters and Sculptors (New York,
N.Y.)
1913
5 ½ x 3 ½ in.
Walt Kuhn, Kuhn Family Papers, and Armory Show
Records, 1859-1978, bulk 1900-1949, Archives of
American Art, Smithsonian Institution

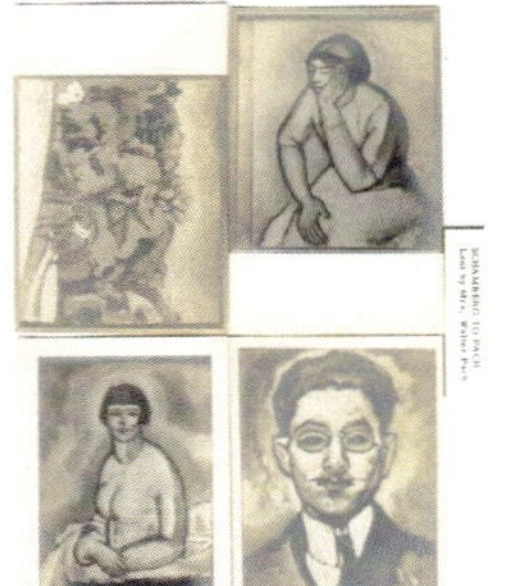

83. Morton Schamberg letter to Walter Pach on 4 postcards,
handwritten
August 23, 1912
3 ½ x 5 in. each postcard
Walter Pach papers, 1857-1980, Archives of American Art,
Smithsonian Institution

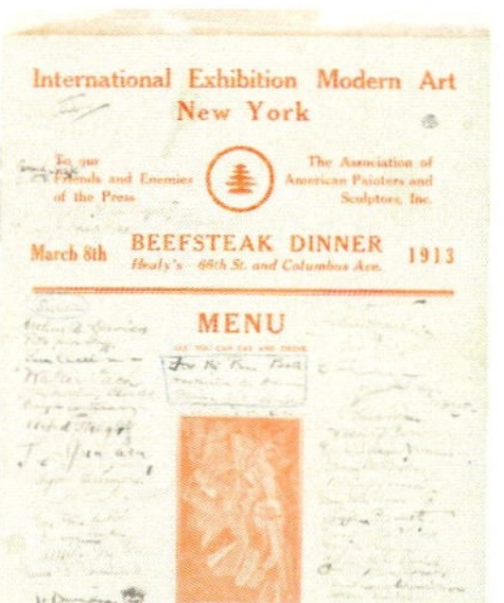

84. International Exhibition of Modern Art dinner menu
signed by guests, Association of American Painters and
Sculptors (New York, N.Y.)
March 8, 1913
14 1/8 x 11 in.
Walt Kuhn, Kuhn Family Papers, and Armory Show
Records, 1859-1978, bulk 1900-1949, Archives of
American Art, Smithsonian Institution

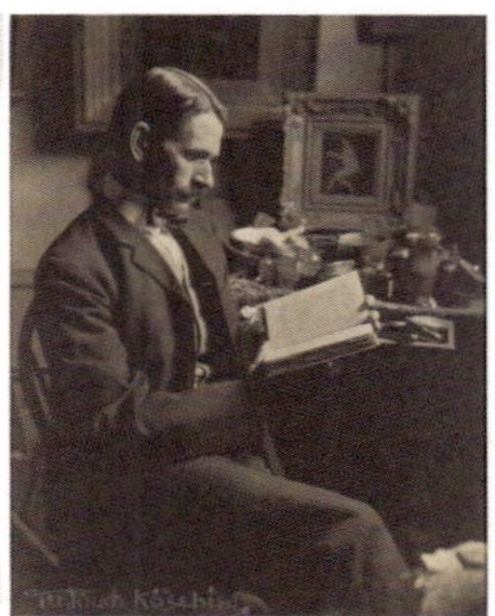

85. Gertrude Käsebier
Portrait of Arthur B. Davies, ca. 1908
platinum photographic print
7 ½ x 6 in.
Ferargil Galleries records, circa 1900-1963, Archives of American, Smithsonian Institution

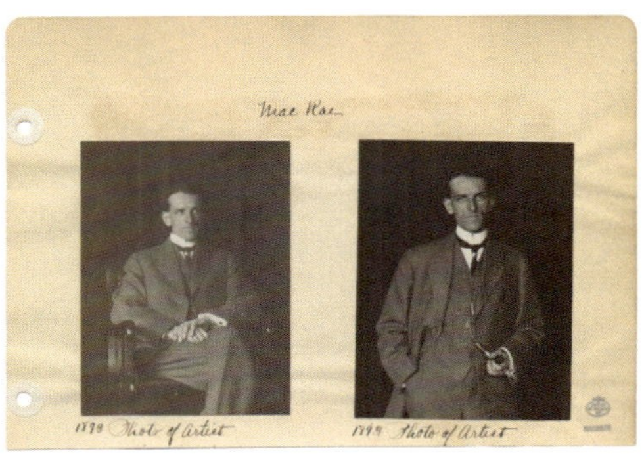

86. Unidentified photographer
Portrait of Elmer L. MacRae, ca. 1893
photographic print
13 ¾ x 9 ½ in.
1913 Armory Show, 50th Anniversary Exhibition Records, 1962-1963, Archives of American Art, Smithsonian Institution

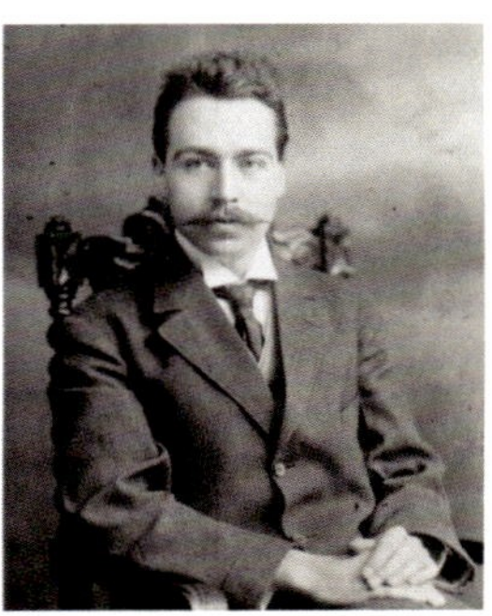

87. Pach Brothers
Portrait of Walter Pach, ca. 1909
photographic print
10 ¼ x 8 7/10 in.
Walter Pach papers, 1857-1980, Archives of American Art, Smithsonian Institution

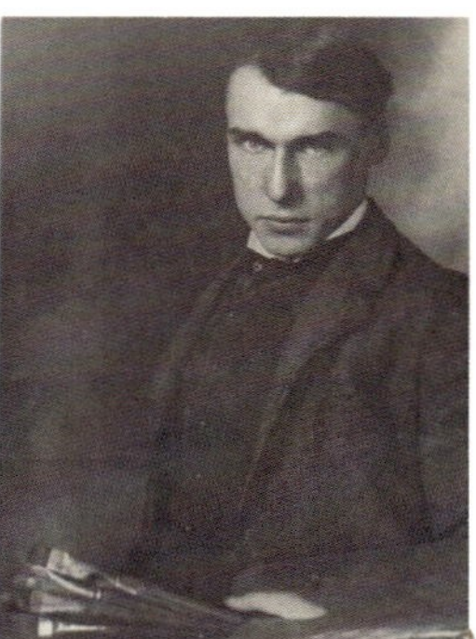

88. Pangborn Pangb
Portrait of Walt Kuhn, 1904 or 1905
B&W photographic print
8 ¼ x 10 ¼ in.
Walt Kuhn, Kuhn Family Papers, and Armory Show Records, 1859-1978, bulk 1900-1949, Archives of American Art, Smithsonian Institution

† *Charter Members*

§ *Exhibition of Independent Artists*

* *Exhibits catalogued but not received: Artists that were asked to participate and included in the catalogue but were then listed in the supplement as "not received".*

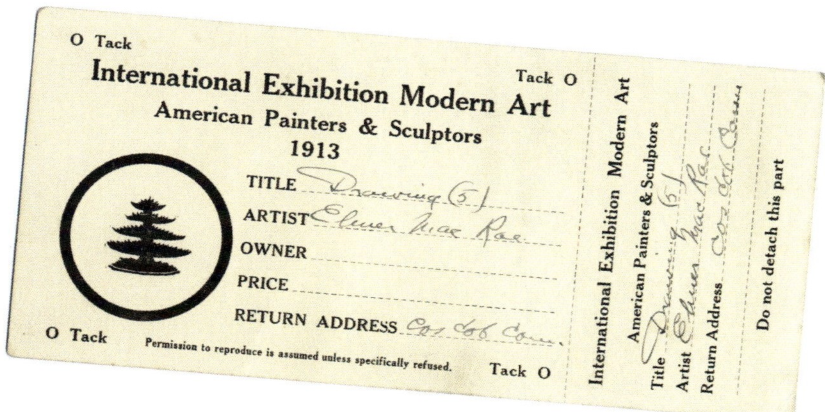

Fig. 21
Armory Show label for a drawing by Elmer MacRae, Greenwich Historical Society Library and Archives

Abendschein, Albert (1860- ?)

Aitken, Robert Ingersoll (1878-1949) §

Alger, John H. (1879- ?)

Anderson, Karl (1874-1956) †

Ashe, Edmund Marion (1867-1941)

Barkley, Florence Howell (1880-1954) §

Barnard, George Grey (1863-1938)

Beach, Chester (1881-1956)

Beal, Gifford (1879-1956) *

Becker, Maurice (1889-1975)

Beckett, Marion H. (1886-1949)

Bellows, George (1882-1925) †§

Bickford, Nelson N. (1846-1943)

Bitter, Karl (1867-1915) *

Bjorkman, Olaf (1887-1946)

Bluemner, Oscar (1867-1938)

Borglum, Solon (1868-1922)

Boss, Homer (1882-1956) §

Brewer, Bessie Marsh (1884-1952)

Brinley, D. Putnam (1879-1963) †§

Brown, Bolton (1864-1936) §

Brown, Fannie Miller (1893-?)

Bruce, Patrick Henry (1881-1936)

Burlin, Paul (1886-1969)

Burroughs, Edith Woodman (1871-1916)

Butler, Theodore Earl (1861-1936)

Carles, Arthur Beecher (1882-1952)

Cassatt, Mary (1844-1926)

Cesare, Oscar (1885-1948)

Chaffee, Jr., O. N. (Oliver Newberry) (1881-1944)

Chanler, Robert Winthrop (1872-1930)

Chew, Amos (n.d)

Churchill, Alfred Vance (1864-1949)

Cimiotti, Jr., Gustave (1875-1969)

Clymer, Edwin L. (1871-1949) *

Coate, Harry W. (n.d.)

Cohen, Nessa (1885-1976)

Coleman, Glenn O. (1887-1932) §

Coluzzi, Howard (n.d.)

Cory, Kate Thompson (1861-1958)

Crisp, Arthur Watkins (1881-1974)

Crowley, Herbert (n.d.)

Currier, J. Frank (1843-1909)

Cutler, Carl Gordon (1873-1945)

Dabo, Leon (1864-1960) †§

Dasburg, Andrew (1887-1979)

Davey, Randall (1887-1964)

Davidson, Jo (1883-1952) †

Davies, Arthur B. (1862-1928) †§

Davis, Charles Harold (1856-1933)

Davis, Stuart (1892-1964) §

Dawson, Manierre (1887-1969)

Dimock, Edith (1876-1955) §

Dirks, Rudolph (1877-1968)

Dolinsky, Nathaniel (1890-1980)

Donoho, Gaines Ruger (1857-1916)

Dreier, Katherine S. (1877-1952)

Dresser, Aileen King (n.d.) §

Dresser, Lawrence Tyler (n.d.) §

Dreyfous, Florence H. (n.d.)

du Bois, Guy Pène (1884-1958) †§

Duffy, Richard H. (1881-1953)

Eberle, Abastenia St. Leger (1878-1942)

Eddy, Henry Brevoort (1872-1935)

Eells, Jean (n.d.)

Engle, Amos W. (1880-1926)

Esté, Florence (1860-1926)

Everett, Lily (1889-?)

Foote, Mary (1872-1938)

Fraser, James Earle (1876-1953)

Frazier, Kenneth (1867-1849)

Freund, Ernest Arthur (1890-1923)

Fry, Sherry E. (1879-1966) †

Fuhr, Ernest (1874-1933) §

Gaylor, Samuel Wood (1883-1957)

Glackens, William (1870-1938) †§

Glintenkamp, Henry I. (1887-1946) §

Goldthwaite, Anne (1869-1944)

AMERICAN ARTISTS IN THE 1913 ARMORY SHOW *continued*

Gussow, Bernard (1881-1957)
Gutmann, Bernhard (1869-1936)
Hale, Philip L. (1865-1931)
Halpert, Samuel (1884-1930)
Harley, Charles R. (1864-?)
Hartley, Marsden (1877-1943)
Hassam, Childe (1859-1935)
Haworth, Edith (1878-1953) §
Henri, Robert (1865-1929) †
Higgins, Eugene (1874-1958)
Hoard, Margaret (1879-1944)
Hopkinson, Charles (1869-1962)
Hopper, Edward (1882-1967) §
Howard, Cecil De B. (1888-1956)
Humphreys, Albert (1863-1922) §
Hunt, Mrs. Thomas (n.d.)
Huntington, Margaret Wendell (1867-1958)
Johnson, Grace Mott (1882-1967)
Karfiol, Bernard (1886-1952)
Keller, Henry (1869-1949)
King, Edith (1884-1975)
Kleiminger, Adolph (1865-1945)
Kleinert, Hermine E. (1880-1943)
Kramer, Edward Adam (1866-1941) †
Kroll, Leon (1884-1974)
Kuhn, Walt (1877-1949) †§
Lachaise, Gaston (1882-1935)
Lawson, Ernest (1873-1928) †§
Lee, Arthur (1881-1961)
Lie, Jonas (1880-1940) †
Londoner, Amy (1878-1953) §
Luks, George (1867-1933) †
Lundberg, August F. (1828-1938)
MacKnight, Dodge (1860-1950)
MacRae, Elmer Livingston (1875-1955)†§
Mager, Gus (1878-1956) §
Manigault, Edward Middleton (1887-1922)§
Marin, John (1870-1953)
Mase, Carolyn (1880-1949)
Maurer, Alfred Henry (1868-1932)
McComas, Francis (1975-1938)
McEnery/Cunningham, Kathleen (1885-1971)
McLean, Howard White (1879-1952) §
Meltzer, Charlotte (n.d.)
Miller, Kenneth Hayes (1876-1952)
Mowbray-Clarke, John (1869-1953) †
Muhrmann, Henry (1854-1916)
Murphy, Hermann Dudley (1867-1945)
Musselman-Carr, Myra (1871-?)
Myers, Ethel (1881-1960)
Myers, Jerome (1867-1940) †§
Nankivell, Frank Arthur (1869-1959) †§
Niles, Helen James (1865-1940)
Organ, Marjorie (Mrs. Robert Henri)(1886-1931)
Pach, Walter (1883-1958) §
Paddock, Josephine (1885-1964) §
Pelton, Agnes (1881-1961)
Pepper, Charles Hovey (1864-1950)

Perrine, Van Dearing (1869-1955)
Phillips, Harriet Sophia (1848-1929)
Pleuthner, Walter Karl (1885-?)
Pope, Louise (n.d.) §
Potter, Louis (1873-1912) §*
Powers, Thomas E. (1870-1939) *
Prendergast, Maurice (1858-1924) †
Preston, James (1873-1962) §
Preston, May Wilson (1873-1949)
Putnam, Arthur (1873-1930)
Rasmussen, Bertrand (1890- ?)
Reuterdahl, Henry (1871-1925) §
Rhoades, Katharine Nash (1885-1965)
Rimmer, William (1816-1879)
Robinson, Boardman (1876-1952)
Robinson, Theodore (1852-1896)
Rogers, Mary C. Gamble (1882-1920) §
Rohland, Paul (1884-1953)
Roiné, Jules Edouard (1857-1916)
Rook, Edward Francis (1870-1960)
Rumsey, Charles Cary (1879-1922)
Russell, Morgan (1886-1953)
Ryder, Albert Pinkham (1847-1917)
Salvatore, Victor W. (1885-1965)
Schamberg, Morton L. (1881-1918) §
Schumacher, William Emile (1870 - 1931)
Shaw, Sydney Sale (1879-1946)
Sheeler, Charles (1883-1965)
Sloan, John (1871-1951) †§
Sprinchorn, Carl (1887-1971) §
Stella, Joseph (1877-1946)
Stevens, Frances Simpson (1894—1976)
Stinemetz, Morgan (1890-?)
Taylor, Henry Fitch (1853-1925) †
Taylor, William Nicholson (1882-1945)
Tucker, Allen (1866-1939) †
Twachtman, Julian Alden (1882-?)
Twachtman, John Henry (1853-1902)
Vonnoh, Bessie Potter (1872-1955)
Wagner, Fred (1864-1940) *
Walkowitz, Abraham (1878-1965)
Walts, Frank M. (active 1912-1935)
Ward, Hilda (1878-1950) §
Warshawsky, Alexander (1887-1945)
Weber, F. William (1865-1905)
Webster, E. Ambrose (1869-1935)
Weir, Julian Alden (1852-1919)
Whistler, James Abbott McNeill (1834-1903)
White, Charles (1878-1918)
Wilson, Claggett (1887-1952)
Wolf, Leon (n.d.)
Wortman, Denys (1887-1958)
Yandell, Enid (1870-1934)
Young, Art Henry (1866-1943)
Young, Mahonri Macintosh (1877-1957) †
Zorach, Marguerite (1887-1968)
Zorach, William (1887-1966)